FAME AMID THE RUINS

FAME AMID THE RUINS

ITALIAN FILM STARDOM IN THE AGE OF NEOREALISM

Stephen Gundle

First published in 2020 by
Berghahn Books
www.berghahnbooks.com

© 2020, 2025 Stephen Gundle
First paperback edition published in 2025

All rights reserved. Except for the quotation of short passages
for the purposes of criticism and review, no part of this book
may be reproduced in any form or by any means, electronic or
mechanical, including photocopying, recording, or any information
storage and retrieval system now known or to be invented,
without written permission of the publisher.

Library of Congress Cataloging-in-Publication Data

Names: Gundle, Stephen, 1956– author.
Title: Fame amid the Ruins: Italian Film Stardom in the Age of Neorealism / Stephen Gundle
Description: New York: Berghahn, 2020. | Includes bibliographical references and index.
Identifiers: LCCN 2019037398 (print) | LCCN 2019037399 (ebook) | ISBN 9781789200010 (hardback) | ISBN 9781789200027 (ebook)
Subjects: LCSH: Motion picture actors and actresses --Italy--Biography. | Celebrities--Italy--Case studies. | Fame--Social aspects--Italy. | Realism in motion pictures. | Motion pictures--Italy--History--20th century.
Classification: LCC PN2687 .G68 2020 (print) | LCC PN 2687 (ebook) | DDC 791.4302/80922 [B]--dc23
LC record available at https://lccn.loc.gov/2019037398
LC ebook record available at https://lccn.loc.gov/2019037399

British Library Cataloguing in Publication Data
A catalogue record for this book is available from the British Library

ISBN 978-1-78920-001-0 hardback
ISBN 978-1-80539-744-1 paperback
ISBN 978-1-80539-923-0 epub
ISBN 978-1-78920-002-7 web pdf

https://doi.org/10.3167/9781789200010

To Paul Ginsborg

Contents

List of Illustrations — ix

Acknowledgements — xiii

Introduction — 1

Part I. Italian Cinema and Society, 1945–52 — 17

1. Postwar Cinema and the Challenges of Democracy — 19
2. The Film Industry from Fascism to the Cold War — 34
3. The Transformation of the Star System — 51
4. The Public, Film-Going and the Stars — 73

Part II. Stardom, Anti-Fascism and Neorealism — 93

5. Massimo Girotti: Proletarian Apollo — 95
6. Clara Calamai: The Suspension of Glamour — 114
7. Aldo Fabrizi: Nostalgia and Popular Culture — 132
8. Anna Magnani: Authenticity and the Star Persona — 150
9. Andrea Checchi: Shadows of Defeat — 173

Part III. Popular Idols for New Times — 191

10. Totò: Jester of the Republic — 193

11. Silvana Mangano: Beauty and Stardom — 216

12. Amedeo Nazzari: The Hero Domesticated — 240

13. Silvana Pampanini: Dream Girl of the Masses — 261

14. Raf Vallone: The Physiognomy of Fame — 282

Part IV. Reconfigurations of Stardom — 301

15. The Non-professional Actor and Low-Definition Stardom — 303

16. Co-productions and International Stardom — 323

Conclusion — 344

Bibliography — 349

Index — 362

Illustrations

2.1 Anna Magnani and Vittorio De Sica at the rally in defence of Italian cinema in Rome, *La Settimana Incom*, February 1949 (author's own collection). 43

3.1 Two protagonists of Fascist cinema, Fosco Giachetti (left) and Amedeo Nazzari (middle), in the war film *Bengasi* (Augusto Genina, 1942), the only one of the period in which they both featured (screenshot by the author). 55

4.1 The popular magazine *Hollywood* functioned almost like a fan club for filmgoers. Lavishly illustrated, it almost always pictured American stars on the cover (author's own collection). 87

5.1 Postcard portrait photo of Massimo Girotti, the young star c. 1942 (author's own collection). 100

5.2 Massimo Girotti as Christian martyr Sebastian, the future saint, in *Fabiola* (Alessandro Blasetti, 1949). The actor became a 'proletarian Apollo' for neorealists but was also configured as a 'queer Adonis' (screenshot by the author). 109

6.1 A deglamorized Clara Calamai in the kitchen, in *Ossessione* (Luchino Visconti, 1942). The actress feared her image had been damaged by this process but later understood that it had widened her repertoire (screenshot by the author). 117

6.2 Clara Calamai as the sensual courtesan Fulvia in her first major role, in the period film *Ettore Fieramosca* (Alessandro Blasetti, 1938) (author's own collection). 122

6.3 Clara Calamai as a dissatisfied bourgeois wife and frustrated pianist in *Amanti senza amore* (Prelude to Madness, Gianni Francolini, 1948) (screenshot by the author). 129

7.1 The Roman comedian Aldo Fabrizi as Don Pietro during a gag in a shop selling religious articles, in *Roma città aperta* (Rome Open City, Roberto Rossellini, 1945) (screenshot by the author). 135

7.2 Aldo Fabrizi (centre) in a dramatic role as a father seeking his daughter amid the postwar underworld of black marketeers, prostitutes and deserters, in *Tombolo, paradiso nero* (Tombolo, Dark Paradise, Giorgio Ferroni, 1947) (screenshot by the author). 139

8.1 An actress amongst the crowd: Anna Magnani as Pina (centre), moments prior to her tragic death, in *Roma città aperta* (Rome Open City, Roberto Rossellini, 1945) (screenshot by the author). 151

8.2 Anna Magnani as the feisty market stallholder Elide in *Campo de' fiori* (Mario Bonnard, 1943), one of two pre-1945 films in which she acted opposite Aldo Fabrizi (screenshot by the author). 160

8.3 Anna Magnani at the inaugural Nasto d'argento (silver ribbon) ceremony in 1946, at which she received the award for best supporting actress for her role in *Roma città aperta* (Rome Open City, Roberto Rossellini, 1945) (author's own collection). 162

9.1 Andrea Checchi, the young actor while still a student at the Centro sperimentale film school, 1938. His performance in *I grandi magazzini* (The Big Store, Mario Camerini, 1939) brought him to the attention of Giuseppe De Santis and others (author's own collection). 181

9.2 Andrea Checchi as a factory boss who lends support to the Resistance in *Achtung! Banditi!* (Carlo Lizzani, 1951) (screenshot by the author). 188

10.1 Totò played a living corpse or an automaton in some of his prewar performances. He toyed once more with the macabre in *Totò cerca casa* (Totò Seeks a Home, Steno and Monicelli, 1949) when his homeless family finds accommodation in a cemetery (screenshot by the author). 195

10.2 Totò with the showgirl Isa Barzizza, who appeared alongside him in numerous stage shows and several films (author's own collection). 207

10.3 Prince Antonio De Curtis (Totò) at home. The actor sought to draw a sharp distinction between his public and private personae but was not always consistent in doing so (author's own collection). 210

11.1 An elegant young Silvana Mangano, a contestant at the Miss Lazio pageant, 1947. It is likely that she presented herself in a similar way at the audition for *Riso amaro* (Bitter Rice, Giuseppe De Santis, 1949) (author's own collection). 218

11.2 Silvana Mangano dances the boogie woogie in her breakthrough role as a misguided rice worker in *Riso amaro* (Bitter Rice, Giuseppe De Santis, 1949) (screenshot by the author). 220

11.3 Silvana Mangano signing autographs at the 1952 Venice film festival. Meeting fans and satisfying their requests for autographs were among her least favourite activities (author's own collection). 235

12.1 A polished Amedeo Nazzari on the cover of *Cine illustrato*, 15 February 1948 (author's own collection). 245

12.2 Amedeo Nazzari returns from Argentina to take the lead male role opposite Silvana Mangano in *Il lupo della Sila* (The Wolf of the Sila, Duilio Coletti, 1949), *La Settimana Incom*, April 1949 (author's own collection). 252

13.1 Silvana Pampanini in period costume on the cover of *Le Ore* magazine. The actress was one of the most popular cover girls of the late 1940s and early 1950s. Many of her films had a feel of belle époque Paris (author's own collection). 265

13.2 After becoming a mother out of wedlock in *La schiava del peccato* (Slave of Sin, Raffaello Matarazzo, 1954), Silvana Pampanini is obliged to earn her living as a factory worker (screenshot by the author). 276

14.1 Raf Vallone as wronged farmer Francesco in *Non c'è pace tra gli ulivi* (No Peace under the Olive Tree, Giuseppe De Santis, 1950) (screenshot by the author). 289

14.2 The one-time professional footballer Raf Vallone returned to the game in the popular drama *Gli eroi della domenica* (Sunday Heroes, Mario Camerini, 1953) (screenshot by the author).   296

15.1 After playing the unemployed worker Antonio in *Ladri di biciclette* (Bicycle Thieves, Vittorio De Sica, 1948), Lamberto Maggiorani lost his regular job and became a builder's labourer (author's own collection).   313

15.2 Carlo Battisti (right), in the title role, and Maria Pia Casilio (left) were the two main non-professionals to be cast in *Umberto D* (Vittorio De Sica, 1952) (screenshot by the author).   315

16.1 Glamorous French stars Michèle Morgan and Henri Vidal were engaged by producer Salvo D'Angelo to take lead roles in the epic film *Fabiola* (Alessandro Blasetti, 1949) (screenshot by the author).   327

Acknowledgements

This book has been several years in the making, and the materials employed in it have been gathered over a far longer period of research into Italian cinema and society dating back to the 1980s. Over that time, I have accumulated many debts towards fellow scholars, librarians and archivists and my students at Royal Holloway – University of London and at Warwick, as well as film enthusiasts who have been kind enough to share with me their thoughts about the Italian stars of the postwar period. I should like to mention first a number of colleagues in different disciplines and countries, who have provided me with inspiration either through their work or in person, or both: Gian Piero Brunetta, David Ellwood, Albertina Vittoria, Michela De Giorgio, Patrizia Gabrielli, Pierre Sorlin, Franco Minganti, Ruth Ben-Ghiat, David Forgacs, Robert Gordon, Guido Bonsaver and the late Patrick McCarthy and Alberto Farassino. Between 2016 and 2019, I have had the privilege of working on an AHRC project on Italian film producers with Karl Schoonover, Stefano Baschiera, Barbara Corsi, Marina Nicoli, Vanessa Roghi, Michela Zegna and the late Chris Wagstaff. The work we have conducted together has informed the approach adopted in this book, especially in relation to the film industry. For conversations, stimulating short-term collaborations and suggestions, I wish to thank Mariapia Comand, Emiliano Morreale, Jean A. Gili, Louis Bayman, Mariapaola Pierini, Jacqueline Reich, Pauline Small, Catherine O'Rawe, Dana Renga, Sergio Rigoletto, Reka Buckley, Katia Pizzi, Natalia Piombino, Maddalena Spazzini, Alessandra Antola Swan, Silvia Magistrali, Agnese Bertolotti, Rossana Capitano and the late Nina Rothenberg.

Among the institutions whose resources I have used are: Cineteca di Bologna; Biblioteca dell'Archiginnasio, Bologna; Biblioteca Nazionale di Firenze; Biblioteca Nazionale di Roma, Biblioteca Chiarini, Centro sperimentale di cinematografia, Rome; Centro documentazione Rizzoli, Milan; Biblioteca Sormani, Milan; Margaret Herrick Library, Los Angeles; Wisconsin Center for Research in Film and Theater, Madison Wisconsin; Harry Ransom Research Center, Austin Texas. Among those who have provided me with special assistance in these institutions are Michela Zegna at the Cineteca di Bologna and Cristina Bariani and Sonia Orlandi at the Centro documentazione Rizzoli.

I first tackled some of the issues and personalities discussed here in the context of a project that David Forgacs and I conducted in the early 1990s. This was published as *Mass Culture and Society in Italy from Fascism to the Cold War* (Bloomington: Indiana University Press, 2007). Just as I was able to greatly expand the reflections on the film stars of the Fascist period contained in that volume in my previous Berghahn book, *Mussolini's Dream Factory: Film Stardom in Fascist Italy* (2013), so here I have done so on those of the postwar years.

It would not have been easy to write this book without many visits to street markets, used bookshops and fairs of printed ephemera, not to mention hours spent trawling eBay for old magazines, articles and images. I am grateful to the many stallholders and sellers of printed ephemera who have shared anecdotes with me and sometimes allowed me to study material without buying it.

Over the years, I have relied on the assistance of people who were able to go into archives and libraries when I was not easily able to travel. Fabrizio D'Alessio provided me with practical help with research in Rome, while Martina Barbieri assisted me in the search for illustrations.

I wish especially to thank Simona Storchi for sharing valuable insights into some of the stars in this book and for commenting on drafts of some chapters. While I have been at work on the book, our son Alessandro, age ten, has discovered the films of Totò. His favourite is *Totò le Moko*, one of the great Neapolitan comedian's best.

The book is dedicated to Paul Ginsborg, my Cambridge PhD supervisor and then friend and colleague. I first learned much of what I know about postwar Italy from him, and I have always sought to emulate his humane approach to scholarship. It is thanks to his early willingness to allow me to explore cultural and media issues alongside political history that I have been able to develop an approach to Italian cinema that combines several disciplinary concerns.

Introduction

It is a hot, sunny day in Rome, and a large number of women are gathering at the Cinecittà film studios with their young daughters. Raised voices fill the air with an atmosphere of expectation. The girls are waiting to be auditioned for a part reserved for an 8-year-old in a new film to be directed by Alessandro Blasetti. The women have clearly been waiting for some time. At the much-anticipated summons, they push through the open doors of the studio, leaving only one of their number outside desperately searching for her daughter. This mother, Maddalena Cecconi, is a lower-class woman from the Pietralata district, a home visitor who dispenses injections. She is a keen cinema-goer, who wants to get her daughter Maria into the movies. As soon as she has located the wandering girl and bustled her into the studio, she starts to elbow her way to the front of the throng. Before long, she gains the director's attention and secures an opportunity for Maria to show off her limited gifts. A novice at the audition game, Maddalena will soon discover that a whole world of dance and music teachers, drama instructors, dressmakers and hairdressers exists to feed the aspirations of the ambitious parents and prepare their children for the entertainment industry. She will also find out that there are unscrupulous individuals who claim to have special access to directors and who, for money, will advance the cause of this or that girl. One of them, a cynical and somewhat peripheral character named Annovazzi, seeks to seduce Maddalena and profit financially from her dreams. He has sensed that Maria, unlike many of the girls who have been trained to the point that they appear to be already professionalized, is an unpolished innocent. Indeed, for all her mother's passionate promotion, she is a plain child who seems to lack nearly all of the requisites for the advertised role. Maddalena's husband does not share her ambition and remonstrates with her about her obsession with their daughter's career. He seeks repeatedly to persuade her that she is wasting her time. Yet she must learn for herself that fame is not a golden chalice and that a movie role, even if it is obtained, does not solve all life's problems. It is when she peeps at the director and his team viewing the screen test – and realizes that some of them are laughing derisively at Maria's tearful failure to perform – that she wakes from her dream. Amid loud cries and expressions of desperation, she flees the studio. When she is tracked down and informed that Maria is being offered the part, she refuses the money that is offered to her. Chastened, she instead embraces a normal life for her away from the limelight.

Luchino Visconti's *Bellissima* (1951) is one of two or three films that are often said to mark the end of postwar neorealism. It is a film that is informed by none of the hopeful optimism that inspired the first works to appear after the end of the war. There is no idea of cinema as a witness, as the cultural arm of the anti-fascist Resistance, or as a contributor to the building of a new democratic Italy. Though some of the practices associated with neorealism mark the film – including scenes shot in the Pietralata quarter of Rome and the use of some non-professional actors and choral elements – the focus on a real event or problem (which had once been unemployment, homelessness etc.) is here turned on cinema itself. The director is played by real-life director Alessandro Blasetti, who, though he is shown to be kindly, was enraged when he discovered that his entry is to the tune of the charlatan's theme from Donizetti's opera *L'elisir d'amore*.[1] Visconti does not portray the medium as an instrument of emancipation and collective engagement but rather as a tool of oppression due to its capacity to distort and individualize demands for social mobility. By the year it was made, much had changed in Italy, and the passion for reform had dissipated. No longer was the country struggling to emerge from the ordeal of dictatorship, civil war and foreign occupation. No longer were the political forces cooperating to rebuild and lay the foundations of a stable democracy. No longer were artists, writers and film-makers convinced that they could contribute to the weaving of a new reformist texture in civil life. And no longer was the film industry in a state of suspension. Though the material and moral scars of Fascism and war remained, reconstruction was well advanced, and a republican constitution had been established. Political leadership was in the hands of the Christian Democrats, a force that enjoyed the backing of both the Church and the United States. This powerful support had ensured that the party secured nearly 50 per cent of the vote in the watershed 1948 election. The left, which had confidently expected to set the agenda in postwar Italy, had been ousted from power. While the Socialists and Communists still counted on a high level of support in the north and centre of the country, they were confined to opposition. The refurbishment of state support for the film industry contributed to a situation in which impulses to political change and social reform were replaced by a drive to uncomplicated entertainment.

Bellissima belongs to a small group of films made at the time about cinema and the mass media, all of them exposures of the reality underlying the alluring imagery. It is a text that portrays a world in which everyday life has been moulded by practices of media consumption with negative effects. Stardom and its lure figure prominently among these. The film is about the mechanisms of fame and the passions and ambitions that are fuelled by it. It comments on the neorealist practice of non-professional casting while also itself being cast in part in this way.[2] In addition, the film offers an indicator of the state of the star system at the start of the 1950s, since the main roles were attributed to Anna Magnani (Maddalena), the actress who had established herself in 1945 as the face of neorealism and shortly thereafter became Italy's number one box office draw, and to Walter Chiari (Annovazzi), an actor normally employed in comedies whose growing popularity among the young was seen by the producer Salvo D'Angelo – who had lost money on Visconti's previous film, *La terra trema* (The Earth Trembles, 1948) – to offer a guarantee of success at the box office.[3]

Visconti had wanted to work with Magnani ever since he had sought to cast her in his 1942 film *Ossessione*.[4] He was intrigued by her vital energy and emotional intensity, her ability to blend the theatrical with the ordinary and by her utter dedication to her art. *Bellissima* was his third film, after *Ossessione* and *La terra trema*. The plot outline written by the writer and cultural organizer Cesare Zavattini provided him with the opportunity he had been looking for. For all its critical thrust, the film is something of a star vehicle. It is constructed around Magnani and the persona she had built up over several films. In homage to Magnani's by now well-established histrionic performance mode, she was provided with opportunities to enter fully into the part of the working-class housewife. The production team worked with her in this regard, as the writer Suso Cecchi d'Amico, who revised Zavattini's story to meet the director's requirement that the initially lower middle-class Maddalena should become working class, later revealed.[5] Her black costume was allegedly acquired from a woman who was stopped in the street and offered money in return for her clothes. Moreover, Magnani was personally involved in the selection of the non-professional actors who would play her character's husband and daughter. Gastone Renzelli, who played blunt husband Spartaco, was an abattoir worker whose strong physique and handsome countenance won her approval. She took little Tina Apicella, who played Maria, so much to her heart that she even asked her parents if she could adopt her (the request was refused).[6] The director abandoned his custom of absolute perfectionist directorial control for her. The actress was allowed to freewheel and to improvise, and in one domestic scene, Maddalena/Magnani reflects on the nature of performance as she grooms herself in front of a mirror.[7] Visconti would continue his exploration of Magnani's star persona in the episode he directed of the film *Siamo Donne* (All About Love, 1953). Also conceived by Zavattini, the film was intended to reflect, in a series of episodes, on a real aspect of the life of a number of famous actresses.

Much to D'Angelo and Visconti's chagrin, *Bellissima* was not a box office success. Though Magnani was still highly respected as an actress, her star appeal had waned, and the film did nothing to relaunch it. Her character was in keeping with the 'woman of the people' persona she had established in *Roma città aperta* (Rome Open City, 1945), but by the early 1950s this persona had already been re-proposed on several occasions and had become something of a cliché. Furthermore, as the disruptions of war receded, it was no longer in tune with the social and cultural climate in the country. A new generation of female stars emerging from beauty contests was asserting itself. Magnani would henceforth find most success abroad, notably in her Oscar-winning role of Serafina the feisty Italian widow in Daniel Mann's *The Rose Tattoo* (1955). The 26-year-old Walter Chiari drew little benefit from the film either, beyond the kudos of working with an acknowledged master.

Bellissima highlights some of the problems that film directors belonging to the neorealist school had with stars and stardom. In principle, they did not like stars and what they signified in terms of cinema's relationship with its audiences. Stars were a product of an undemocratic strain in mass culture, Zavattini argued, which promoted heroes and exceptional individuals over ordinary men and women.[8] The aim of neorealist film-makers was to demystify cinema and turn it into a tool of collective emancipation and progress. Hence, stories were derived from recent real experiences or were inspired by social problems. Actors, where possible, were drawn from popular theatre or were taken from everyday life. Magnani was a case apart because she was seen as a star of a different type, almost an anti-star, who had gone beyond convention to turn screen acting into art. Though in radical counter-tendency to the norms of commercial film-making, neorealism would have an immediate impact and a lasting influence on Italian cinema. But the moment of its flowering was only ever a relatively brief and partial experience, even if it constituted one of the most glorious and important in film history. It was also less dramatically external to conventional film production than legend would have it. From the start, neorealist directors had to come to terms with – or rely on – many pre-existing talents, competences, structures and channels of support. These included technical staff, studios, writers, production companies (sometimes) and artistic personnel, all of which were part of a wider film industry. Stars, who had briefly seemed irrelevant, would soon make a return as the industry recovered and began to expand.

This book is concerned with the place of stars and stardom in postwar cinema and society. It seeks to address a series of questions about the role of stars in the complex period of political transition and economic reconstruction that came after five years of war, nearly two of civil war, a double foreign occupation and the end of a dictatorship that had lasted for more than two decades. How did established stars manage the turbulent transition from dictatorship to democracy, from war to peace, from autarky to competition? What consequences did the return of Hollywood stars have for domestic Italian stars and stardom? What impact did neorealism's efforts to abolish or refashion the star system have? Did new stars emerge against or through these efforts? How far did the star system that was taking shape in the early 1950s represent a substantial break with that which had been in place in the early 1940s? What were its hallmarks and distinctive features? Did star typologies change in terms of their gender, age, social extraction and appearance? How did performance styles change in the period? How important were film stars in actively shaping postwar Italian identity?

The mere existence of these questions is an indicator of how far Italy between 1945 and 1953 was a highly mediatized society. Despite the claim that neorealist films emerged in an industrial void, regular production resumed soon after the end of the conflict, and a small number of companies were re-establishing themselves. Though some postwar films, perhaps especially some belonging to, or influenced by, neorealism, present an image of the country as backward, Fascism had promoted a great expansion of the mass media.[9] Postwar films show us hunger, homelessness, ragged clothing, exploitative working conditions and unemployment, phenomena of displacement and general suffering, but they also feature radio, advertising and commercial initiatives, the press, popular music of various types and, of course, cinema itself. The striking growth of cinema as a leisure activity in the postwar years was driven by commercial forces, political and cultural actors, including the Church and the parties, and by audience demand. Cinema represented a window on the world, a form of citizenship, a distraction, a place of socialization and of erotic awakening.[10] It was a collective experience and a trigger for the individual imagination. The stars were implicated in all of these and therein lies their importance. They offer a unique way of understanding a society and its media during a crucial period of transition. The star system was a barometer of the different impulses and experiences. It bore witness to established affections, desires for change, hopes and aspirations as well as vanities and disappointments.

The Study of Italian Stars and Stardom

In recent years, stars and stardom have become an important topic of study. Once, interest in the industrial aspects of film-making, cinema as a mass entertainment and the popular consumption of films was largely confined to the disciplines of sociology and economics. Political science was concerned with cinema only insofar as it became an instrument of propaganda or an area of government regulation ad intervention. History paid little attention to the mass media and its products, though the sub-discipline of film history gained much ground from the 1980s. In its initial phases as an academic discipline, film studies was more concerned with film as art than commerce, and in consequence the processes of film production and distribution received little systematic attention. For all these reasons, the study of stars was mainly left to journalists and popular writers. Richard Dyer's pioneering text *Stars* (first published in 1979), which for many years would constitute the essential reference point for all studies of stars and stardom in the English-speaking world, marked a significant shift.[11] Though mainly concerned with Hollywood, Dyer acknowledged a debt to European sociologists like Edgar Morin and Francesco Alberoni, who, two decades earlier, had focused on the social processes and functions of stardom,[12] as well as to an older generation of scholars and theorists, and academics of his own generation who were engaged in opening up a new field of inquiry. Dyer remained keenly interested in film texts, but he was well aware that stardom could not be studied solely through them. If their significance was to be grasped, then attention needed to be paid to everything from fan letters and advertising posters to personal biographies, public images and physical characteristics. His key aim was to understand stars as cultural symbols, to interpret the ideas that were associated with them and to assess their power in lending visibility to oppositional currents and alternative values. Questions of national cinema interested him less.

In the study of Italian cinema, stars occupied, if anything, an even less prominent position that they did in the study of Hollywood. Neorealism, its auteurs and their successors constituted the main focus, while genres and popular cinema came a distant second.[13] The industry was tackled by specialists in film economics and those keen to denounce the role of the state or of capital or both. Almost the only people to write about stars were journalists and a handful of sociologists of the Alberoni school.[14] In the 1980s and 1990s, Italy's leading film historian, Gian Piero Brunetta, was at the forefront of efforts to widen the perspective on cinema's role in Italian society. In his many works, it is not simply an art but also a collective experience, a force for modernization, a commercial activity, an instrument of Americanization, a sphere of cultural conflict, a focus of identity and a locus of memory. In his histories of Italian cinema, stars receive some treatment and even dedicated chapters.[15] Working within a sociocultural framework, feminist film scholars like Giovanna Grigniffini approached the question from the point of view of the representation of women, with female stars acting as forces for change in a context in which barriers to emancipation remained strong.[16]

In recent years, things have changed. Star studies have diversified to bring more clearly into focus the factors bearing on the production and circulation of star images, the role of the actor's labour in contributing to these and the specific historical contexts in which given stars have prospered.[17] A variety of cultural and historical approaches have shed light on the way in which stars have functioned as economic agents, diplomatic forces, cultural ideals and national symbols. While, in Italy, most work on stars still takes place around festivals and in journalism, there have been some innovations. It is significant that a number of chapters on stars have been published in the official multi-volume, multi-author *Storia del cinema italiano*, which began to appear in the early 2000s. In contrast to volumes edited between the 1970s and the early 1990s for Marsilio by Lino Miccichè, Giorgio Tinazzi and others, which accorded serious attention to the film industry and to genre production, but which completely lacked any attention to stars,[18] the monumental volumes of this collective history give some space to the theme. This is not to say that the matter has been tackled exhaustively. A close examination of the contents of the volumes shows that often it is approached obliquely, through a focus on actors (volumes on 1934–39 and 1940–44), on stars who constitute exemplars of approaches to acting (volumes on 1949–53 and 1965–69) or via individuals of exceptional note such as Vittorio De Sica, Alida Valli or Totò. The only volume that offers a variety of approaches is the one dedicated to the period 1945–48, though together these treatments occupy fourteen pages out of 514 (minus appendices). Even in the overarching volume entitled *Uno sguardo d'insieme*, the theme of the actor is preferred to that of the star.[19] This is not to suggest that actors are not an important topic. On the contrary, there is ample scope for more work on performance, casting, the screen actor's craft, as well as gesture and voice. But the study of stars takes in a range of issues that goes beyond these. In particular, it necessarily involves matters of marketing, promotion, genre, press and other media coverage, reception and cultural and political meaning.

Though significant chapters and articles have appeared in Italian, only a few stars have been the object of systematic attention. The Neapolitan comedian Totò has been the subject of a number of book-length studies,[20] while another comic actor, Alberto Sordi, has been the subject of several volumes.[21] Female stars have on the whole received more attention than the men, though the biographical approach has been dominant. A special issue of the film magazine *Bianco & Nero* dedicated to Alida Valli, and based in part on the actress's private papers, constitutes a rare example of sustained study.[22] Fandom remains under-researched, though Federico Vitella and Reka Buckley have produced a number of innovative articles on this theme.[23] On the whole, political and cultural historians have not granted stars much status. Even in books and series on national identity, they hardly figure at all. In the publisher Il Mulino's series *Identità italiana*, the only star to merit a volume is the indisputably significant Amedeo Nazzari, whose heyday was in the 1930s and 1940s.[24]

In the English-speaking world, several studies have appeared in recent years. Angela Dalle Vacche's explorations of female stars of silent cinema opened up a neglected field.[25] Marcia Landy's *Stardom Italian Style; Screen Performance and Personality in Italian Cinema* offered a view of the changing qualities of Italian stars from the silent era to the early twenty-first century.[26] Centred on screen performance rather than extra-textual factors, the book highlighted the importance of bodies and was unusual in stressing direction – even to the point of taking directors themselves to be stars.[27] Buckley's articles on Gina Lollobrigida, Elsa Martinelli and Italian glamour offer important close readings of key stars and star images.[28] In contrast to Landy, she stresses the public images of stars and their relationships with the fashion world, the press and fans. Jacqueline Reich's book-length studies of Marcello Mastroianni and Maciste offer new perspectives on masculinity and stardom,[29] which have also been developed by Catherine O'Rawe in relation to contemporary cinema.[30] Reich and O'Rawe's co-authored *Divi: la mascolinità nel cinema italiano* provides the first overtly gendered reading of Italian male stardom, starting from the premises that 'Mediterranean masculinity is defined in the public rather than the private sphere' and that 'the forms of modern masculinity are fragile, unstable and constantly subject to uncontrollable changes'.[31]

Stardom is a theme that I have returned to on several occasions since the publication of my article 'Sophia Loren: Italian Icon' in the *Historical Journal of Film, Radio and Television* in 1995 and my chapter on 'Fame, Fashion and Style: The Italian Star System' in David Forgacs and Robert Lumley's edited volume *Italian Cultural Studies: An Introduction*.[32] Most recently, in *Mussolini's Dream Factory: Film Stardom in Fascist Italy*, I sought to draw attention to the neglected phenomenon of interwar stardom.[33] My intention was to assert the importance of film stars in the study of Fascist society while, at the same time, drawing on the historiography of Fascism to illuminate the understanding of the film stars of the period. I explored the lives and careers of a number of prominent stars using a wide range of primary materials including the press, publicity, public and private archives, memoirs, and published interviews as well as film texts. Though I sought to address the postwar fate of the individual stars and to analyse popular memory of the stars of the period, I did not deal directly with the way stars were contested, debated and reconfigured by the cinema of the post-fascist period or the ways in which a transition occurred between one star system and another. These are the central topics of the present volume.

Themes and Method

Italian cinema of the years between 1945 and 1952 has been extensively studied. It has always been the main focus of scholars in the English-speaking world, and it is probably fair to say that more has also been published about it in Italian than on any other period in the national cinema's history. The reason for this is not mysterious. The films that have been grouped together by critics under the label of neorealism won almost immediate international recognition. At a vital moment in world history, they constituted a hugely influential body of work that connected cinema with the social and with ideas of citizenship. They pioneered a new method of film-making that was tied to the exploration of social questions. They also helped change the image of Italy in the eyes of the country's people and the world. Through films like *Roma città aperta* (Rome Open City, Roberto Rossellini,

1945), *Paisà* (Roberto Rossellini, 1946), *Sciuscià* (Vittorio De Sica, 1946) and *Ladri di biciclette* (Bicycle Thieves, Vittorio De Sica, 1948), a country that had been the ally of Nazi Germany for much of the war, and that was regarded with suspicion by Allied governments, managed to attract great sympathy for the sacrifices and sufferings of its people. Neorealism was and remains a cultural tendency of great significance, and for this reason it continues to be the subject of research and publications.

Sometimes, though increasingly less frequently, there has been a tendency to see neorealism as being synonymous with the whole of Italian cinema of the immediate postwar years. This convention in turn has been used to judge later films in terms of how far they matched up to earlier work. Alan O'Leary and Catherine O'Rawe, and also Aine O'Healy, have deplored what the latter calls 'the embalmment of realism as the gold standard of Italian film-making'.[34] By now, it is well established that neorealism rose and fell in a context in which commercial cinema, though seriously weakened by the disruptions and conflicts of the final two years of the war, was also producing and distributing films that had no aim but to entertain. Despite a desire on the part of some critics and ideologues to mark a clear distance between the films of a small group of neorealist masters and the rest of Italian cinema, neorealist film-makers were never completely isolated or separate from the usual channels of film production and distribution. Ideas along these lines that were advanced cautiously in a volume edited by Alberto Farassino in 1989 have been brought into the mainstream in recent work by Stefania Parigi and by Francesco Pitassio and Paolo Noto.[35] Of the three most prominent directors, only Roberto Rossellini could be argued to have operated consistently outside the industry. But, even in his case, this could be contested. Though he was undoubtedly the least commercially minded (and commercially successful) of the trio, he on occasion acted as his own producer, he worked with professional actors – stars even – as well as non-professionals, he sought finance for his films from conventional sources (including Samuel Goldwyn and RKO, once he linked up with Ingrid Bergman) and his films were presented and released in a conventional way. *La terra trema* (The Earth Trembles, 1948), Visconti's first film of the period, following his 1942 debut *Ossessione*, was a radical rejection of most tenets of commercial cinema, though – like the star vehicle *Bellissima* – it was produced by Salvo D'Angelo, whose Universalia company was an offshoot of the Vatican-sponsored Orbis. In the same period, D'Angelo pioneered Italian-French co-productions with the blockbuster *Fabiola* (Alessandro Blasetti, 1949). As for De Sica, his innovative and widely praised postwar films were informed by his long experience as an actor in light comedies. Though several of his films were essentially self-produced, they were made to a high professional standard in all respects except the casting.

Not surprisingly, there were a number of attempts to break the pattern of commercial film production. However, channels of alternative production, such as the partisans' association ANPI's support for Giuseppe De Santis's *Caccia tragica* (1947) and the cooperative of authors and spectators that made Carlo Lizzani's first films, were problematic and short-lived. Within a short time, production companies that were keen to develop strategies for different segments of the market intervened to support the projects of novice directors like De Santis, Lizzani, Pietro Germi and Renato Castellani, who wanted to take cinema into new and more socially aware directions. Such support injected resources but came at a cost, which manifested itself in pressure, for example, to cast established stars or to build new ones. Though producers were less resistant than some directors to casting stars who had made their names in the 1930s or early 1940s, they were also happy to endorse efforts to create new stars. They mostly understood that the social, economic and political conditions of the late 1940s were so different that inevitably there would have to be adjustments to the star system, even if they were initially sceptical of De Santis's declared aim to 'produce the neorealist star, the national popular star system in which the audience can see itself sublimated'.[36]

Fascist cinema had produced a number of stars who resonated with the public, and by the early 1940s there was a functioning star system that served to add commercial appeal to the dominant comedy, musical and dramatic genres. After the fall of Mussolini in 1943, and the interruption of film production, the stars were left largely to fend for themselves. A few opted to quit cinema and withdraw into private life, but most expected to resume their careers and did not see themselves as in any way contaminated by an association with the regime. In reality, very few stars would make a successful transition into postwar cinema that was anything more than short-lived.[37] Within a few years, a new star system was taking shape that largely excluded prewar names, though some were able to continue working, even at a high level, albeit without any special glamour. The reasons for this transition may seem obvious. A closer examination of the situation reveals a complex picture to which the position of production companies, the preferences of directors, the tastes of the public, personal choices and opportunities, existing star images and the challenges of Hollywood all contributed.

Most stars of the late Fascist period were under contract to one production company or another, with the state-owned Cines company having the most illustrious roster. The lack of continuity in production in the postwar years led to a situation in which old agreements fell by the wayside and few performers received the sort of attention and range of offers that had once been afforded them. Most passed from one film to another with little continuity, many contracts being confined to one film. Some had assistants or family members to guide them, but agents did not become commonplace until well into the 1950s. David O Selznick's recruitment of Alida Valli in 1946 led to a legal dispute with Minerva, which claimed to have her under contract,[38] but this was a rare instance of an artist whose strong commercial value was relatively undimmed. Comedy performers were the first to be tied to production companies on account of their box office appeal and the serial nature of much of their work.

Most stars operated at several levels of cinema. After her triumphant performance as the tragic Pina in *Roma città aperta*, Anna Magnani made a series of popular comedies in which she varied or reprised the persona she established in that film. Nazzari, the greatest star of the Fascist period, was bypassed by the leading neorealists but much appreciated by producers, who were keen to harness his continuing box office appeal. Although the transition was anything but smooth, his completion of the passage from prewar to postwar stardom ensured that an extensive overhaul in the star system was configured as an evolution. Aldo Fabrizi worked with Rossellini in *Roma città aperta* and *Francesco giullare di Dio* (Francis, God's Jester, 1950) while also acting in drama and comedy and turning to direction for *Emigrantes* (Emigrants, 1949). This ability to move across genres and between auteur works and popular cinema means that the stars offer a unique insight into the workings of the film industry and cinema's relationship to society, as well as into the rise and fall of neorealism.

This book will seek to situate the trajectories of the stars in a specific social, political and cultural context. It will explore performances, lifestyles and public images for the purpose of explaining how stars were perceived, how they won favour, established personae and became public figures and collective symbols. It will also examine the various factors that contributed to significant shifts in the mechanisms of recruitment of screen actors and to the qualities that they required. Whereas most prewar actors had a background in the theatre or had studied at the Centro sperimentale film school, many postwar stars had little training and had to learn screen acting on the job. This applied both to the younger women who entered the world of cinema after winning beauty contests or working in advertising or for photoromance magazines and to the men who were recruited from the world of sport. The de-professionalization of film acting was a result of both the concern of directors associated with neorealism to widen the pool from which screen performers were drawn and the postwar shift to post-synchronized sound. Though deskilling gave rise to criticism and protest, it was a key element of the way cinema represented everyday milieus in a realistic way and explored national characteristics and aspirations.

The book is divided into four parts. Part I addresses issues relating to the postwar context. Separate chapters deal with the efforts of film-makers to rise to the opportunities and challenges of the return to democracy, the situation of the film industry, the star system in general and the public. The next two parts explore in detail the case studies of ten stars.

Part II is dedicated to five stars who began their careers under Fascism and who, with greater or lesser success, continued working in the postwar years. Inevitably, there are several possible candidates for close examination who are omitted for reasons of space. By opting to cover Massimo Girotti, Clara Calamai, Anna Magnani, Aldo Fabrizi and Andrea Checchi, I have had to leave out others, including Gino Cervi, Alida Valli, Isa Miranda and Carlo Ninchi. While I have written elsewhere about Miranda and Valli,[39] I hope at some point to be able to render justice to Cervi and Ninchi. Checchi's inclusion requires some explanation, since he was neither a big star nor did he leave a significant mark on the popular imagination. He features because he was identified by some contributors to neorealism, notably De Santis and Lizzani, as the ideal face of a cinema that was no longer dominated by the twin poles of propaganda and escapism. His downbeat manner made him suitable, it was felt, to represent the new age of the common man. This intention was barely realized, though Checchi did appear in leading roles in several postwar films. His failure to become a popular favourite provides insights into the nature of postwar stardom and the changing tastes that bore on it.

Part III is concerned with three stars who emerged in the postwar years – Silvana Mangano, Silvana Pampanini and Raf Vallone – and two actors who began their screen careers in the 1930s: Totò and Amedeo Nazzari. The comic actor Totò worked almost entirely in variety theatre and revues until he made a series of highly successful films in the late 1940s. From then, he became one of the film industry's most bankable stars. The reinvention of Nazzari, for reasons outlined above, was one of the more striking developments of the 1950s. In all cases, the film careers of the selected stars are examined solely in relation to the period up to 1952, even though some of them had far longer careers.

In Part IV, two important themes are explored: the role of the many non-professional actors who were recruited to cinema in this period and the ways in which the internationalization of film production affected the star system.

This study draws on a wide range of sources. Film texts are accorded due importance and many are closely scrutinized. Press sources are extensively used to study the wider public images of stars and to capture contemporary perceptions of them. I have also drawn on archives, memoirs, biographies, collections of testimonies and interviews. Publicity material and posters are a valuable source for anyone exploring star images, and I have made recourse to these where possible. Exhibition catalogues, volumes on single stars and collections of journalistic pieces have provided further material.

Notes

1. See Faldini and Fofi, *L'avventurosa storia del cinema italiano: raccontata dai suoi protagonisti, 1935–1959*, 248. Visconti pacified Blasetti by writing to him explaining that his intention was to suggest that, in the final analysis, all directors were charlatans, including himself.
2. The film's storyline was conceived by the writer Cesare Zavattini, one of neorealism's architects and its chief theorist and promoter, after he witnessed the scenes that accompanied the open auditions for the part of a young girl in Blasetti's film *Prima Comunione* (Father's Dilemma, 1950). See Faldini and Fofi, *L'avventurosa storia*, 248.
3. Testimony of Suso Cecchi d'Amico in ibid., 247.
4. The actress withdrew on account of her pregnancy and was replaced by Clara Calamai (see Chapter 6).
5. Testimony of Suso Cecchi d'Amico in Faldini and Fofi, *L'avventurosa storia*, 248.
6. Governi, *Nannarella*, 157–58.
7. For a discussion of this scene, see Marcus, 'Visconti's *Bellissima*: the Diva, the Mirror and the Screen', 9–17.
8. C. Zavattini, 'A Thesis on Neo-Realism' (1952), in Overbey, *Springtime in Italy: A Reader on Neo-Realism*, 73, 76.
9. Forgacs and Gundle, *Mass Culture and Italian Society from Fascism to the Cold War*, Chapter 7.
10. Ibid., Chapters 1 and 2.
11. Dyer, *Stars*.
12. Morin, *Les stars*; Alberoni, *L'elite senza potere: ricerca sociologica sul divismo*.
13. This situation was forcefully lamented in O'Leary and O'Rawe, 'Against Realism: On a "Certain Tendency" in Italian Film Criticism', 107–28.
14. For example, Rositi, 'Personalità e divismo in Italia durante il periodo fascista', 9–48.

15. Brunetta, *Storia del cinema italiano: dal 1945 agli anni Ottanta*, 247–60; Brunetta, *Cent'anni di cinema italiano*, Chapters 13 and 22.
16. G. Grignaffini, 'Il femminile nel cinema italiano: racconti di rinascita', in Brunetta, *Identità italiana e identità europea nel cinema italiano dal 1945 al miracolo economico*, 357–87; Grignaffini, 'Female Identity and Italian Cinema of the 1950s', in Bruno and Nadotti, *Off Screen: Women & Film in Italy*, 111–23.
17. See, for example, P. McDonald, 'Film Acting', in Hill and Church Gibson, *The Oxford Guide to Film Studies*, 30–50; Baron and Carnicke, *Reframing Screen Performance*; McLean, *Being Rita Hayworth: Labor, Identity and Hollywood Stardom*; Bolton and Wright, *Lasting Screen Stars: Images that Fade and Personas that Endure*.
18. Among these are Miccichè, *Il neorealismo cinematografico italiano*; Tinazzi, *Il cinema italiano degli anni '50*; Zagarrio, *Dietro lo schermo: ragionamenti sui modi di produzione cinematografici in Italia*.
19. F. Pitassio, 'L'attore', in Bertetto, *Storia del cinema italiano: uno sguardo d'insieme*, 192–207.
20. See Chapter 10 of this volume.
21. For example, Livi, *Alberto Sordi*; Schiavina, *Alberto Sordi: storia di un commediante*; Fofi, *Alberto Sordi: l'Italia in bianco e nero*.
22. Comand and Gundle, 'Alida Valli', 586.
23. See Chapter 4.
24. Gubitosi, *Amedeo Nazzari*.
25. Dalle Vacche, *Diva: Defiance and Passion in Early Italian Cinema*.
26. Landy, *Stardom Italian Style: Personality and Performance in Italian Cinema*.
27. A decision criticized by O'Rawe in her 2010 review article 'Italian Star Studies', 286–92.
28. Buckley, 'National Body: Gina Lollobrigida and the Cult of the Star in the 1950s', 527–47; Buckley, 'Elsa Martinelli: Italy's Audrey Hepburn', 327–40; Buckley, 'Glamour and the Italian Female Film Stars of the 1950s', 267–89.
29. Reich, *Beyond the Latin Lover: Marcello Mastroianni, Masculinity and Italian Cinema*; Reich, *The Maciste Films of Italian Silent Cinema*.
30. O'Rawe, *Stars and Masculinities in Contemporary Italian Cinema*.
31. Reich and O'Rawe, *Divi: la mascolinità nel cinema italiano*, 6–7.
32. Gundle, 'Sophia Loren: Italian Icon', 367–85; S. Gundle, 'Fame, Fashion and Style: The Italian Star System', in Forgacs and Lumley, *Italian Cultural Studies: An Introduction*, 309–26.
33. Gundle, *Mussolini's Dream Factory: Film Stardom in Fascist Italy*. The volume grew out of a 2002 chapter 'Film Stars and Society in Fascist Italy' published in Reich and Garofalo, *Reviewing Fascism: Italian Cinema, 1922-1943*.
34. O'Leary and O'Rawe, 'Against Realism', 107–28; O'Healy, 'Towards a Transnational Approach to the Study of Contemporary Cinema', 268–71.
35. Farassino, 'Neorealismo: cinema italiano, 1945-1949'; Parigi, *Neorealismo: il nuovo cinema del dopoguerra*; Pitassio and Noto, *Il cinema neorealista*.
36. M. Giusti, 'Mignone è partito: divi attori e caratteristi', in Farassino, *Neorealism*, 67.
37. See S. Ambrosino, 'Il cinema ricomincia: attori e registi fra "continuità" e "frattura"', in Farassino, *Neorealismo*, 65–66.
38. Pellizzari and Valentinetti, *Il romanzo di Alida Valli*, 91.
39. See Gundle, *Mussolini's Dream Factory*, Chapters 5 and 10 and Gundle, 'Alida Valli in Hollywood: From Star of Fascist Cinema to "Selznick Siren"', 559–87 as well as Comand and Gundle, 'Alida Valli'.

PART I
Italian Cinema and Society, 1945–52

CHAPTER 1
Postwar Cinema and the Challenges of Democracy

The period between the liberation of Rome in 1944 and the exclusion of the parties of the left from government in the spring of 1947 witnessed a flowering of cultural initiatives of all sorts. With the anti-fascist political parties having formed a government of national unity, the overriding task was to defeat the Nazis and their Fascist allies in the north of the country and restore democracy. At the same time, artists and intellectuals began to think out ways in which they could contribute to the rebirth of the nation after twenty years of dictatorship. Though cinema was not among the most established of arts, it would emerge as the field in which the boldest and most influential reflections on the situation of the country would take place. Thanks to the resources that Fascism had invested in a range of infrastructures and institutions, and the centralization that it had imposed on film production, there was a significant community of practitioners, writers and critics based in the capital who were involved with the medium. Throughout the country, there was a cinematic culture that had grown steadily in the interwar years. Though the industry remained largely in private hands, the involvement of the state had seen various initiatives flourish. Numerous young intellectuals had been drawn to cinema through magazines and the student activities of the Cineguf (Fascist University Cinema Groups). They had begun to think out the future direction of the country in relation to it. The hostility they felt towards the dominant culture, whether conventional or fascistic, would not only inform and sustain significant innovations in cinematic practice; it would help propel cinema to a position of unprecedented cultural prominence in the postwar years.

While some film-makers simply wanted to get back to work, many were concerned to try to find new ways of making films that reflected the specific conjuncture of the nation. There was clearly a need to rethink cinema's relationship to society and politics, for not only had the dictatorship fallen but the forms of state support that had sustained the industry and contributed to the development of a culture of film had disappeared. This meant that new types of political involvement were needed or that film-makers needed to turn to commercial companies or find ways of engaging civil society. However, it was not just a matter of finance. There were also urgent questions of film content and film style. Genre films could still be made, for sure, though some were products of the specific social and cultural situation of the Fascist period, but contemporary drama could not but take account of recent and unfolding events. The war and the experiences of both civilians and military personnel were no longer to be seen through the prism of the regime; rather they needed to be represented in ways that took account of the country's new alignment, its return to democracy and the collapse of Fascism's ultranationalism. The first priority was to provide witness to the suffering and sacrifices that war and foreign occupation had entailed. The second was to explore the efforts of the Italians to contribute to the liberation of their country and to face the many problems that war and dictatorship had left behind. These involved decisions about subject matter, storytelling, values and personnel.[1]

The innovations that occurred in film-making practice would have a lasting impact on Italian film aesthetics, on the relationship of cinema to society and on casting and the performance of actors. The current known as neorealism would become the defining trend within Italian cinema in the years between 1945 and 1952. It would include some of the most important films made in the immediate aftermath of war and would dominate critical discourse at least until the end of the 1950s.[2] This chapter will explore the place of new ideas about the role of cinema in the particular situation of the period after the fall of Fascism and the end of the Nazi occupation. This was characterized not only by cultural ambitions but by political conflicts, economic displacement, Allied control over the communications apparatus and efforts to recommence commercial film production.

Fascism, War and Foreign Occupation

The fall of Mussolini in July 1943 marked a watershed in the Italian film industry. The announcement that the man who had led the country for twenty years had been deposed and arrested was confirmed by the news that the Fascist Party had been abolished and that a royal government headed by Marshall Badoglio was now in office.[3] These developments came completely out of the blue to many people in the film industry. The sudden removal of figures and institutions that had been seen as permanent provoked disorientation and even panic.[4] While some critics, directors and even actors who had been cultivating opposition to the regime joined ordinary Italians in rejoicing at the fall of dictatorship and what many hoped erroneously would be the end of the war, others looked to the future with trepidation. The film industry had established itself as a zone of privilege with close links to the dictator's circle. The Duce himself had taken a keen interest in cinema, once he had been persuaded of its usefulness, while his son Vittorio had been involved in film production and had acted as editor of a film magazine, *Cinema*.[5] Producers and others had become accustomed to calling on officials and the minister in charge at the Ministry of Popular Culture on Rome's Via Veneto to seek favours. Industry personnel and prominent artists were integrated into the Fascist system and were expected, when required, to don uniforms, attend meetings and rallies, provide lustre to galas and generally provide adornment to the public activities of the regime. Actors and especially actresses were expected to attend diplomatic gatherings and meet foreign officials at the Venice festival, as well as provide comfort to serving soldiers and their wounded counterparts through autographed postcards and hospital visits.[6] In the new situation, film production ceased almost immediately, with some films being interrupted before they were completed. The arrest of key officials and uncertainty over financial guarantees and distribution effectively pulled the plug on one of the country's most florid industries.

Fascism had used state power and resources to stabilize the economy and reinforce Italy's weaker industries. Cinema was among these as it had declined markedly in the later 1920s and struggled to make an effective transition to the sound era. As a result, it was closely bound up with Fascism or, more precisely, with the state. For both economic reasons and ideological reasons, the regime decided to invest in a medium that had the capacity to communicate the Fascist message, as well as to offer entertainment that was deemed to be compatible with that message, to Italians and to foreigners. After taking over the Luce Institute in 1925 and turning it into the main vehicle of visual propaganda, it created institutions including the Venice film festival in 1932, the Centro sperimentale film school in 1935 and inaugurated the Cinecittà studio complex in 1937. It adopted measures that promoted the growth of larger companies and provided them with financial incentives and support while employing preventive censorship to encourage quality productions and eliminate potentially undesirable works. The

Fascists did not believe in the sort of state-run cinema that existed in the Soviet Union or Nazi Germany, but the balance between private enterprise and state intervention progressively tilted in favour of the latter. When the state took over the Cines production company and turned it into an instrument for the type of cinema that had long been championed by Luigi Freddi, the key official in the sector,[7] it set the tone for the rest of the market. Its output, along with other Italian and foreign films, was handled by the distribution organization ENIC, which was granted a monopoly over the purchase and distribution of foreign films in Italy from 1939. In protest, the major American companies decided to withdraw entirely from the market. In response, Italian film production increased year by year until, by 1942, it was able to cover over 56 per cent of the market.[8]

The period from July 1943 until the end of the war in April 1945 is one that was marked by a substantial inactivity of the industry. Only a handful of films went into production in this period, most with some form of institutional support. After the Germans freed Mussolini from imprisonment in the Abruzzo region, invaded the country and installed the one-time dictator at the head of a puppet republican regime based in the north of the country, Freddi was given the task of establishing a new film production centre in Venice. Despite heavy inducements, only a small number of directors, actors and technical personnel joined him in this venture, which would see the completion of just sixteen films, none of which would be released before the end of the war.[9] In Rome, where the Germans requisitioned much of Cinecittà's technical equipment, particular pressure was brought to bear on those who had not gone north. Two films that entered production in 1943, *La porta del cielo* (The Gates of Heaven, Vittorio De Sica, 1945) and *I dieci comandamenti* (The Ten Commandments, Walter Chiti, 1945) were made under the auspices of the Vatican. These productions were a harbinger of greater Vatican involvement in this sector in the postwar years.[10]

Italians who continued to go to the cinema in this period, despite air raids and curfews, were presented with mixed fare. In the north, under Nazi occupation, German films mingled with recent Italian ones and a few American ones that had not been removed from distribution. The task of the press was 'to keep up the sense of entertainment as an amusement and to provide support for the production' that was undergoing relocation and relaunch in Venice.[11] Distraction not propaganda was the priority at a time when everyday life was undergoing major disruption. In the south, where the Allies, having landed in Sicily in July 1943, were expanding step-by-step the territory under their control, audiences were presented with a package of films supportive of the Allied war effort, which were distributed by the Psychological Warfare Branch (PWB).[12] Otherwise, cinemas showed Italian films that had been granted the Allied seal of approval and some old films of various provenance that had remained in the hands of distributors and exhibitors. In both the German-occupied north and the Allied-occupied south, the authorities in charge placed great importance on the newsreels that accompanied films.

The liberation of Rome in June 1944 marked a significant step towards the rebirth of film-making. It meant that free discussions could occur, that those who had sought refuge in the countryside could return to the capital and that concrete proposals could begin to be formulated. The critical impulses that had begun to take shape in regime publications in the early 1940s were developed in a range of new publications. Some efforts to start film-making again got underway, all of them outside Cinecittà, which, like the Tirrenia complex near Pisa, had been commandeered by the Allies and turned into a refugee camp.[13]

The tentative resumption of production did not occur in complete freedom. The Americans asserted control of the communications apparatus and had clear views of their own about Italian cinema. Up until the mid 1930s, Hollywood films had occupied around 75 per cent of Italy's screens, a position they lost following creation of the monopoly over the purchase of foreign films and the withdrawal in protest of the major companies.[14] The Allies were greatly concerned about the way the mass media had been employed to bolster Fascism. There was a strong belief that free trade should be restored and that the return to democracy would be aided by the distribution of films emanating from the democratic nations. Hollywood executives were embedded within the PWB, and their concern to democratize the communications apparatuses was indistinguishable from their desire to re-establish their hold in a lucrative market. The Americans were also perturbed by the reappearance in key roles of the same men who had filled key roles under Fascism.[15] They feared that the institutions and laws created by the regime would also survive if swift action was not taken to abolish them.

Neorealism and Film Practice

These fears were not ungrounded, for within the state there were some officials who were pushing for the maintenance of the status quo. But the situation was different in the industry, where nearly all of those who were actively interested in the resumption of Italian cinema were already looking beyond Fascism. Though the involvement of the regime had contributed to a situation in which the medium was seen as a tool for national cultural promotion, there was no desire to continue in any form with the dictatorship's political design. The prominent and privileged place that cinema occupied in public affairs from the mid 1930s meant that conformism, if not outright enthusiasm, had been the norm as long as the regime was in place, though industrialists had pushed for a reduction of political inference. Nevertheless, the field had given rise to a current of critical activity in the late Fascist period. The state film school, the Centro sperimentale di cinematografia, had become a hotbed of nonconformist ideas, and theoretical debates published in the journal *Cinema* in 1941–43 about the future of Italian cinema had pointed in the direction of realism. Especially among younger writers and critics, there was a strain of disaffection, which evolved into opposition. As Giuseppe De Santis later noted, the group around *Cinema* sought to bring 'the search for truth and for reality' to cinema.[16] 'Immersing ourselves in our time is the most healthy and constructive thing one can do today', they had urged.[17]

Various ideas had been developed in the early 1940s, and some of these had found some application in films such as Visconti's pioneering *Ossessione*, which was shot in the summer of 1942 and had provided the first occasion for antifascists to put some of their ideas into practice.[18] The fall of the regime was the beginning of a new phase that would, it was hoped, allow their ideas to flourish in a democratic context. Foreign occupation and war in the peninsula put off this reckoning and created new circumstances that could not have been foreseen. The great calamity of Italy's war and the Nazi invasion was followed by a national awakening that gradually involved more and more people, especially in the final stages of the conflict in the spring of 1945. It meant that Italians could, with justification, claim that they had made a decisive contribution to their own liberation and did not owe everything to the Allies. The Resistance was a movement that was cross-class and that involved intellectuals, students, workers and peasants. Though the communists were the largest political force within it, a wide spectrum of opinion was represented in its organisms and among its fighters. To function, the Resistance needed a broader movement around it of people who were prepared, at great risk, to help partisans, to cover for them, protect them and provide them with food and succour.[19] Thus it was configured as a national uprising, even if much of the south was excluded from it and many people preferred to bide their time and avoid the risks of involvement. The Resistance movement would prove to be crucial in providing an impulse to innovation insofar as it revised the context in which film-makers conceived their role. De Santis was always insistent that the socially engaged cinema of the postwar years 'began with the Resistance'.[20] It would provide the more politicized members of the film world with their first theme, as well as a means of achieving the sort of engagement with the real life of the country that they had been calling for.[21]

Plans for films dealing with the experience of war and occupation began soon after the Allies entered Rome. De Santis himself began planning a film with Carlo Ponti, then an executive producer with Lux, but, distrusting the untested director, the latter eventually withdrew and the project was aborted. Soon after the liberation of the north in April 1945, De Santis, Carlo Lizzani and others headed for Milan, where they joined the staff of *Film d'oggi*, a magazine that, it was envisaged, would take up the battles launched a few years earlier in *Cinema*.[22] It was there that they began work on Aldo Vergano's film *Il sole sorge ancora* (The Sun Still Rises), which would be released in early 1946. In Rome, the situation was also evolving, though under the close supervision of the Allies. The Cultural Association of Italian Cinema (ACCI), which was formed in December 1944 with the aim of addressing artistic, cultural and technical issues, had taken on the task of reviewing the role cinema had played under the regime. While many once prominent professionals kept their heads down, the directors Alessandro Blasetti and Mario Soldati, the actor-director Vittorio De Sica, the actress Isa Miranda and others testified publicly about their activities and undertook acts of self-criticism. Blasetti had at one time been an architect of Fascist policy on cinema, but he had distanced himself from the regime and now turned his attentions to the great themes of the day. Mario Camerini's light comedies had played into the escapist culture the regime had fostered in the entertainment sphere, but he had never been regarded as a supporter. Now, he was given responsibilities by the Allies for de-fascistising cinema and proclaimed his socialist beliefs. Though he had not been party to the debates of the early 1940s, he engaged actively with the challenges facing cinema and addressed current themes.

It would come as a considerable surprise to long-standing anti-fascists when it transpired that the first film to tackle the topics of war and Resistance would be directed by Roberto Rossellini. The director of a trilogy of Fascist propaganda films,[23] Rossellini had only turned towards the *Cinema* group late and for this reason was regarded with suspicion and some hostility by more political elements, who saw him as an opportunist.[24]

The making of *Roma città aperta* amid great practical difficulties would come to be seen as a heroic achievement.[25] The director certainly exaggerated when he claimed that in Rome everything had been destroyed: 'almost all the producers had disappeared. Here and there various attempts flourished but the ambitions were very limited.'[26] Some producers were holding back, but others, however, were active – perhaps most notably those engaged in regional initiatives that aimed to create centres of production in several major cities.[27] However, conventional production was suspended, and Rossellini felt that 'it was this state of affairs that allowed us to undertake work of an experimental character'.[28] 'We enjoyed great freedom, the absence of an organised industry favoured the most exceptional initiatives. Any project was alright', he claimed.

Roma città aperta would be important for the way in which it presented a picture of the Italian people as united in their opposition to the Nazi occupation. It depicted the Resistance as a movement of the whole nation, regardless of religious and political differences.[29] Glossing over the support that had been given to Mussolini's regime and to most of the collaborationism with the Nazis that had occurred in Rome, it highlighted the great sacrifices that had been made in the struggle for freedom. The battle against oppression that it so vividly explored would contribute to marking a new beginning in national history. It was also significant for the innovations it brought to film-making. Unlike most commercial films up to that point, it was conceived and made in a collaborative way. The screenplay was crafted by several authors, who shared a sense that they were participating in something important.[30] Stories of real people and actual events and places were woven into the text. The first half especially provided an unprecedented depiction of everyday life infused with drama and danger.[31] The film continued the practice pioneered in *Ossessione* of reconfiguring actors and stars in order to take a stand against their conventional use. Like Visconti, Rossellini did not dispense entirely with established names but he went further in this regard because he did not downscale conventional stars but instead cast two popular comedy stars (one of whom had never played a leading role) in highly unfamiliar dramatic roles. His powerful and original film was hailed on its release in September 1945 as the first product of a new school of Italian cinema. It was the first effort to situate cinema in the role of witness, a function that would be further developed in *Paisà*, which Rossellini made the following year. The fact that the two films were made largely outside of conventional channels fuelled anti-industrial attitudes. It tended to be forgotten that much of the second half of *Roma città aperta* was studio-bound or that the cinematography and soundtrack were the work of experienced professionals. Those who expected the parties of the left to dominate government were hopeful that one day all films could be freed from the constrictions of commercial practices and pressures. Intellectuals and the people would work together to create a new type of collective cinematic experience.[32]

Observation and research were integral to neorealist film-making. 'We were anti-fascists; we insisted on analysis of the reality and the humanity that surrounded us', claimed De Santis of the *Cinema* group.[33] This became a systematic practice, and real events or newspaper articles often provided the initial inspiration for the treatment of a problem or issue.[34] These led to investigations and the gathering of first-hand information. Attention to detail in terms of environments, costumes and so on followed from this, as did other practices. On location, local people were tapped for information and invited to work as extras or supporting players. Though filming in real locations was often done quickly, attention was paid to specificities of place, atmospheres and events.[35] Above all, there was a desire to grant prominence to ordinary protagonists. As De Santis put it, 'not by chance the protagonists of neorealism are – for the first time in Italian cinema – all those people who took part in the Resistance, from the fishermen to the workers, to the artisans, to the small and medium intellectuals etc.'[36] Even *Ossessione* had only placed them strategically in the background.[37] Now backgrounds became foregrounds in a desire to engage spectators in new ways of looking at the world around them and thinking about their place in it. Lizzani later observed that there was a decisive move away from the use of common people as a 'colourful and passive chorus around this or that protagonist'. Rather, they were given 'moments of protagonism': 'chorality in other words was no longer decorative and hierarchically-ordered, but conflictual, lacerated, emotional and subject to change.'[38]

Film-makers wanted to draw people into cinema, or to a certain type of cinema, that promoted democracy as a meaningful practice and a shared value.[39] This was approached through a furious engagement with the present moment that aligned watching with witnessing.[40] As Ruth Ben-Ghiat has perceptively observed, many postwar Italian films offered a unique sense of 'the experience of living through a liminal moment'. They 'sprang from the exigency of working through a crisis of signification caused not only by the war's dislocations but also by the end of a Fascist-era system of meaning that had permeated Italian life for twenty years'.[41] The films display a keen awareness of 'the legacies of Fascist and wartime violence, the need for a recovery of humanitarian values, the importance of testimony and language, and the war's effects on gender roles'.⁴² Feelings of anxiety, loss and displacement are balanced by a search for emotional connections. 'The injunction to replace Fascist hardness with *tenerezza* (tenderness) runs through many neorealist interrupted reunions of many postwar films reflecting the actualities of contemporary Italian society'.⁴³

Engaged and Popular Cinema

Neorealist cinema would soon come to be shrouded with what Paolo Noto and Francesco Pitassio have called 'a mythical and heroic aura'.⁴⁴ The current's close association with Italian culture's opposition to barbarism and totalitarianism, its humanitarian perspective and its emphasis on understanding over ideological contrasts won it wide recognition. The stylistic novelty and immediacy that characterized the depiction of everyday reality underscored its contribution to the reframing of the country's image. The portrayal of the energy and vitality of the Italian spirit in the aftermath of war and at a time of material scarcity and social displacement accorded it a fundamental place in the reconfiguration of national identity following twenty years of Fascist dictatorship. The recasting of the Italians as victims and everyday heroes rather than fanatical supporters of Mussolini would have a significant impact abroad. It showed a commitment to national renewal that was part of a larger mobilization of collective energies in the direction of reconstruction and reform.

The distinctive features of neorealist films were decisive to the way the new cinema won recognition. So too were some of the criticisms that were levelled at aspects of conventional film-making. The hostility towards screen heroes, stars and even actors was a striking aspect of this. The screenwriter Cesare Zavattini was at the forefront of the attack on the cult of the exceptional figure, which he saw as undemocratic and bound up with commercial cinema. Throughout this period, he lost no opportunity to argue that stars were an aspect of an idea of cinema that had had its time; all the films he made with De Sica between 1946 and 1956 featured non-professionals in the leading roles.⁴⁵ 'I confess that I have a long-standing and in part unjustified aversion to actresses and actors', he wrote in his diary. 'With tears in my eyes, I would beat them *in a public square*, without doing them too much harm, while forcing them to say *I am worthless.*'⁴⁶ Yet neorealist directors and writers had all learned their trade inside the institutional or commercial worlds of Fascist cinema. They were schooled in conventional film-making and were accustomed to certain practices and devices. They might have rejected stars but 'rarely were intentions manifested in a coherent manner', Stefania Parigi argues. 'Rather they appear almost always bound up with the residues of the production canons of the past.'[47] Neorealism did not abolish or even oppose genre, regardless of what some critics argued. Instead, it mixed many different currents, inspirations and practices.[48] For Lizzani, the new way of seeing produced 'a grid of new narrative structures'. There was not so much an abolition of genre as 'a profound re-shuffling of "genres"'. There was, he argues, 'a healthy confusion: grotesque and dramatic, tragic and comic'.[49] Neorealism, from this perspective, was 'the fruit of an explosive hybridisation' of different genres, cultural currents and aesthetics.[50]

Recent studies have drawn attention to the persistence within films of situations and tropes drawn from mainstream cinema, including, most obviously, melodrama, which, as Louis Bayman has observed, is 'the Italian form par excellence'.[51] Ben-Ghiat argues that, 'it was the desire to convey current emotional climates in an honest manner that led neorealists to depart from realism when necessary, making recourse to genres such as the melodrama and the gangster film and borrowing from the stylistic conventions of expressionism'.[52] In other words, eclecticism was not necessarily the result of auteurist flaws or the product of commercial pressures. It was also part of the attempt to 'express the real distress and challenges faced by many Italians living in a fractured and incoherent situation, deprived of any centre of orientation',[53] for commercial cinema had developed a range of tools and strategies that could not be entirely renounced in the effort to win the attention of audiences. Thus, the films associated with the current present a mixture of new themes and old narrative devices, new atmospheres accompanied by conventional soundtracks, and new faces and some familiar ones.

One of the difficulties in establishing how many films can be described as neorealist lies in the fact that elements of melodrama, the western and other established tropes and practices infiltrated even the works of directors who championed the movement.[54] Another is that films that were not driven by any special mission or purpose also included scenes shot in real locations, references to recent wartime experience and actors drawn from popular theatre and from life. The tendency towards realism quickly generated situations, approaches and solutions that were drawn on by commercial cinema to pep up comedies and melodramas.

Neorealism, Parigi argues, was not a distinct presence so much as 'a composite and aerial imaginary, in the sense that is can deposit itself almost anywhere, or rather can infiltrate the most diverse works with smaller or larger elements'.[55] 'It presents itself, in other words', she argues, 'as a depository of commonplaces, symbols and mythologies that relate to two distinct but not separate trajectories: cinematographic work on the one hand, and iconic and thematic reference points on the other'.[56] The first series consisted in essence of screenplays based on recent history or new events, the presence of non-professional actors and the use of real exteriors. The second included such things as war and resistance, destroyed cities, lower class people, ragged clothes, the desperation of returned soldiers, hunger and poverty, prostitution and unemployment.

Both trajectories could be found in a popular film like Mario Mattoli's *La vita ricomincia* (Life Starts Over, 1946), though the balance tipped decisively towards the second. Mattoli had been one of the most prolific wartime directors, the creator of a series of melodramas 'that spoke to the heart'.[57] Shot in part on location in Naples, the film recounted the story of an officer returning home to find that his wife had prostituted herself in order to procure medicine for their seriously ill son. It included strong references to the war, the impact of the occupation on families, the challenges facing returning soldiers and unemployment, as well as prostitution. However, the film is a melodrama in which two established names, Alida Valli and Fosco Giachetti, play characters very similar to their usual types.[58] Neapolitan actor-playwright Eduardo De Filippo plays a comedic supporting role while Valli herself performs a popular song in a musical interlude.

Not all the commercial films of the period incorporated elements of the neorealist imaginary. There was strong evidence of a persistent demand for entertainment, demonstrated by the fact that most of the Italian films that entered distribution following the war were conventional. Musicals, comedies and adventure films dominated, while there was still demand for white telephone films. The positive reception received by the first American films was also a sign that escapist entertainment had not lost its appeal. Among the top box office earners of 1946–47 were *Aquila nera* (Return of the Black Eagle, Riccardo Freda, 1946) and Carmine Gallone's screen adaptation of Verdi's *Rigoletto*, while *Paisà* occupied ninth place.[59] Freda's film was a Pushkin adaptation about a soldier who returns home and, in the guise of a masked bandit, wreaks vengeance on an evil landowner. A great admirer of Hollywood cinema and a keen believer in the idea of the screen hero, he wanted to show that it was possible to make adventure films in Italy that were as good as those coming from America.

Freda, who had directed his first film in 1937, was a representative of that part of Italian cinema that had no sympathy with efforts to widen the range of issues and people represented. He considered *Roma città aperta* 'something accidental and absolutely uninteresting'.[60] Realism, in his view, was 'the worst possible form of artistic expression'. 'My film', he later boasted, 'exploded like a bomb to destroy the fetid vapours of neorealism'.[61] It 'overwhelmed the last resistance of a cinema that was anchored to sordid human miseries'. His films spoke to the parts of the country that disliked seeing ragged and humble individuals, prostitutes and the unemployed on screen or that had not been affected by the national uprising of the Resistance. It was precisely from these sectors of opinion that the Christian Democrats would draw much of their support. The revival of commercial cinema in the late 1940s would occur in the context of political changes that saw the forces of the left decline in influence. Pressures for reform were replaced by a desire to restore stability and lay the bases for economic growth. Yet the innovative themes and practices of the immediate postwar years left a significant mark on both working practices and the iconography of Italian cinema. People formed in the school of neorealism would continue to play key roles in the sector for years to come. Their absorption by a reviving industry that was seeking ways to compete with Hollywood and its stars was proof not only that production companies had made a return but also that they were more flexible and dynamic than anyone had imagined possible. With the support of government, they would contribute decisively to the resurrection of a national cinema that had seemed to be fatally damaged by the fall of Fascism and whose revival had been obstructed by the Allies.

Notes

1. For a selection of recent reflections on neorealism, see Carluccio, Morreale and Pierini, *Intorno al neorealismo: voci, contesti, linguaggi e culture dell'Italia del dopoguerra*.
2. D. Forgacs, 'The Making and Unmaking of Neorealism in Postwar Italy', in Hewitt, *The Culture of Reconstruction: European Thought, Literature and Film, 1945-1950*, 51–66.
3. On 1943, see Gentile, *25 luglio 1943*.
4. See Gundle, *Mussolini's Dream Factory: Film Stardom in Fascist Italy*, 261–63.
5. Sedita, 'Vittorio Mussolini, Hollywood and Neorealism', 431–57.
6. Gundle, *Mussolini's Dream Factory*, 87–92.

7. For Freddi's account of his role, see Freddi, *Il Cinema*.
8. Quaglietti, *Storia economico-politica del cinema italiano 1945–1980*, 289. See also Forgacs and Gundle, *Mass Culture and Italian Society from Fascism to the Cold War*, 125–27.
9. See G. Ghigi, 'Il cinema di Salò', in Laura, *Storia del cinema italiano*, Vol.VI 1940–1944, 50–53.
10. See Treveri Gennari, *Postwar Italian Cinema: American Intervention, Vatican Interests*, 64–72.
11. Brunetta, *Storia del cinema italiano 1895–1945*, 531.
12. Forgacs and Gundle, *Mass Culture and Italian Society*, 218–20.
13. The former would remain out of action until 1947, the latter until 1949.
14. Forgacs and Gundle, *Mass Culture and Italian Society*, 151–52, 206–7.
15. Brunetta, *Storia del cinema italiano: dal 1945 agli anni Ottanta*, 26n.
16. Giuseppe De Santis in Gili and Grossi, *Alle origini del neorealismo: Giuseppe De Santis a colloquio con Jean A. Gili*, 29.
17. C. Lizzani, 'Vie del cinema italiano', *Cinema*, 25 February 1943; Gili and Grossi, *Alle origini del neorealismo*, 75.
18. See B. Torri, 'Il caso *Ossessione*', in Laura, *Storia del cinema italiano*, Vol. VI, 1940–1944, 176–86.
19. See Cooke, *The Legacy of the Italian Resistance*.
20. De Santis in Gili and Grossi, *Alle origini del neorealismo*, 96.
21. Ibid., 120.
22. Giacci, *Carlo Lizzani*, 44–45.
23. See Ben-Ghiat, 'The Fascist War Trilogy', in Forgacs, Lutton and Nowell-Smith, *Roberto Rossellini: Magician of the Real*, 20–35.
24. Gili and Grossi, *Alle origini del neorealismo*, 84–86; S. Parigi, 'Fuochi incrociati sulla trilogia del dopoguerra', in Martini, *L'antirossellinismo*, 48–49.
25. The film has been extensively discussed and studied. For two selections of essays, see Gottlieb, *Robert Rossellini's Rome Open City*, and a special issue of *Journal of Italian Cinema and Media Studies* 6(3) (2018).
26. Cited in Rondolino, *Rossellini*, 71. See also Wagstaff, *Italian Neorealist Cinema: An Aesthetic Approach*.
27. A. Farassino, 'Neorealismo, storia e geografia', in Farassino, *Neorealismo: cinema italiano 1945–1949*, 23–24.
28. Cited in Rondolino, *Rossellini*, 71.
29. See Forgacs, '"Rome, Open City": Before and After Neorealism', 301–13 and Gordon, *Rome Open City*.
30. Lizzani, *Il mio lungo viaggio nel secolo breve*, 88–90.
31. Forgacs, '"Rome, Open City"', 303.
32. S. Gundle, 'The Communist Party and the Politics of Cultural Change in Postwar Italy, 1945–50', in Hewitt, *The Culture of Reconstruction*, 15–17.
33. De Santis in Gili and Grossi, *Alle origini del neorealismo*, 62.
34. Zavattini, quoted in R. Ben-Ghiat, 'Italian Film in the Aftermath of War and Dictatorship', in Biess and Moeller, *Histories of the Aftermath: The Legacies of the Second World War in Europe*, 160.
35. Lizzani, *Il mio lungo viaggio*, 81 on *Germania anno zero*.
36. De Santis in Gili and Grossi, *Alle origini del neorealismo*, 120.
37. Minghelli, *Landscape and Memory in Post-Fascist Italian Film: Cinema Year Zero*.
38. Lizzani, *Il mio lungo viaggio*, 93.
39. Ben-Ghiat, 'Italian Film', in Biess and Moeller, *Histories of the Aftermath*, 159.
40. Schoonover, *Brutal Vision: The Neorealist Body in Postwar Italian Cinema*.

41. Ben-Ghiat, 'Italian Film', in Biess and Moeller, *Histories of the Aftermath*, 158.
42. Ibid., 158.
43. Ibid., 159, 161.
44. Noto and Pitassio, *Il cinema neorealista*, vii.
45. The exception was *Stazione Termini* (1953), produced by David O. Selznick and starring Jennifer Jones and Montgomery Clift.
46. Zavattini, *Diario cinematografico*, 65. The entry is dated 28 May 1948.
47. Ibid., 181.
48. Lizzani refers to neorealism's 'profound re-shuffling of "genres"' in *Il mio lungo viaggio*, 93.
49. Lizzani, *Il mio lungo viaggio*, 93.
50. Ibid., 92.
51. Bayman, *The Operatic and the Everyday in Postwar Italian Film Melodrama*, 2.
52. Ben-Ghiat, 'Italian Film', in Biess and Moeller, *Histories of the Aftermath*, 159–60. On American genre influences, see Campari, 'America, cinema e mass media nel neorealismo italiano', 62–69.
53. Ben-Ghiat, 'Italian Film', in Biess and Moeller, *Histories of the Aftermath*, 159–60.
54. Wagstaff, 'The Place of Neorealism in Italian Cinema from 1945 to 1954', in Hewitt, *The Culture of Reconstruction*, 67–87.
55. Parigi, *Neorealismo: il nuovo cinema del dopoguerra*, 90.
56. Ibid. See Gundle, *Mussolini's Dream Factory*, Chapters 9 and 10, and Spinazzola, *Cinema e pubblico: lo spettacolo filmico in Italia 1945–65*, 10, 19.
57. C. Cosulich, 'In viaggio dal fascismo al antifascismo', in Cosulich, *Storia del cinema italiano*, Vol. VII 1945–1948, 45.
58. See Gundle, *Mussolini's Dream Factory*, Chapters 9 and 10.
59. Spinazzola, *Cinema e pubblico*, 10, 19.
60. Freda, *Divoratori di celluloide: 50 anni di memorie cinematografiche e non*, 91.
61. Ibid., 79.

CHAPTER 2
The Film Industry from Fascism to the Cold War

The period in which the Cinecittà studios were not available to film-makers is sometimes taken to be one in which little conventional film production took place. Several sound stages had been destroyed in wartime bombardments, while others were badly damaged.[1] With refugees camped in the grounds and the regular looting of everything from bricks to bathroom equipment, further deterioration occurred. It would not be until 1947 that some studios could be used again. In fact, the picture is more complex. There were several privately owned studios in Rome that were undamaged. Though money was scarce and the previous system of subsidies was no longer in force, production never ceased completely, and a handful of producers was keen to get to work as soon as possible after liberation. The production companies that had prospered in the later Fascist years did not disappear, though most reduced or suspended their production activity during the last two years of the war and the first year or so of peace. In addition, cooperatives were formed and some initiatives flowered outside of Rome.

The production context of the immediate postwar years presented some challenges to companies seeking to re-establish the industry, whether in continuity with past practices or on some new basis reflecting the changed political, economic and social situation. Larger enterprises that had come to occupy an important place in the market since 1939, like Lux, Titanus, Scalera and Excelsa-Minerva, approached these challenges in different ways. While the first two would emerge as the dominant players in the new context, the others would – for different reasons – soon decline. However, these companies were not alone. Several smaller but nonetheless serious ones entered the field, while a wider range of individuals and new companies also embarked on film production, though often their role was short-lived. Some of this opening up of the production sector occurred because the barriers set up under Fascism no longer existed. The success at home and especially abroad of some of the first postwar releases also induced new collaborations and initiatives.

Old habits were to die hard, however. The industry had developed and prospered thanks to the role of Fascism in creating institutions and laws that sustained and protected national production. In July 1944, film producers joined with distributors and processing companies to form the industry association ANICA. Dominated by figures who had been active under the regime (the second president, Eitel Monaco, had fulfilled a similar function in the 1930s before becoming director general of cinematography at the Ministry of Popular Culture in 1941), it wasted little time in seeking to win the backing of political forces for state support and protection. Though formal acknowledgement of the doctrine of free trade was never lacking, calls for support were insistent. As the governments of national unity gave way to the polarization of the Cold War period, the field of cinema once more became deeply politicized. New laws passed in 1947 and 1949 restored significant aspects of the system of support first adopted by the regime and contributed to renewed government interference. Yet they also formed the basis for the remarkable ascendancy of the Italian industry in the years that followed.

The Film Industry after Fascism

Fascism reinforced state authority and created many new para-state apparatuses. In the field of cinema, it first created the Venice film festival in 1932, then the Centro sperimentale film school and the Cinecittà studio complex, respectively in 1935 and 1937. It intervened in distribution and exhibition and brought the Cines production company into the public realm. An entire system of support for the industry was instituted, which culminated in the Alfieri law of 1938 and the establishment of a state monopoly over the acquisition of foreign films for distribution in Italy.[2] For both economic and ideological reasons, the regime decided to invest in an industry that had the capacity to communicate the Fascist message, or at least to offer entertainment that was deemed to be compatible with that message, to Italians and to foreigners. Between the mid 1930s and the early 1940s, Italian film production increased year by year until, by 1942, it was able to cover well over half of the market.[3] The regime adopted measures that promoted the growth of larger companies and provided them with financial incentives and support, but it did not nationalize companies unless, as with Cines, they were failing.

In the view of Luigi Freddi, the key Fascist official in the field, the role of the state was to encourage and to direct, if necessary by example. Preventive censorship provided a tool whereby producers could gain advice prior to committing funds to a project. In his time as director of Cines, which was refounded in 1941–42 as part of a systematic state presence in all sectors of the industry, he pursued his belief in dignified, quality productions. The aim was to set the tone for the market rather than dominate it.[4]

The production sector expanded greatly as a consequence of state intervention. As a result, it acquired a stability that it had not known since the death in 1931 of Cines founder Stefano Pittaluga. In the early 1930s, a range of smaller and medium companies that did not own their own production facilities dominated the industry.[5] With American product meeting much of the market's requirements, most of these made no more than four films per season. The withdrawal of the American majors from the market greatly enhanced the demand for product. It had two effects on the sector. On the one hand, by greatly reducing the competition, it encouraged companies that had hitherto mainly focused on distribution to venture into production. The Titanus company, which had been founded in 1928, entered production with the variety comedian Totò's first films in the late 1930s. It then moved into other comedies and melodramas.[6] The Lux company was founded in 1934 by Riccardo Gualino, an industrialist with wide interests in textiles, transport and other spheres.[7] Formed of two separate but related companies – one French and one Italian – its initial activity was also more in distribution than production, but the conditions created by the Alfieri law favoured its entry into the latter sector.[8] It quickly became known for the high quality of its output, which was aimed especially at middle-class consumers in big cities. The regime also persuaded other industrialists to enter the field to place it on a more solid economic footing. The Scalera brothers, who were engaged in the construction industry, were personally invited by Mussolini to move into cinema. Between 1939 and 1942, their company produced an average of nine films per year, many of them costume dramas. Production companies became so influential that they demanded to be released from Freddi's interference and in 1941 succeeded in having him replaced as director-general of cinema by Eitel Monaco, who had since 1935 headed the National Fascist Federation of Entertainment Industrialists.[9]

The arrival of the Allies in the capital presented companies with a new situation to which they responded vigorously. The formation of ANICA can be read as a declaration of intent. But the conjuncture was not propitious. Deprived of the economic support and privileges that they had enjoyed as long as Fascism was in power, unable to access the studio complex that was the best and most widely used in the country, and faced with a highly disrupted domestic market, film companies were reluctant to lay many plans for the immediate future. Infrastructure had been destroyed, personnel dispersed, equipment lost or damaged and capital was lacking. Moreover, the Americans appeared to be in no hurry to facilitate the resumption of film production. While directors could discuss projects and writers could get to work without delay, the business of film-making needed a more secure situation to resume, even on a provisional footing.[10] For this reason, it was not until the war finally came to an end in the whole peninsula that more than two or three films entered production. Nearly all of those were films that had been started and left incomplete in mid 1943. Nevertheless, the film world was vibrant and, eighteen months after Mussolini was first toppled, there was a strong desire to realize new projects. The magazine *Star* listed sixteen production companies that were based in Rome and that were waiting for the right moment to set to work.[11] There were also a striking number of regional initiatives. With the removal of the pressure towards centralization, companies were formed in Naples, Sicily and elsewhere. Cinema was an activity that attracted many and not only because of the potential for making money. Soon after the war finally ended in the north, the newly formed partisans' association, ANPI, looked to cinema as a way of spreading awareness of the sacrifices of the Resistance.[12]

The Excelsa company was among the first to resume its activities. It plunged into the production of many types of films, including *Roma città aperta* (Rome Open City, Roberto Rossellini, 1945) and Mario Mattoli's *La vita ricomincia* (Life Starts Over, 1946), along with literary adaptations, comedies and opera films. Carlo Ponti, who mainly worked as an executive producer for Lux, made Mario Camerini's *Due lettere anonime* (Two Anonymous Letters, 1945) for the company. The Catholics had long cultivated an interest in cinema, and they too were swift to act. The Orbis company was established in 1945 by the Catholic Cinema Centre. It represented, Daniela Treveri Gennari has observed, 'a concrete attempt on the part of the Vatican to intervene in film production'.[13] Universalia was born as an offshoot of Orbis. Founded by the Sicilian Salvo D'Angelo, it sought greater freedom than the Catholic Cinema Centre allowed, while remaining firmly in the Vatican's orbit.[14] In addition, a range of small and independent producers also inserted themselves in the fluid situation, including the Americans Rod Geiger, who contributed to the production of *Roma città aperta*, and Paolo William Tamburella, who contributed to *Sciuscià* (Vittorio De Sica, 1946).

Film Companies of the Postwar Years

Excelsa, One of the most significant companies in the immediate postwar years, was so active because its parent company was the long-established distributor Minerva. It was the strong position occupied by Minerva in national and international distribution that had sustained Excelsa and allowed it to engage in an eclectic series of productions. However, it would only be a major player for a short period. In May 1947, a fire caught hold at the warehouse and offices of its parent company, killing some twenty-five people and destroying its library of films. This seriously weakened its position. Though the company continued to make films until 1956, after the fire it was reduced to a marginal place in the industry. By contrast, Lux would quickly emerge as a significant force. It had developed integrated structures of production and distribution. Between 1945 and 1948, it was responsible for around one ninth of the total number of films produced in Italy (36 out of 302), and many of its titles performed strongly at the box office. It was known for the strict organization of the production process and the control it maintained over budgets, but also for the flexibility of its operations.[15] Projects were developed and followed by producers who were not company employees but who were associated with it. Carlo Ponti, Dino De Laurentiis and others exercised a degree of autonomy that allowed Lux to maintain a regular system of genre production while exploring new avenues and artistic endeavours. Unlike other companies, Lux had no studios of its own and simply rented facilities as and when they were needed. A powerful force in distribution at home and abroad, the company soon became the most important in the Italian market.

Scalera also developed ambitious plans. However, the company was the most compromised by the close relationship it had enjoyed with the Fascist regime.[16] It came under attack for moving its operations to Venice, where it installed the 'Cinevillaggio' established by Freddi during the Italian Social Republic. After the war, it launched into swashbucklers after the success of Riccardo Freda's *Aquila nera* (The Return of the Black Eagle, 1946) showed that adventure films in costume still enjoyed success with audiences. However, the four films of this genre produced by Scalera all flopped. Though two opera films did better, its output was seen as marked by certain old-style clichés in content and an overly theatrical performance style, reflecting a rigid studio system. A programme of international collaborations, which included *Cagliostro* (Black Magic, Gregory Ratoff, 1949), starring Orson Welles, and the latter's *Othello* (1951),[17] did little to shake off its associations or fuel its fortunes. While it remained strong in distribution and its studios were remunerative, the company's own productions and co-productions did not do well. With rising debts, the company was declared bankrupt in 1952.

Titanus, the fourth 'major on the Tiber' to adopt Barbara Corsi's label, was the last of the major companies to embark on a programme of production.[18] It abstained altogether from any involvement in production in the years between 1945 and 1949. Instead, it underwent a significant reorganization and invested resources in its Farnesina studios and a dubbing facility that it had acquired from Metro Goldwyn Mayer in 1935. The oldest of the four companies, and the only one with strong roots in Neapolitan cinema, as well as the one with the strongest presence in the distribution field, it opted to bide its time. From 1949, Goffredo Lombardo steadily turned it into a significant presence, especially in the field of popular cinema.[19] For Mino Argentieri, it developed a type of cinema that was remunerative but 'low profile aesthetically, culturally and industrially' in order to create a safety net for the business as it began to move into higher profile productions.[20]

The size and resources of the larger companies gave them crucial advantages over the many new production companies that were established in 1945 and the following years (159 in total up to 1949), most of which were of little or no substance. Those that persisted usually did so because they could count on the support of backers in industry or the aristocracy. Also significant was a variety of experienced players, like the Vatican-supported D'Angelo, as well as independent producers like Giuseppe Amato and Luigi Rovere, who were keenly observing the postwar market.[21] Unlike those who launched themselves into film production with little or no preparation, and who often made one film, they had a solid knowledge of the industry. Regional production companies flourished as a direct consequence of the removal of a strong government role and of Cinecitta's temporary demise as the prime focus of production.[22] They shared a concern to break the stranglehold of the capital over the entire sector and saw that new cinematic practices favoured them.[23] Fortunato Misiano's Romana Film was an example of a company that developed a specialized interest in popular cinema, especially melodramas and musical films with a Neapolitan flavour.[24]

The Italian industry in this period was not precisely reinventing itself; rather it was undergoing a form of revitalization that involved both innovation and consolidation. Many producers were cautious in their assessment of the type of film that Italian audiences were ready to embrace, but others were willing to engage with the new currents that were engaging with the problems and challenges of the moment. Lux, in particular, would prove adventurous. This was just as well for, as Alberto Farassino has shown, the costs of most neorealist films were higher than those of other films due to location shoots and the consequent need to transport personnel and equipment.[25] Despite the rejection of an idea of a film 'industry' among the more socially committed film-makers and critics, and some interesting experiments in terms of independent and cooperative production and distribution, the only stable system of making and distributing films was provided by private companies. Few film-makers were in a position to turn down the offers of producers who could support production in a systematic way.

The biggest challenge facing producers was constituted by the Americans. Though Italian companies were not opposed to a situation in which, to quote Farassino, cinema was turned from a national priority into 'a family affair of private industry',[26] the lack of state intervention left them exposed to unequal competition. The period between 1945 and 1946 saw the major studios re-establish their Italian operations. Many of the men who had run branches of companies before the war returned to perform the same functions.[27] The close surveillance of the market by Hollywood and American government departments has been described by Brunetta as a highly aggressive policy that was aimed at the destruction of the Italian industry.[28] In reality, the Americans gave little thought to their Italian counterparts, who they regarded as small fry. But, undoubtedly, the sheer volume of American films meant that those seeking to promote the rebirth of Italian cinema had to contend with powerful obstacles. The Hays Office representing the American film industry was alert to any reappearance of protectionism in Europe and engaged directly in negotiations with governments to prevent any obstacles being placed in the way of the studios' activities. In its view, only voluntary restrictions on free trade were acceptable, but it was unable to ensure that the behaviour of member companies conformed to voluntary agreements or influence the smaller companies, which were not part of the Motion Picture Export Association (MPEA).[29] Thus the Italian production sector was forced to fend for itself. The decision to abolish all Fascist laws on cinema in 1945 provided no 'indications concerning the reorganisation of production' or the role of state organisms.[30] In these circumstances, early ambitions faltered. In 1947–48 the 'crisis of production' became so severe that a broad coalition of industry forces was united in demanding government intervention. Two years after the war, some 60 or more Italian films were being released annually, but these counted for just 13 per cent of box office.[31] Moreover, with so many foreign films in distribution, lots of Italian films had to wait for release, and some only found willing exhibitors in second-run cinemas or in the suburbs.

Politics, International Relations and the 'Andreotti Law'

The abolition of all legislation protecting and supporting the film industry was soon followed by pressure to restore elements of the regulation and privileges that had been obtained previously. Industry interests, organized in the producers' association ANICA, were well aware of the leverage they had acquired in the 1930s, and their very identity was bound up with this.[32] According to Marina Nicoli, the industrialists 'had created an economic/industrial policy that gave them the benefits of an independent private organisation, but with state funding'.[33] This 'paracorporative strategy' was adapted to the new context. ANICA's role was to assert the existence of the industry and claim a right to be heard by political forces and governments at home and in the USA. Winning the ear of the powers that be was essential if the film business was to win legitimacy as an industry. The association had to accept that there could be no return to the past system of protectionism if it was to persuade, first, other sectors of the industry and then the authorities that support for production was necessary and would benefit all.[34]

Politicians were active in brokering the agreement with France in October 1946 that, after an initial trial period, would blossom into fully-fledged co-production accords that would become a key platform of the recovery and growth of the industries of both countries.[35] Government officials were engaged in addressing a series of administrative, technical and financial issues arising from the war, which were a necessary preliminary to the establishment of cultural projects in common. Co-operation was seen by both industries as a vital precondition for the conquest of foreign markets. Initially, it was intended that co-operation should occur only at the highest level with the films involved being selected on the basis of quality. The films were meant to be prestige projects that would bring lustre to the parties involved. In fact, not all met this criterion, though it is fair to say that collaboration would prove to be most systematic at the level of the art film.

The evolution of the joint Allied-Italian Temporary Film Commission into the Secretariat for Press, Entertainment and Tourism, attached to the prime minister's office, heralded the beginning of the reassertion of government control over cinema. It also marked the start of a complex jockeying for position between interest groups who approached the whole issue of cinema policy from different points of view – national, cultural and economic. The government was the inevitable interlocutor because the industry remained quite fragile. No Italian production company was vertically integrated, and the exhibition sector did not even cover all municipalities in the more advanced north and centre of the country.

The Christian Democrats, whose leader De Gasperi held the office of prime minister between December 1945 and August 1953, would be the force most tasked with resolving questions relating to cinema. With Giulio Andreotti occupying the post of undersecretary with special responsibility for the central office for cinema from 1947 to 1953, there was great continuity in the treatment of film industry affairs. Nicoli argues, basing herself on a text by Luigi Chiarini, that 'he chose to exercise his power in a latent way, so that he became labelled "The Great Invisible Man"'.[36] Certainly, he proved an able and astute mediator between different interests and the quiet forger of a new system of governmental domination that in some respects was not so different from the old one.[37]

The political context in which this occurred was significant. The onset of the Cold War led to the closer links between the government and Washington and to the exclusion in May 1947 of the Socialist and Communist parties from the anti-fascist coalition that had taken office following the liberation of Rome. With the first general election of the postwar years to be held in April 1948, the Christian Democrats were keenly interested in winning support from business interests. Andreotti took measures in favour of the film industry, backing action to ensure that cinemas reserved the mandatory number of days to Italian films, while also winning the trust of cinema owners, distributors and the Italian branches of the major American studios, who opposed limitations on the free circulation of American films. However, these were not sufficient to prevent the left from accusing the party of being subservient to the United States and effectively mobilizing various sectors of the film industry against it before, during and after the election, which accorded the Christian Democrats a historic victory.[38]

A large rally attended by 20,000 people was held in Rome's Piazza del Popolo in February 1949 at which Anna Magnani, Vittorio De Sica, Gino Cervi and many others were joined by Giuseppe Di Vittorio of the CGIL trade union to demand

Figure 2.1 Anna Magnani and Vittorio De Sica at the rally in defence of Italian cinema in Rome, *La Settimana Incom*, February 1949 (author's own collection).

support for Italian cinema (see Figure 2.1). The rally was held one week after the head of Lux and president of the producers' union, Riccardo Gualino, wrote a letter to the government stating that if a new law were not passed within two months, producers would have to cease all activity. The left parties were convinced that the government would never be able to impose the protectionist measures that the sector was calling for because of its indebtedness to the Americans following their massive involvement in the election campaign. There was a widespread view that the government would fail to take decisive action also because of Catholic hostility to neorealism and the apparent preference for Hollywood family films in the growing circuit of parish cinemas.

In fact, this did not happen. As Ennio Di Nolfo showed, the American government overrode Hollywood's desire to reduce the Italian film industry to insignificance and re-establish the dominant position in the market that it had occupied in the early to mid 1930s.[39] The political desire to see the economy of a key western ally recover and embark on a period of sustained growth led it to allow the adoption of certain measures of support, in opposition to Hollywood's interests. In addition, though the DC may have been beholden to the Americans, its dominant position was also due to its position as the party that represented the interests of Italian industry. Since its expansion in the prewar years, the film industry was a component of that. The key economic players, in short, had the ear of government, even if film workers and artistic personnel did not.

The result was the 1949 law 'Disposizioni per la cinematografia', popularly known as the 'Andreotti law', which has been credited with saving the industry and initiating its most florid period, while it has also been attacked for ensuring the elimination of the radical currents that developed after the war. Barbara Corsi has suggested that the law was 'a daring synthesis of the ideas of Freddi and Alfieri' (Alfieri being the Fascist minister who was the architect of the 1938 law that instituted the controls that led to the Americans boycotting Italy).[40] While there was no backtracking from the principle of free trade on which the USA insisted as the foundation of all postwar trade agreements, it gave rise to the partial rebirth of the state controls over cinema and the state-regulated cinema market that had prevailed under Mussolini.

The law, which remained in force until 1954, guaranteed protection and subsidies to producers while centralizing all power of decision on cinema matters in the Central Office, a close relation of the Fascist General Directorate for Cinema. Scripts were submitted for approval by a commission before the granting of subsidies and certification of a film's nationality. Thus, a system of preventive censorship was restored. The certainty that support would be forthcoming for productions that received the green light provided stability as well as an invitation to new forces to enter the production sector. In contrast to Freddi's concern to avoid fragmentation, pluralism prevailed and nothing was done to prevent the proliferation of film companies, even though some of them were little more than speculative operations. The measures facilitated the industrial expansion of Italian cinema, with parts of the sector undergoing a transition from an 'artisanal' stage of development to a properly 'industrial' one, but the sector was also brought into a relationship of permanent dependency on the state. According to Argentieri,

> *the practice of subsidies, from which Italian cinema would never again free itself, became routine with the result that entrepreneurs were continually subject to blackmail (a simple gap between one legislative provision and another was enough to unleash panic and reduce production) and Italian cinema was forced to wrestle with American companies in the domestic market rather than engage with it in a constructive way.*[41]

The left was highly critical of the law and its effects. The government and its allies were installed as cinema's gatekeepers insofar as they were able to a large degree to determine which films were made. Consequently, blame for the demise of neorealism was laid at its door. Depoliticization was the order of the day and entertainment preferred to any form of social criticism. Almost worse in the Cold War period from the left's point of view was the effect the law had in bringing American companies into the country to produce or commission the production of their films. By placing controls over the export of capital earned on the distribution of American films, the law obliged the companies to invest in Italy and assist the development of its film industry.[42] At first the Americans were reluctant to embark on what they called 'runaway' productions because of the difficulty of keeping full control over the making of films. But a combination of the desire to use blocked funds, the lower costs with respect to Hollywood and the growing economic importance of European markets as the domestic one shrank led to a pattern of such productions, many of them with ancient world settings. Though the left would remain influential among writers and directors, attempts at alternative production strategies failed. Political defeat and the industrialization of Italian cinema meant that the working practices changed. As a result, a gap opened between many declarations of principle and the practice of individuals whose wish to work of necessity engaged them in negotiation and compromise.

The Ascent of a National Industry

In the late Fascist period, film producers had baulked at what they saw as excessive government intervention. They did not now oppose the passage of legislation that subjected the whole industry to government interference and control because it also provided them with the guarantees they had been seeking. It signalled that from this moment forth the survival and prosperity of the industry became a matter of national interest. Producers thus worked to derive maximum advantage from the situation. One of their key ambitions was to gain regular access to international markets. As Corsi notes,

> *already at the start of 1947, when ANICA made the first approach to the Ministry for Foreign Trade to include the category "film" in trade negotiations, the secretary general Monaco was perfectly aware that an effective strategy of export required advanced methods such as publicity and the gathering of statistical data on foreign markets, and above all some fundamental requirements of industrial planning.*[43]

ANICA asserted itself as a powerful sectoral organization that included some 180 companies operative in production and distribution, among them the distribution affiliates of the American majors, a fact that signalled the international vocation of the key Italian players and the good relations established with the American film exporters' association, the MPEA.[44] It preferred centralization to decentralization on the basis of a conviction that resources needed to be concentrated if the industry was to assert itself as a powerful force. Thus, the initial postwar proliferation of regional initiatives gave way to a determination to reinforce Rome as the sole industrial pole, as had been the case under Fascism. The move signalled that once more the Hollywood model was king.

To relaunch Italian cinema along American lines signified concentration, volume and scale. The return of Cinecittà to its original function as the most important centre of production was the key element in a reorganization and modernization of the industry's infrastructure. That the first film to be made there was a large-scale project produced by the Universalia company in collaboration with French interests was a sign of the new direction. Blasetti's *Fabiola* was an edifying story of the birth of Christianity made with huge means and featuring an all-star cast including Michèle Morgan.⁴⁵ Great publicity was given to every stage of the film's making and to its launch in March 1949. In the view of the producer D'Angelo, the film was intended to mark the start of a long-term collaboration between two complementary industries with the aim of merging the two countries into one market.⁴⁶

The industry was in fact particularly sensitive to the demands of the domestic market. Its efforts to find themes and narrative formulas that went over well with both the traditional film-going audiences of the big cities and the new less sophisticated filmgoers of the south and the provinces were supported by investment in the development of a functioning star system. The industry's declining interest in director-led productions that appealed to an intellectual elite was endorsed in an article published in the trade journal *Cinespettacolo*, which hailed the need to produce films for mass audiences, who chose to pay to see a title on the basis of its theme and its stars, rather than the name of its director.⁴⁷ An important transition occurred when the Titanus company adopted some film-making practices pioneered in the postwar years, such as the exploration of lower-class experiences and non-studio locations, as aspects of popular comedy. As Alberto Abruzzese argued, despite the controversy that such developments gave rise to, this was not so much a question of political defeat or ideological betrayal as industrial progression.⁴⁸ A key factor was the insistence of exhibitors on commercial products of predictable appeal.⁴⁹ Historically, this category had always preferred films of this type, whether Italian or American, and it could be counted on to support the national industry only in so far as it gave them what they wanted. As the average cost of each film rose and the technical quality of it improved, they provided more consistent backing to national production, though prestige American films always provided the best guarantee of good returns.

By the early 1950s, Italian cinema was well on its way to being organized as a mass entertainment industry. The number of films produced grew from 71 in 1949 to 146 in 1953, an expansion that was fuelled by the growth of the exhibition sector.⁵⁰ According to official figures, some 6,551 auditoria were operating in 1948, a figure that rose to 7,545 in 1949 and to 9,502 in 1953.⁵¹ No longer were Italian films the poor relation in their own home; by 1953 their share of the market had doubled from 17.3 per cent in 1949 to 38.2 per cent, a figure that would rise further in the years that followed.[52] Due to the foreign strategies of single companies and the enterprise of ANICA, which actively engaged in promoting and distributing Italian films abroad, exports also increased by several hundred per cent. The industry was by this time an important economic sector and one that was dominated by stable companies with ambitious plans for further development and even greater influence abroad. The split of executive producers Carlo Ponti and Dino De Laurentiis from Lux in 1951 to found their own company heralded the first step in the direction. With quality productions geared to the national market and a programme of spectacular big-budget productions aimed at the international market, they did not so much take Hollywood as their model as seek to compete directly with it on its own familiar ground.

Notes

1. Burchielli and Bianchini, *Cinecittà: la fabbrica dei sogni*, 62–63.
2. Forgacs and Gundle, *Mass Culture and Italian Society from Fascism to the Cold War*, 130, 151–52; Corsi, *Con qualche dollaro in meno: storia economica del cinema italiano*.
3. Quaglietti, *Storia economico-politica del cinema italiano 1945–1980*, 289. See also Forgacs and Gundle, *Mass Culture and Italian Society*, 125–27.
4. F. Bono, 'Verso un gruppo di Stato: Cinecittà, ENIC e Cines', in Laura, *Storia del cinema italiano*, Vol. VI 1940–1944, 370–80 and Argentieri, 'La struttura dell'esercizio', in Laura, *Storia del cinema italiano*, Vol. VI 1940–1944, 421.
5. Nicoli, *The Rise and Fall of the Italian Film Industry*, 124.
6. Germani et al., *Titanus: cronaca familiare del cinema italiano*, 50–54.
7. See Farassino and Sanguineti, *Lux Film: Estetique et systeme d'un studio italien*; Caponetti, *Il grande Gualino: vita e avventure di un uomo del Novecento*.
8. Caponetti, *Il grande Gualino*, 346–47.
9. Bono, 'Verso un gruppo di Stato', in Laura, *Storia del cinema italiano*, 368.
10. U. Rossi, 'La fasticosa ripresa', in Cosulich, *Storia del cinema italiano*, Vol. VII 1945–1948, 392–93.
11. Sei, 'Cosa fanno?', *Star*, 23 June 1945, 5.
12. Giorgio Agliani, a former partisan commander with a business background, produced Aldo Vergano's *Il sole sorge ancora* (Outcry, 1946) and De Santis's *Caccia tragica* (Tragic Hunt, 1947) with the backing of the partisans' association ANPI. See Gundle et al., *Dream makers: come i produttori hanno fatto grande il cinema italiano*.
13. Treveri Gennari, *Postwar Italian Cinema: American Intervention, Vatican Interests*, 65.
14. Ibid., 66.
15. B. Corsi, 'Le majors sul Tevere', in Cosulich, *Storia del cinema italiano*, 391–92.
16. Scaccabarozzi, 'Nuove ricerche e analisi intorno a Scalera Film', 104–8.
17. Ibid., 109–10.
18. B. Corsi, 'Le majors sul Tevere', in Cosulich, *Storia del cinema italiano*, 391–92; Germani, *Titanus*; Di Chiara, *Generi e industria cinematografica in Italia: il caso Titanus (1949–1964)*.

19. Ibid., 22–23.
20. M. Argentieri, 'La Titanus e il mercato', in Zagarrio, *Dietro lo schermo: ragionamenti sui modi di produzione cinemtografici in Italia*, 22–23.
21. It is evident from many entries in the diary of Steno (Stefano Vanzina) that these men were regularly meeting with writers and directors. See Steno, *Sotto le stelle del '44*.
22. V. Zagarrio, 'L'industria italiana tra crisi della produzione e boom dell'esercizio', in Cosulich, *Storia del cinema italiano*, 369.
23. Ibid., pp. 368–69.
24. Della Casa, *Romana Film: Fortunato Misiano e la sua avventura nel cinema*.
25. A. Farassino, 'Il costo dei panni sporchi: note sul "modo di produzione" neorealista', in Zagarrio, *Dietro lo schermo: ragionamenti sui modi di produzione cinematografici in Italia*, 135–44.
26. A. Farassino, 'Neorealismo, storia e geografia', in Farassino, *Neorealismo: cinema italiano, 1945–1949*, 40.
27. Quaglietti, *Ecco i nostri: l'invasione del cinema americano in Italia*, 70.
28. Brunetta, *Storia dl cinema italian: dal 1945 agli anni Ottanta*, 80.
29. Forgacs and Gundle, *Mass Culture and Italian Society*, 156.
30. Farassino, 'Neorealismo, storia e geografia', in Farassino, *Neorealismo: cinema italiano, 1945–1949*, 40.
31. C. Zanchi, 'L'industria cinematografica italiana nel primo dopoguerra', in Miccichè, *Il neorealismo cinematografico italiano*, 87.
32. Nicoli, *The Rise and Fall*, 141.
33. Ibid.
34. Ibid., 142.
35. C. Burucoa, 'Gli accordi di coproduzione (1946–1995)', in Gili and Tassone, *Parigi-Roma: 50 anni di coproduzioni italo-francesi (1945–1995)*, 18–20.
36. Nicoli, *The Rise and Fall*, 143; Chiarini, *Cinema quinto potere*.
37. For Andreotti's testimony, see *Giulio Andreotti – Il cinema visto da vicino/la politica del cinema* (Istituto Luce DVD, 2016).
38. In the election, Antonio Pietrangeli, a promoter of grass-roots film circles and a future film director who had been a contemporary of Andreotti's at high school, stood for the Democratic Popular Front. He was not elected, and following the election, he was no longer received by Andreotti.
39. E. Di Nolfo, 'La diplomazia del cinema americano in Europa nel secodo dopoguerra', in Ellwood and Brunetta, *Hollywood in Europa: industria, politica, pubblico del cinema 1945–1960*, 35; see also, Forgacs and Gundle, *Mass Culture and Italian Society*, 137–39.
40. Corsi, *Con qualche dollaro in meno*, 49–50.
41. Argentieri, 'La Titanus e il mercato', in Zagarrio, *Dietro lo schermo*, 19–20.
42. Forgacs and Gundle, *Mass Culture and Italian Society*.
43. Corsi, 'La ripresa produttiva', in De Giusti, *Storia del cinema italiano*, Vol. VIII 1949–1953, 144.
44. See Nicoli, *The Rise and Fall*, 148–51.
45. See L. Pellizzari, 'Fabiola di Alessandro Blasetti', *Cineforum* 284, 55–62.
46. C. Burucoa, 'Gli accordi di coproduzione (1946–1995)', in Gili and Tassone, *Parigi-Roma*, 19–20.
47. W. Ruffili, 'Perchè il pubblico va al cinema?', *Cinespettacolo*, 2 February 1949.
48. Abruzzese, 'Per una definizione del rapporto politica-cultura', in Miccichè, *Il neorealismo cinematografico italiano*, 52–58.
49. See Freda, *Divoratori di celluloide: 50 anni di memorie cinematografiche e non*, 79.

50. Nicoli, *The Rise and Fall*, 153.
51. Ibid., 150–51.
52. On the comparative popularity of American and Italian films in the domestic market, see Treveri Gennari, *Postwar Italian Cinema*, Chapter 5.

CHAPTER 3

The Transformation of the Star System

In her book on star personae and star performances in Italian cinema, Marcia Landy suggests that there were significant continuities between the cinema of the prewar and war years and the postwar period.¹ Actors as well as cinematographers and writers who were active under Fascism formed the backbone of the industry after the war, she argues. However, while some actors maintained their popularity through this turbulent period, others did not, and no star image was unaffected. The altered conditions of production, combined with the experience of war and the return to Italy's screens of the Hollywood stars, cast Italy's established stars in a new light. While few were contaminated by close personal association with the regime, the position of privilege they had occupied exposed some to criticism. Moreover, the conditions of spectatorship were affected by social and material circumstances, with the result that some tastes and expectations were modified. Moreover, neorealism did not simply stand in opposition to stardom. Landy argues that it 'was responsible for new stars in the context of a changed cultural and political landscape'.² The 'hybrid character' of films, which used 'preexisting cinematic forms' for 'different ends', she continues, 'played a significant role in revivifying and enhancing popular actors from previous years such as Anna Magnani, Aldo Fabrizi and Massimo Girotti'.³ It also 'produced a new galaxy of stars' through the enthusiastic reception of many of the new performers who debuted in postwar films'. Overall, far from abolishing star figures, as some critics had hoped, Landy argues that neorealism 'had a transforming effect on stardom, reinvigorating it and producing different cultural models'.⁴

Stardom is not usually given much attention in studies of Italian cinema of the immediate postwar period.⁵ In the years before the emergence of a new and predominantly female star system in the 1950s, perhaps only Anna Magnani, the heroic and tragic Pina in Rossellini's *Roma città aperta* (Rome Open City, 1945), has been extensively written about, though more often as 'anti-star' than star.⁶ Giuseppe De Santis's 1949 film *Riso amaro* (Bitter Rice) is regarded as having marked the first appearance in postwar Italy of an American-style star type in the form of Silvana Mangano, a former beauty pageant winner who played a naive and corruptible rice-weeder.[7] Needless to say, the situation was far more complex than this, and a whole series of circumstances, practices and events needs to be considered if the transformation that the Italian star system underwent between the fall of Mussolini and the growth in national film production from the end of the 1940s is to be properly investigated. Landy's suggestive chapter, together with an earlier overview by Gian Piero Brunetta, provides a starting point for detailed analysis of these questions.[8]

In this chapter, attention is paid to the way in which patterns of stardom changed during the postwar transition. Neorealist practices are considered in relation to commercial pressures, the role of production companies, the powerful example of Hollywood stardom and the broader context of transition in popular aspirations and culture. Class bore significantly on the emergent star system, but so too did the collapse of petit bourgeois respectability, the emancipation of women and the crisis of Fascist masculinity. Geography was significant too, as the stars who prospered during and after the reconstruction predominantly hailed from the south.

The Fascist Star System

The star system that took shape in Italian cinema in the 1930s was often compared, and not usually favourably, to the American star system. Faced with the dominance by Hollywood of Italy's screens, production companies selected actors for feature films on the basis of their resemblance to American stars or star types. Given the condition of Italian cinema in the mid 1930s, these efforts were not always successful. The stars who were most popular were those, like Vittorio De Sica, who developed a persona that included recognizable Italian qualities; in his case these were musicality and a certain Neapolitan spirit.[9] The formation of the Centro sperimentale film school provided a channel of recruitment different from the theatre, and many of the younger actors who appeared in features in the second half of the 1930s, and especially after the rise in production from 1939, had been students there. It was a source of some surprise and not a little satisfaction that these new faces went over well with the public and were able adequately to fill the gap left by the Americans when the boycott began.[10]

For Fascist officials and journalists, the issue of stars was a thorny one.[11] On the one hand, there was a feeling that the film star was an American phenomenon, a product of commercial cinema that should not be imitated in Italy. What the country needed were screen actors able to embody and communicate the best Italian values. For this reason, it was not uncommon to encounter criticism of the shallow, polished types who inhabited the cosmopolitan worlds of the Cines comedies of the early 1930s or the 'white telephone' films of later years. On the other hand, it was acknowledged that stars not only attracted audiences to films; they also had the power to root ideas in the popular mind and to shape perceptions and aspirations. Because Fascism had no intention of abolishing commercial film-making, stardom as a promotional tool inevitably prospered as production increased. In consequence, hostility in the regime to the phenomenon was replaced by a pragmatic desire to shape stars, to harness them to national objectives and to use them as role models and examples.[12]

This is not to say there were not issues that presented problems. One was the question of glamour, which observers already identified with American cinema.[13] Here too there was ambivalence. Instinctively, some critics recoiled from the 'cold and uninviting' beauty that was manufactured by the studios and that was seen as synthetic and inhuman. Jean Harlow, for example, was described by critic Giacomo De Benedetti as 'a masterpiece of embalming' or sculpted marble.[14] 'Chemically pure beauty' was seen extraneous to Italian culture both because there was no knowledge of how to achieve it and because it did not accord with the preference for types of beauty that expressed regional traits or national qualities. Yet, when it came to fashion, which was a key component of Hollywood glamour, there was wide agreement that cinema needed to be used to promote Italian textiles and garment production at home and abroad. The question of how actresses should dress, on screen and off, was discussed at length in the press, and significant efforts were made to develop an idea of cinematic fashion that could serve as proof of the capabilities of Italian designers and the quality of Italian textiles.[15]

Though there was general satisfaction with the leading stars of the 1940s, there were still reservations about how far they were representative of the Italian people. Luigi Freddi had called for new actors to be selected on a continuous basis from among 'the middle, educated classes, who are distant from banal, snobbish and parvenu habits'.[16] The problem was that some of the stars were too middle class. Many of the young women who came to the fore, whether via the Centro sperimentale or through other routes, were refined and delicate. In keeping with the cosmopolitan style that continued to be the hallmark of many comedies, they had a northern appearance. Indeed, a number of them, including the blondes Assia Noris, Irasema Dilian and Vivi Gioi, were foreign by birth and, though they were accepted by Italian audiences, they were utterly unsuitable for use in films with propagandistic intents. The director Alessandro Blasetti had called, as early as 1930, for the Italian female star of the near future to be a 'woman of the people',[17] but the dominant type remained middle class and northern through the war years. Nevertheless, a handful of female stars had more earthy qualities. Blasetti had cast the exuberant Leda Gloria in rural-themed films including *Terra madre* (Mother Earth, 1931), in which she plays a peasant girl who marries a wealthy landowner, though in some other films she presented different qualities. Both Luisa Ferida and Doris Duranti were dark-haired actors whose intensity was harnessed to good effect in a number of roles. Duranti in particular played primitive, passionate women in films including *La figlia del corsaro verde* (The Daughter of the Green Pirate, Enrico Guazzoni, 1940), *Carmela* (Flavio Calzavara, 1942) and *Giarabub* (Goffredo Alessandrini, 1942). However, her characters more often than not were femme fatales rather than everyday women. This was an image that Duranti, in contrast to other stars, was pleased to confirm in her flamboyant off-screen persona.[18]

The Fascist star system was dominated by leading male actors who took top billing and who earned the most. Both Amedeo Nazzari and Fosco Giachetti had a background in theatre, but they transcended this to become the most prolific and effective screen performers (see Figure 3.1). While the performance style of many was, in Brunetta's view, 'stuck halfway between theatre and cinema', they managed to develop a professionalism that was better than the 'rather flat' average.[19] The Sardinian Nazzari rose to fame as the star of military films, notably *Cavalleria* (Cavalry, Goffredo Alessandrini, 1936) and *Luciano Serra pilota* (Luciano Serra pilot, Goffredo Alessandrini, 1938).[20] Tall, handsome and robustly built, he carefully cultivated a positive screen persona suited to heroic leading roles. He was often compared to Hollywood actors; a slight resemblance to Errol Flynn did him no harm, though he admired Gary Cooper for his quiet composure. However, Nazzari was seen as a thoroughly Italian type. His persona had an instinctive courage; honesty and loyalty were combined with a strongly patriotic feeling. He cultivated a film-star image and he appeared, alongside the rising star Alida Valli, in a promotional short entitled *Cinque minuti a Cinecittà* (Five Minutes at Cinecittà, 1940) in which his open-top luxury sports car was on prominent view. Giachetti was physically slighter than Nazzari and less versatile as an actor. But his rich, distinctive voice and the intensity he brought to his roles brought him great popularity.[21] He too played military roles and indeed he made his name in three films, all directed by Augusto Genina, in which he played captains: the desert-set drama *Squadrone bianco* (White Squadron, 1934), the Spanish civil war-themed *L'assedio dell'Alcazar* (The Siege of the Alcazar, 1936) and *Bengasi* (1942), a tale of the World War II conflict between the Italians and the British in Africa. Though admired by women, Giachetti's characters are almost always reserved types who are most comfortable in homosocial environments.

Both Nazzari and Giachetti played in propaganda films and received honours and privileges. Though they each are said to have declined invitations to join the National Fascist Party,[22] this did not prevent them from being aligned with the regime. Nazzari, Brunetta has argued, was seen as 'the Mussolinian hero par excellence' (albeit 'unjustly'), and Giuseppe Gubitosi has further commented on

Figure 3.1 Two protagonists of Fascist cinema, Fosco Giachetti (left) and Amedeo Nazzari (middle), in the war film *Bengasi* (Augusto Genina, 1942), the only one of the period in which they both featured (screenshot by the author).

the 'complementary nature – within the collective imagination – of the myth of Mussolini and the personality of Nazzari'.[23] The actor, it has been suggested, represented a sort of super-Italian, an Italian as Italians would have liked to be, and for this reason his persona was endowed not only with patriotic connotations but was readily incorporated into Fascist ultranationalism. Giachetti was drawn even more into his screen image. Whereas Nazzari was able to keep a certain distance between his image and his roles through the variety of the former and his film-star persona, Giachetti was ultimately more closely identified with his roles, something that would mark him even into the postwar period.[24]

Italian film stars of the war years were not remote or aloof. Despite occupying a place of note in the regime's system of communications, they were shown in the press as sharing the experiences and sacrifices of the Italian people.[25] They took public transport, lived modestly and made contributions of various sorts to the war effort. The female stars visited the wounded in hospital, sent autographed postcards to soldiers and donated subscriptions to film magazines. Though they were insulated from the sufferings of much of the population, they established a common feeling with filmgoers in this period that complemented the popularity they won through their screen performances. This would ensure that, though the return of the Americans at the end of the war would present a major challenge, their place in Italian affections would not disappear along with the regime that had facilitated the development of national cinema into a force to be reckoned with. This did not mean, however, that they would all be able to continue with their careers in coming years, even though, as Brunetta observes, not only new actors would emerge from the ruins of war; 'old actors would return to life too'.[26]

Civil War, Occupation and the Return of Hollywood

The overthrow of Mussolini in 1943 and the subsequent impact of war and foreign occupation on the peninsula would have relatively little immediate impact on the star system. Though actors were no longer engaged in a regular series of productions, and indeed were suddenly reduced to idleness, the film press continued to supply keen fans with news and pictures of their favourites. Magazines published in Milan like *Film* and *Primi piani* sustained the efforts of the Italian Social Republic to establish a production centre in Venice, but they did not seek to draw a line between the handful of well-known actors who accepted Freddi's inducements to go north and the majority who, on the basis of various pretexts, refused to do so. Rather there was an attempt to provide an illusion of continuity by appropriating the pattern of stardom that had been established in previous years. There was no anathema against those who had opted to stay in Rome (indeed this choice was never disclosed) but rather an annexation of their popularity. Only in the final months of the war, when the limited pages and infrequent publication of magazines indicated that they were suffering from a shortage of material and a lack of advertising, did this attitude give way to expressions of venom against those stars who had failed to join the Salò venture. It was not on any principled grounds that Nazzari and Giachetti had withheld their support but because their exorbitant demands had not been met, the journalist Marco Ramperti claimed, adding that 'they wore the uniforms of heroes in the past, but now we know they were no more than mercenaries'.[27]

The majority of actors who stayed in the capital were thrust into a limbo that would last at least until the liberation. During the Nazi occupation of Rome, some performers were pressured to join in with the entertainment of the troops, while others went into hiding or left the capital for the countryside. During the period of relative idleness, several of the young female stars wed, including Alida Valli (who also gave birth to her first son), Marina Berti, Clara Calamai, Maria Denis and Vivi Gioi. In the weeks prior to the liberation of Rome, some provided practical assistance to the Resistance, among them Valli and Isa Miranda, whose husband Alfredo Guarini was a coordinator for the Communist Party. The arrival of the Allies in Rome and the establishment of a new government formed by the anti-fascist parties raised hopes that film production would soon recommence. It also signalled the start of a process of filtering and selection of artistic personnel that would continue into the second half of 1945. This process took several forms: the Allies were most concerned with Fascist propaganda films and those who had made them; the film community was concerned to settle accounts internally and purge itself of compromised elements; left-wing critics were keen to review the talent pool as it had been formed during the preceding period and select those best able to contribute to a cinema for the democratic era.

With so few films in production, many actors either took to the theatre or participated in the many public events that signalled the growth in leisure of the liberation period. As Christine Geraghty has noted, long breaks between the release of films create opportunities for stars to develop a celebrity persona by working in other media.[28] This serves to maintain a public profile and provide alternative or additional sources of income. Though she was not thinking of Italy at war's end, something of this occurred, as idle stars joined in celebrity football matches, acted as judges at beauty competitions, took part in inaugurations, engaged in other promotional initiatives and made themselves available to the press for photo features and profiles. With few stars under valid contracts, and no system of agents and mediators, the stars themselves or, if they were lucky, personal secretaries, arranged these stunts. Wherever they went, the stars were greeted by friendly crowds and asked for autographs. But the situation was worrying. Though the return of Hollywood films to Italy's screens would not occur in massive proportions until 1947, it was preceded by the whole paraphernalia of the star system in terms of promotion, publicity, press materials and strategies of public engagement, including competitions and radio interviews. Distributors exploited the fact that the stars of Hollywood stood for the spirit of the liberation in the way that boogie woogie provided its soundtrack. *Star*, *Hollywood* and the other magazines that began publishing in 1944–45 rarely featured an Italian actor's face on the front or back cover. While articles often displayed a commitment to the rebirth of Italian cinema, the photographic imagery derived predominantly from Hollywood.[29] The smiling faces of Veronica Lake, Dorothy Lamour, Rita Hayworth, Bette Davis and others beamed out from magazines, while photographs of anonymous bikini-clad starlets filled inside pages. Accompanying text was often lifted directly from the press books and other material supplied by the American agencies, but there were also articles by Italians on American cinema and its stars. American ideas of elegance, leisure, prosperity, health and fitness testified to the superior standard of living of the most powerful country in the world. New models of beauty were propagated in association with the stars,[30] while gossip pieces, features on home and private life and depictions of sport and leisure invited identification with them.

The impact of Hollywood was widespread thanks in part to the favour with which the favourites of the 1930s were remembered. But it was not only through familiar names that the charm and appeal of its stars was reaffirmed. Especially intriguing were the new faces, who seemed best to capture something of the moment, like Rita Hayworth and Tyrone Power. A product of the star alchemy of Harry Cohn, the head of Columbia, a smaller studio, Hayworth introduced in her 1945 film *Gilda* an unprecedented combination of qualities that tantalized and scandalized in equal measure. She was neither a vamp nor a girl next door, Glauco Viazzi noted, but both; she blended innocence and sex appeal.[31] Fashion specialist

Gion Guida argued that, 'Gilda speaks a universal language that crosses all frontiers and is in direct communication with the spectator thanks to that very special passport called *sex appeal*.'[32] Some were not entirely persuaded. A seasoned observer like the former Fascist Ramperti, who, after a period of imprisonment,[33] resumed his press work, struggled to make sense of her. 'Throughout the world, her beauty is cited as the most splendid, the most exciting, the most beautiful!' he wrote, but anyone seeking a glimpse of her décolletage was likely to be disappointed: the fact is, he argued, 'that a similar masterpiece of a bosom has not been seen by anyone, yet everyone swears that there is nothing like it on earth, that it is a the "atomic bosom", the bosom-phenomenon, the "Gilda", the *nil mirari*, the eighth wonder of the world and so on'.[34] Glamour, as a seduction based on illusion, remained a quality that was difficult to grasp,[35] though some saw its power. It would not be long before articles appeared bemoaning the detachment of Hollywood from the Italian situation. But there was no doubting the extraordinary attraction that was exercised by Hayworth and her bullfighter co-star in *Blood and Sand* (Rouben Mamoulian, 1941), the handsome Power, who was a regular visitor to the peninsula from 1947 (see Chapter 4).

Italian stars occupied what can only be termed a subordinate position. With production at a low ebb and no company even attempting to compete with the Americans in the area of publicity, the press coverage they received was occasional and unsystematic. The initiative lay with journalists rather than press or publicity agents. Pictures of Italian actresses, including Maria Denis, Elsa De Giorgi, Clara Calamai and others, posing in bathing costumes did not so much confirm their status as stars as situate them at the decidedly lower level of starlet. Only their recognizable faces distinguished them from the mass of American 'cheesecake' shots. Ambivalence towards their past position in the entertainment world of the regime was underlined by the practice of asking actresses to write 'Letters to . . .' columns (for example, in *Star* Mariella Lotti 'wrote' to Veronica Lake almost apologizing for having succeeded while the Americans were absent).[36] The fact that they featured at all, it might be said, demonstrates that journalists and readers alike felt affection for familiar faces who had been part of a shared culture through the difficult years of the war. For some, the limbo period of magazine celebrity masked the beginning of a decline that would end in oblivion. With the modesty of their professionalism thrown into relief, stars like Assia Noris, Maria Denis, Laura Solari, Charetta Gelli, Lilia Silvi, Roberto Villa and Antonio Centa, either immediately or in short order, would exit the film industry. Giachetti, Isa

Miranda and others would find work in secondary roles, but their star aura did not survive far into the postwar era. Alida Valli, Rossano Brazzi, Valentina Cortese and a handful of others were talent-spotted by Hollywood and migrated there temporarily, while Spain lured Irasema Dilian, Miriam di San Servolo (sister of Mussolini's lover Claretta Petacci) and some others, including Nazzari. Others, including Aldo Fabrizi, Gino Cervi, Vittorio De Sica and Totò benefited from the relaunch of production and the ability with which they consolidated or renewed an older popularity. A handful benefited from the remoulding and relaunch to which they were subjected by neorealism. All of them, however, would have to contend with a new alignment of stars who would emerge in the 1940s or early 1950s; these owed their prominence to processes and opportunities that had nothing to do with the prewar film industry and were more closely attuned to the specificity of the new situation of the postwar years.

Neorealism's Approach to Stars and Stardom

The critics who, in their articles for *Cinema*, sought to outline a future direction for Italian cinema were not sympathetic to stars and stardom. Visconti's article 'Anthropomorphic Cinema', which appeared in the Autumn of 1943, outlined his approach to working with actors.[37] This was centred on his working on their 'human qualities' to build his characters 'so as to make a unity of the man-actor and the man-character'. 'Until now', he continued, 'the Italian cinema has had to endure actors; it has left them free to magnify their vanity and errors, while the real problem is to use their originality and the actuality of their true nature'.[38] His task as a director was to strip away the mannerisms, habits and presumptions of professional actors in order to get to the human being that lay at the core.[39] Although he did not spell it out, it was clear that among the 'vanity and errors' of actors was their sense of their own star image and, by extension, the way this was harnessed by directors and production companies.

This preoccupation fed into the casting of *Ossessione* (Luchino Visconti, 1943). Giuseppe De Santis, who collaborated on the film, later revealed that he and other members of the *Cinema* group had identified Andrea Checchi as a possible standard-bearer of a new type of cinema. He was a 'realistic actor', whose very physique 'offered us a link to the great school of French cinema';[40] he had an everyday look about him and a physical presence that was completely unexceptional. Rather than the 'angel-type' Massimo Girotti, who was Visconti's choice, they would have preferred to see Checchi cast as the wanderer Gino in the film. However, when it came to Anna Magnani, who Visconti saw as the ideal actress to cast as Gino's adulterous lover Giovanna, on account of her intensity and informality, De Santis and others found her 'not sufficiently attractive for a story of this sort'.[41]

These differences of opinion suggest that, while there was agreement that actors needed to be used in a new way, it was not always obvious how this should be translated into practice. The requirement of physical beauty could not be abolished, it seemed, only suspended in the case of this or that character. Visconti was more preoccupied with achieving authenticity with his female actors, while his younger collaborators retained some conventional ideas about feminine beauty. The attitude to male actors was the reverse; Visconti preferred the ideal; De Santis and company the real.

Non-professional actors offered a possible means to achieve the abolition of the inauthentic layers that impeded the realization of the impression of reality. They had been used in a number of films of the 1940s, notably the military films of Rossellini and Federico De Robertis, and this led to increasing interest in them. In 1943, Visconti argued that they had 'a fascinating simplicity' and even that 'they often have more genuinely healthy qualities because, being less corrupt, they are often better men'.[42] However, there was little consistency also over the use of them. The director employed professionals in the leading roles in all his films, save *La terra trema* (The Earth Trembles, 1948). For his part, Rossellini would make ample use of non-professionals in *Paisà* and some later films, while casting well-known actors, who he significantly transfigured, as the two leads in *Roma città aperta*. From 1949, he made a series of films with Hollywood émigré Ingrid Bergman. De Sica cast non-professionals in the leading roles in all his films of the 1946–54 period but often surrounded them with a professional supporting cast. The issue of non-professional actors is addressed in more detail in Chapter 15.

Fundamentally, what the film-makers belonging to the new current in Italian cinema wanted to do was to rethink the role of the actor. 'While the reconstruction of cinema seemed unable to do without cinematographers, directors, scenographers who had worked in the previous cinema, the actor was seen as being completely dispensable', Brunetta argues.[43] The desire was to effect a series of breaks: with the personnel of Fascist cinema, with established performance modes and with the imperatives of commercial cinema. There was also a concern to interrupt the process whereby screen actors became surrounded by a star aura, a factor that simultaneously removed them from the realm of the everyday and increased their contractual value. It was necessary to widen the pool of people performing on screen if new themes were to be introduced and cinema were to be taken into areas of the country and society that had been ignored or under-represented. All neorealists shared a conviction that cinema's mission was to tell the truth, and they were sure that this could be fulfilled principally by engaging with 'reality'. Real men and women could offer a different type of presence to the professional actor and create a more authentic atmosphere. There was a class aspect to this. While Freddi had wanted to reinvigorate the ranks of Italian cinema's talent by means of the recruitment of 'elements who either belonged to the educated classes or had lived in moral circles',[44] postwar innovators were more interested in the working class, in line with the shake-up of social relations heralded by the end of Fascism, Resistance and the formation of democratic mass political parties. While they too felt little sympathy for the theatrical-Bohemian milieu, cinema was seen not as an affair of the more comfortable urban classes but of the whole people. Class would, in fact, prove a problematic issue for film-makers as they sought to bring the lower classes to the screen. Neither of neorealism's two most famous 'workers', Massimo Girotti and Raf Vallone, was actually of working-class extraction; both had been university students, and they came to cinema via the world of sport.

Soon after the liberation of Rome, articles began to appear in newly founded film magazines that reviewed the qualities and potential of the country's screen actors. For Antonio Pietrangeli, who would author two incisive articles for *Star*, the issue was not whether any actors were politically compromised but simply whether they were any good or not.[45] The future director Pietrangeli was a keen supporter of neorealism, and he would be active in organizing local film circles. He stood as a candidate for the left in the 1948 election but was not elected. Overall, he took a dim view, finding many actors inexpressive and lacking both character and artistic sensitivity. Amedeo Nazzari, who had emerged as the leading male star after the withdrawal of the Americans in 1939, was once more seen as an inferior Errol Flynn who had scarcely developed since his debut. This 'wooden, clumsy star' found a counterpart in Fosco Giachetti, who was denounced as immobile save for a few nervous twitches, making him at once implacable and ridiculous. Girotti could not be taken seriously after he had played a silly Tarzan type in Blasetti's fantasy *La corona di ferro* (The Iron Crown, 1941). The women fared no better. Maria Denis, Mariella Lotti, Vanna Vanni and others were deemed to lack authenticity, talent or both. The worst of all was Assia Noris, who was found to be 'always the same and unpleasantly simpering, sickly sweet and artificial'. Her unusual accent lay 'somewhere between the exotic and the mannered', while her range was confined to 'monotonous and doll-like movements of staring eyes and stereotyped smile'. Pietrangeli argued that these actors were bad because they were overly theatrical – that is, literary, sentimental, rhetorical and histrionic. However, not all were similarly limited. As he saw it, Checchi and De Sica shared with Gino Cervi and Carlo Ninchi sincere, humane and moral qualities, which were also to be found in Calamai and Valli, in addition to Isa Miranda and Marina Berti.

The actors of the 1930s had been recruited for the most part from the theatre, and this had given rise to unflattering comparisons with American screen actors.[46] Though, as Peter Krämer and Alan Lovell observe, an 'intimate relationship' between theatre and film acting obtained widely, including in the United States,[47] the specificity of cinema meant that, in more advanced industries, there was no simple passage from one to the other. Italian cinema seemed to suffer from, on the one hand, an artistic subordination to the theatre and, on the other, a desperate desire to imitate certain aspects of the American star system. For example, the serial production of polished and beautiful young starlets who seemed similar to each other drew critical comment.[48] The Centro sperimentale film school had made a difference to the quality of performance of the younger actors who studied there, while a handful of men had emerged from the world of sport. But the actors of the prewar and war years had been worked so hard that they had become overfamiliar. Their mannerisms and general polish associated them closely with the mode of production of the cinema of the time. Even with some transfiguration, it was difficult to imagine that they could suddenly be made to seem like anything other than the modest professionals that they were; a higher dose of naturalism was the best that could be obtained. In order to widen the talent pool, the sphere of recruitment needed to be expanded.

However, the injection of a new sense of purpose impacted in a number of ways on performers and performances. First, the anti-fascist impulse in postwar cinema meant that neorealist films were often structured around the telling of stories that acquire the value of testimony. The approach to the themes of guilt and retribution that consumed Italian society in the immediate postwar years led to an exploration of new, less elaborately verbal modes of communication. Silences played a part, due to the desire to avoid 'reproducing the sounds of Fascist speech'.⁴⁹ For Ruth Ben-Ghiat, 'the silences and ellipses of this cinema, its reliance on body and gesture, are solutions to the problem of utilizing a still "contaminated" language' but also need to be seen 'in function of the different relationship of the protagonist to his or her setting':⁵⁰ 'Neorealist films situate the act of speech in the body and dramatize its effects in the family and the community, rebuking the disembodied authoritarian commands issued via radio by Mussolini and other Fascists'. An actor, André Bazin noted, had 'to *be* before expressing himself'.⁵¹ The shift away from the studio bore on this, for, he added, 'the natural setting is to the artificial set what the amateur actor is to the professional'. 'The experience of war, genocide, and poverty had left many people ashamed of the shining light and eager happiness of entertainment films', writes David Thomson.⁵² 'It was a time for reality' and 'nowhere was that urge stronger than in Italy'.

Casting became integral to this. In the Fascist period, several sometimes incompatible imperatives conditioned casting: the need for actors trained in screen acting who would be capable of rivalling the star appeal of the Americans, the demand that actors should look and behave like positive Italian racial types, and the preference for men and women recruited 'from real, true life', who were 'endowed with fresh spontaneity and fertile creativity'.⁵³ The Centro sperimentale had helped form new actors, but now those critical of the cinema of the regime sought to avoid using actors associated with it in any way, or at least avoid employing them in ways that bore continuity with the past. New faces were needed, and this led to more competitions in the press, a new relationship with popular theatre and to open auditions and casual scouting. The basic idea, which had a noble pedigree going back to Greek theatre, was that, in a properly dramatic situation, 'a simple human presence [is] enough'.⁵⁴ It was underscored by the emergence in seventeenth-century Europe of the idea of the individual as a being endowed with an essential 'true' core.⁵⁵ The emphasis on the body, which was both cause and consequence of the reduced emphasis on speech, assisted the passage from the professional to the non-professional actor, since only the body of the non-actor offered the promise of an authentic engagement with reality. The idea was that the screen character should be as close as possible to a real person, and this person should not seem to be acting at all. They should simply stand for the community of people from which they emerged.

In principle, the recourse to non-actors should have led to a simplification of casting. In reality, the opposite was often the case. As Bazin noted, with reference to *Ladri di biciclette* (Bicycle Thieves, 1948),

> De Sica hunted for his cast for a long time and selected them for specific characteristics. Natural mobility, that purity of countenance and bearing that common people have ... He hesitated for months between this person and that, took a hundred tests only to decide finally, in a flash and by intuition, on the basis of a silhouette suddenly come upon at the bend of a road.[56]

In fact, Lamberto Maggiorani, the factory worker who took the lead role in the film, was not chosen in precisely this way;[57] the idea of the flash of intuition was a romantic view that confirmed Bazin's belief that neorealism did away with all the artifices and falsity of cinema and its conventional preliminaries.

Maggiorani unquestionably had presence; he could hold the spectator's attention, and his granite-like face was inexpressively expressive, a little like that of Giachetti. His own life experiences had stamped on his countenance the desperation that his character feels over the theft of his bicycle and the consequent loss of his newly acquired job. However, while his silences were eloquent, like the majority of non-professional actors of the period, he had to be dubbed by a professional, since few amateurs could deliver even limited lines to an acceptable standard. Foreign films were routinely dubbed, but the practice of post-synchronized sound became standard in postwar cinema in Italy due to a variety of economic and cultural conditions, including location shoots and the scarcity of sound-recording trucks (most of the few in use had been requisitioned by the Germans).[58] With even the professionals adding their voices after the completion of editing, it was a simple step to eliminate the biggest hurdle to the assimilation of the amateur.

The Emergence of a New Star System

The relative lack of success at the box office of neorealist films after their initial impact led to pressures to substitute innovative casting practices with more conventional star casting. The major companies and the leading producers were always convinced of the role of big names in drawing an audience to a film. Some of the directors who inserted themselves in the current of neorealism – without having contributed to its development as an idea – were swift to adapt. For example, Alberto Lattuada acceded to Dino De Laurentiis's insistence that Nazzari rather than Checchi be cast in the leading role in *Il bandito* (The Bandit, 1946) because he was well loved by the public.[59] Directors including Blasetti, Camerini and Mattoli showed no interest in experimenting with non-professionals; their films relied on casts featuring actors who were well established. The popularity of comedy, and the success of comic actors like Fabrizi, Macario and Totò, signalled a pattern of taste that producers were keen to exploit. The latter was the first actor whose contractual obligations would be traded between companies. Variety theatre would become a more important basin of recruitment than it had ever been before, with showgirls as well as comedians being drawn into cinema. The pressing need to develop female stars capable of challenging the Americans led to the opening up of selection processes. The new names who would come to the fore did so via different routes, all of them with some element of public endorsement. The Miss Italia beauty pageant, launched in 1946, would be the most institutional of these, though various sorts of searches for new faces also played a part. The 1947 contest was won by Lucia Bosè ahead of Gina Lollobrigida, Gianna Maria Canale and others, all of whom would enter the movies. Silvana Mangano and Sophia Loren would also first come to attention though this means. By the early 1950s, Italian cinema could boast a new, predominantly female, star system with genuine box office appeal that could compete with the Americans at home and abroad.[60]

However, the direction of postwar cinema was never set aside. Though the heyday of the non-professional was brief, the continued use of natural settings and lower-class milieu demanded a certain type of actor who looked and felt at ease in such contexts. Consequently, the stars who emerged in the period that saw production once more increase were often new recruits who lacked the professional training and experience of most actors of the prewar period. They were not quite non-professionals, selected to play one part and then return to their regular lives, but nor were they fully-fledged actors, since they did not perform to consistent professional standards or with their own voices. Their limitations as actors were offset by the type of film in which they featured and the emphasis on presence and body, which was a direct example of the impact of neorealism. Indeed, the relative irrelevance of voice in their stardom – to the extent that several Italian and foreign actresses were dubbed by a handful of voice actors, the most well regarded of whom was the versatile Lydia Simoneschi – confirms the absolute pre-eminence of body and the focus on beauty and sex appeal. In the production of their star images, they were typically presented as unassuming and informal.

The de-professionalization of some aspects of screen acting contributed to the widespread clamour to break into the movies that was a feature of the postwar years. It was as though anyone could win a role in a film. For some young women, beauty contests offered a special platform, as juries often included representatives of the film world. Such contests flourished on a grand scale and were widely followed.[61] They complemented an emphasis on women's appearance and beauty in the press and other media.[62] Despite restrictions on women's consumption, the idea of the screen actor as representative of the people did not eradicate the long-standing belief that the movies were the easiest route to riches. The new stars of the postwar years, while preserving their accessible demeanour and informality, soon also exhibited the material benefits of their newly acquired status. Stories of origin were important components of their images though, and in these stories the role of the beauty contest or the casual encounter with a producer or director was central. In reality, the transition from a pageant catwalk to film set was rarely straightforward; often there were intermediary steps (Lollobrigida and Loren both worked in photoromances, while Mangano worked as a model while attending auditions). But the pageant was the crucial first step towards it. The buzz around such contests showed that the film community had learned to scout more widely than before for possible screen talent, and this underlined the idea that stardom was a community phenomenon that was democratic and shared.

The women who would emerge as protagonists and supporting cast members in Italian films from the late 1940s looked very different from those of the 1930s or early 1940s. They were less demure, more ostentatious; they transmitted an air of lived experience rather than the studio. Though, following the example of Anna Magnani, they generally looked more Italian due to their darker hair and commonplace features,[63] they also incorporated aspects of the American starlet. The focus on body stemmed certainly from the neorealist redefinition of the role of the actor and the actor's body in the construction of film narratives; but, reflecting the postwar tension between impulses to collectivism and to commercialism, it was also influenced by the shift that occurred in American glamour from fashion to sex appeal.[64] The wide diffusion of cheesecake shots in magazines was a consequence of the war-time rise of the pin-up, a female image created specifically for American servicemen to cheer their morale via a combination of titillation and sweetheart purity.[65] In Italy, as elsewhere in western Europe, there were reservations about the way American actresses were created and launched with big money 'in exactly the same way as a razor blade or a toothpaste'.[66] But, more and more, commercial practices were embraced by ambitious producers like Dino De Laurentiis and Carlo Ponti. After being cast in a leading role in *Riso amaro* (Bitter

Rice, Giuseppe De Santis, 1949), the former's protégée Silvana Mangano, more than anyone, was cast and promoted with Hayworth in mind via pin-up style film stills and the slogan 'l'atomica italiana' (a reference to the picture of Hayworth that allegedly adorned the atomic bomb dropped by the Americans on Bikini Atoll during a nuclear test in July 1946). Her impact was strikingly immediate compared to the slower build-up of all other postwar stars. A few years later, the resonance of Gina Lollobrigida's performance as a murderous beauty in the episode 'Il processo di Frine' ('The trial of Frine', of *Altri tempi* [Olden Times], Alessandro Blasetti, 1952) proved that beauty had become the Italian film industry's chief weapon in the conquest of both domestic and foreign markets.[67]

The shift in the criteria that were used to select and cast screen characters was regarded as disconcerting by some members of the film business. Considerable effort had gone into building up the professionalism of screen actors in the 1930s and early 1940s, and this had been hailed as a positive development. Changing methods of recruitment and casting had led to a decline in the quality of acting that was tantamount to de-professionalization. The cinema owners' magazine *Ciak*, for example, voiced the concern that the transition in the star system, and above all the stress on physical beauty, had led to a lowering of standards:

> *For some time now in Italy, the better actors are, the more they are undervalued and their place is taken by elements of dubious value. In Italy only the good-looking make progress; in Italy there is a strange pattern ... which means that a fine pair of legs or a Herculean chest, which are maybe more static even that the statues of the Foro italico – to the point of driving the poor directors who have to guide them mad – are valued more highly than the artistry of valid actors who the public still remembers fondly.*[68]

It regretted that fine actors like Andrea Checchi, Lea Padovani, Roldano Lupi and Fosco Giachetti were being neglected. 'Distributors mostly say No to Lea and only occasionally Yes, if she is accompanied by some statue from the Foro Italico ... For our distributors, a name is necessary, a name however that has not been made through artistic ability but [by means of] physical qualities'. Checchi 'does not have an athletic upper body, but rather top quality artistic gifts'. There were too many new faces, the magazine complained, with little to offer beyond youth and beauty. Their 'happy-go-lucky performances' were only 'redeemed thanks to the cure-all of the valorous Italian dubbing business'.[69]

This sort of lament was unusual within the exhibition sector, for professional attributes counted for little in the marketing of films. It was the commercial appeal of stars that made an impact at the box office. The press agent Vittorio Calvino, who was instrumental in promoting Lux films before moving to the Titanus company, would remark in 1955 that 'film advertising has been travelling for years along the predictable track of the star system. From a commercial point of view, a film's worth depends on the box office standing of the actors who play in it'.[70] 'Creating or reinforcing the aura of the star', he continued, 'this is the main task of those who are concerned with film publicity'. If a star was possessed of great beauty, then their job was easier. In the age of mass entertainment, screen personalities were not only necessary vehicles of the film industry; they embodied the dreams and desires of millions and, as one journalist remarked, audiences in Italy preferred qualities that were 'absolutely natural and spontaneous, the fruit not so much of study or research as of a gift from birth that has flowered spontaneously and revealed itself all of a sudden'.[71] For this reason, new stars carried a value that would soon lead to increases in the costs of film production.[72] Yet, it should not be overlooked that altered patterns of recruitment and modifications to the genre system heralded changes in the very nature of screen acting in order to align performance more closely with everyday life. To express regret about the passing of a style that, to quote Brunetta, had remained 'half way between theatre and cinema' was to ignore both the efforts of many directors to work with actors to break with old performance modes and the contributions of those actors who had been willing to accept the challenge of innovation.[73] While non-professionals may have been largely eliminated by the process of industrialization of film production by the early 1950s, the reflection on actors and stars that had led to their employment persisted and manifested itself in a number of films that sought to expose the illusory nature of the cinematic dreams.[74]

Notes

1. Landy, *Stardom Italian Style: Screen Performance and Personality in Italian Cinema*, Chapter 3.
2. Ibid., 85.
3. Ibid.
4. Ibid.
5. For example, it does not feature at all in Haaland's stimulating 2012 study, *Italian Neorealist Cinema*. See, however, Ambrosino, 'Il cinema ricomincia: attori e registi fra "continuità" e "frattura"', in Farassino, *Neorealismo: cinema italiano, 1945–1949*, 61–66.

6. Magnani is dealt with in most histories of Italian cinema, including Landy, *Stardom Italian Style*. Among recent articles are Culhane, 'Street Cries and Street Fights: Anna Magnani, Sophia Loren and the Popolana', 254–62; Chiappetta-Miller, 'Projecting the Diva's Voice: Anna Magnani in Visconti's *Bellissima*', 364–76 and contributions by Francesco Pitassio and Sergio Rigoletto to the special issue of *Journal of Italian Cinema and Media Studies* on Rome Open City: Rupture and Return 6(3) (2018).
7. See, for example, Buckley, 'Glamour and the Italian Female Film Stars of the 1950s', 267–89; Carman, 'Mapping the Body: Female Film Stars and the Reconstruction of Postwar Italian National Identity', 322–35.
8. See the chapter on actors and stars in Brunetta, *Storia del cinema italiano: dal 1945 agli anni Ottanta*, 247–60.
9. See Gundle, *Mussolini's Dream Factory: Film Stardom in Fascist Italy*, Chapter 6.
10. Brunetta, *Storia del cinema italiano*, 248.
11. Gundle, *Mussolini's Dream Factory*, 48–53.
12. Ibid., 48–58.
13. Ibid., 75–80. On glamour more generally, see Gundle, *Glamour: A History*.
14. A. De Benedetti, 'Dive, machere e miti del cinema' (1936), in De Benedetti, *Al cinema*, 155.
15. On the place of fashion under Fascism, see Paulicelli, *Fashion under Fascism: Beyond the Black Shirt*. Lupano and Vaccari, *Fashion at the Time of Fascism: Italian Modernist Lifestyle, 1922–1943*.
16. Freddi, *Il cinema*, 279.
17. Blasetti, quoted in T. Kezich, 'Gli attori italiani dalla preistoria del divismo al monopolio', in Caldiron, *Storia del cinema italiano*, Vol. V, 1930–1934, 383.
18. On Duranti, see ibid., pp. 86–87; Masi and Lancia, *Stelle d'Italia: piccole e grandi dive del cinema italiano dal 1930 al 1945*, 69–73; and Duranti, *Il romanzo della mia vita*. In contrast to the dominant ethos, she embraced a glamorous personal style. She made no secret of her liaison with the Minister of Popular Culture, Alessandro Pavolini, though of course this was never mentioned in the press.
19. Brunetta, *Storia del cinema italiano*, 252, 247.
20. On Nazzari, see Gubitosi, *Amedeo Nazzari*; Casavecchia, *Amedeo Nazzari: il divo, l'uomo, l'attore*.
21. On Giachetti, see Gundle, *Mussolini's Dream Factory*, Chapter 9.
22. For Nazzari's refusal, see S. Casavecchia, 'Amedeo Nazzari: il divo, l'uomo, l'attore', in Casavecchia, *Amedeo Nazzari: il divo, l'uomo, l'attore*, 12. For Giachetti's relations with the regime, see Gundle, *Mussolini's Dream Factory*, 212–13.
23. Brunetta, *Cent'anni di cinema italiano*, 212; Gubitosi, *Amedeo Nazzari*, 71.
24. Gundle, *Mussolini's Dream Factory*, 281; Ambrosino, 'Il cinema ricomincia', in Farassino, *Neorealismo*, 65–66.
25. Ibid., 87–90.
26. Brunetta, *Storia del cinema italiano*, 250; Ambrosino, 'Il cinema ricomincia', in Farassino, *Neorealismo*, 64–66.
27. M. Ramperti, 'I mercenari', *Primi piani*, August 1944, unnumbered page.
28. C. Geraghty, 'Re-Examining Stardom: Questions of Texts, Bodies and Performance', in Gledhill, *Reinventing Film Studies*, 183–201.
29. This is confirmed in Rigoletto, '(Un)dressing Authenticity: Neorealist Stardom and Anna Magnani in the Postwar Era (1945–48)', 391.
30. See Harris, '"In America è vietato essere brutte": Advertising American Beauty in the Italian Women's Magazine *Annabella*, 1945–1965', 35–53.

31. Viazzi, 'Gilda non è una vamp' (1948), in Viazzi, *Scritti di cinema 1940–1958*, 219–21.
32. G. Guida, 'Gilda', *Cine moda*, 6 April 1947, 7.
33. See Ramperti, *Quindici mesi al fresco*.
34. M. Ramperti, 'L'anima è il seno di Rita Hayworth', *Cine-cocktail*, 10 March 1949, 5–7.
35. On glamour and Italian glamour, see Gundle, 'Hollywood Glamour and Mass Consumption in Postwar Italy', 95–118 and Buckley, 'Glamour and the Italian Female Film Stars', 267–89.
36. *Star*, 24 March 1945.
37. L. Visconti, 'Anthropomorphic Cinema' (1943), in Overbey, *Springtime in Italy: A Reader on Neo-Realism*, 84.
38. Ibid., 84.
39. On the search for authenticity in neorealism, see Rigoletto, '(Un)dressing Authenticity', 390–91.
40. Gili and Grossi, *Alle origini del neorealismo: Giuseppe De Santis a colloquio con Jean A. Gili*, 49.
41. Ibid., 49.
42. Visconti, 'Anthropomorphic Cinema' in Overbey, *Springtime in Italy*, 84.
43. Brunetta, *Storia del cinema italiano*, 248.
44. Freddi, *Il cinema*, 279.
45. A. Pietrangeli, 'Gli attori', *Star*, 23 September 1944, 5–6. The second part was published in the issue of 30 September 1944.
46. For Brunetta, 'This star system, that was decked out in darned and second-hand clothes, was forced to promote actors to the level of stars of production that American cinema would not even have enrolled as extras or in the lowest category of western', *Storia del cinema italiano*, 248.
47. Krämer and Lovell, *Screen Acting*, 1.
48. See, for example, Emmeci, 'Parliamo un po' delle nostre attrici nuove', *L'Eco del cinema*, January 1941, 3–4.
49. R. Ben Ghiat, 'Italian Film in the Aftermath of War and Dictatorship', in Biess and Moeller, *Histories of the Aftermath: The Legacies of the Second World War in Europe*, 161–62.
50. Ibid., 161.
51. A. Bazin, 'Vittorio De Sica: metteur en scène' (1948), in Cardullo, *André Bazin and Italian Neorealism*, 78.
52. Thomson, *Why Acting Matters*, 144–45.
53. Freddi, *Il cinema*, 281.
54. Thomson, *Why Acting Matters*, 146.
55. Rigoletto, '(Un)dressing Authenticity', 390.
56. Bazin, 'Bicycle Thieves' (1948), in Cardullo, *André Bazin and Italian Neorealism*, 69.
57. On Maggiorani, see Chapter 15.
58. S. Masi, 'Il dopoguerra dei tecnici', in Cosulich, *Storia del cinema italiano*, Vol. VII 1945–1948, 356–58.
59. See Faldini and Fofi, *L'avventurosa storia del cinema italiano, 1935–1959*.
60. On this, see G. Grignaffini, 'Female Identity and Italian Cinema of the 1950s', in Bruno and Nadotti, *Off Screen: Women & Film in Italy*, 111–23; Buckley, 'The Female Film Star in Postwar Italy'.
61. See Gundle, *Bellissima: Feminine Beauty and the Idea of Italy*, 118–21, 131–41.
62. Gabrielli, *Il 1946, le donne, la repubblica*, 8.
63. Pitassio, 'L'attore', in Bertetto, *Storia del cinema italiano: uno sguardo d'insieme*, 202–3.
64. Gundle, *Glamour: A History*, 253–54.
65. Gundle, *Bellissima*, 108–12.
66. Anon., *Festival*, 28 February 1953.

67. Gundle, *Bellissima*, Chapter 7.
68. ANGALF, 'Svalutazzione dei valori: strano fenomeno della cinematografia italiana', *CIAK*, 22 September 1953, 6.
69. Ibid., 6.
70. V. Calvino, 'Baci sulla carta', *Cinema*, 10 August 1955, 763.
71. S. Guarnieri, 'Campioni e dive' (1956), in Aristarco, *Il mito dell'attore: come l'industria della star produce il sex symbol*, 49.
72. See U. Lisi, 'Le paghe degli attori' (1955), in Aristarco, *Il mito dell'attore*, 286–302.
73. Brunetta, *Storia del cinema italiano*, 252.
74. Ibid., 253. Among the films reflecting on cinema are *Bellissima* (Luchino Visconti, 1952), *Siamo Donne* (Of Women and Love, 1953) and *La signora senza camelie* (The Lady Without Camelias, Michelangelo Antonioni, 1952).

CHAPTER 4

The Public, Film-Going and the Stars

Cinema was the single most popular form of commercial mass entertainment in the period between the mid 1930s and the mid 1950s.[1] Throughout the years considered in this book, many more cinema tickets were sold in the north and centre of the country than in the south. While Naples, Bari and the Sicilian cities of Palermo and Catania witnessed levels of film consumption that were equivalent to those of northern cities, rural areas of the south and islands generally had far lower levels than similar areas in other parts of the peninsula. Yet film-going increased steadily in more rural areas and especially the south, as more cinemas were built and there was an increase in the number of parish cinemas. The role of the Americans in the liberation of Italy brought many southerners into direct contact for the first time with the unfamiliar but enticing sounds, images, rituals and consumption practices that were manifestations of plenty. The Allied occupation brought home the idea of the land of prosperity, which had informed the mass emigration from Italy's poorer regions in the late nineteenth and early twentieth centuries. The glittering attractions of Hollywood, which was made up of extravagant publicity, beautiful stars and a materialist dreamworld, fuelled the lure of cinema.

Before the war, young middle-class men and women residing in provincial capitals and larger towns were most likely to be frequent cinema-goers. Popular film culture was largely an expression of those who read film magazines, shared news and opinions of their favourites and styled themselves in ways reminiscent of them.[2] After the war, the enthusiasm for Hollywood that had prospered in the interwar years was renewed, as is testified by descriptions of the fans of heart-throb Tyrone Power, who came to Italy in 1947 to film *Prince of Foxes* (Henry King, 1949) and married in Rome in 1949. However, the social disruption of war and occupation created new expectations on the part of wider categories. The passion for cinema among the mass population was one manifestation of this. The spread of the medium was accompanied, driven even, by the numerous competitions, beauty contests and searches for 'new faces', which proliferated in the 1940s. These attracted thousands of entrants and caught the imagination of many more. In a context in which aspirations were rising following hardship, cinema was not just a realm of fantasy and imaginary projection but a promising source of possible personal enrichment and fulfilment.

This chapter will look at the ways in which older and newer practices of stardom impacted on popular leisure and aspirations. The changing composition of the postwar film-going public will be explored in relation to the efforts of political and religious forces to harness or obstruct the appeals of both Hollywood and Italian films. The final section will consider the development of fan culture and the way some stars built relations with the public.

The Film-Going Public

Despite shortages and disruptions resulting from the conflict, the box office figures for the immediate postwar years do not betray any decline in film-going either with respect to the prewar or the war years.[3] Indeed, despite anecdotal evidence that cinema lost some of its appeal as a leisure activity during the period of Allied bombing, the figures remain remarkably constant. The total number of tickets sold remained stable at around 459m between 1942 and 1946. After that, significant increases are registered each year, with 608m being reached in 1949 and 738m in 1952.[4] An all-time high of 819m tickets would be sold in 1955. Over this period, provincial capitals always account for over 50 per cent of tickets sold, though the share drops step by step with respect to smaller centres from 59 in 1945 to 52 in 1955. In the twelve major northern cities, the number of tickets rose from 120,761,000 in 1942 to 172,147,000 in 1951, while in the major southern cities it increased over the same period from 60,903,000 to 107,978,000. While the north remained dominant, the rate of increase in film-going in the south was significantly higher. A number of factors drove these increases. First, there was the general expansion of commercial leisure in the postwar period as people sought to enjoy new freedoms and put the privations of the conflict behind them. Second, the competition between film companies and distributors to exploit an expanding market led to the construction of new, often larger, cinemas, which, as production increased, showed a greater number of releases than before. Third, the development of film promotion and the film press brought the excitement of cinema to ever wider areas and sectors of the population, drawing them to the medium. This keyed in with aspirations for material improvement that followed both individual and familial paths. Fourth, the intense political competition that marked the reconstruction and early Cold War periods witnessed sustained efforts by the parties of the left on the one hand and the Catholic Church and the Christian Democrats on the other to establish their influence in the field of leisure. In different ways, both intervened to promote and to some degree influence the way in which cinema was consumed and to control or channel its social impact.[5]

Urban audiences did not all encounter cinema in the same way. There was a significant differentiation based on the type of cinema and the area in which it was located. A three-tiered distribution structure of first-, second- and third-run cinemas corresponded in larger cities like Turin and Bologna to a concentric urban geography.[6] New releases were shown for a limited time in comfortable theatres located in city centres, where they were located amid shops and bars. After this, they would be taken up by less comfortable but cheaper cinemas situated in residential suburbs. Finally, films would reach the urban periphery, where, often in less than perfect condition, they would be shown in spartan settings to audiences paying a low ticket price. According to Gian Franco Vené, this structure had become entrenched on a class basis in the 1930s, when a trebling of ticket prices in first-run cinema relegated working-class spectators to suburban cinemas.[7] In rural areas, all cinemas were second or third-run.

The city in which cinema occupied the most central position in social and cultural life was the capital, Rome. With its population of over 1.5m and 250 permanent cinemas, it was the largest market for films in the country, beating Milan by some distance.[8] Moreover, Romans went to the cinema on average more often than the residents of other cities, reaching a peak of thirty-five times per year in 1956. Because the city was also the centre of the film industry – and therefore the site of studios, production and distribution company offices, ancillary services and numerous professional and industry associations including ANICA and AGIS as well as the offices of some film publications – cinema was a diffuse experience that impacted on everyday work and life in more intense and regular ways than elsewhere.[9]

A recent study of postwar Roman audiences by Daniela Treveri Gennari and others has shed light on the way in which the tripartite division of cinemas worked in practice.[10] First-run theatres, which screened new releases first, generally attracted 'a more sophisticated and elegant crowd'.[11] People were struck by their comfort and décor, their perfect sound systems and their cleanliness – all of which were evoked decades later in their memories.[12] Second-run cinemas could also be large and comfortable. Tickets cost less though, and the cinemas were usually located nearer to spectators' dwellings; indeed, they were often remembered as being local and familiar, almost like an extension of the home.[13] Third-run cinemas had a distinctly lower-class image; the audiences were likely to be noisy and unruly, and women might find themselves molested.[14]

Observers of cinema audiences in the 1940s noted a certain reshuffling in terms of the social composition. With the economic dislocations of the war and foreign occupation, phenomena of upward and downward mobility had an impact. Black marketeers eager to flaunt their new-found wealth invaded cinemas, theatres and restaurants once reserved for the urban elite, bringing a certain change of tone. Genova's Cinema Grattacielo was an example of a cinema that had entered the social imaginary of the city before the war as 'the symbolic opulence of an accessible but refined luxury, of Progress with a capital P that was translated into the eminently visible forms of mirrors, lifts and escalators'.[15] Social commentator Irene Brin noted than even in 1941 there was a certain social promiscuity in audiences; alongside elegant, bejewelled ladies could be seen 'calm and dignified women of the people'.[16]

There can be no doubt that there was great enthusiasm for cinema in the years following the war. Some of this was strictly associated with the return of Hollywood. As Mario Quargnolo noted in his volume on cinema-going in the northern city of Udine, 'once the war was over, the passion for cinema exploded again without limit. When – in May 1945 – American cinema returned to Udine in the form of a very mediocre musical film starring Betty Grable (a pin-up of the period) and spoken in English to boot, the success was enormous.'[17] When *Gone with the Wind* finally reached the city in 1951 (after having opened in Rome and Milan in 1949), it occupied one huge 1,500 seat cinema for a record one month. The same film figures prominently in the memories of spectators interviewed by Treveri Gennari and her colleagues.[18] Hollywood offered a sense of scale and spectacle that was exceptional and that attracted keen filmgoers of all classes who were eager to be the first to experience novelties.

Cinema was magical for many spectators in that it lifted them out of the everyday realm. Treveri Gennari's witnesses spoke of cinema being 'a place outside of this world, magic' or 'a fascinating place which was not part of life'.[19] Larger cinemas had 'a screen that captured you', giving one spectator the sense that 'while I was sitting in the cinema I felt part of the film.' But cinema was also part of the texture of community life, a place one went with family members, with friends or with one's boy- or girl-friend. Witnesses interviewed by David Forgacs, myself and our collaborators in the early 1990s often associated trips to the cinema with courtship and intimacy.[20] The same themes recur in more recent historical work. Cinema in this sense was a collective experience that provided a sense of community spirit and vivid moments of personal experience.

The enthusiasm for cinema spread even to small centres. As Gian Piero Brunetta observed, 'cinema fever spread almost by contagion, and the gigantic glow expanded seamlessly from one end of the peninsula to the other, communicating a sense of festivity, of the capillary spreading of a new mass rite that was at once fascinating and frightening, a bearer of civilisation and of corruption at the same time'.[21] For the lower classes, the great desire to be part of the experience of cinema was part of a wider wish to be part of a process that was associated with economic advancement. This collective movement unleashed 'a consumeristic spiral, a series of chain reactions between the demand for entertainment and the supply that grew year by year and which seemed to have no readily predictable saturation point'.[22]

Italian films offered a type of experience that was decidedly different from Hollywood. They were more realistic, and they offered scenes, stories and personalities that audiences found closer to their own lives.[23] For some, there was a sort of patriotic identification with the exploration of one's own country that was radically different from the high-register type of nationalism presented in the grand gestures and sacrifices of Fascist war films. However, significant sections of both the middle class and the popular audience preferred escapism. If cinema owners found that their habitual customers did not react well to films laced with realism, they rejected them unilaterally.[24] As the bulletin of the cinema owners' association AGIS asserted in 1949,

> the vast Italian audience does not like to linger over their poverty and everyday miseries... it prefers to be transported to unusual places, fantastic, luxurious or old-fashioned environments. If they are placed in their everyday life, they prefer the strong emotions of laughter or of drama because they know their own life and do not enjoy watching it on the screen even if it is portrayed with art and cleverness.[25]

Only when neorealism and popular cinema were synthesized was the audience for Italian films unified and the film industry able to compete seriously with Hollywood in the domestic market.[26] This process began when the Titanus company discovered the formula of the domestic melodrama, which was launched by *Catene* (Chains, Raffaello Matarazzo, 1949) and was consolidated with the same company's rural comedy series, which began with *Pane, amore e fantasia* (Bread, Love and Dreams, Luigi Comencini, 1953).[27]

The Audience and the Stars

Stars and genre had an important influence on the films that people chose to see. Gender preferences were largely predictable in keeping with the strong division that had been culturally and politically institutionalized under Fascism and that by all accounts persisted into the postwar years.[28] When asked, several decades later, to name their favourite films, some respondents to a survey immediately mentioned stars, citing a mixture of American and Italian names: Frank Sinatra, Anna Magnani, Rossano Brazzi, John Wayne, Dean Martin, Gina Lollobrigida, Amedeo Nazzari and others.[29] Italian female stars were named more often than their American counterparts, while male star preferences were distributed evenly between Italy and the USA. It is striking that no French or British star was cited. These responses testify to the success of Italian cinema in producing stars who resonated with the public. There has long been an assumption that American and Italian stars functioned in different ways. While Hollywood stars were dream figures, Italian stars were accessible and familiar. Brunetta writes that

> *Italian stars never needed to be brought down to earth in the press to an everyday level of existence, for the simple reason that they never aspired to reach the rarefied plane of Olympus, nor did they produce a stellar glow. All the actors or stars of the postwar period, whether they liked it or not, had to bathe in the waters of neorealism and accept some of its fundamental traits.*[30]

Treveri Gennari finds that audience memories are coloured by a similar dichotomy 'between the familiar and the inaccessible'.[31] On the one hand, Anna Magnani is remembered as 'not only the actress they may have seen in the variety shows in local cinema theatres, but also she is the star most similar to Roman women, as well as the artist that interprets women like the ones you would meet in daily life; she is not "uncommon" and she is always described as natural and spontaneous' and Gina Lollobrigida is praised for her beauty; on the other hand, Rita Hayworth and Marlon Brando are idols, figures of a 'forbidden dream'.[32]

There is a sense in which observations of this type have become widely accepted. Italian stars, like many European film actors, were fundamentally different from American stars because they were not products of studio manufacture. They emerged more spontaneously and were less subject to the sort of packaging that might result in a complete change of image, name and personal biography. Though great efforts were made by the studios to lend Hollywood stars an everyday dimension, Italian stars hailed from specific, known places and often maintained that sense of coming from somewhere as part of their persona. The fact that they featured in films that for domestic audiences were set in identifiable, familiar locations also contributed to the conviction that they were 'like us'. To some degree, there was a measure of continuity from the 1930s, when Italian actors had first acquired the reputation for being typical and spontaneous, with attitudes and lifestyles that were modest by comparison with the Americans. Neorealism simply consolidated this divergence and embraced it as a distinguishing feature in a way that would feed into the wider commercial cinema.

However, while these differences corresponded to something real, it would be misleading to suggest that Italian stars did not unleash dreams and channel the aspirations of the public. All stars to some extent combine the ordinary and the exceptional, the real and the unreal. Production companies were using star names to promote films in the 1940s, and this practice was extended in the following decade.[33] The way in which the postwar Italian stars first emerged served simultaneously to underline their familiarity and to diffuse the appeal of cinema as a vehicle for the realization of everyone's dreams of fame, wealth and personal fulfilment. The lack of any formal training and the stress on physical beauty that was a particular hallmark of many of the young female stars who came to the fore led many young women to think that recognition and fame were within their grasp. The extraordinary clamour that surrounded the beauty contests of every type that flourished in the 1940s bore witness to the desires of young women (and their families) for material improvements.[34] They also served as a focal point for the shift that was occurring in the idea of Italian feminine beauty from modesty and natural charm centred on the face to sex appeal located in the legs, the bust and general attitude.[35] The diffusion of American beauty products and notions of beauty complemented this shift even if it was not responsible for it.[36]

Although discourses of the natural would never be eclipsed, and indeed were incorporated into the official narratives of the Miss Italia beauty pageant by its founder and chief promoter, Dino Villani, they existed alongside, and to some degree in subordination to, a wider preoccupation with the commercial appeal of beauty. The journalist Orio Vergani observed that, 'For Villani, Miss Italia is nothing other than a "living poster", a sort of three-dimensional affiche, brought to life by a flashing smile. In short, a young woman is chosen by means of a competition to compete with thousands of beautiful young women that we have seen on posters in half a century of commercial art.'[37] 'The beautiful living and smiling women selected from the ranks of aspirants for the title of Miss Italia . . . carry the signature of Dino Villani', Vergani continued. 'He did not paint them, but discovered them and, in a certain sense, "invented" them, directing on to their faces the projector of an advertising slogan.'

On the one hand, the transition to flesh and blood women from the fantasy figures of the advertising posters of the first half of the century, and inventions like Boccasile's popular illustrations of the Signorina *Grandi firme* cover girl between the wars,[38] was heralded by the changes that occurred in the social position of women, including the conquest of the vote;[39] on the other hand, the intervention of commercial organizations and practices was a product of the level of development reached by media industries that were no longer subject to the restrictions of the Fascist period. Step by step, they were evolving complex structures and repeatable procedures.

The glamour of the Italian stars would always be to some extent different to that of the Americans.[40] The particular typology of feminine beauty that came to be associated with postwar Italian cinema was heavily traded on in the export of Italian films; stars like Silvana Pampanini and Silvana Mangano were imbued with 'starlet appeal' even as they acquired the star's capacity to impact on the box office.[41] In the Italian context, however, they would soon acquire the trappings of wealth and success that would be so appealing for the public. Even Anna Magnani would live up to her image as a star in her wardrobe, furs and personal appearances. While an established star like Amedeo Nazzari had elaborated a star lifestyle, including an opulent home, in the prewar years, the new-found prosperity of the younger female stars was highly suggestive. They would be bombarded with letters requesting money or advice from young men and women as they steadily refined their images and embraced a fashion dimension.[42] Though few of them would be deemed conventionally elegant, the Roman fashion designer Emilio Schubert developed a mode of star dressing that complemented their specific appeal and contributed to the elaboration of an Italian idea of glamour.[43]

The impact of stardom, and particularly female stardom, on personal consumption, self-image and style would be considerable. In the interwar years, the expansion of cinema and of the press linked to it provided alternative modern reference points to those imparted by the Catholic Church and the Fascist regime.[44] Hair styling, cosmetics, dress, interpersonal behaviour and personal attitudes were influenced by a medium that presented itself overtly as a school of modernity. After the war, both American and Italian stars would be studied closely by the young. The lookalike photo contests that were run by film magazines testify to the continuing appeal of star culture but also to a turnover in the actors who were the objects of imitation. As cinema audiences expanded, the appeal of the northern-looking female stars proposed by Hollywood and the blondes of interwar Cinecittà declined, to be substituted by the new, more accessible faces of postwar cinema that had emerged from life rather than formal performative routes.

Catholics, Communists and the Stars

Postwar Italian society was highly politicized and both Communists and the Catholics built mass organizations that extended into the cultural sphere.[45] Both invested considerable energy in cinema, but they did so in different ways. To use Brunetta's words, for the left, films came first, then cinema as an economic and cultural phenomenon; for the Catholics, it was the other way round.[46] Thus the two forces moved in ways that were quite distinct, even if the ultimate objective – to shape and influence the impact of cinema on the mass of the population – was fundamentally the same. The Catholics had been wary of the negative influence of cinema for decades, and this attitude was very evident after the war. As early as 1945, Pope Pius XII called on young people to mobilize against the attacks on Christian life that were everywhere evident, above all in the field of entertainment.[47] The Church resisted all attempts to turn cinema into an instrument of collective reflection on the present and recent past. It deployed its own structures and those of a variety of sectoral lay associations to condition the experience of cinema. With the Christian Democrats securely installed in government, they were able to assert their influence at many levels. In 1945, there were 359 parish cinemas operating in the country; by 1949 the Association of Catholic Cinema Managers (ACEC), whose members included both the representatives of parish cinemas and commercial owners, claimed to control 3,000 auditoriums.[48] There was a specialist Catholic film press, an organization (the Catholic Cinema Centre) that assessed and classified each new release on the basis of its suitability for different audiences, as well as a network of circles that promoted discussion on cinematic culture.

The left operated in a way that was more concerned with public opinion and with the interests of the various sectors of the film world. It made itself the chief defender of a film industry that was struggling to be reborn and the promoter of the new currents to have emerged after the war. In the period before 1949, the Communists successfully mobilized all sectors of the film world in demanding government action to aid the national industry and give Italian cinema a chance to compete with the huge Hollywood presence. While the Catholics deployed their forces at every level from central government down to the remote parish, the left counted mainly on an alignment of directors and writers who were associated with neorealism and a variety of press organs, which included specialist journals, the national party press and local publications. Left-wing critics would continue to champion realism in more or less dogmatic forms after adoption of the Andreotti law, with Visconti emerging as the symbol of a cinema that was still committed to engagement.[49] Though it could not and did not seek to build a network of cinemas even in areas of particular strength, it promoted the formation of film circles, which were organized in a national federation in 1947.[50] Though these would never succeed in their broad aim of forming a new type of aware popular filmgoer, and would decline in the late 1940s, circles provided an important stimulus to the development of cinematic culture, especially in the smaller centres of the south.[51]

Neither the Catholics nor the Communists were very keen on stars. The Catholic press had published disapproving articles about fandom before the war, and young people who entertained unrealistic fantasies about cinema and its stars were often subjected to reproval or pity.[52] Similar condemnations were issued in the postwar years. The most important exception was for the stars of Hollywood. The alliance between the Church and the Americans, which provided the DC with such powerful credibility and resources in the 1948 election, meant that American movies were largely exempt from the general critique of cinema that emanated from some Catholic quarters. Hollywood stars had been mobilized in support of the DC in the election campaign and, despite a certain reluctance, they had been joined by Hollywood's most recent Italian recruit, Alida Valli.[53] Hollywood stars who came to Italy were often embraced by the Church. In the month of their Rome marriage, February 1949, Tyrone Power and Linda Christian were pictured in the press in the company of Prime Minister De Gasperi and were received by Pope Pius. Stars who professed the Catholic faith, like Gary Cooper and Irene Dunne, were guaranteed coverage in the popular Catholic weekly, *Famiglia Cristiana*.[54]

For the Communists, stardom presented the same sort of problems as it had for the neorealists. It was essentially a commercial and predominantly American phenomenon that was antithetical to a genuine critical and popular cinema. Hollywood was seen, especially after the onset of the Cold War, as a tool of cultural imperialism along with swing music and ballpoint pens.[55] Hardliner Pietro Secchia denounced US corporations for 'invading our country with their books, their films and their low level ideological goods'.[56] There was a strong perception that the American films that were being screened in Italy were being filtered for their ideological content with the deliberate aim of providing audiences with a distorted world view. By showing violence and through the exaltation of the bourgeoisie, property and money, the commodification of dreams and the falsification of history, American cinema was attempting to deviate and disperse energies that were needed in the struggle to improve the economic and social conditions of the masses.[57] However, stars like Humphrey Bogart, Lauren Bacall, Spencer Tracy and Katherine Hepburn, who took the defence of the 'Hollywood ten' and who were accused by McCarthyites of being Communists, were regarded with favour, along with a long-standing favourite Charlie Chaplin.

The left-wing women's magazine *Noi Donne* understood better than most that Hollywood stars had considerable appeal even for working-class audiences and that this was not always a bad thing. The images of female protagonism in the films of the 1930s and 1940s were of interest to women who were fighting bigotry and discrimination not only in society but sometimes even in the parties of the left. The magazine never referred to 'stars' but always to talented actresses who had been able to overcome the corruption of the industry in which they worked. 'Bette Davis has become, with tenacity and great strength of will, the greatest actress of the American screen despite the organisation of Hollywood cinema', it was observed,[58] while Joan Crawford was another fine actress who had achieved success 'working even at the cost of humiliating experiences'.[59] Katherine Hepburn was praised as someone 'whose entire artistic life has been and continues to be one of struggle against a vulgar and conventional cinematic world'.[60] By contrast, stars like Betty Grable and Rita Hayworth, who were seen as products manufactured by the commercial mechanisms of American cinema, were dismissed without much ceremony.[61]

As far as Italian stars were concerned, there was a variety of attitudes. Though far more interest was shown in film directors than actors, the latter were sometimes drawn into Communist initiatives. Massimo Girotti and Raf Vallone, for example, signed petitions, gave electoral endorsements and took part in party initiatives. Italian stars were given ample coverage in the popular left-wing press and were seen as far better influences than most Hollywood stars. There was a widespread awareness among those who were most in contact with popular opinion and grass-roots activists that the culture of stardom was not only rooted in the way people encountered cinema but that is was becoming more so. Here and there, the unmediated enthusiasm for stars even crept into the Communist press. In *La Verità*, organ of the Communist organization in the city of Modena, admiration for Greer Garson and Greta Garbo betrayed the persistence of dreams formed in the interwar years.[62] The same paper had praised *Riso amaro* (directed by party member Giuseppe De Santis but nonetheless the source of polemics) for its protagonists Silvana Mangano, 'the new marvellous, provocative Italian beauty', and Vittorio Gassman, 'the actor whose voice and charm drive women crazy'.[63]

The Communists sought to insert themselves in the texture of popular culture. They never wanted to find themselves cut off from activities and rituals that were attracting great enthusiasm among the young. Thus they sought to provide outlets for the widespread passion for dancing, which was condemned as immoral by the Catholics, and to gain a foothold in the beauty contest craze and the associated passion for getting into the movies. After various local contests took place, the illustrated weekly *Vie Nuove* organized its own national competition as a rival to Miss Italia. The competition ran for several years and was hugely popular, though it caused some opposition among Communist women and hardliners.[64] The aim of the organizers was to intercept individual aspirations and direct them back towards collective objectives. Thus bathing costumes were not worn at Miss *Vie Nuove*, and little attention was paid to the physical charms of the participants. However, national juries were composed of such luminaries as the writers Alberto Moravia and Elsa Morante, directors like Blasetti, Visconti and De Santis, actors including Girotti and Fosco Giachetti, as well as Simone Signoret and Yves Montand. If local winners could expect to be feted for an evening and perhaps receive a subscription to the magazine as a prize, national winners were rewarded with sewing machines and radios in addition to being offered a screen test. According to the Communist film journalist Ugo Casiraghi, the aim of the competition was to contribute to Italian cinema's search for new faces;[65] a search that he hoped would produce new actors who rejected the commercial mechanisms of stardom. This sense of mission would inevitably wane as the industry recovered, to be replaced by efforts to annex the stars to the left.

It would be misleading to suggest that the Catholics and Communists had little influence on the popular reception of stardom. Both mediated it and channelled it to some degree in so far as it impacted on their core followers. They were able to establish preferences for given stars, building meanings into their star personas that were significant within a specific subcultural ambit. But they were never able to control fully the engagement of filmgoers with the stars, as few of these did not read the commercial press or go to cinemas of whatever run they could afford. Stars had a capacity to cut through ideology and present appeals and suggestions that were no less powerful for their being disapproved of by this or that authority.

Fans and Fandom

Relatively little has been written about the film fandom of the postwar years. The few studies that exist tend to focus on the period from the mid 1950s.[66] While Federico Vitella has mainly addressed the fans of American stars, Reka Buckley has written about the fan cults of Gina Lollobrigida, Claudia Cardinale and other female stars.[67] One of the major objects of postwar fandom was Tyrone Power. Power, who had starred opposite Hayworth in the bullfighting drama *Blood and Sand*, was especially popular with the young. When he went to Turin in November 1947, *Hollywood* magazine announced that his hotel was besieged by schoolgirls aged between twelve and eighteen: 'the girls shouted his name (they did not chant Tee-ro-nay, but Tai-rone – the high school element was preponderant)'.[68] With his dark good looks, he provided Italian boys with their most accessible model since Rudolph Valentino. His popularity would remain high, reaching a peak at the time of his Rome wedding to the Italian-educated starlet Linda Christian in 1949.[69] The enthusiasm around the wedding was an expression of the particularly intense relationship that subsisted in the capital between the film industry and its stars and the public.[70] Elsewhere, encounters with stars were altogether rarer and therefore perhaps even more significant when they happened. Some witnesses in Calabria interviewed in the early 1990s recalled seeing Nazzari and Mangano during the filming of *Il lupo della Sila* (The Wolf of the Sila, Duilio Coletti, 1949). Three male interviewees from near Cosenza were deeply affected, especially by the real-life vision of Nazzari: 'I was a small boy, of course. I saw him as a great man', said one of them.[71]

Dating the starting point of postwar fan culture is not easy and perhaps not advisable, as some practices and indeed some star cults predated the war.[72] But Scarlini and Paloscia argue that the origins of fandom lie in the public's response to the first Miss Italia beauty pageant in 1946.[73] This view has been endorsed by Buckley, who observes that the public present in Stresa 'called for Silvana Pampanini – rather than the judges' favourite Rossana Martini – to be crowned the winner'.[74] While Martini's film career would be brief and unremarkable, Pampanini would go on to become a leading star and a popular favourite. The growth of the phenomenon of fandom was plotted in specialist publications including *Cinema nuovo*, which found that Italian stars were the object of interest from people of both sexes and every age and social background,[75] though not to an equal degree. While the Roman Pampanini would build a national fan base, Yvonne Sanson, the star of a popular series of melodramas, would have a regional following concentrated in the south. Stars whose careers would blossom later like Gina Lollobrigida and Sophia Loren would add a significant international dimension.[76] The construction and perpetuation of the star cult depended on a number of institutions and practices. In the absence of fan clubs on American lines – that is, associations created and sustained by big studios – the press played a crucial role. Vitella argues that the magazine *Hollywood* (see Figure 4.1), which was published by the Milanese publisher Vitagliano between 1945 and 1961, 'performed the principal functions [of the absent clubs], responding often successfully to the pressing demands of a pattern of consumption that was not necessarily any more passive than that found in other countries'.[77]

While the film circles and specialist journals were aimed at an educated audience, or at least an audience interested in reflection and criticism, and positioned themselves as 'cultural', a magazine like *Hollywood* was aimed more simply at the enthusiast – that is, someone 'whose only interest while leafing through its glossy pages was in finding things that appealed to him or her'.[78] Thus, while

Figure 4.1 The popular magazine *Hollywood* functioned almost like a fan club for filmgoers. Lavishly illustrated, it almost always pictured American stars on the cover (author's own collection).

the former commented on the phenomenon of fandom – for example, through articles on the fan letters of Yvonne Sanson and on autograph hunters[79]– the latter was immersed in it. From the start, it made the coverage of stars and stardom its main purpose, the title indicating a desire to exploit most especially curiosity about American stars after seven years of absence. Much of the illustrated press gave ample coverage to Hollywood stars, but *Hollywood* was entirely oriented in this direction, to the point that it resembled an American-style fan magazine. The content was geared to the needs of the readers, whose primary interest was in illustrated material. Photographs dominated its pages and took many forms, including portraits, film stills and leisure shots. Photographs of particular stars were published at the request of readers, with the size of the reproduction being a key indicator of their current popularity.

Fans were well known to like assembling their own albums of pictures and articles cut from the press, and *Hollywood* catered to this. Indeed, 'among the most fervent enthusiasts, there was the custom of buying two copies at a time, one to consult and then maybe bind in a volume with other issues from the same year, and one destined to the true star cult in all its forms (albums, collections, wall posters etc.)'.[80] The letters page played a key role in meeting the demand of readers for information about their favourites and engaging in a dialogue about them, including indications of which stars were most likely to reply to letters and tips about how to write to them. The sense of a community of fans sharing the same values and interests linked the magazine and its readers. Indeed, this was institutionalized in the section of the letters page that allowed for swops of photographs, cuttings and old periodicals. The use of the informal '*tu*' form of address was the rule. *Hollywood* also offered its readers opportunities to adopt star looks and embrace star styles.[81] This was a direct continuation of practices begun in the prewar years, which were now resumed and more widely embraced.[82] There were also periodic referendums to establish the hit parade of Hollywood and Italian stars, the results of which were prominently published and followed by comments and discussion.

While the most popular film weekly carried out the functions of a fan club, the stars also communicated directly with their fans. Whereas American stars could often rely on their studios to respond to fan letters, send out autographed photographs and organize fan clubs, Italian stars had to establish their own procedures for maintaining a relationship with their admirers. In many cases, family members took a leading role, though secretaries could also be involved when the volume of mail grew. In the interwar years, female stars were known to be far more likely to respond to their fans than the men, some of whom remained rather aloof from the whole celebrity phenomenon.[83] This was no different in the postwar period. Some stars were known for their engagement with their fans and were much appreciated for this. Silvana Pampanini cultivated an accessible image, posing as the friend of her followers, and in this way she consolidated a female fan base that might have been alienated by some of her transgressive screen roles.[84] Those who wrote to her were far more likely to receive a response than from other stars, such as Silvana Mangano. The initiative was her own, for she was assisted only by her father, while Mangano's career was directed by a dynamic producer. Stars used the press to feed their admirers nuggets of information and insights into their personal lives, constructing an impression of intimacy in which the reader imagined they were engaged in a one-to-one relationship rather than a one-to-thousands one. At the same time, fans knew that they were one of many and often had to be satisfied with general acknowledgements of their existence, as when stars were pictured surrounded by their mail or in the act of signing photographs, or when they issued blanket declarations of gratitude for the attention and gifts they received.

Though the phenomenon studied by Vitella and Buckley was in its nascent phase in the period covered by this book, the cult of Italian stars seems to have been more radicated and long-lasting than those that flourished around the Hollywood stars. The popularity of Tyrone Power, while intense, was also brief; the decline after his highly publicized wedding was rapid. Italian stars may have lacked some of the magic of the Americans, but they had other advantages: their films spoke more directly to the experiences of audiences, they emerged from milieus that were familiar, their values and tastes were recognizable, they were more accessible and responsive, their successes were a cause of pride and their rites of passage more closely aligned with those of ordinary Italians. At a time when the country was passing from reconstruction to growth, they accompanied people on the road to a better future and assisted them in consigning the experience of war and dictatorship to the past.

Notes

1. Forgacs and Gundle, *Mass Culture and Italian Society from Fascism to the Cold War*, 42.
2. Ibid., 73–80; Gundle, *Mussolini's Dream Factory: Film Stardom in Fascist Italy*, 101–6.
3. Forgacs and Gundle, *Mass Culture and Italian Society*, 42–45.

4. The figures in this paragraph are taken from ibid., 42–45. All figures are rounded up or down to the nearest million. These figures in turn are elaborated from the *Lo spettacolo in Italia* (SIAE, Rome) yearbooks.
5. S. Gundle, 'From Neorealism to *luci rosse*: cinema, politics, society, 1945–85', in Baranski and Lumley, *Culture and Conflict in Postwar Italy*, 204–11.
6. Forgacs and Gundle, *Mass Culture and Italian Society*, 42.
7. Vene, *Mille lire al mese: la vita quotidiana della famiglia nell'Italia fascista*, 283.
8. Treveri Gennari and Sedgewick, 'Memories in Context: The Social and Economic Function of Cinema in 1950s Rome', 83.
9. This is captured well in Colonna, *Personaggi e interpreti*, 13–33.
10. 'In Search of Italian Cinema Audiences in the 1940s and 1950s: Gender, Genre and National Identity', AHRC research project 2012–16, Principal investigator: Daniela Treveri Gennari.
11. Treveri Gennari and Sedgewick, 'Memories in Context', 96.
12. Ibid., 94.
13. Ibid., 95.
14. Ibid., 96.
15. I. Brin, 'Quelli del Grattacielo', *Film*, 6 September 1941, 8.
16. Ibid., 8.
17. Quargnolo, *Quando i friulani andavano al cinema*, 122.
18. Treveri Gennari, '"If You Have Seen it, You Cannot Forget!": Film Consumption and Memories of Cinema-Going in 1950s Rome', 61.
19. Treveri Gennari and Sedgewick, 'Memories in Context', 96.
20. Forgacs and Gundle, *Mass Culture and Italian Society*, 67–73.
21. Brunetta, *Storia del cinema italiano: dal 1945 agli anni Ottanta*, 205.
22. Ibid., 206.
23. Treveri Gennari, '"If You Have Seen it, You Cannot Forget!"', 61.
24. V. Camerino, 'La vita del cinema in un piccolo-medio centro del salentino', 38. Cited in Brunetta, *Storia del cinema italiano: dal 1945*, 214.
25. M. Villa, 'Il film italiano', *Bollettino di informazioni dell'Associazione Generale Italiana dello Spettacolo* 71 (1949), 1–15 January.
26. Spinazzola, *Cinema e pubblico: lo spettacolo filmico in Italia 1945-1965*, 102–22.
27. Barzoletti et al, *Modi di produzione del cinema italiano: la Titanus*, 29.
28. Treveri Gennari, '"If You Have Seen it, You Cannot Forget!"', 61.
29. Ibid., 62.
30. Brunetta, *Storia del cinema italiano: dal 1945*, 222n.
31. Treveri Gennari, '"If You Have Seen it, You Cannot Forget!"', 62.
32. Ibid., 62.
33. V. Calvino, 'Baci sulla carta', *Cinema*, 10 August 1955, 763.
34. In 1956, Anna Garofalo noted that the spread of magazine images of high society women also induced feelings of inferiority among the many with limited means. See *L'italiana in Italia*, 95.
35. Gundle, *Bellissima: Feminine Beauty and the Idea of Italy*, Chapter 5.
36. Harris, '"In America è vietato essere brutte": Advertising American Beauty in the Italian Women's Magazine Annabella, 1945–1965', 35–53.
37. O. Vergani, 'Introduction to D. Villani', in Villani, *Come sono nate undici Miss Italia*, 8.
38. See Gundle, *Bellissima*, Chapter 4; and Biribanti, *Boccasile*, 73–110.

39. For a rich exploration of this transition, see Gabrielli, *Il 1946, le donne, la repubblica*.
40. On the nature of Italian glamour, see Gundle, 'Hollywood Glamour and Mass Consumption in Postwar Italy', 95–118; and Buckley, 'Glamour and the Italian Female Stars of the 1950s', 267–89.
41. See Anon, 'Le attrici famose ci sono, ma gli attori?', *Cinespettacolo* 7(5) (1952) December, 5.
42. See Buckley, 'Material Dreams: Costume and Couture Italian Style – From Hollywood on the Tiber to the Italian Screen', in Bondanella, *The Italian Cinema Book*, 133–41.
43. Gundle, 'Hollywood Glamour and Mass Consumption', 95–118.
44. Forgacs and Gundle, *Mass Culture and Italian Society*, 73–78. See also De Grazia, *How Fascism Ruled Women: Italy 1922–1943*, 132–37.
45. See Forgacs and Gundle, *Mass Culture and Italian Society*, 247–68.
46. Brunetta, *Storia del cinema italiano: dal 1945*, 110.
47. E. Natta, 'La molteplicazione delle sale parocchiali', in Cosulich, *Storia del cinema italiano*, Vol. VII 1945–48, 443.
48. Brunetta, *Storia del cinema italiano: dal 1945*, 125.
49. Ibid., 110. On the left and neorealism, see D. Forgacs, 'The Making and Unmaking of Neorealism in Postwar Italy', in Hewitt, *The Culture of Reconstruction: European Thought, Literature and Film, 1945–1950*, 51–66; and S. Gundle, 'Neorealism and Left-Wing Culture', in Bondanella, *The Italian Cinema Book*, 77–83.
50. Tosi, 'L'organizzazione della cultura cinematografica', in Cosulich, *Storia del cinema italiano*, Vol. VII 1945–48, 499.
51. Ibid., 513.
52. Gundle, *Mussolini's Dream Factory*, 114.
53. Gundle, 'Alida Valli in Hollywood: From Star of Fascist Cinema to "Selznick Siren"', 559–87.
54. See S. Gundle, 'Cultura di massa e modernizzazione: *Vie Nuove* e *Famiglia Cristiana* dalla guerra fredda alla società dei consumi', in D'Attore, *Nemici per la pelle: sogno americano e mito sovietico nell'Italia contemporanea*, 235–68.
55. A. Fadeiev, 'L'espansione ideologica dell'imperialismo americano', *Rinascita* 9–10 (1948), 361–62.
56. P. Secchia, 'Il Partito comunista e gli intellettuali', *L'Unità*, 5 February 1948, 3.
57. See S. Gundle, 'Il PCI e la campagna contro Hollywood (1948–1958)', in Ellwood and Brunetta, *Hollywood in Europa: industria, politica, pubblico del cinema, 1945–1960*, 119.
58. M. Mida, 'Bette non teme d'essere brutta', *Noi Donne*, 30 December 1951, 20.
59. Anonymous note, *Noi Donne*, 12 March 1950, 16.
60. V. Marinucci, '"Katie" anticonformista', *Noi Donne*, 26 February 1950, 16.
61. For a fuller discussion of the Communist press's views of American stars, see Gundle, 'Il PCI e la campagna contro Hollywood', in Ellwood and Brunetta, *Hollywood in Europa*, 127–29.
62. Anon., 'I film da vedere', *La Verità*, 25 October 1952, 10.
63. *La Verità*, 24 September 1949, page unnumbered.
64. See Gundle, *Bellissima*, 133–41.
65. Ugo Casiraghi, interview with the author, Milan, May 1986.
66. Scarlini and Paloscia, *Il mondo dei fan club*; Buckley, 'Italian Female Stars and their Fans, 1950s and 1960s', in Burke, *A Companion to Italian Cinema*, 158–78. Much interesting work has also been done by Federico Vitella. See, for example, 'Forbice, album e carta da lettere: *Hollywood* come fan magazine', 51–64; 'Il diario intimo come fonte per la storia del fandom: ritratto di un Bobby-soxer di provincia', 153–60; 'Tirone, la volpe e il Papa: il matrimonio Power-Christian e la fan culture italiana del dopoguerra', in Dagrada, *Anna Cinquanta: il decennio più lungo del secolo breve*, 81–93.

67. Buckley, 'National Body: Gina Lollobrigida and the Cult of the Star in the 1950s', 527–47; Buckley, 'The Emergence of Film Fandom in Postwar Italy: Reading Claudia Cardinale's Fan Mail', 523–59.
68. Vitella, 'Tirone, la volpe e il Papa: il matrimonio Power-Christian e la fan culture italiana del dopoguerra', in Dagrada, *Anna Cinquanta*, 88.
69. Gundle, 'Memory and Identity: Popular Culture in Postwar Italy', in McCarthy, *Italy Since 1945*, 190–92.
70. See Colonna, *Personaggi e interpreti*, 13–31.
71. Forgacs and Gundle, *Mass Culture and Italian Society*, 166.
72. Gundle, *Mussolini's Dream Factory*, Chapter 4.
73. Scarlini and Paloscia, *Il mondo dei fan club*, 26–27.
74. Buckley, 'Italian Female Stars and their Fans', in Burke, *A Companion to Italian Cinema*, 159.
75. Ibid., 175.
76. Ibid., 166.
77. Vitella, 'Forbice, album e carta da lettere', 53.
78. Ibid., 54.
79. S. Martini, 'Mia leggiadrissima Yvonne' (1957), in Aristarco, *Il mito dell'attore: come l'industria della star produce il sex symbol*, 315–19; Renzi, 'La borsa degli autografi', *Cinema Nuovo*, 10 September 1956, 111–13.
80. Vitella, 'Forbice, album e carta da lettere', 56.
81. Ibid., 59–60.
82. See Gundle, *Mussolini's Dream Factory*, Chapter 4.
83. Ibid., 101–6.
84. Buckley, 'Italian Female Stars and their Fans', in Burke, *A Companion to Italian Cinema*, 166–67.

PART II
Stardom, Anti-Fascism and Neorealism

This part of the book examines the trajectories of five actors who were deeply implicated in efforts to reform Italian cinema in order to align it more closely with the reality of the country during and after the war. Two films have been identified critically as watersheds in this attempt to renegotiate the role of cinema and the methods of film-making. These are *Ossessione*, Visconti's 1942 adaptation of James M. Cain's novel *The Postman Always Rings Twice* and *Roma città aperta* (Rome Open City, 1945), Rossellini's epic treatment of the Roman Resistance. In the first film, which was shot in the summer of 1942 before having a short and patchy release in early 1943 and then a proper one after the war, two actors who occupied places in the star system of the autarkic cinema of the later Fascist period underwent a significant reconfiguration. The chapters on Massimo Girotti and Clara Calamai examine the impact of the film on their identities as actors, on their screen images and their careers in the years that followed. These chapters are followed by close analyses of Aldo Fabrizi and Anna Magnani, the two most prominent players in Rossellini's film. Neither was new to cinema, but their roots lay in popular theatre and it was as comedy or character actors that they had previously featured in films. *Roma città aperta* saw them take on dramatic roles for the first time; something that they did so effectively that the film would not only expand their ranges but win them a recognition and a popularity that would make them top box office earners for the rest of the decade. These acts of transformation signalled the unwillingness of directors and writers who had committed themselves to renewal to embrace uncritically the screen actors who populated the films of the 1930s and early 1940s. A new cinema needed new faces and bodies to convey new purposes or, at the very least, faces and bodies that did not simply bring to mind previous roles and personas. The films have been much studied, but they are not usually written about from the point of view of their actors and stars – men and women who were obliged to reinvent themselves and who would become the vectors of a new style of acting and a new mode of being a film star. In some cases, most notably that of Calamai, it would not prove easy to shake off an established image; in that of Magnani, the transfiguration would lead to a popularity that would be closely bound up with the period of the war and postwar transition and would prove unable to move decisively beyond it. The final chapter in the section looks at the case of Andrea Checchi, an actor who was identified from an early date as having the sort of undistinguished, everyday air that the champions of neorealism would seek for their films. Each chapter reflects on the way that a cinema that sought to abolish stars, and which positioned itself against the star system, was compelled to engage in a constant negotiation over stardom and to deal with the pressures of industry needs, public expectations and the personalities of the actors themselves.

CHAPTER 5
Massimo Girotti
Proletarian Apollo

Massimo Girotti was the first and, in some respects, the only male star of neorealism. He appeared in the early films of several neorealist masters, bringing to them qualities that had first tentatively come to the fore in his performances in both the commercial and the propaganda cinema of the Fascist period. The ways in which the actor's attributes were taken over and remodelled by anti-fascist directors illustrate the extent to which these opted, or were obliged, to work with established talent, and the ways in which they sought to reconfigure or harness this. Visconti would be the most important director in Girotti's career, even though he only starred in one of the director's films and took a small supporting role in another.[1] He was first noticed and admired by Visconti while both were working on the film *Tosca* (which began under the direction of Jean Renoir in 1942 and was finished by Carlo Koch, war events having obliged the Frenchman to leave Italy). In that film, Girotti had a small part – that of a nationalist revolutionary, to which he was expected to bring his handsome presence and little else. By then, the actor was already making his mark, having made his debut at the age of 21 in Mario Soldati's satire of the film world and its stars, *Dora Nelson* (1939). He was not yet a professional, having still been a student of engineering when he did a screen test for Soldati, although he had a background in amateur and student theatricals. Soldati had said he wanted 'a very good looking youngster, but with a virile, manly face'.[2] In other words, he was seeking the antithesis to the then popular teenage heart-throb Roberto Villa, who communicated a sweet, virginal air.[3] After his first film, Girotti continued to study and take part in inter-university water polo matches, switching his degree course to Law as it allowed him more time for his film work. By the time Visconti cast him as the wanderer Gino in *Ossessione* (1943), he was a rising star. He had appeared in some seven films; one them, Rossellini's aviation drama *Un pilota ritorna* (A Pilot Returns, 1942), as protagonist.[4]

Girotti first came to public attention in Alessandro Blasetti's medieval blockbuster *La corona di ferro* (The Iron Crown, 1941). A studio-bound extravaganza that mixed elements of mythology, literature and history, the film starred the versatile Gino Cervi in the role of Sedemondo, the usurper of his brother's throne, Blasetti's lover Elisa Cegani as Sedemondo's spiritual daughter Elsa, and Luisa Ferida as the warrior princess Tundra. Girotti's character Armonio is a medieval Tarzan-type, who, following his abduction as a child, has been raised by lions. Armonio enjoys a relationship with both of the rival princesses, a platonic one with Elsa and a physical one with Tundra, with whom he is united at the conclusion of the story. Armonio is established in the course of the narrative as the most perfect and accomplished of men; he is brave, handsome, agile, virile, sensitive, true and strong. He wins the favours and affection of women, torments Sedemondo's soldiers with his sling and lasso, overcomes the strongest of Tundra's loyalists (played in comic key by the one-time world heavyweight boxing champion Primo Carnera) and outsmarts and kills the evil prince Eriberto (Osvaldo Valenti) in a tournament whose prize is Elsa's hand. Throughout, Girotti is dressed in little more than a loincloth. His harmonious, athletic physique distinguishes him from the heavy, awkward or disquieting screen presence of the other male characters.

After *La corona di ferro*, Girotti later acknowledged that the fan letters arrived 'by the sackful: a thousand, two thousand, maybe six thousand a week; and the women who hadn't seen me at the cinema were all taken with me because of the vast quantity of photographs that were published everywhere' (see Figure 5.1).[5] These generally showed him bare-chested and highlighted his long straight legs, clear eyes and regular profile. The press, too, noted that girls no longer looked at the 40-year-old De Sica, or even the still popular Villa; it was Girotti who drew their attention.[6] It was evidently these physical qualities that commended him to Visconti. Although Giuliana Minghelli has recently disputed Geoffrey Nowell-Smith's assertion that *Ossessione* is a film about the destructive power of physical passion,[7] there is no doubt that, for his film to work, the director required actors who could convey the passion of Gino and Giovanna in a plausible and realistic way. In adapting James M. Cain's pulp novel *The Postman Always Rings Twice* for the screen and transferring the location from California to northern Italy, he wanted to explore a range of issues that had been raised by the young contributors to *Cinema* magazine in the preceding two years. The film was intended as a manifesto for a new Italian cinema, one that was more attuned to the reality of the country, its people and their relationship with the landscape. An American pulp novel might seem an unlikely starting point for such a project, and some of Visconti's leftist supporters expressed concern about the melodramatic plot and also the decadent French air that permeated the portrayal of the doomed lovers. Nonetheless, the film deals with the themes of freedom, solidarity and betrayal in real locations, which are largely unembellished by cinematic niceties or a stock supporting cast. Girotti later reflected on the unfamiliar experience that the film was for himself and Clara Calamai, who played the adulterous Giovanna:

> *Neither of us was really aware that we were contributing to the birth of a masterpiece. In all sincerity, we were disconcerted by Visconti's unusual methods. I was coming from a film like* La corona di ferro, *where the fantasy setting provided a frame for my athletic silhouette and my heroic doings. Clara came from* La cena delle beffe *[The Jester's Supper, 1942], in which her superlative beauty was emphasised by luxurious gowns and jewels.*[8]

Both films were directed by Blasetti, a great champion of Cinecittà and the most prominent film-maker of the period. Visconti demanded authenticity and took his actors outside the studio. Far from glamorizing them, he sought to strip them of their conventional armoury. He shouted at them and bullied them, demanding take after take until he achieved the desired effect. Girotti was aware of the political agenda that informed the film and of the anti-fascist persuasion of the director and his screenwriters. He was drawn into contact with leftists at this time and grew more political in the months that followed. He understood that the shoot was challenging because of the particular meanings that Visconti wanted to extract from the dialogue in order to highlight the deeper themes of the film. 'With me, he revealed his intentions fully', Girotti said; 'I knew him quite well and we talked a lot.'[9] Only several decades later would Girotti reveal that some of the tension on set was not solely due to the nature of the film project but also to the sexual relationships in course between himself and both Visconti and Calamai.[10]

Girotti's character was a wanderer, a vagabond, who is sucked into a murderous drama by an unhappy wife whose charms he is unable to resist. He is a practical man and a former soldier who has fallen on hard times and lives by expedients. He is not the 'positive hero' of the film – he is too weak and easily led for that – but his ambiguity and vulnerability are real and involving. Girotti succumbs to Giovanna, is picked up on the train by a travelling showman known as 'lo spagnolo' (the Spaniard) and flirts with an easy-going dancer come prostitute.

He is torn between different forms of love and camaraderie and passes between these without ever fully realizing their implications. His virile presence was vital to the realization of the character of Gino. A handsome innocent, he has in some way to be a blank canvas who speaks little and communicates largely with his body. For everyone to find him attractive, even desirable, he needs to embody some physical ideal, albeit one that is ruggedly devoid of any 'glamour and polished mannerisms'.[11] When Gino first wanders into the kitchen of the roadside inn and petrol station, drawn by the singing voice of Giovanna, he has just been ousted from the back of the truck on which he caught a free ride and branded a tramp by the inn's owner, Bragana. However, when the latter's down-trodden younger wife turns to look at him, the camera immediately zooms into a close-up of his handsome face. Although his impoverished status does not entitle him to disport himself with confidence, he is clearly a man aware of his good looks and what they entitle him to. While his light eyes and open face suggest ideal qualities, his athletic body, revealed by the simple vest he is wearing, lends him a more sexual appeal. 'You are built like a horse', exclaims Giovanna as she hungrily feasts her eyes on him.

The character of Gino, it may be argued, retains a certain American-ness inherited from the source material. The figure of the vagabond recalls the America of the Depression and was not familiar to Italian experience. The vigorous physicality of the role also brings to mind the self-sufficiency and independence of Cain's American male characters, even if this aspect would largely be absent from the Hollywood adaptation of the novel (directed by Tay Garnett in 1946). As an actor without formal training, Girotti had few theatrical mannerisms and was inspired rather by the examples of screen masculinity furnished by the American stars of the day. His athleticism was of a type taken for granted in Hollywood where it had been turned explicitly into a trope by Douglas Fairbanks and the swimming champion-turned-actor Johnny Weissmuller (the first cinematic Tarzan). Girotti prospered because this type or model was almost entirely absent in Italian cinema. Many male actors were tall and endowed with regular, appealing features; many, too, played characters who were morally upright and courageous. But none possessed that fluidity of movement and rugged physical presence that was associated with the Americans. Amedeo Nazzari was always fully clothed while Fosco Giachetti, who did not mind occasionally exposing his upper body, was lean and sinuous rather than powerfully muscular. Only Girotti was able plausibly to play a boxer, yachtsman or footballer.

Girotti's first film in a leading role was Rossellini's propaganda feature *Un pilota ritorna*, in which he played an intrepid war pilot who manages to escape from capture in Greece, seize a British plane and fly under fire back to his own camp. In 1942, Rossellini was still a protagonist of Fascist cinema. Nonetheless, he was beginning to experiment with an anti-rhetorical style that incorporated some of the spirit and feel of ordinary life. For example, the production had initially envisaged that the film's central character would be selected from among the entrants to a competition launched for the purpose. In the end, only the supporting players were cast in this way, but Girotti was obliged to blend with a supporting cast of real pilots and airmen, whose stories and experiences were an integral part of the film. This custom of blending professionals with non-professionals to enhance the feel of reality was relatively new. It would become more widespread in the immediate postwar years, when it was taken as a mark of democratization.

Un pilota ritorna was proposed and supported by Mussolini's son Vittorio (cited in the credits as Tito Silvio Mursino, an anagrammatic pseudonym) and was clearly propagandistic in intent. Girotti's character, Lieutenant Rossati, is an airman from beginning to end; he is shown to enjoy the privileges and share the camaraderie of the officer corps, most of whose members are older than him and who know they risk their lives in every mission they undertake. The film's opening titles explain that it is dedicated 'with a fraternal heart to the pilots who did not return from the skies of Greece'. At a critical moment in the fortunes of Italy's war effort, the film turned Girotti into a vehicle for the official values of the regime. By means of his stardom and physical beauty, the film was best able to fulfil its aim to 'make known the heroism of our air force',[12] even if, the actor later stated, 'little glory is associated with combat' and rather it is 'a world-weary sense of the destructiveness of war' that prevails.[13] Rossellini's inclusion of a chaste romantic interlude, and its abrupt truncation, served to humanize the pilot. It also confirmed Girotti as a sensitive romantic hero. The interruption of a burgeoning heterosexual relationship in the context of war had been presented before, notably in *L'assedio dell'Alcazar* (The Siege of the Alcazar, Augusto Genina, 1940), but this was the first time the hero was visibly affected by it. For Ruth Ben-Ghiat, 'the extreme close-up of his face in the film's final shot conveys his inner conflict.'[14] It would be an early sign of the softening of masculinity that would become more widespread in postwar films.

After the liberation of Rome in 1944, when critics began to assess the potential of Italy's cinematic talent, no mention was made of *Un pilota ritorna*, or indeed

Figure 5.1 Postcard portrait photo of Massimo Girotti, the young star c. 1942 (author's own collection).

of the other propaganda films that the by now anti-fascist Rossellini had made. Though some felt that his Tarzan type roles had done him no good,[15] Girotti's contribution to *Ossessione* became his calling card. Later observers, among them Michel Azzopardi, have noted that, as Gino, he exhibited 'the traits of a proletarian Apollo'.[16] *Ossessione* had taken him from a propaganda context and placed him in a critical one. Thanks to it, he had the potential to become the symbolic actor of democratic Italy for left-wing directors.[17] Yet some critics were not entirely persuaded by the figure of Gino. Pietro Bianchi saw the film with other critics in June 1943 and wrote: 'the protagonist Massimo Girotti wore on his head a French-style cap unknown to our proletarians ... he wandered around a sun-drenched Emilia and the roads of the Adriatic coast with a "non-Italian" spirit.'[18] The Viscontian conjunction of decadentism and realism jarred. The future director Steno (Stefano Vanzina), too, would refer in his diary of 1944 to the 'autarkic French types' of *Ossessione*.[19] But the impact of the film, among film-makers if not the public, was enormous. De Sica is known to have seen the film as he was preparing *I bambini ci guardano* (The Children are Watching Us, 1943), and others, too, felt it licensed them to transgress what had hitherto been the non-negotiable limits of what could be presented on screen.

Girotti's beautiful body became something of a cinematic trope in the years between the war and the early 1950s.[20] On a variety of occasions, he appeared semi-naked, removed his shirt, wore a sleeveless vest or otherwise displayed his finely contoured muscles. This repeated exposure occurred in very different contexts, which ranged from the fantasy of *La corona di ferro* to a beach scene in *La famiglia Brambilla va in vacanza* (The Brambilla Family Go on Holiday, Carl Boese, 1942), from *Ossessione* and the postwar melodrama *Fatalità* (Fatality, Giorgio Bianchi, 1947) to the Biblical epic *Fabiola* (Alessandro Blasetti, 1949). The final role in which his muscular body was deployed for effect was Riccardo Freda's *Spartaco* (Sins of Rome, 1953), a film that disappeared from circulation after the Americans bought up the rights for 50,000 dollars in order to eliminate comparison – or perhaps competition – with their own treatment of the story, *Spartacus*, starring Kirk Douglas and directed by Stanley Kubrick.[21]

Alexander Garcia Düttmann sees Girotti's body as 'a meaningless sign' – that is to say 'a sign that wants for nothing and needs no signifier to justify its existence'.[22] 'This unruffled self-sufficiency ... has about it something of the innocence and patience of the saint', he adds.[23] Within some film texts, this may be the case, but male bodies and their representation were not at all innocent under

Fascism. Thus, it is not possible to abstract the actor's body so lightly from the cultural and political context in which it acquired visibility. Far from being devoid of meaning, it was significant symbolically because of the importance of the male body to Fascist aesthetics. This is not to say that there was a complete appropriation on the part of the regime of the faces and figures of cinema or that there were not other dynamics at work – among them sport and consumerism. But the deployment of Girotti in propaganda and anti-fascist cinema as well as entertainment genres means that it is legitimate to discuss him in relation to the political transitions that occurred over this period and the aesthetic displacements that these entailed.

Beauty was a key feature of modern masculinity. For George Mosse, 'modern masculinity was to define itself through an ideal of manly beauty that symbolized virtue.'[24] This was so because of the Enlightenment idea that the body was a visible embodiment of a person's inner qualities. In his study of masculinity and aesthetic modernism in Fascist Italy, John Champagne interrogates the representation of the male body in the visual and figurative arts.[25] He suggests that, in order to escape the effeminizing implications of the twentieth-century commodification of beauty, Fascism adopted two strategies: cultural battles against perceived negative elements and recourse to Greco-Roman ideals. These did not necessarily lead in the same direction though. As Mosse notes, Winckelmann's view of the ideal body as consisting of balance, proportion and moderation implied a degree of posed passivity that was unsettling.[26] Fascism aimed to correct this by emphasizing the army, the party and the school. Generic ideals were formed from a mixture of sources, which included Roman statuary and patriotic painting. Though Mosse takes the view that beauty was less important in Italy than in Germany,[27] nevertheless 'men's bodies in all their well-sculpted nudity became fascist symbols.'[28] In terms of broader ideals of masculine beauty, absorbed and rearticulated by Fascism, Girotti was in line with a tradition that had become Fascist in inflection but that was not solely and uniquely Fascist. Youth, vigour and vitality marked 'the graphic and sculptural representation of patriotic heroes that spread everywhere in Italian cities in the late nineteenth century'.[29] In *Tosca*, Girotti makes an uncredited appearance as one of a band of patriots who penetrate the Castel Sant'Angelo fortress in Rome in the guise of blacksmiths. Their aim is to free the condemned prisoner Angelotti, and this they do by knocking out a guard and smuggling out Angelotti dressed as one of their number. Girotti is briefly seen as he slips out of his shirt to make the disguise (and is greeted as

'Massimo' by the surprised Angelotti, played by Adriano Rimoldi). The camera's exploration of the surfaces of his body serves to highlight a patriotic aesthetic that Fascism had taken up and re-elaborated within contemporary visual culture. Girotti, after all, measured up to Fascist male iconography in ways that neither Mussolini nor most male film stars did.[30] Visconti's task was to mould Girotti in such a way that his beauty would become detached from both Fascism's purposes and cinematic convention. For the cinematography of his film, he rejected the most respected names of the time and instead opted for Aldo Tonti, an artisan master who was capable of realizing the atmosphere he wanted without recourse to conventional solutions.[31]

The actor's primary image in *Ossessione* and other films is ostensibly as an object of heterosexual desire. The central storyline concerns his doomed relationship with Giovanna, and a subplot sees him win the sympathy of a young dancer. But the heterosexual narrative of Visconti's film overlies a homosexual one, which is subtextually present in the relationship between Gino and the figure of the Spaniard, and which inflects the political subtext.[32] Tension emerges between the two characters when Gino's suitcase falls open to reveal women's clothes belonging to Giovanna, suggesting a fit of jealousy on the Spaniard's part. When the latter furtively holds up a candle to cast an admiring eye over Gino's sleeping body, we know that he is harbouring desire for him. When the two work together, it is the Spaniard who takes the active role running his fairground show while Gino is reduced to walking around like a sandwich-man with advertising boards strapped to him. He is explicitly a display object to be noticed. For William Van Watson, 'Gino's subjectivity is under siege from Visconti's homoerotic sensibility, which insists on objectifying him.'[33] Although some critics have been more nuanced than Nowell-Smith, who frankly states, 'the Spaniard is a homosexual',[34] there has long been a recognition that there is something 'equivocal' or 'ambiguous' about this character that detracts from – or complicates – the intentions of some scriptwriters to have him stand as the positive character of the film.[35] One of the writers, Giuseppe De Santis, interviewed in 1977, admitted, 'you can clearly see that a particular pleasure is taken by the director in Massimo Girotti's body, his vest and his fine shoulders; there is a homosexual complicity.'[36]

This is true, but the implication that Visconti could not restrain himself from giving expression to his sexual orientation ignores the fact that he was as committed to the film's political message as its writers. Unlike these, he saw that he could effectively articulate the cinematic critique of Fascism on several planes.

By queering the disenfranchised former soldier Gino, he could also tackle Fascist hyper-masculinity. This was an exceptionally subtle operation that showed an appreciation of the contradictions of the regime's cult of masculinity. As recent critics have observed, the homosociality of Fascism could not but on occasion enter the realm of the homoerotic, and not always could this be kept at bay by homophobia.[37] Champagne has argued that, by turning the male body into 'an object of erotic contemplation', Fascist aesthetics inadvertently brought with them 'a "feminization" of the male body (feminization understood here as a cultural and historical encoding of the body as object of pleasure, recipient of the gaze, and so forth)'.[38] Derek Duncan has further observed that 'the public celebration and display of the male body raises questions of how men looked at each other', and these did not always find answers that were fully in line with the militaristic objectives of the regime.[39] The Spaniard's gaze can be seen as precisely as an example of such questioning.

Visconti's operation would not have been possible had the actor Girotti not been eminently pliable. The passivity that allowed Gino to be objectivized seems also to have been a trait of the young and relatively untested Girotti. Though he was a sportsman who offered an image of the type of virile activism that Fascism encouraged, he was no soldier of the cause. His disposition was indolent and distracted. 'I was an unenthusiastic student who only barely managed to pass from one year to the next; I did not care much for study', he later said.[40] He was drawn to the shiny world of Hollywood and often skipped classes and sports training to go to the movies. He was well aware that he owed his breakthrough in cinema to his physical appearance more than any achievement. 'They chose me because I was handsome, because I was 1.8m tall, I had light coloured eyes, slim thighs and broad shoulders. I did not know how to work or to do anything. They just wanted me to move, to walk or to look; nothing else was required of me. I felt wrong, alienated from myself.'[41] Girotti's beauty was taken over by Fascism without it belonging to the dominant 'hyper-phallic discourse of virility'.[42] By the same token, it could be taken up and used for other purposes once the Fascist edifice began to crumble and after it finally fell.

Girotti spent the final period of the war away from Rome in the Abruzzo region, where he joined Visconti, Rossellini and others in political discussions about the country's future. After the liberation of Rome, he turned to the theatre, like many, to maintain some activity until film production recommenced. Once it did, he was in demand, and he was cast in a number of important projects, including the first films of De Santis and Pietro Germi, as well as a variety of commercial projects. However, efforts to assert him as the leading male star of the new era were hampered by that fact that his god-like good looks contrasted with the pursuit of the ordinary. Beauty may have been bound up with dynamics other than Fascism, but in the immediate postwar years male beauty was a debased coinage. Thus Girotti's depthless handsomeness was cast by some as empty or uninteresting. He is often weaker than a leading man should be; he loses women to other men or is in some way overshadowed by them.

An early example of this is offered by *Desiderio* (Desire, 1945), a film that was begun in Rome by Rossellini under the title 'Scalo merci' and then continued with shooting relocated to the Abruzzo region and later finished by Marcello Pagliero (the hero Manfredi in *Roma città aperta*). His role was a bland one; he is the dull husband of a homely woman who is driven to erotic distraction by his sister-in-law, a woman who has returned to the rural family home after leading a life of supposed vice in the capital. Despite his best efforts to impress her, the sophisticated sister, played by Elli Parvo, only ever toys with him and never deigns him with any serious attention. In *Fatalità* (Fatality, Giorgio Bianchi, 1946), his character Vincenzo is also rejected by a woman, in this case his restless young wife, played by Maria Michi (who took the role of the corrupt Marina in *Roma città aperta*). Paola is bored by her husband's intense involvement in his river transport business near Rome. Though she does not intend to be unfaithful, her head is turned by Renato, a new employee with a chequered past and unfulfilled ambitions. She at first resists his overtures, then conspires to run away with him, before realizing the folly of this whim once the pair are alone in a hotel room in Rome.[43] Vincenzo is so wrapped up in his business that he notices nothing until after Paola's flight. Unaware that she has changed her mind on the brink of committing adultery, he tracks her down to the hotel room and, fired by jealousy and violated honour, kills her. Though the opening shot of the film is of Girotti bare-chested as he dresses in the morning, his erotic appeal is never developed. Indeed, he is repeatedly shown in banal situations (domestic environments, a bowls game), and his relations with his wife are desexualized to the point that the two barely touch each other and never kiss.

The earthy loner Renato is played by Amedeo Nazzari, who had been the leading male star in Italian cinema before 1943. The two actors had previously made three films together: *Harlem* (Carmine Gallone, 1943), *Apparizione* (Apparition, Max Neufeld, 1943) and *Un giorno nella vita* (A Day in the Life, Alessandro Blasetti,

1945). In the earlier films, unsurprisingly, the older Nazzari was always the more potent and compelling figure. In *Apparizione*, he even played himself – Amedeo Nazzari film star – who goes to some lengths to persuade a young fan to return to her jealous mechanic fiancé after he catches her posing for a photograph with him and she resolves to end the engagement. Girotti plays the petulant mechanic. After 1945, Nazzari was no longer bolstered by a film industry and had to seek out new roles. But his maturity and popularity helped him maintain his ascendancy over younger rivals. In *Un giorno nella vita*, the two men play partisans, but Nazzari is the leader of the group while Girotti is merely a wounded fighter. Though Nazzari was eleven years older and struggled to adapt his persona to the new era, he remained a force to be reckoned with. Still in the 1952 film *Un marito per Anna Zaccheo* (A Husband for Anna Zaccheo, Giuseppe De Santis), he seduces the eponymous Anna, a beautiful would-be career girl, while Girotti, who plays a romantic young sailor who aspires to marry her, is left distraught and empty-handed.

In seeking to explain why Girotti, despite what might have seemed propitious circumstances, failed to oust Nazzari from his pre-eminent position in Italian cinema, reference needs to be made to the rich and intense humanity that the latter projected. While Girotti's Gino was more seduced than seducer, Nazzari was never subordinate to anyone. Despite his prominence in Fascist-period cinema, he differed from the shallow actors who populated the effervescent 'white telephone' comedies. In some respects, he was well equipped to perform the role of witness in a reconfigured cinema. By contrast, Girotti seemed to lack a hinterland. Physically, the two men were also different. While both were tall and strong, and shared something with leading American actors, Nazzari was more typically Italian in appearance. Though he hailed from the province of Macerata, in the central Marche region, where his parents had run a pharmacy, Girotti looked like a northerner. With his light brown hair and blue eyes, he corresponded to a physical type that was not widespread in Italian cinema in the Fascist period or afterwards. His regular features and physical beauty lifted him into a realm that seemed to be devoid of specificity. Paradoxically, it was he – and not Nazzari – who most resembled the American actors, which Italian cinema was no longer seeking to copy. The regional origins of his characters were extremely variable, when they were specified at all. On several occasions he was Roman, while on others he was from the central Romagna region, Liguria or Venice. He spoke an unaccented Italian that was inoffensive and functional rather than richly characterful. Moreover, there was a class issue. While Girotti played mechanics, soldiers and sportsmen, he was never confined to the type of working-class role Azzopardi had in mind when he described him as a 'proletarian Apollo'. He plausibly played a policeman, a magistrate, a doctor and the owner of a transport company. This mobility was a useful resource for an actor but indeterminacy was not necessarily an advantage in the class-inflected and unvarnished cinema of the period.

Nevertheless, he featured widely, especially in more popular neorealist films. He was an actor with whom many directors aligned with the current they felt they could use to combine the requirements of a new type of cinema with certain commercial demands. De Santis overcame the reservations he had had at the time of *Ossessione* to cast him as the lead in his debut film,[44] *Caccia tragica* (Tragic Hunt, 1947), a working-class drama about returning soldiers and the struggles of agricultural cooperatives (which is discussed in Chapter 10). Two of the most significant films he made in the late 1940s were directed by Pietro Germi, who had been Blasetti's assistant and who embraced the former's artisanal approach to filmmaking. For Lino Miccichè, Germi always stressed 'his own diversity with respect to the cinematic mainstream of the moment'.[45] He did not share the progressive political stance that came to be associated with the movement's practitioners and nor did he conceal his admiration for American cinema. Both films, *Gioventù perduta* (Lost Youth, 1947) and *In nome della legge* (In the Name of the Law, 1948) were at one level inquiries into social problems: the postwar amorality of youth in the former and the Mafia in the latter. At another, they were thrillers, centred on the battle of a lone man of the law to bring wrongdoers to justice and re-establish rightful order where it had been challenged. The realism of the former was, for Miccichè, 'more Fordian than Rossellianian'.[46] In both instances, Girotti played the noble hero in his struggle. The director used him to incarnate 'the idea that he was constructing in these years of the positive hero',[47] an ambition also pursued, albeit without an acknowledgement of the social, by the reactionary director Riccardo Freda.[48] In the first film, Girotti is a police officer who is charged with uncovering a series of crimes that have been committed, it is suspected, by a band of bored and materialistic middle-class students. In the second, he is a magistrate sent to a remote Sicilian town where the Mafia is the sole acknowledged authority. Girotti's roles in both films were 'American', in keeping with the generic characteristics of the films.

In *Gioventù perduta*, a remodelled gangster movie, his character is morally complex, since he infiltrates the students' environment and strikes up an amorous friendship with the innocent sister of the prime suspect, who he eventually kills in a street shoot-out. Yet, there is no real ambiguity in his conduct and nor could there be, it has been argued, given his 'respectable face'.⁴⁹ In the end, the sister appears to forgive both his deception and his killing of her evil sibling, and their *'addio'* becomes transformed into a hopeful *'arrivederci'*. Although Girotti wears a suit throughout, his body remains a crucial, if unexhibited, signifier of his moral purpose, for, as Sesti observes, in Germi's cinema, 'the body is at the service of a vision, not the other way round. Cinema itself is felt as a physical presence'.⁵⁰

In *In nome della legge*, he is in effect the sheriff, the man alone who must show great moral and physical courage in a context in which it is in short supply. Indeed, the film has been called 'Italy's only true western.'⁵¹ He is supposedly Sicilian himself, though there is no trace of an accent in his speech. He also looks different, a tall and handsome man of light colouring who wears crisp suits rather than crumpled work clothes. 'He introduces into the landscape – sometimes explicitly, but more often in subterranean, nearly imperceptible fashion – a constant element of unreality, by way of the crevasses in the hat covering his face, and the double-breasted suit that stands out against the whitewashed walls and barren ravines, and the defenceless yet unstoppable gait of an outsider of unknown origins', Mario Sesti has remarked.⁵² He is brought into conflict not just with organized crime but with the town's ruling class, which exhibits a disregard for the economic interests of the citizenry and dominates the timorous authorities. Only a loyal policeman and the wife of a sinister baron have any sympathy for his endeavours and seek to help him.

Girotti did not incorporate his private life into his image. Few were aware before the later 1950s that in 1942 he had married Marcella, a fellow student, and they had two children, who were born in 1948 and 1951. Instead, he harnessed his celebrity to politics. In the political battles that characterized the late 1940s, he was firmly identified with the left. He claimed that anti-fascism was 'in my blood'.⁵³ He joined the Italian Communist Party, and his fame was harnessed by the party to boost its popularity among the workers. The party newspaper *L'Unità* reported in December 1948 that he had donated Lit. 20,000 to the 'Una Befana felice a un bimbo infelice' (An Epiphany present for an unhappy child) campaign. In April 1949, it was announced that he would go to Paris as the delegate from an Emilian section of the party to the conference of the Peace Front, and in 1950 it was stated that he had signed the Stockholm appeal against the use of the atomic bomb. His name was regularly listed in the years that followed among the donors to progressive causes.⁵⁴ With these stances, he joined intellectuals whose cultural

Figure 5.2 Massimo Girotti as Christian martyr Sebastian, the future saint, in *Fabiola* (Alessandro Blasetti, 1949). The actor became a 'proletarian Apollo' for neorealists but was also configured as a 'queer Adonis' (screenshot by the author).

tastes as well as politics he shared. He amassed a personal art collection, which included works by the modernist masters Morandi, De Pisis and Picasso.[55] In later years, he would be pictured with them at his villa in Rome's Monte Mario district.

In his heyday, Girotti came to be seen as the ideal actor for 'every character that demands engagement, sincerity and vigour'.[56] 'His face of a sad angel, his athletic form, his restrained, human playing' suited him to play partisan, bandit, worker, boyfriend, husband or lover, one observer remarked. He was the 'type of man everyone – whether male or female – would like to meet'. Abroad, he was labelled the 'new Valentino' and the 'new George Raft',[57] while his own Hollywood favourites were Spencer Tracy, Henry Fonda and, for his overall physical presence, Burt Lancaster.[58] However, he lacked the rugged feel of Raft and Lancaster, the moral weight of Tracy or the intensity of Fonda. His gaze is often absent, and suggestions of thoughtfulness are seldom combined with demonstrations of intelligence. Only on very rare occasions did he constitute the central focus of a film.

Though, as Giulio Cesare Castello argued, 'his clear, thoughtful eyes can express uncertainty, interior fragility, but also tranquil decision', this was mainly a result of screenplays that set up a contrast between his characters and compromised ones.[59] A certain vulnerability constituted one of his key traits, which meant that he could seem almost a supporting player, as in *Molti sogni per le strade* (The Street Has Many Dreams, Mario Camerini, 1948) and *Vortice* (Vortex, Raffaello Matarazzo, 1953), in which he was overshadowed respectively by Anna Magnani and Silvana Pampanini. In *Natale al campo 119* (Christmas at Camp 119, Pietro Francisi, 1948), he plays a Venetian gondolier who becomes a rich visitor's lover only to be abruptly discarded when the woman and her older husband leave the lagoon city. In *Anni difficili* (Difficult Years, Luigi Zampa, 1948), he is defenceless or passive as a soldier of the Fascist period who is repeatedly called up to war and finally fails to return home.

For Alberto Abruzzese, the image that encapsulates 'the sense of Massimo Girotti' occurs in Blasetti's Biblical drama *Fabiola* (1949). The film was a Franco-Italian coproduction, the first blockbuster to be filmed at the newly reopened Cinecittà. In some respects, it recalled the director's *La corona di ferro*, in which Girotti had first made his name. This time he lends his 'gentle, beautiful body' to the Christian martyr Sebastian and is bound to a tree and shot with arrows (see Figure 5.2). The scene is composed pictorially to maximize the synthesis of beauty and suffering. This, Abruzzese argues, is because his beauty was taken over by cinema and was sacrificed to it.[60] In European art, St Sebastian was infused with homoeroticism, and it is difficult to imagine that this was not a factor in the casting. The persistent display of Girotti's athletic body ensured that the homoerotic quality that had first become attached to him in the Fascist period remained an undercurrent of his persona. On several occasions in the course of his long career, it was incorporated into the diegesis of his films.[61] In *Spartaco*, the zoom of *Ossessione* is repeated when he is eyed up by the daughter of a rich Roman general, and he is also given an erotically charged public whipping. Even before the celebrated case of Visconti's film he had been surveyed at the beach and drawn into male horseplay in *La famiglia Brambilla va in vacanza*. These momentary incidents would become inscribed in Girotti's screen persona and lent him an ambiguity that could be mobilized in various ways by directors seeking to query or reflect on modern masculinity.

The last significant film of the neorealist period in which he took the leading male role was Antonioni's debut film *Cronaca di un amore* (Chronicle of A Love,

1950). He was paired with Lucia Bosè, a Milanese shop girl whose extraordinary beauty and poise had led to her winning the Miss Italia title in 1947. Echoes of *Ossessione* permeate a narrative in which a tragic death hangs over two former lovers who meet again some years later.[62] While Girotti's character Guido is a good-looking, unsettled man, his former lover Paola has settled down in Milan with a wealthy older man. The ostensibly accidental death of Guido's fiancée during a drunken evening at which all three were present continues to haunt him. The guilt that torments Guido is evidently an allegory for the complicity of the Italians with Mussolini's regime. He is a weak man whose fluid inconsistency is ably contrasted by Antonioni with the cold hardness of bourgeois Milan and the icy perfection of the fashion-piece Paola. Though the death in a road accident of Paola's husband finally leads him to take a decisive stance and to reject the chance to get back together with her, he is fundamentally an irresolute individual who struggles to cast off the past. In short, the film, which perplexed critics and received a tepid initial response,[63] thrust him back into the Fascist era while ostensibly freeing him of it.

Girotti's contribution to *Ossessione* had consecrated him in the eyes of a generation of film-makers that was seeking to express opposition to Fascism[64] and positioned him to play a key part in the construction of a cinema that aspired to be at once popular and engaged. As a 'proletarian Apollo' whose secret subtext was that of a 'queer Adonis', he was the male actor who held out the prospect of a transition from Fascist aesthetics to a more democratic iconography by inflecting beauty with vulnerability and indeterminacy. Yet, by December 1952, the industry magazine *Cinespettacolo* was already lamenting that no replacements had yet been found for Girotti and Nazzari, as though he was a figure of the past.[65] When Visconti made the Risorgimento melodrama *Senso* in 1954, he cast him in the smallest of roles, barely more than a cameo. The beautiful male body still carried some residual historical value, but it could not be deployed innocently in contemporary films.

Notes

1. Until he was offered a further role (in *L'innocente*, 1976), long after his star status had given way to a more prosaic reputation as an actor of dependable quality.
2. Quoted in A. Sanzio, 'Il quarantenne che piace', *Luna*, 10 August 1961, 13.
3. E. Ferri, '"Finalmente non sono più un divo"', *Novella*, 11 September 1966, 27–29.

4. In this film, Pietro Bianchi wrote, he 'showed that he had potential'. See Bianchi, *L'occhio di vetro: il cinema degli anni 1940–43*, 131. Review published 18 May 1942.
5. Ferri, '"Finalmente non sono più un divo"', 28.
6. C. Musso, 'La lanterna di De Sica', *Star*, 19 August 1944, page unnumbered.
7. Nowell Smith, *Luchino Visconti*, 17; Minghelli, *Landscape and Memory in Post-Fascist Italian Film: Cinema Year Zero*.
8. M. Girotti, 'Le dieci donne della mia vita', *Annabella*, 31 July 1960, 22.
9. Faldini and Fofi, *L'avventurosa storia del cinema italiano: raccontata dai suoi protagonisti, 1935–1959*, 64–65.
10. Alberico, *Il corpo gentile: conversazione con Massimo Girotti*, 103–4. In his obituary, John Francis Lane wrote that the actor 'suffered from Visconti's amorous attention', *The Guardian*, 7 January 2003. Lane's own gay chronicles appear in his 2013 memoir *To Each His Own Dolce Vita*.
11. Bacon, *Visconti: Explorations of Beauty and Decay*, 15.
12. Brunette, *Roberto Rossellini*, 19.
13. Girotti, 'Le dieci donne della mia vita', 21–22.
14. R. Ben-Ghiat, 'The Fascist War Trilogy', in Forgacs, Lutton and Nowell-Smith, *Roberto Rossellini: Magician of the Real*, 26.
15. A. Pietrangeli, 'Gli attori', *Star*, 23 September 1944, page unnumbered.
16. Azzopardi, *Massimo Girotti: un acteur aux cent visages*, 25.
17. Ibid., 27.
18. Bianchi, *Maestri del cinema*, 343.
19. Steno, *Sotto le stelle del '44*, 160.
20. He later remarked: 'Even in *Ossessione*, which I believe to be my most important film, the best one in which I have appeared, I was expected first and foremost to be beautiful', he later observed. 'The wretch who leads me to kill her husband was infatuated with me; she lost her head for my body.' Ferri, '"Finalmente non sono più un divo"', 28.
21. Azzopardi, *Massimo Girotti*, 49.
22. Düttmann, *Visconti: Insights into Flesh and Blood*, 18.
23. Ibid., 18.
24. Mosse, *The Image of Man: The Creation of Modern Masculinity*, 5.
25. Champagne, *Aesthetic Modernism and Masculinity in Fascist Italy*, 4.
26. Ibid., 34.
27. Mosse, *The Image of Man*, 161.
28. Ibid., 161.
29. Banti, *Sublime madre nostra: la nazione italiana dal Risorgimento al fascismo*, 36.
30. See Gundle, Duggan and Pieri, *The Cult of the Duce: Mussolini and the Italians*, Chapters 10–13.
31. Gili and Grossi, *Alle origini del Neorealismo: Giuseppe De Santis a colloquio con Jean A. Gili*, 42–43.
32. Ibid., 39.
33. W. Van Watson, 'Luchino Visconti's (homosexual) *Ossessione*', in Reich and Garofalo, *Re-Viewing Fascism: Italian Cinema, 1922–1943*, 185.
34. Nowell-Smith, *Luchino Visconti*, 23.
35. Van Watson, 'Luchino Visconti's (homosexual) *Ossessione*', in Reich and Garofalo, *Re-Viewing Fascism*, 181–82.
36. Gili, *Alle origini*, 40.
37. Ibid., 14.
38. Champagne, *Aesthetic Modernism*, 36.

39. D. Duncan, '*Ossessione*', in Forbes and Street, *European Cinema: An Introduction*, 94–106.
40. Ferri, '"Finalmente non sono più un divo"', 28.
41. Ibid., 28.
42. Ibid., 96.
43. The hotel overlooks the Trevi fountain and is known today as Hotel Fontana.
44. Gili, *Alle origini*, 49.
45. L. Miccichè, 'Prima della "trilogia grottesca"', in Miccichè, *Signore e signori di Pietro Germi*, 25.
46. Ibid., 25.
47. M. Girotti, 'Le dieci donne della mia vita'; Aprà, 'Per una revisione di Pietro Germi', in Miccichè, *Signore e signori*, 56.
48. See Freda, *Divoratori di celluloide: 50 anni di memorie cinematografiche e non*, 85.
49. Spinazzola, *Cinema e pubblico: lo spettacolo filmico in Italia 1945–65*, 29.
50. Sesti, *Pietro Germi: Life and Films of a Latin Loner*, 44–45.
51. Ibid., 24.
52. Ibid., 77.
53. Alberico, *Il corpo gentile*, 95.
54. See *L'Unità*: 10 December 1948, 16 April 1949, 22 June 1950, 3 January 1953. Eventually, he let his membership lapse while remaining a sympathizer. Alberico, *Il corpo gentile*, 96.
55. However, he was not a faithful husband. In 1960, he admitted that he had enjoyed liaisons with many of the women he had worked with. Massimo Girotti, 'Le dieci donne della mia vita', *Annabella*, 31 July 1960, 19–22. Only in his final interview did he reveal that he had also had a sexual relationship with Visconti.
56. Sanzio, 'Il quarantenne che piace', 16.
57. Anon., 'Massimo Girotti', *Cine revue*, 26 October 1956, 14–15.
58. Anon., 'Massimo Girotti séducteur tranquille', *Cinémonde*, 5 November 1954, 15.
59. Castello, *Il divismo: mitologia dell'attore*, 409–10.
60. A. Abruzzese, '"L'eccellenza dell'italianità"', in Alberico, *Il corpo gentile*, 10.
61. His later roles would continue to mine the current of ambiguity marking his screen image. In Pasolini's *Teorema* (1968), he is seduced along with the rest of the bourgeois family by Terence Stamp's handsome intruder. In his final film, *La finestra di fronte* (Facing Windows, Ferzan Ozpetek, 2003), he plays an elderly amnesiac Jew who gradually recalls the circumstances of the death of his male lover during the time of the Nazi occupation of Rome. In treating the theme of memory, and in evoking war-time traumas, the film indirectly references what would remain the actor's best-known role.
62. For a perceptive analysis of this film's take on the Fascist past, see Minghelli, *Landscape and Memory in Post-Fascist Italian Film: Cinema Year Zero*, Chapter 4.
63. See Tassone, *I film di Michelangelo Antonioni*, 68–69.
64. Lizzani, 'Postfazione', in Alberico, *Il corpo gentile*, 121.
65. Anon, 'Le attrici famose ci sono, ma gli attori?' *Cinespettacolo*, 20 December 1952, 5.

CHAPTER 6

Clara Calamai
The Suspension of Glamour

By the time she was cast as the dissatisfied innkeeper's wife Giovanna in *Ossessione* (Luchino Visconti, 1943), Clara Calamai had established herself as one of Cinecittà's leading stars. Not only had she worked with many directors in historical and contemporary dramas, but she had forged a screen type that aroused the interest, and sometimes adoration, of critics and the public. Some of this rested on an armoury of sumptuous costumes, elaborate cosmetics and glamorous cinematography, which marked her out from the numerous *ingénues* who rose to fame in the early 1940s. Calamai stood for elegance, worldliness and sex appeal. Her flawless oval face and poise contributed to the reputation she acquired in a relatively short time as the 'glamour queen' of Italian cinema. On the face of it, therefore, she was an unusual choice to play the part of Giovanna. It is well known that Visconti's first choice was Anna Magnani, who at that time was a lesser-known variety actress who had only made supporting appearances in films. Calamai, by contrast, was one of the most visible and 'official' names of the Italian cinema (she was under contract to the state production company, Cines). While she was not closely identified with the regime in the way that some actresses of the period were,[1] she was unavoidably drawn into some of its social events and had allegedly attracted the attention of foreign minister Galeazzo Ciano and Mussolini himself. Inevitably, she was drawn closer to the Mussolini circle when she was cast alongside Claretta Petacci's sister Myriam in the latter's debut film *Le vie del cuore* (Loves' Ways, Camillo Mastrocinque, 1942).[2] Her screen persona was sufficiently dark for her to be cast without difficulty in a story of adultery and even murder. However, she was not the sort of actress one might readily associate with menial work and humdrum routine.

Calamai came into consideration, according to Visconti's collaborator Gianni Puccini, when 'we saw a casually "realistic" photograph of her wearing ordinary clothes and with her hair mussed up'.[3] 'Luchino's intuition led him to see the future Giovanna in that photograph', he added. It is probable that Puccini was referring to one of the images that accompanied an article by the critic and future director Luigi Comencini, published in *Tempo* magazine in September 1941.[4] Comencini had mused on the actress's unusually powerful screen image, while the accompanying photographs showed her in a series of real-life situations. Further evidence that left-inclined critics and film-makers were beginning to think about how the actress could be remodelled is provided by an article that Puccini himself wrote for *Cinema* in October 1941, in which he had noted something that separated Calamai's person from her established persona and voiced the hope that 'one day we would like to see her dishevelled'.[5] Thus, when a pregnant Magnani was obliged to withdraw with the shoot already underway, immediate moves were made to have Calamai replace her. The production company ICI had anyway preferred a name of proven box office appeal ('with la Calamai the French market was guaranteed',[6] Giuseppe De Santis later claimed), and Libero Solaroli, the director of production, swiftly made arrangements with Cines.[7] He personally went to Milan, where Calamai was appearing on stage, to collect her and take her to the set in Ferrara.

Though some reports have Calamai reluctant to take the part, her acquiescence in this hasty operation indicates that she was aware of the prestigious nature of *Ossessione*, even though Visconti was making his directorial debut. Yet she was not prepared for the radically different film-making experience that was in store for her. Visconti had thought Magnani well suited to the part of a passionate and tousled woman of the people. There was little doubt that Calamai could be transformed, since her range was known to be reasonably wide, and there was a chameleon quality to her, but turning her into a *popolana* was a challenge. The actress later acknowledged that 'Visconti feared that my transformation would not be easy because I had a face that was flawless, usually made-up and, in a word, "refined".[8] He began by messing up her hair, experimenting with different arrangements and proceeded by eliminating her customary heavy make-up. Though the actress would later say that she fell in love with an uninterested Visconti during filming, she was shocked by his disregard for the well-being of his actors, and when she first saw rushes of herself in the guise of Giovanna, she cried desperately.[9] As Girotti later observed, 'Visconti forced her to act without makeup, in a plain little black dress and flat shoes' (see Figure 6.1). Moreover, he terrorized his actors, forcing Girotti into 'endless takes' of a slap to Calamai's face.[10] Not only was she by this stage accustomed to being treated with a certain regard, and had a reputation for vocal objection when her treatment fell short of her expectations,[11] she feared that her widely acknowledged beauty had been destroyed, with ruinous consequences for her star image. Girotti later recalled that 'the first set photographs worried us; they showed two ordinary, scruffy creatures with faces of the type that you can see on any street corner. Clara and I spoke about it as we thought of quitting the film after the first scenes.'[12] However, they decided to persist and gradually came to understand what was required of them and to immerse themselves in their roles. Girotti, who – unlike Calamai – was drawn into the political discussions that accompanied filming, acknowledged that some of the difficulties derived from efforts to adapt the protagonists' style of acting to the film's subtext. 'The main theme of the film was freedom and you cannot imagine what that meant in that particular moment', he observed. 'This theme obviously could not be writ large, rather it emerged from the dialogue taken as a whole, and the dialogue was written with a particular intent while maintaining a balance between the said and the unsaid. The way things were said was important. From a technical point of view, it was very difficult.'[13]

As far as Calamai was concerned, *Ossessione* heralded a significant departure from her regal image. At the same time, it somehow turned her, one critic argued, into 'something recognisably ours'.[14] Yet it may be suggested that the much discussed transformation of the actress was not as complete as is implied by discussions of the film, which portray it as a watershed. Recent writing about the film has drawn attention to continuities between Calamai's performance and her screen persona as well as between these and an older tradition in Italian cinema (her emphatic acting in the part has even been seen to owe a debt to the diva tradition).[15] In her analysis of the film, Giuliana Minghelli refers to Giovanna as a 'black-clad femme fatale' who 'belongs' in the dark interiors of the inn, and to Calamai's 'gleaming with black brilliance'.[16] These two elements overlap and fuse in Minghelli's analysis, when she refers to 'glamorous and unhappy Giovanna'.[17]

Giovanna's 'fatal' status is established from her very first scene, when the sound of her voice singing a popular melody lures Gino to the door of her kitchen, where he catches sight of her shapely legs swinging as she works.[18] Though Calamai was unhappy with her transformation at Visconti's hands from queen to run-down skivvy, in fact, in Giovanna's flirtatious manner with Gino and her discontent with her lot and her marriage, there are traces of the typical Calamai character. Giovanna is the active player in the relationship with the wanderer Gino. She is nervous, neurotic, modern. If she is 'fatal' it is because she is dissatisfied. Her

Figure 6.1 A deglamorized Clara Calamai in the kitchen, in *Ossessione* (Luchino Visconti, 1942). The actress feared her image had been damaged by this process but later understood that it had widened her repertoire (screenshot by the author).

values may be petty bourgeois and materialistic, but she is self-possessed and is aware that her beauty is still a resource. She has kept her figure after her marriage and resisted becoming pregnant by a man from whom she would rather escape. There is an air of eroticism about her that chimes with the decadent, French-influenced feel that some leftist critics found in the film. For De Santis, there was a certain erotic concentration on Calamai's feet, which Visconti borrowed from Renoir – for example when Giovanna first tires after fleeing with Gino, complaining that her feet hurt, or when she walks barefoot in the inn.[19]

From the point of view of the anti-fascist makers of the film, Giovanna was not a properly positive figure. By this choice, it might be noted, they betrayed a disinclination to make a woman the bearer of their political project. But her position is rendered complex by the fact that the film's positive character, the Spaniard, had, Mario Alicata and orthodox leftists felt, been turned by Visconti from a mainly political symbol into something sexually ambiguous.[20] No sympathy is due Giovanna because her actions are dictated solely by personal and material concerns. Yet her husband Bragana, a belligerent man of conventional views who has been a soldier in the Bersaglieri regiment, is not made sympathetic either – because he is a Fascist, as he reveals during a fleeting moment of banter with Gino. Giovanna's desire to rid herself of an authoritarian husband is a desire that matched that of Visconti and his collaborators to rid Italy of Fascism. This was not the first time Calamai had played an unscrupulous woman of ambition, but the context of *Ossessione* lent a cultural and political significance to her roving eye and desire.

Though, for contractual reasons, Calamai returned to roles of a conventional type (such as the American socialite Peggy in Poggioli's *Le sorelle Materassi* [The Materassi Sisters], 1944),[21] playing Giovanna threw her a lifeline into the postwar, post-fascist era; it gave the actress a chance to rebuild her career in an uncertain but radically different context. Yet Calamai would not manage to assert herself as the first-choice actress of any of the directors most associated with the neorealist current. Thus, *Ossessione* was not quite the decisive watershed for her that it has often been claimed to be. While her glamour may have been stripped away, the femme fatale aspects of her persona proved to be less superficial than some assumed. Indeed, the melodrama of Visconti's film, if anything, appropriated them and affixed them to the actress more strongly than before, precisely because they were cast in a realist mould. The dramatic downscaling from queenly perfection to quotidian banality, and the shift from the constructed artificiality of Cinecittà to the imperfect reality of real-life locations, masked what was in fact a modest change from glamorous femme fatale to troubled dark lady. In this respect, Calamai's transformation can be compared with the one that would be effected by Ingrid Bergman in 1949, when she abandoned Hollywood to make *Stromboli* with Rossellini, ostensibly leaving behind an entire mode of film-making while in fact preserving the peculiar mix of the sensual and the spiritual that had always characterized her screen persona.[22]

In 1945, Rossellini began work on *Roma città aperta* (Rome Open City, 1945). Once again, Magnani was the preferred choice for the main female part, that of the spirited woman of the people Pina. But, because of a dispute over whether her pay would match that of Aldo Fabrizi, she initially refused the role, with the consequence that shooting began with Calamai in the part of Pina. Screenwriter Sergio Amidei revealed that some of Rossellini's collaborators favoured Calamai,[23] but the experience of making a film in conditions that were even less conventional than those of *Ossessione*, however, proved problematic for the actress. In keeping with her prima donna reputation, she was very demanding in terms of the level of organization she required, something that was difficult to offer in the very particular circumstances under which the film was made. Before long, Magnani came round, and Calamai was forced to step aside, her substitution being endorsed by the producer Giuseppe Amato, who had bought the foreign distribution rights.[24]

Given the strong Roman cast that Magnani gave to her character and the utter identification in popular memory of the actress with the part, it is impossible to imagine what Calamai's Pina might have been like. But this is not to diminish her, for, by the same token, it is difficult to imagine Magnani as Giovanna. The geographical setting would have been an issue and so too would Giovanna's beauty and refined tastes. Calamai's Giovanna is not truly a *popolana*; because she is aspirational and materialistic, she is endowed with a petty bourgeois demeanour. The materialistic characters that Magnani would play in her postwar comedies, unlike the intense and self-obsessed Giovanna, were brash and vulgar. Calamai was clearly better suited to the role, despite her limited experience in playing ordinary women.

Though she would not figure in the founding film of neorealism, Calamai would instead appear in *Due lettere anonime* (Two Anonymous Letters, 1945), the first postwar film made by Mario Camerini, the director of many escapist comedies in the 1930s, which would be released four months after Rossellini's film, in December 1945. The film is unusual because, unlike films belonging to the neorealist canon, it explicitly addresses the guilt of Italians and their complicity with Nazism. A vocal critic of *Roma città aperta*'s whitewashing of Italian responsibilities during the Nazi occupation, Camerini struck a stance with the film that could not but arouse hostility.[25] Calamai is again a lower class woman who commits murder, and again the victim is marked as a fascist type, in this case a fellow worker to whom she has given herself after assuming that her one-time fiancé had fallen on the Russian front. Unlike many other people at the printing business where both work, the man collaborates with the occupying Nazis to advance his career and enrich himself. When she realizes that her lover is a collaborationist who has caused her former fiancé (who, in the meantime, has returned from Russia and taken up with the Resistance) to be imprisoned, she kills him. The film includes newsreel footage of the liberation of Rome, which occurs within the film's diegesis after the woman has been arrested and imprisoned for her act. The action concludes on a close-up of her distraught face staring out from behind the bars of her cell –

an image that would by widely used on posters advertising the film. Even though her former fiancé, played by Andrea Checchi, assures her that she will soon be free – after all, given the political context, her action cannot be regarded as requiring punishment – her pained expression tells us that she will always be haunted by her past. By her inattention to her boyfriend's associations, and despite her own contributions to the Resistance, she will struggle to win full redemption.

The film had a very limited impact compared to *Roma città aperta*, and it has no critical reputation. The critic Pietro Bianchi argued that, although the film was indisputably well made, the characters were too reminiscent of the humble men and women of the director's comedies of the 1930s.[26] Their behaviour and concerns seemed trivial when set against the dramatic events of 1943–44. Among the actors, Calamai received particular praise, since 'she returns to the type of role she played in *Ossessione*, that is a girl of the people and not a femme fatale.' 'Closed in a difficult part, in a character who acts without clear motivation, she manages to fill it out persuasively', he observed.[27] The observation is interesting on two counts; first, because it shows that, in the eyes of a contemporary critic, the realistic setting eclipsed the melodramatic nature of aspects of the plot and, second, because it shows that the down-to-earth Calamai blinded even expert spectators to the residual persistence of the femme fatale in her everyday characters.

Following the relative failure of this film, Clara Calamai was at a crossroads in her career as a film actor. An article by the future director Dino Risi in *Tempo* magazine in January 1946 labelled her, with a nod to Pirandello's *Six Characters in Search of an Author*, 'a personality who has not yet found her author.'[28] This judgement confirms that, despite the fact that she had departed from her previous roles and established what would become the neorealist template of the dishevelled, unpolished ordinary woman, she had not asserted a new physiognomy. As Risi saw it, Calamai remained in some way a product of the autarkic cinema that had prospered following the withdrawal of the Americans from the Italian market in 1938. She had been typecast as Cinecittà's 'glamour queen', 'the Freudian beauty of cinema as dream'. 'She wore that apparent personality before the misty eyes of high school students and white-collar workers.' However, Risi continued, developing a train of argument that granted her a real core, 'she was never truly a femme fatale, not because there was any element of irony in her performances but simply because it did not suit her.' While performing, 'she seemed almost to be apologising with her eyes. In fact, it was her eyes that saved her: restless, feverish, suffering eyes; a woman's eyes.'[29]

The *Tempo* article was accompanied by photographs of the actress at home in Milan, posing in various guises, and out shopping, where she was the object of the stares of passers-by and fellow shoppers, who were struck as much by her fur coat as her distinctive profile. The impression given by both article and the images is that Calamai was somewhat isolated and defenceless, a star still in her own eyes as well as those of others but one who, however, was no longer privileged and was obliged to perform her own chores and not just give the impression that she did so for publicity reasons. Risi captured some essential points about an actress who appeared to have made the transition from Fascist commercial cinema to neorealism but who, in reality, never found a stable place in the cinema of the postwar years. At the time of this magazine feature, she was evidently not working, and the article served to remind filmmakers of her availability. The 'parabola' referred to in the title ('la parabola di Clara') did not seem to be one that was on the ascendant.

Any discussion of the postwar career of Clara Calamai is bound to explain why an actress who was widely assumed to stand on the brink of a new phase in her career failed to fulfil her promise. For Carlo Lizzani, Calamai was herself to blame for her downward turn. Though she had rejected overtures to join Luigi Freddi in his efforts to establish a Fascist film-making nucleus in Venice after the Nazi invasion, she did not throw herself into the new opportunities that came her way. 'For *Il sole sorge ancora* we asked Clara Calamai, who in that moment, from the point of view of her career, got everything a bit wrong', Lizzani asserted.[30] 'She rejected the role in *Il sole sorge ancora* and so the part was given to Elli Parvo, a good actress of the period who had filled the lead role in *Desiderio*.' Lizzani also blamed her to some degree for failing to seize her chance with *Roma città aperta*, though he conceded that she had poor guidance and was not always cast well.[31] Other factors also contributed, including the actress's failure to cultivate relations within the film world (the fact that she was living in Milan in 1946, though the reasons were straightforward and personal, itself speaks volumes), some unfortunate choices of roles and developments in her personal life. Changes in class relations and the public articulation of female beauty also did not work in her favour.

Calamai was associated with glamour, despite *Ossessione*, because of the supporting and leading roles she had played across a variety of genres including historical drama, the best known of which were Blasetti's *Ettore Fieramosca* (see figure 6.2) and *La cena delle beffe* (The Jester's Supper, 1942) and Gallone's *La regina di Navarra* (The Queen of Navarra, 1942). She had figured in melodrama (Poggioli's period piece *Addio giovinezza!* [Goodbye Youth, 1940] and Matarazzo's

Figure 6.2 Clara Calamai as the sensual courtesan Fulvia in her first major role, in the period film *Ettore Fieramosca* (Alessandro Blasetti, 1938) (author's own collection).

Hitchcockian *L'avventuriera del piano di sopra* [The Adventuress from the Floor Above, 1941], as well as Mattoli's *Luce nelle tenebre* [Light Amid the Darkness, 1941]) and adventure (the Salgari adaptation *I pirati della Malesia* [The Pirates of Malaysia, Enrico Guazzoni, 1941]). In mid 1942, she was fresh from the scandal of briefly appearing topless in one of Alessandro Blasetti's star-driven historical films, the screen adaptation of Sem Benelli's Renaissance-set play *La cena delle beffe*. Though the film itself was not a huge success, according to director Riccardo Freda this unprecedented exposure 'massively enhanced the popularity of the actress'.[32]

From almost the start of her screen career, she played courtesans and vamps (see Figure 6.2). Born in 1909 in Prato (though publicity often asserted 1915),[33] she was older than the large cohort of girl actresses and never played uncomplicated parts. She was often cast as the older – or certainly more sophisticated – woman who seduces or fascinates a younger man, sometimes subtracting him from the love of a simpler younger woman (examples include *Addio giovinezza!, Io, suo padre, Addio amore!* [Farewell Love! Gianni Franciolini, 1943] and, in its own way, *Ossessione*). For audiences of the time, she embodied an idea of sex appeal – that is to say, a distillation of qualities that included indexical factors beginning with physical beauty and including screen presence, plus plot and character factors such as suggestive situations and seductive gestures, and elaborate, personalized photography. She also offered something of a blank canvas. She had no trademark hairstyle or even colour and could switch from her natural dark hair to blonde and back again with ease. Observers sought to put their finger on the way these elements combined. Writing in 1941, Comencini noted that she had precisely the '"filling" power' that was necessary for cinema to 'tug the spectator from the idea of the white wall' or blank screen.[34] She had, he said, the photogenic qualities that in his view were quite simply 'the ability to bear enlargement'. Blasetti would define *fotogenia* in 1944 as 'having elements – it does not matter how many or which ones – to please, in the final analysis, the public and, preliminarily, he who has the task of predicting its preferences'.[35] This meant that she could enliven even modest films: 'her appearance on screen is like a breath of fresh air; the screen suddenly brightens up and, even when she is not acting, her persona creates a sort of polarisation that is centred precisely on her person.'

To try and uncover the secret of this unusual appeal, the magazine sent a photographer to capture her at home, at the swimming pool and in other situations.

The aim, Comencini wrote, was to pursue an inquiry that went in the opposite direction to her emergence and affirmation in cinema. In other words, to go to the root of her screen presence, deconstructing it, rather than exploring the finished product. Comencini was of the view that, like Marlene Dietrich, Calamai was relaxed and controlled in front of the lens. Her physical movements 'always maintain an elegant game of lines and attitudes (look at her hands that compose a harmonious design at all times) while her face, which is always alert, preserves that mild expression of self-satisfied irony which derives from the self-confidence she displays when faced with the scrutiny of the photographic lens'.[36]

For Comencini, Calamai was a consummate screen actor. 'Knowing how to communicate intimate feelings on the screen via the visible part of one's personality is not a gift that everyone possesses', he wrote.

> *If you think about it, a theatre actor is always working in the same dimension; he always acts with his whole body, while in the cinema it happens that you have to act with no more than a movement of the eyelashes. Clara Calamai's eyelashes are a very important part of her face; they open and close like butterfly wings and they perfectly animate the flash of the eyes which, in the cinema, even with the advent of sound, is always more persuasive than speech.*[37]

In short, she was a properly cinematic presence whose image was based on a close and harmonious interplay of the physical, the performative and the arts of the cinematographer and director. In any event, the result was compelling, as the reactions of her devoted admirers testify. In 1941 Ettore Palmieri wrote:

> *I have seen* Le sorprese del vagone letto *three times and now, here I am, besotted and glued; glued, that is, to the image of Clara. Clara who emerges radiant from the foam of the bubble bath; Clara subtle and wriggling; Clara with the eyes like traffic lights positioned at the crossroads of damnation; Clara with the explosive bosom – a pink explosion – and of the voice full of shadows – nocturnal shadows, propitious of sexual contraband – Clara, perfidious and tempting, the prelude to an abyss, the scaffold or hell.*[38]

Laura Mulvey's seminal reflections on the way in which the image of the female star is dissected and fragmented by the film production process for the visual pleasure of the spectator who is principally conceived as male were developed in relation to Hollywood cinema.[39] They have not been applied systematically to the Italian cinema of this period, not least because in Fascist Italy it was not just the male gaze that was dominant but the male everything. Yet there can be no doubt that Calamai was subjected to a similar process of disarticulation. Discussion of her physical characteristics focuses on different parts of her body, in keeping with the way in which they were highlighted or deployed in various films. The eyes drew most comment, but her legs and hands were the subject of debate in a way that was not the case with any other star of the period. To this list would be added her breasts, following their controversial fleeting exposure in Blasetti's *La cena delle beffe*. Though the scene was one of humiliation rather than titillation, it would remain one of the most memorable of the actress's career and one that would definitively consecrate her place as one of the most sexually charged stars in a cinema that was heavily constrained by official morality and politically inspired censorship.[40] With *Ossessione*, Visconti emphasized her feet.

Beauty would always be her key to character. While her costumes could be eye-catching and sumptuous, particularly in historical films, they were always trumped by her intriguingly individual face. Her dark hair gave her a domestic feel that was underlined by a down-to-earth name and surname once Blasetti persuaded her to abandon the exotic-sounding stage surname of Mais, which she had used for her first small roles. But her skin was alabaster, and it was her eyes and mouth that were central to her expressive power. The former were dark and large, framed by high eyebrows and set off by layered mascara, which maximized their animation. The latter was furnished with teasing lips and white teeth more perfect than many in Italian cinema; her smile was captivating, while its absence instantly established a mood of melancholy. Though her look was individual and more mature than that of many of Cinecittà's actresses, this did not diminish perception of her as a beauty. The journalist Adriano Baracco, writing in *Film* in 1942, observed that 'everyone who knows her judges her to be one of the most beautiful women in Italy',[41] while a comment in the magazine *Cinema* described her as passing for 'the Juno of our cinema' – that is, the highest female god in ancient Roman religion, the sister of Saturn and companion of Jupiter, goddess of all things feminine, including fertility and marriage.[42] Not by chance was she often compared to another, more famous Tuscan, the Mona Lisa. The actor Rossano Brazzi, who knew her as a teenager, commented that 'she had the slim figure of a mannequin',[43] while the costume designer Gino Sensani once said that she was the only Italian actress who walked like a Renaissance woman.

Calamai often brought a degree of composure to the scenes in which she appeared. Even her modern characters are not usually very mobile or athletic. If she is seen walking, it is commonly for a few seconds or a short distance. There is a degree of indolence and, were it not for her sleek figure and active intellect, one might even say sedentariness to her that is reflected in numerous scenes across many films in which she is seated or confined to an interior space. This Italianate composure, which in historical films never turns into stiff stateliness, allows the camera to dwell on her and bring out the expressiveness of her face. Given the importance of her eyes to her screen presence, it is not surprising that she is often engaged in the act of looking; she looks in order to take stock or to size up situations. Strikingly, given the anatomical dissection to which the camera subjected her, her looking sometimes serves to counter a male gaze or to construct a point of view. Often we spend more time looking at her looking than we do seeing what she is looking at. For this reason, her looking cannot properly be regarded as functional; rather it is a feature of the way in which her identity as a femme fatale was visually established. She looks because she claims the power to do so and because she does not suppress her desire. For example, in *Io, suo padre* (I, The Father, Mario Bonnard, 1939), it is she who notices the handsome young boxer Masetto and engineers a meeting with him and not vice versa. No other female star of the period exercised so consistently this prerogative of choice – which would also characterize her character in Visconti's film.

Despite her difficulty in claiming a place in postwar cinema, Calamai was still a name to be reckoned with. In 1946, she starred in three films of very different genres. One of these, Duilio Coletti's melodrama *L'adultera*, would bring her official recognition in the form of a Nastro d'argento (Silver Ribbon) award for best actress from the film journalists' union (SNGCI) under the founding presidency of Mario Soldati. Shot in the Scalera studios in Rome with the cinematography of Ubaldo Arata, *L'adultera* would echo aspects of the plot of Visconti's film, with Calamai's character, the ambitious peasant beauty Velca, abandoning her beloved in order to marry a wealthy landowner. After the latter discovers that the child he believes to be his is in fact that of the lover, with whom Velca has resumed relations after some years of unhappy marriage, he kills him. In consequence, Velca goes mad with remorse. An adaptation of Tullio Pinelli's 1941 play *I padri etruschi*, the film captured the intense contrast of ambitions and interests, while its rustic flavour situated it within the regional current that was beginning to flourish in postwar cinema. Despite the award given to the lead actress, the film was butchered by the censors and is rumoured to have been destroyed. No version of it has been seen since the 1940s.

Il tiranno di Padova (The Tyrant of Padua, 1946) would return her to the historical genre in which she made her name. Directed by Max Neufeld, a prolific director of Austrian origin of the 1930s and 1940s, whose Italian career was almost at an end, the film was an adaptation of Victor Hugo's 1835 play. Set in Padua in 1549, it features Calamai as Tisbe, the daughter of a couple of travelling players whose beauty causes conflict and controversy. A bewitching dancer, she captivates the tyrant Angelo, who covers her in jewels and introduces her to his court painter, for whom she will pose. With the Mona Lisa on display in his studio, the artist compares her smile to that of Leonardo's celebrated portrait. The audience is offered the chance to compare Calamai to the enigmatic sixteenth-century Florentine beauty whose image had been widely used that same year to sanction and publicize the victory in the first Miss Italia contest of a girl from Florence, Rossana Martini.[44] Tisbe receives the tributes of the male courtiers but the whispered condemnation of the women who see her as an ambitious courtesan. In a see-through tunic, she performs in a neoclassical dance at court, which underlines her grace and allure while offering audiences an ample glimpse of her breasts. However, she never succumbs to the overtures of the tyrant and induces the nobleman she truly loves to kill her when she realizes that he is pledged to Angelo's discontented wife.

The last film of any significance that she would make in this period was *Ultimo amore* (Last Love), directed by the former head of the Centro sperimentale Luigi Chiarini in 1946 and released in 1947. This was another film that looked back as much as it did forward. The film opens with a priest, Don Peppino, played by Carlo Ninchi, who is seeking the relatives and friends of three airmen who perished during the war on the same ill-fated flight. Calamai plays Maria, a showgirl who had a short but meaningful relationship with one of the pilots, Lieutenant Rastelli, played by Andrea Checchi. Believing that she has been forgotten by her lover, she is mortified to learn that he is dead. As so often, Gino Sensani's costumes serve to enhance Calamai's allure. She is first seen in the dressing room of a theatre, where she is wearing a scintillating backless top with exposed midriff and a billowing skirt adorned with sparkling stars and stripes. Her dark hair is pulled back off her face to reveal the melancholic expressiveness of her porcelain features. In flashback, her encounter with the pilots and her relationship with Rastelli are portrayed. She is alluring and fashionable; her carefree and sophisticated attitude fascinates the young men, not least when she laughs with natural abandon. 'Did you know you are truly a fascinating woman', a pilot says to her in a moment of intimacy, 'you could do well in the cinema ... you look exactly like Luise Rainer.' The film recreates the atmospheres of Rossellini's aviation drama *Un pilota ritorna* (A Pilot Returns, 1942) and situates them in the past, a past that continues to cast a shadow over the present. The shadow is not that of Fascism, because the airmen are killed as they seek to prevent their planes from falling into German hands. Rather it is the shadow of war and the legacy of suffering it has left.

When he visited the set of the film, the critic Gian Luigi Rondi was struck by Calamai's appearance, which was less overtly sexualized than he recalled from having seen her in *La cena delle beffe*. Seeking something to say, he could think of nothing better than 'You are as beautiful as ever!' to which she replied with annoyance: 'It's too soon to be astonished by that.'[45] In fact, though by now aged 38, an age that at the time was considered mature, the actress was still cast as the seductress, and different parts of her body were subjected to scrutiny as they had been earlier in the decade. This applied both to *Ultimo amore* and *Amanti senza amore* (Loveless Lovers, Gianni Franciolini, 1947). Adapted from Tolstoy's 'The Kreutzer Sonata', a short story about a marriage with echoes of *Anna Karenina*, the film sees Calamai play Elena, a former pianist who marries a medic with whom she finds she has little in common (see Figure 6.3). Given her love of the piano, the focus on her hands is more than justified, but the camera also explores her face and profile; it dwells on her hair, which is sculpted more than arranged, and she is glimpsed disrobing at her dressmaker's. Some shots of the bombed buildings of Genoa lend the film a contemporary feel, but the protagonists are without exception well-to-do, while Calamai's beauty is marked as unequivocally bourgeois. Though she plays a mother for the first time, her character is self-contained and utterly uninterested in her daughter. The typecasting resulting from her by now long string of seductress roles was not to be shaken off.

Calamai's postwar career has been termed 'a modest epilogue' to the one that culminated before the fall of Fascism.[46] As Giulio Cesare Castello wrote in 1957, 'postwar cinema offered her little', and the enchantment she cast in the early 1940s was not renewed. While her characters remained generally dark and seductive, and she preserved her reputation as an actress of passion and temperament, it proved impossible to give her persona a fully democratic inflection. On a personal level, she distanced herself in several respects from the world of cinema. Her marriage in 1945 to an aristocratic air force officer, Count Leonardo Bonzi,

Figure 6.3 Clara Calamai as a dissatisfied bourgeois wife and frustrated pianist in *Amanti senza amore* (Prelude to Madness, Gianni Francolini, 1948) (screenshot by the author).

marked a change in her status. An explorer and documentary producer who had belonged to Italo Balbo's Atlantic crossing expedition and had fought in Africa, Bonzi was also a lawyer and landowner with substantial properties in several cities and an estate in Tuscany. He steered his wife firmly away from any association with the left-wing currents that were influential in postwar cinema and society and advised her to turn down roles that could have hitched her more firmly to neorealism. Imagining he was guiding her towards more fruitful work, he in fact set the seal on her premature decline.

Notes

1. M.P. Fusco, "'È vero, Luchino mi prese a schiaffi a mi imbrutti", ma quanto lo amavo!', *La Repubblica*, 15 November 1981, 25. In the Fascist period, she lived modestly with her mother in the Prati quarter, preferring to save her earnings rather than spend them. To avoid the attentions of

Ciano and, by her account, Mussolini himself, she was obliged to avoid the social scene, including even the Venice film festival.
2. D. Cimagalli, ' "Il mio seno nudo scandalizzò gli italiani' ", *Gente*, 23 March 1989, 145.
3. Quoted in Faldini and Fofi, *L'avventurosa storia del cinema italiano: raccontata dai suoi protagonisti, 1935–1959*, 62–63.
4. L. Comencini, 'Clara Calamai', *Tempo*, 25 September 1941, 23.
5. Puck (Gianni Puccini), *Cinema*, 25 October 1941, quoted in E. Lavagnini, 'Noi e Clara', in Moscati, *Clara Calamai: l'ossessione di essere diva*, 71.
6. Gili and Grossi, *Alle origini del Neorealismo: Giuseppe De Santis a colloquio con Jean A. Gili*, 51.
7. Libero Solaroli, quoted in Faldini and Fofi, *L'avventurosa storia*, 63–64. Solaroli actually says that Calamai was under contract to ENIC, but given that this was the state distribution company, it is probable he meant Cines. Calamai, on the same page in this volume, specifies that her contract was with Cines.
8. Quoted in Faldini and Fofi, *L'avventurosa storia*, 64.
9. Quoted in Fusco, '"È vero . . .'", 25.
10. Rondi, *Un lungo viaggio: cinquant'anni di cinema italiano raccontati da un testimone*, 47.
11. For example, Carlo Ludovico Bragaglia said that, during the shooting of *La guardia del corpo* (The Bodyguard), she refused to be photographed from behind conversing with De Sica until it was explained to her that this was necessary to achieve the desired shot-reverse shot result. Quoted in Lavagnini, 'Noi e Clara', in Moscati, *Clara Calamai*, 71.
12. M. Girotti, 'Le dieci donne della mia vita', *Annabella*, 31 July 1960, 22.
13. Quoted in Faldini and Fofi, *L'avventurosa storia*, 64–65.
14. D. Risi, 'Parabola di Clara', *Tempo*, 31 January 1946, 12.
15. D. Duncan, 'Ossessione', in Forbes and Street, *European Cinema: An Introduction*, 101.
16. Minghelli, *Landscape and Memory in Post-Fascist Italian Film: Cinema Year Zero*, 21, 25.
17. Ibid., 26.
18. The mermaid's song is the instrument by which she lures sailors to their deaths, though the female voice in cinema has served different purposes. For example, in Ophuls' *La signora di tutti*, it stands for truth against the inauthenticity of the visual image. See Gundle, *Mussolini's Dream Factory: Film Stardom in Fascist Italy*, 124–26.
19. Gili and Grossi, *Alle origini del neorealismo*, 42.
20. See Guido Aristarco's 1943 articles on the film in Laura, *Storia del cinema italiano*, Vol. VI 1940–1944, 632–33.
21. Fusco, '"È vero . . .'", 25. 'I became that character', she claimed, 'I remember I cried desperately on Poggioli's shoulder when, after *Ossessione*, I had to play a stupid, shallow American girl in *Le sorelle Materassi*. I just could not accept it after Giovanna.'
22. See S. Gundle, 'Saint Ingrid at the Stake: Stardom and Scandal in the Bergman-Rossellini Collaboration', in Forgacs, Lutton and Nowell-Smith, *Roberto Rossellini: Magician of the Real*, 64–67.
23. Amidei cited in Moscati, *Clara Calamai: l'ossessione di essere diva*, 75.
24. Ibid., 75.
25. Germani, *Mario Camerini*, 135.
26. Bianchi, *L'occhio di vetro: il cinema degli anni 1945–1950*, 25–26.
27. Ibid., 26.
28. Risi, 'Parabola di Clara', 12.
29. Ibid., 12.
30. Lizzani in Faldini and Fofi, *L'avventurosa storia*, 119.

31. The actress was very particular about her roles in this period, writing in December 1946 to De Santis, with whom she was planning a film that remained on the drawing board, that she 'absolutely [did] not want to play an unsympathetic or evil character'. Centro sperimentale di cinematografia, Fondo Giuseppe De Santis. Letter from Calamai to De Santis, 31 December 1946. The film was entitled 'Ultimo amore' though it is not clear if this is the same project that would subsequently be directed by Luigi Chiarini.
32. Quoted in Lavagnini, 'Noi e Clara', in Moscati, *Clara Calamai*, 73.
33. Information on Calamai's early life is taken from F. Capello, ' "Tutti impazzivano per me ma non ho avuto l'unico uomo che amavo: Luchino Visconti' ", *Gente*, 8 August 1986, 80–86 and Cimagalli, '"Il mio seno nudo"', 143–47.
34. Comencini, 'Clara Calamai'.
35. Blasetti, 'L'attore nel cinema' (1944), in Blasetti, *Scritti sul cinema*, 168.
36. Comencini, 'Clara Calamai', 25.
37. Ibid., 25.
38. Castello, *Il divismo: mitologia del cinema*, 420.
39. Mulvey, 'Visual Pleasure and Narrative Cinema', 6–18.
40. See D. Forgacs, 'Sex in the Cinema: Regulation and Transgression in Italian Films, 1930–1943', in Reich and P. Garofalo (eds), *Reviewing Fascism: Italian Cinema, 1922–1943*, 159–61.
41. A. Baracco, 'Clara Calamai, scandalo per bene', *Film*, 18 April 1942, 7.
42. Anon., untitled comment, *Cinema*, 25 July 1942, cited in Moscati, *Clara Calamai*, 93.
43. Quoted in I. Moscati, 'Vita pubblica e privata di una contessa', in Moscati, *Clara Calamai*, 52–53.
44. See Gundle, *Bellissima: Feminine Beauty and the Idea of Italy*, 86–92.
45. Rondi, *Le mie vite allo specchio: diari 1947–1997*, 13.
46. Innocenti, *Le signore del fascismo*, 148.

CHAPTER 7

Aldo Fabrizi
Nostalgia and Popular Culture

The Roman actor Aldo Fabrizi was already a film star by the time Rossellini cast him as the dignified and heroic priest Don Pietro in *Roma città aperta* (Rome Open City, Roberto Rossellini, 1945). A popular variety theatre performer, who had extended his audience in the course of the 1930s through radio and gramophone discs, he had made three films in 1942–43: *Avanti c'è posto* (Welcome Aboard, Mario Bonnard, 1942), *Campo de' fiori* (Mario Bonnard, 1943) and *L'ultima carrozzella* (The Last Carriage, Mario Mattoli, 1943). It was a measure of the popularity he already commanded that he was the undisputed protagonist of each of these. Not only was he the lead actor, he also contributed to the screenplays and worked with the directors to ensure that the stories and the settings emanated an authentic air of everyday Rome. The producer Giuseppe Amato first had the idea of giving this popular actor the chance to debut in cinema in comedy dramas that were set among the Roman lower class, which was the actor's preferred milieu, indeed his natural habitat. *Avanti c'è posto* cast Fabrizi as a well-meaning ticket seller on the trams who befriends a pretty servant girl whose purse is stolen amid the shoving and pushing of the passengers. In *Campo de' fiori*, he is a fishmonger and stallholder in the famous Roman open-air market who seeks to win the favours of an aristocratic lady to whom he supplies fish. Finally, in *L'ultima carrozzella*, he is the driver of a traditional horse and carriage and fervent opponent of motorized taxis who is landed in trouble after he gives a ride to a popular entertainer who leaves her suitcase behind in her rush to catch a train. The films were set among the poor and not so poor folk of the lower-class quarters of Rome. With their slim stories based on plausible everyday events and wide variety of encounters and conflicts, interwoven with unfulfilled aspirations and personal frustrations, the films consecrated Fabrizi as the central figure in a new current in Italian cinema, that of the dialect comedy. This contrasted with the polished studio-bound fare of the late

Fascist period and for the first time took the cameras systematically out into the streets and used real locations.

When Rossellini was thinking of offering Fabrizi the part of the priest Don Pietro in the film he was planning based on episodes of the Nazi occupation of Rome, he turned to Federico Fellini. The young writer and humourist had contributed to the scripts of Fabrizi's films and knew the actor well. From the moments of pathos in *Avanti c'è posto* and the other films, Rossellini and his writer Sergio Amidei perceived that he was more than a comic performer. He was capable of conveying a range of emotions and of injecting a moral dignity into his characters. Though many histories of Italian cinema trace the connection between the three dialect comedies and neorealism, the difficulty of drawing a known performer with a very distinct profile and view of the creative process into the effort to make cinema into a tool of reflection on the turbulent events that had beset the nation should not be underestimated. Fabrizi's films were immensely popular, but they divided seasoned observers. They were recognized by some critics for their genuine air and praised for the spirit they shared with the tales of the great nineteenth-century poet of the Roman lower class Gioacchino Belli, or even the master of the satirical monologue and creator of social types Ettore Petrolini, who had died in 1936. But others deplored their 'falsity', 'incongruences' and 'superficiality'.[1] Fabrizi was deemed to be more of a personality than an actor and one who 'lacks the ability to get to the bottom of things; ... he is good observer, but a superficial one'.[2] Moreover, as a performer who was also a writer, Fabrizi was used to exercising a high measure of control over his material and to selecting carefully the projects on which he worked. He told Fellini that he knew that he could make people laugh but was unsure he could make them cry.[3] Though he was greatly moved by the stories that Rossellini planned to weave together in the film that would become *Roma città aperta*, he was cautious about risking his name and reputation in a project that while undoubtedly worthy also seemed flimsy and experimental.[4] Like other characters in the script, Don Pietro was modelled on a real-life character, in this case Don Morosini, a priest who had been executed by the Nazis for aiding the Resistance.[5] The inclusion of scenes of torture and death ensured the film would be remote from Fabrizi's usual idiom.

The story that he demanded the sum of one million Lire for his contribution to the film has been told many times.[6] It paints a picture of an artist who was motivated by financial gain, who was utterly uninterested in the innovative promise of the film and who perhaps doubted its solidity as a project. Yet it also shows a man who was aware of the value of his star name and the importance this would have in the marketing of the film. Perhaps it indicates that he wanted to test the seriousness of Rossellini. Fabrizi took pride in having founded a new genre of Roman popular cinema and did not want to spoil or sell this primogeniture cheaply. The fact that Anna Magnani, his co-star and sparring partner in *Campo de' fiori* and *L'ultima carrozzella*, was to take the key female role of Pina must have made him think that Rossellini was exploiting the popularity of a double act of proven commercial value and that for that he should pay.

In the end, Fabrizi settled for far less than the one million Lire he had initially demanded. But the film brought him numerous benefits, since, after a difficult opening in Italy, it would end up as the top box office earner of the 1945–46 season.[7] It showed him in a new light as a dramatic actor, and it brought him for the first time to the attention of an international audience. Thanks to the film, he greatly enhanced his reputation as an actor who was able to endow ordinary characters with a rich humanity and even nobility. However, he did not gain the universal plaudits that were bestowed on Anna Magnani. Magnani, who had objected to his bossy domination of the set on *Campo de' fiori* and *L'ultima carrozzella*, became a key contributor to the director's new way of making cinema, which relied on a measure of spontaneity and intense improvisation. Thus, she was integral to the film and was seen as deserving of a share of the creative merit for it in a way that Fabrizi was not. In later years, he would complain resentfully that 'everyone won prizes except me'.[8]

Avanti c'è posto and the other early films had presented a 'cleaned-up' Fabrizi with respect to the rude stage performer who was known for his colourful expressions and ribald humour. In its portrayal of a sensitive and caring tram operative who tries and fails to win the heart of the girl he has protected from her cruel employers, the film had allowed Fabrizi to explore the quiet suffering of a man who is not quite as ordinary as he looks. As Don Pietro, the respected local priest who does not hesitate to lend his help to the anti-fascist Resistance, Fabrizi was praised for the sobriety of his performance. He too was playing in drama for the first time, yet unlike Magnani, who underwent a transformation to turn herself into Pina, he effected limited, if significant, adjustments to his screen persona to become the priest. To be sure, Don Pietro's emotional journey as he experiences the life of the quarter, comes into contact with the Resistance, is arrested and compelled to witness torture before being executed is dramatic in the extreme, but it is punctuated by moments of comedy. Indeed, almost all the moments of light relief that are embedded in the texture of *Roma città aperta* involve the pop-

Figure 7.1 The Roman comedian Aldo Fabrizi as Don Pietro during a gag in a shop selling religious articles, in *Roma città aperta* (Rome Open City, Roberto Rossellini, 1945) (screenshot by the author).

ular actor. Within moments of his first being introduced, as he referees the boys of his parish during a noisy kickabout in the churchyard, the ball bounces high and lands on his head amid much hilarity. The humour continues with a gag, to which only the spectator is privy, about a naked female statuette in a shop selling religious artefacts (see Figure 7.1). It culminates shortly before Pina's death, with the famous scene in which her altar boy son compliments Don Pietro for the *padellata* (whack with a frying pan) that he has administered to a garrulous, bed-ridden old man who refuses to keep quiet as they hide weapons during a Fascist search. However, steps were also taken to mark the priest's spirituality. Although Fabrizi was already by this time known for his culinary indulgences (*L'ultima carrozzella* includes a scene in which the imprisoned coachman passes the time dreaming up a menu composed of his favourite dishes), Don Pietro is the only Italian adult male character in Rossellini's film who is never seen eating or caught thinking about food.

In later years, Fabrizi would engage in a polemic at a distance with the director over the paternity of neorealism and even over who was responsible for *Roma città aperta*'s evolution from a series of documentary episodes into a long feature. The actor dismissed efforts to grant Rossellini the status of creative genius who had revealed hidden possibilities in comedy actors. Not only did he argue that it was he who had discovered Rossellini, not the other way round; he claimed that the transformation of a series of episodes into a fully-fledged feature with a coherent narrative had been his idea, which Fellini and Amidei subsequently embraced.[9] When he was asked, in the 1970s, if *Roma città aperta* was his favourite among the many films he had made, he replied with irritation and cited instead a minor work: 'No. The film I like most and of which I was director, writer and creator is *Marsina stretta* [The Tight Jacket], an episode of the 1954 film *Questa è la vita*, adapted from the novellas of Pirandello. It is one of the three episodes of *Questa è là vita* [Of Life and Love], a comedy drama from 1954.'[10] For his part, Rossellini claimed that he had had to work hard to reign in Fabrizi's histrionic tendencies; for example, dissuading him from 'crying like a calf' during the execution scene.[11]

Despite these controversies, observers have concorded that Fabrizi's playing of Don Pietro was one of the high points of his career. The understated dignity of the priest, his firm moral convictions and the gentle courage he displayed in adversity turned him into what Brunetta calls 'a symbol of the new Italy'. What Fabrizi offered was 'a personification into which the humble variety actor, albeit of the type that Bertolt Brecht appreciated, poured all his untameable lower-class temperament'.[12] In priest's garb, Gian Luigi Rondi argued, the dialect actor appeared transformed; he was 'vital and credible'.[13] Fabrizi himself never accepted this and rejected both the originality and the quality of neorealism.

> As for neorealism, let's just forget about it. It had as many fathers as a bastard child. In any case, you filmed in the street because there was no money to pay the rent on studios. Then it turned out that it was neorealism, with those poor penniless actors who have remained penniless. I have made better films than that, from the acting point of view: Giovanni Episcopo, Marsina stretta, and Vivere in pace, for example.[14]

Fabrizi would only perform on one other occasion in a Rossellini movie, when he was cast as the tyrant Nicolaio in the director's treatment of Francis of Assisi and his devoted followers, *Francesco giullare di Dio* (Francis, God's Jester, 1950).

The director did not flatter him with this casting but rather sought to exploit his tendency to become mannered and his unenviable reputation for going over the top. Fabrizi was the only professional actor in the film's cast, and his histrionic performance was widely criticized. But, as Peter Brunette observes, 'his acting – over-acting, really – is precisely what is necessary to augment the structural opposition between the brothers' simplicity and Nicolaio's worldliness.'[15] 'His performance is purposely foregrounded, made self-reflexive ... and thus serves, itself, as part of the film's meaning.'

Despite the resentment it gave rise to, *Roma città aperta* unquestionably opened a new phase in Fabrizi's career and brought him many opportunities. Between 1946 and 1950, he was a top box office draw; he made eleven films, and he would be the lead actor in all of them.[16] There were light or comic aspects to several of them, while a significant number harnessed his new-found credibility as a dramatic actor. The first of these was *Mio figlio professore* (My Son, the Teacher, Renato Castellani, 1946), the story of a school porter and widower who devotes himself to raising and educating his only son so that he will one day become a teacher. The film begins with the boy's birth in 1919 and proceeds over the next twenty and more years until the son becomes a teacher in his father's very school, a development that leads first to friction and embarrassment and then to the now elderly father's self-sacrificial abandonment of his post. The father and son theme had already been explored on several occasions in Italian cinema; for example, in *Luciano Serra pilota* (Luciano Serra, Pilot, Goffredo Alessandrini, 1938), *Io suo padre* (Me, His Father, Mario Bonnard, 1939), *Giarabub* (Augusto Genina, 1942) and so on and two years later would famously form the core of *Ladri di biciclette* (Bicycle Thieves, Vittorio De Sica, 1948). However, this was the first film to tackle the topic in relation to issues of class and social aspiration. Like Balzac's Père Goriot, Fabrizi's character becomes less relevant and respected as his offspring ascends the social ladder.

The narrative included the familiar Fabrizi trope of disappointment in love, but otherwise the film was anything but formulaic. Written by a team that included the author of many effervescent comedies, Aldo De Benedetti, the no less experienced Emilio Cecchi, the young Suso Cecchi d'Amico and the director Castellani, as well as Fabrizi himself, it was a curious mixture of the sort of aesthetically refined literary adaptation that had prospered in the early 1940s – in which Castellani had specialized – and the focus on ordinary, everyday people that began around the same time and to which Fabrizi himself had so decisively contributed. The cast was no less heterogeneous. Around Fabrizi in the central role of the school porter were some familiar character actors (including Nando Bruno, Don Pietro's sexton from *Roma città aperta*) and the near identical Nava sisters (Diana, Lisetta and Pinuccia), who at the time were a popular turn in stage revues. In addition, a range of prominent intellectuals, including Mario Soldati, Paolo Monelli, Francesco Jovine, Gabriele Baldini, Ennio Flaiano and Ercole Patti, made their screen debuts in small roles, mostly as teachers or state officials. Pietro Bianchi found Fabrizi's performance to be 'superlative and moving', while Giulio Cesare Castello lauded his 'human warmth and communicative manner' (though at the same time warning that he was 'dangerously inclined to overdo it'). For the first time, comparisons were made with prominent international character actors like Emil Jannings and Charles Coburn.[17] Over the years, he would also be likened to Wallace Beery and termed 'a Charles Laughton made in Trastevere'.[18]

Most of the films that followed were productions of at least average quality that developed either the literary strain or the current of contemporary drama laced with comedy. The four films that were released in the course of 1947, which would prove to be the actor's golden year, testify to the eclectic nature of his activity. He played a sharp-witted peasant in Luigi Zampa's war drama *Vivere in pace* (To Live in Peace), a tormented clerk led astray by an adventurer and driven to murder the faithless woman he marries in an adaptation of Gabriele D'Annunzio's *Il delitto di Giovanni Episcopo* (The Crime of Giovanni Episcopo, Alberto Lattuada), a prisoner of war waiting to be sent home in *Natale a campo 119* (Christmas in Camp 119), Piero Francisi's multiregional comedy set in a prison camp in California and a widowed father desperate to save his daughter from a life of perdition in *Tombolo, paradiso nero* (Tombolo, Dark Paradise, Giorgio Ferroni) (see Figure 7.2).

Of these, the most memorable was *Vivere in pace*, which performed strongly at the box office and won three Nastri d'argento (Silver Ribbon) prizes while also achieving recognition abroad, winning the best foreign film award from the New York Film Critics' Circle. The film reprises something of the feel of Rossellini's war trilogy (indeed Gar Moore and John Kitzmiller, who had respectively appeared in the Naples and Rome episodes of *Paisà*, also feature in the cast as American GIs, while Heinrich Bode, who was the Austrian deserter in *Roma città aperta*, plays an English soldier), though the story has a touch of the fable about it, and the dominant mood is one of tragicomedy. Set in a mountain village during the final stages of the Nazi occupation, the film treats Fascism and war as absurd intrusions into the everyday life of a peace-loving community that is populated with good-

Figure 7.2 Aldo Fabrizi (centre) in a dramatic role as a father seeking his daughter amid the postwar underworld of black marketeers, prostitutes and deserters, in *Tombolo, paradiso nero* (Tombolo, Dark Paradise, Giorgio Ferroni, 1947) (screenshot by the author).

humoured stock figures, most of whom are played by familiar character actors. As in *Roma città aperta*, Fabrizi, who takes the part of a well-meaning patriarch known as Uncle Tigna, performed a double act with Nando Bruno, who had played his gruff sexton in the earlier film and who here was the local Fascist official. For the first time he was also paired with the feisty and maternal Ave Ninchi, who plays his wife. It is the relationships between Tigna's family, the village community, the German officer stationed there and Allied soldiers in hiding that form the core of the drama. The community protects the Allied soldiers, and Fabrizi also seeks to assist the German official when he aims to make his escape in civilian clothes ahead of the arrival of the Americans. Both pay with their lives.

Like *Roma città aperta*, this and other films took Fabrizi outside of the realm of the dialect comedy and forced him into contexts in which he was obliged to engage with the terrible challenges and choices that war and foreign occupation had brought. The ability he showed to inhabit parts with feeling and sensitivity situated him at the heart of efforts to renew Italian cinema. According to Gian Piero Brunetta, 'the meeting with Rossellini and neorealism showed that, together with Anna Magnani, he was the professional actor best equipped to adapt to the different types of poetic in course. He had responded perfectly to the demands of directors like Rossellini, Zampa, Lattuada, Blasetti and Castellani and had given rise to portraits that were much richer and more complex than in the past.'[19] 'He contributed to the task of constructing the new Italian while succeeding in underlining the difficulty of completely casting off the social conditions and legacies of the past', Brunetta continued.

In contrast to Magnani, Fabrizi never became a political symbol and nor did he identify in any way with any party or current. Though he received government approval for his film *Emigrantes*, the premiere of which was attended by ministers and officials, he did not even urge the Italians to go to the polls at election time in newsreels, as others did. However, certain expectations stuck to Fabrizi's screen persona after *Roma città aperta*. For example, it would have been inconceivable for him to be cast as a Fascist, even of the village variety played by Nando Bruno.[20] There was a certain pathos about his persona; defeat or death marked the conclusions of the dramas into which he was drawn. In the case of *Vivere in pace*, it was decided at the last minute, after the film had been completed and edited, that his character had to meet his end. 'In vain the popular Aldo begged and the script authors protested. "He's got to die" was the sentence. And in a great hurry Fabrizi was killed off and a conclusion was invented with cypresses and tombstones.'[21] The success of the film with critics and the public suggested to some that while the purer forms of neorealism struggled to make headway at the box office there might be scope for hybrid versions that maintained links to conventional forms of popular entertainment. The screenwriter Suso Cecchi d'Amico, who was one of four (including Fabrizi) to be credited for the script, saw the potential. 'Call it rose-tinted neorealism if you like ... it could give rise to a current', she commented.[22]

Fabrizi had great potential as a key figure in this possible current because of the way he synthesized tragedy and comedy. There was really no need for his screen persona to take on political meanings, because his physical being was his most essential signifier. The evident gulf between his round, fleshy face and stout body, on the one hand, and the Fascist ideal of the lean and fit warrior male, on the other, meant that he was a symbol of an Italy that was resistant to Fascism's efforts to carry out what Emilio Gentile has dubbed an 'anthropological revolution' and turn the Italians into a warrior people.[23] He was physiologically anti-fascist because he belonged to an older Italy that had perhaps been caught up in the momentary enthusiasms that the regime had unleashed but that was not in any sense transformed by them. If his characters had ever been supporters of Fascism, it was out of indolence rather than conviction.

Born in the Campo de' fiori district in 1905, Fabrizi was a product of a Roman popular culture that had a language, a poetry and distinctive culinary traditions, all of which the actor embraced. Despite its close proximity to, and partial subjugation by, both ecclesiastical and temporal power, this culture possessed dignity and traditions. Fabrizi's father had been a poor carriage driver who had not had enough money to pay for treatment when he contracted bronchitis after his cart got overturned into a stream one winter.[24] After his father's death, when the young Aldo was aged only eight, he went to work with his mother on a fruit and vegetable stall, beginning a long series of jobs that would see him employed as a stable boy, street corner newspaper seller, post office porter, assistant typographer, coachman, ticket seller on the trams, watch-repairer, cook and painter, among others.[25] The variety gives a sense of the economic instability of the lower class in a city with little real industry but also of the adaptability of a boy who was obliged from the youngest age to contribute to the budget of a family that included three younger sisters. His familiarity with the subaltern worlds of districts like Campo de' Fiori and Trastevere provided him with rich inspiration as his career as a writer and performer got underway. 'In the evening', he recounted, 'I used to write little poems. During the day, I worked and kept my eyes open'.[26] His earliest sketches in verse were returned to him because the stage speaker who was supposed to perform them rejected them on the grounds that they were not funny. As a result, he performed them personally at the Cinema Corsi in Rome in 1930 during the Festival of San Giovanni. Those sketches became famous, and from there he rose through *avanspettacolo*, theatre, cinema and revues, taking on the roles of actor, writer, composer and director.[27]

Fabrizi boasted that his family had been Roman for seven generations, and his ability to convey the humours and attitudes of the lower class was unrivalled. His version of a popular Roman culture founded on common sense, everyday slyness and a view of life infused with tolerance and irony was forged through life experiences and his work in popular theatre. He refined and polished his act to the point that, with minimal effort, he was able to eliminate from his gestures and his characters' lines any evidence of actual performance.[28] At the theatre, he developed a gallery of characters – the tram driver, the conductor, the footballer, the photographer, the porter, the skier and the waiter – that he re-proposed on the radio in a regular lunchtime slot on *Radio Sociale* between 1932 and 1940.[29] They were also incorporated into larger-scale stage shows and revues, to which he would return in 1944 in the shows of the Circo equestre Za Bum, organized by the Neapolitan theatre and film director Mario Mattoli.

Fabrizi's early films stood as testimony to the ability of the film industry to absorb the stars and modes of entertainment of *avanspettacolo* and the stage revues. Beginning with *Avanti c'è posto*, he would bring to the screen a long series of characters who corresponded to real-life types or categories – characters who could be resigned and cynical but also good-hearted and whimsical. With various shades of emphasis and modest changes of appearance, he became a tram operative, a coachman, a fishmonger, a priest, a porter, a policeman, a builder and many others.[30] Comedy and satire mingled in performances that could be marked by drama or by poetry. Such was the ease with which he could slip into character that 'he had no need to perform or to get into character; he could just be himself and talk about his everyday life', Brunetta has affirmed.

The way an actor like Fabrizi worked differed from that of colleagues who hailed from serious theatre or who had only ever worked in cinema. While it might perhaps not have been exactly true that he had no need to learn lines or find ways to inhabit characters, there was a process of bringing characters to life that involved drawing on a large baggage of personal experience, much of it marked by misfortune. 'Comedy', he once explained,

> is always born from drama. Comedians are always people who have suffered and who suffer a lot, who have been poor like me. Ultimately, you get the audience to laugh by recounting in some way your own troubles. For my part, I can tell you this: I have hardly ever invented anything. Everything I have taken on to the stage has really happened to me.[31]

On another occasion, he explained that a comic actor always had a dramatic side

> because he is part of life and life is made up of highs and lows. It is like a coin; on one side there is comedy, on the other drama. When someone slips over, it is dramatic for him, for the others it is a source of laughter. It seems almost a

law that we are compelled to laugh at the misfortunes of others. The important thing is to get over them.[32]

Then there was a sense, deriving from the *commedia dell'arte*, that a character, like Harlequin or Pantaleone, once defined needed only a template or situation and not a fully-scripted part in order to be able to enter into action. Fabrizi was not exactly a mask in this sense, since he inhabited a range of nuanced characters, but there were sufficient traits in common for them to blend into one another in the popular imagination.

Like many popular actors, he knew his persona so well that he became indistinguishable from it. As his son Massimo noted in a volume of memoirs, Fabrizi 'did not perform exactly; rather he *was*'. He offered

a carefully balanced mixture of intelligence, acumen and humanity, that was not filtered by any theoretical or philosophical pre-supposition. It was not the hard-won result of an apprenticeship, of study in any academy or anything of that type ... The originality of his way of being an actor allowed no room for exact reproduction because any repetition would have produced a different gesture, a different word and a different way of articulating it. That is why Dad disliked scripts and learning lines by heart, even though he had a memory that bordered on the prodigious.[33]

Fabrizi's special art required, and indeed was inseparable from, his distinctive physical presence. Though he claimed that 'at eighteen ... I drew the glances of all the girls because I looked like Rudolph Valentino. I was a slim, muscular heart-throb',[34] by the time he made his screen debut his girth had expanded and he was no longer lean and strong. The words that emerge from his mouth seem as heavy and rounded as his body, while phrases are often begun but not completed, either because their meaning is already clear or because he cannot be bothered to finish them. He emits a long-suffering air born of long acquaintance with the hard realities of life. His characters rarely seem reconciled to their fundamental ugliness. They develop romantic crushes on young women and even attempt to court them, but they are never seen as prospective partners and are destined to intense disappointment. Nor, in truth, are they inclined to accept that their lower-class status acts as a bar to certain relations with higher classes. While the tram worker of *Avanti c'è posto* falls appropriately for a servant girl – though she is too beautiful for him – the fishmonger of *Campo de' fiori* ignores his vulgar colleague Elide (Magnani) and instead seeks to win the favours of a high-class woman who is his customer. One observer noted of the actor that he was 'so anthropologically plebeian as to turn a presumed social inferiority into a mark of aristocracy: vulgar by existential choice, highly refined by artistic vocation'.[35]

Fabrizi was the physical embodiment of a certain type of Roman. He bore the hallmarks of the city's popular culture in his comfortable, jovial demeanour and in his colourful language. His deep Roman roots were evinced by his way of moving and behaving; they informed his indolence and inclination to cynicism. He is oppressed by heat, by financial worries and by petulant officials and family members. Every one of his gestures and attitudes belongs to a cultural humus that is associated with the capital; for example, when raises his hands and makes circular movements with them, or when he goes as if to administer a smack that is then withheld. His chubby hands, in fact, are the most animated parts of his body. His conversations may be lively and passionate, but he may also emit an eloquent sigh or reach an agreement with some accomplice on the basis of little more than a wink and unspoken understanding. For the writer and director Mario Soldati, who acted with him in the film *Mio figlio professore* and observed the way he generated a performance,

> *all the comic and pathetic effects were born from the "belly", from the irresistible contrast between the fat, heavy body and a mysterious agility of movement. I watched Fabrizi puff and blow, huff and puff, sweat, put his hand inside his collar, roll his eyes, open them wide, and suddenly hint almost at a dance step, a light and elegant pirouette.*[36]

He had identified a key trait of the people he somehow incarnated, that desire for recognition and distinction that was expressed in verbal repartee and wit. 'With his array of little moves, Fabrizi ridiculed this passion, that craving of some members of the lower class to move as if "on tip toe".'[37]

The subaltern popular world with its own distinctive characteristics was under threat already when Fabrizi first began to characterize the trades and categories of popular Rome. It would disappear altogether in the rush to prosperity of the post-war decades. Fabrizi's Rome was increasingly one that existed in memory more than in fact.[38] The self-contained and distinctive central quarters that he evoked in films like *Campo de' fiori* were what gave Rome its 'provincial' atmosphere. As

Catherine Brice notes, 'over a long period, Roman leisure pursuits were moments for families, to be enjoyed between friends in a climate of conviviality without the intrusion of elitist pleasures or organised distractions.'[39] But, first, the urban interventions of the Fascist years, which saw old districts demolished to make way for grandiose architectural projects, then the disruptions of war and occupation, followed by a modernization that brought a renewed bout of building and property speculation and a standardization of the retail sector, struck at this social texture.

Nostalgia first featured in Fabrizi's screen work in *L'ultima carrozzella*. His character is a coach driver who is engaged in a battle with motorized taxis that he is destined to lose. The actor very deliberately evoked a world that he knew well, having himself acquired a coach driver's license in 1925. Indeed, the leather cape he wears on screen is the very same one he wore when he exercised this trade. Nostalgic yearning of a different type would mark his first film as director. *Emigrantes* (Emigrants, 1949) was an ambitious project that followed the fortunes of a Roman family compelled by economic circumstances to emigrate to Argentina ('*maledetta la guerra che ci ha ridotti cosi*'). The film, which was produced with Argentine money, sees Fabrizi play Giuseppe Bordoni, a husband who becomes a father for the second time on board the ship that is taking his family to a new life in the Americas. He finds work as a foreman on a building site, and his daughter forms an attachment to her father's handsome employer, but his wife, played by Ave Ninchi, is tormented by nostalgia. The theme is signalled from the moment the couple stop to look over Rome as they prepare to take their leave of it: '*Ammazza, quanta e' bella!*' Fabrizi exclaims. In contrast to the 1935 film *Passaporto rosso* (Red Passport, Guido Brignone), which cast the story of the Italian emigration to South America in a Fascist hyper-patriotic mould, *Emigrantes* offers a low-key variety of patriotism that was pitched, to use the historian Ruggiero Romano's distinction, in terms of the *paese* rather than the *nazione*.[40] It is not the state that animates the sentiments of the migrants but their shared language, culinary customs and sense of mutual solidarity. Accordingly, in the end, Fabrizi is honoured for his work in building houses for his fellow Italians, Ninchi overcomes her chronic desire to return and the family is reconciled to remaining in their new home country.

Emigrantes was a project dear to Fabrizi's heart. It won him recognition and political approval. Pictures show him at the film's premiere at Rome's Cinema Corso shaking hands with the Christian Democrat Mario Scelba and mingling with representatives of the Argentine embassy. However, the film did not received good reviews, and it performed weakly at the box office. The story was held to be insufficiently developed and to make excessive recourse to tear-jerking devices. Writing in *Cinema nuovo*, Guido Aristarco saw the film as a vanity project which Fabrizi had written and directed and in which he had taken the lead role. Likening it to Rossellini's *L'amore*, he concluded, with evident dissatisfaction, that 'maybe immodesty is a characteristic of true artists'.[41]

Nostalgia would permeate much of his work from the late 1940s and would come to mark his public persona. His attachment to the world of the *avanspettacolo*, which was declining rapidly with the postwar expansion of cinema, was reflected in the film *Vita da cani* (A Dog's Life, Steno and Mario Monicelli, 1950), which saw him take on the role of Nino Martoni, artistic director and chief performer of a struggling touring theatre troupe. The film includes some of the actor's stage routines and sees him battle vainly against cinema's lure for his leading ladies and audiences alike. It was a richly comic work that shared some features with Fellini and Lattuada's *Luci della ribalta* (Variety Lights, 1952) in that it was characterized by the same elegiac atmosphere for a world that – as the title suggests – is not itself portrayed with any glamour.

Fabrizi was extremely active in this period, and his apparently natural performance style won praise. His work was varied and extended even to the co-productions that Italian cinema embarked on after the accords with France had been established. He starred as the pretentious owner of a patisserie in the Zavattini-inspired micro-comedy *Prima comunione* (Father's Dilemma, Alessandro Blasetti, 1950), which Salvo D'Angelo produced for Universalia and the Paris-based Franco-London Films. Despite the setback of *Emigrantes*, Fabrizi would persist in directing his own films, alternating personal projects with work in comedies and occasionally dramas directed by others. He proved surprisingly adaptable. In 1950, he won the Best Actor prize at the Venice film festival for *Prima comunione* and would appear over the next few years in films directed by Luciano Emmer and Luigi Zampa, as well as Steno and Monicelli. However, it would be in popular cinema that he would most leave his mark. The series dedicated to the 'Passaguai' family that he directed himself would come to be regarded if not as his best work then as his most typical. Inspired by the characters of A.G. Rossi, the films featured Fabrizi as Peppe Valenzi, a bumbling white-collar worker nicknamed Passaguai (literally 'in trouble', on account of the constant stream of misunderstandings, misfortunes and varied situations that befall him). The series consisted of three films, *La famiglia Passaguai* (The Passaguai Family, 1951), *La famiglia Passaguai fa fortuna* (The Passaguai Family Gets Rich, 1952) and *Papà diventa mamma* (Dad turns into Mum, 1952) (a fourth, entitled *Bruttissimo*, a parody of Visconti's *Bellissima*, was never made). Highly successful, the series marked the abandonment of the social themes that had been a feature of much of his work after *Roma città aperta* and a return to the type of gross gags, vulgar allusions and physical comedy with which he made his name in variety theatre. A large cast of well-known character actors surrounded Fabrizi, giving rise within the thin main narrative to the type of humorous sketch that had been the staple of their stage work.

The Passaguai family, though often hard up, was lower middle class, and various aspects of the humour revolved round the pretensions of this class – that is, its new leisure pursuits and its desire for material comforts and status. The nostalgic strain was evident in an attachment to traditions and in a certain ceremony about social relations. Peppe 'Passaguai' is not in any meaningful sense a modern character, but he nonetheless throws himself into endeavours that signal upward mobility. For example, in *La famiglia Passaguai fa fortuna* he slips easily into the back seat of an outsize open-top American automobile when his friend, the chauffeur, offers him a lift. When he encounters an old friend, he cheerfully pretends that he has had a telephone installed at home, a boast that says much about the real purchasing power of the lower middle class at the time. He also envies the home of his landlord, which is filled with heavy nineteenth-century furniture and ornaments. Peppe Passaguai is heir to the fathers of the comedies of the later Fascist period, like Mariano Bomotti in *Giorno di nozze* (Wedding Day, Raffaello Matarazzo, 1942) or Cesco Brambilla in *La famiglia Brambilla va in vacanza* (The Brambilla Family Goes on Holiday, Carl Boese, 1941). The obsession with money and appearances that is so prominent a theme in those films is reprised and given a specifically Roman comical twist. Though Anna Magnani has always been regarded as Fabrizi's alter ego on account of their memorable pairing in *Roma città aperta*, the Passaguai series confirmed that his ideal screen partner was the heavily built Ave Ninchi. A specialist in roles of irascible but good-natured mature women, Ninchi played his wife on some five occasions.

Fabrizi did not go out of his way to cultivate a private image, though he envied the celebrity status of some of his fellow comics. Indeed, he always complained that the illustrated magazines had no interest in him and that he was never granted a front cover.[42] This was perhaps just as well for, despite the domestic preoccupations of many of his screen characters, he lived apart from his wife and children for much of the period between the later 1940s and the 1950s, taking up residence instead in a series of hotels.[43] However, over time food gradually came to be a central theme of his public image, and his growing physical bulk underscored this. In his diary entry for 8 April 1949, Gian Luigi Rondi recalled being invited to lunch by the actor, shortly after his return from Argentina, in a trattoria where they let him prepare *spaghetti alla carbonara*. 'I like cooking as much as acting', he informed the critic.[44] 'To see him there, he seems good (or good-natured) because, fat as he is with his rounded air, he is the very emblem of the pacific individual who is up for every indulgence', Rondi noted. However, this image was illusory, for 'as soon as he opens his mouth though, with his Romanesque way of speaking that is almost in the style of Belli, you immediately hear biting remarks that lie somewhere between the sly, the malicious and the aggressive.' To those who knew him, Fabrizi had already lost much of his easy-going sociability by the time he made his first movies. 'Behind that peace-loving air', it was said, 'Aldo was unbearably proud, arrogant and bullying'. Colleagues found him rude, grumpy and disrespectful.[45] Though it was once remarked that 'he has too much fat on him to be nasty',[46] it was only his screen persona that was good-humoured and approachable. Instinctively distrustful, he was fearful that any display of goodness might be taken for weakness. His melancholy and his rancour towards the next man was attributed to a childhood marked by poverty and suffering.[47] But it may also be attributed to his sense of himself as the last representative of a dying world. When asked whether he saw Rome as a wife, a lover or a mother, he replied that the city was 'a mother. Once she was a respectable woman. Now the non-Romans have transformed her into a tart. They have infected her with snobbery. Anyway, I still defend her', he confessed with a certain proud resignation.[48]

Notes

1. See the selection of reviews of the three films in Lancia and Melelli, *I film di Aldo Fabrizi*, 27–31.
2. Vice, 'Avanti c'è posto', *Cinema*, 25 September 1942. Cited in ibid., 27.
3. U. Pirro, 'Fabrizi neorealista a caccia del milione', *Corriere della Sera*, 4 April 1990, 17.
4. 'Rossellini convinced himself that Fabrizi would never have been persuaded to put his popularity at risk in a dramatic film full of death and torture.' Pirro, 'Fabrizi neorealista', 17.
5. Federico Fellini, cited in Faldini and Fofi, *L'avventurosa storia del cinema italiano: raccontata dai suoi protagonisti 1935–1959*, 91.
6. Ibid., 90; Brunette, *Roberto Rossellini*, 42; Pirro, *Celluloide*.
7. Spinazzola, *Cinema e pubblico: lo spettacolo filmico in Italia, 1945–1965*.
8. Quoted in Moscati, *Aldo Fabrizi: l'ultimo Re di Roma*, 53.
9. P. Mondini, 'Che guaio il ristorante', *Paese sera*, 6 July 1980, 17.
10. Ibid.

11. Governi, *Nannarella*, 115.
12. T. Kezich, 'È morto Fabrizi, la risata di Roma', *Corriere della Sera*, 3 April 1990, 1–2.
13. Governi, *Nannarella*, 115.
14. P. Fortuna, 'Una minestra a Trastevere', *Epoca*, 30 November 1974, 151–52.
15. Brunette, *Roberto Rossellini*, 136.
16. On Fabrizi's importance in the popular cinema of the period, see Manzoli, *Da Ercole a fantozzi: cinema popolare e società italiana dal boom economic alla neotelevisione (1958-1976)*, 17–22.
17. N. Salvalaggio, 'Aldo Fabrizi racconta i cento mestieri della sua vita', *Corriere della sera*, 1 July 1963, 17.
18. Ibid.
19. G.P. Brunetta, 'È morto Fabrizi, volto ironico di Roma', *La Repubblica*, 3 April 1990, 19.
20. Only much later in his career, in the Franco and Ciccio vehicle, *Gerarchi si muore* (Old Fascists Never Die, Giorgio Simonelli, 1961) would he play a nostalgic old Fascist.
21. E. Bonandini, 'Fabrizi ha da morire', 1947 (unidentified cutting, Centro documentazione Rizoli).
22. Rondi, *Le mie vite allo specchio: diari 1947-1997*, 27.
23. Gentile, *Fascismo: storia e interpretazione*, Chapter 10.
24. P. Poggio, '"Ho capito che era giunta la fine: mi ha baciato le mani e ha pianto in silenzio"', *Gente*, 19 April 1990, 13.
25. L. Gatteschi, 'Aldo Fabrizi: "papà tv"', *La Settimana Incom*, 18 December 1965, 24–25.
26. Ibid.
27. C. Testa, '"Ero un Rodolofo Valentino"', *Oggi illustrato*, 10 March 1971, 75–76.
28. Brunetta, *Cent'anni di cinema italiano*, 374–75.
29. G. Torelli, 'Il poeta degli spaghetti', *Grazia*, 1968, 66 (undated cutting Centro documentazione Rizzoli).
30. Testa, '"Ero un Rodolofo Valentino"', 75–76.
31. Gatteschi, 'Aldo Fabrizi: "papà tv"', 24–25.
32. F. Mondini, 'Che guaio il ristorante', *Paese sera*, 6 July 1980, 17.
33. Fabrizi, *Aldo Fabrizi, mio padre*, 22.
34. Testa, '"Ero un Rodolofo Valentino"', 75–76.
35. Kezich, 'È morto Fabrizi, la risata di Roma', 1–2.
36. Soldati, *Cinematografo*, 410.
37. Ibid.
38. Fabrizi, *Aldo Fabrizi mio padre*, 59–60.
39. Brice, *Histoire de Rome et des Romains de Napoleon 1er a nos jours*, 438.
40. Romano, *Paese Italia: venti secoli di identità*.
41. G. Aristarco, *Cinema nuovo*, 15 June 1949. Cited in Lancia and Melelli, *I film di Aldo Fabrizi*, 58.
42. This was not strictly true. Though it was after his heyday, he appeared on the cover of *La Settimana Incom* 10 January 1953 in the company of Franca Marzi.
43. Fabrizi, *Aldo Fabrizi mio padre*, 58–58.
44. Rondi, *Le mie vite allo specchio*, 82.
45. Carrano, *La Magnani*, 102.
46. Silvo d'Amico, cited in Kezich, 'È morto Fabrizi'.
47. N. Ferreri, 'La comicità di Aldo Fabrizi è fatta di spaghetti e di lacrime', *Oggi*, 31 July 1958, 19–20.
48. P. Mosca, 'La dieta di Fabrizi si chiama telegiornale', *Corriere della sera*, 23 March 1979, 17. See also G. Crescimbeni, '"Povera Roma, tutti pronti a daje addosso"', *Tempo*, 14 March 1976, 15–17.

CHAPTER 8

Anna Magnani
Authenticity and the Star Persona

Few truly memorable film characters have as short a screen life as Pina, the working-class widow and bride-to-be in Rossellini's *Roma città aperta* (Rome Open City, 1945). In fact, Pina exits the film in the 56th minute, after appearing in just eight scenes for a total of less than eighteen minutes. A sense of just how limited Pina's screen time is can be gained from the fact that the Resistance chief Manfredi appears for twenty-eight minutes while the priest Don Pietro is on screen for over thirty minutes. *Roma città aperta* in fact is a choral film. Pina is not a character marked by any special or unusual qualities and nor is she really a co-protagonist. Rather she is a supporting figure who is representative of the women of a lower-class quarter of Rome who are living under the oppression of Nazi occupation. She has an extended family and is a part of the larger communities of her district (see Figure 8.1).[1] Yet Pina is a character who struck a chord with postwar spectators to such an extent that, within a short time, she would be recognized as the most distinctive and original face of neorealist cinema. There are a number of reasons why this was so. Pina is not in any way glossed or glamorized in terms of her age, appearance, clothing or relationships. In her very first scene, she emerges from a crowd of women who have just raided a bakery and, as she elbows her way forward, emits a typical Roman curse of *'Va a morir ammazzato!'* (literally, 'Go and get yourself killed'). She is immediately identified as a working-class woman in her thirties, and we soon learn that she is a widow and a mother who is on the point of marrying for the second time. Though she informs Manfredi that she is a factory worker, she in many ways occupies conventional feminine spheres, leading Mary Wood to insist that the gender hierarchy remains 'firmly in place' in the film.[2] However, she subverts aspects of this by discussing politics in the home, organizing a raid on a bakery and refusing to defer to the German troops who are evacuating her building. Though the raid shows that she is concerned to provide food for her family, this is not taken further; the only people who seem to care about comestibles in the film are mature men – namely her grandfather, who is looking forward to the wedding feast, the local policeman who accepts some stolen bread, and Don Pietro's pragmatic sexton, who makes cabbage soup on the parish stove. As a mother, her manner, her spirit and indeed her appearance are distinct from the established cliché of Italian cinema, which portrayed mothers as elderly, submissive and generally housebound.

Unlike Manfredi and her fiancé, the print-worker Francesco, Pina is not a member of the Resistance. However, she is peripherally engaged in subversive activities that, when the country returned to democratic rule in the postwar years, were widely viewed in a heroic light. She takes part in a sullen everyday resistance to the privations and oppressions of the occupation. Her wedding will take place in church to avoid being married by a Fascist official in the municipality. As Patrizia Gabrielli has argued, women who undertook Resistance activity had to have a high

Figure 8.1 An actress amongst the crowd: Anna Magnani as Pina (centre), moments prior to her tragic death, in *Roma città aperta* (Rome Open City, Roberto Rossellini, 1945) (screenshot by the author).

degree of consciousness because they were not motivated, as many men were, by a concern to avoid being called up to fight in the army of the Nazi-dominated Italian Social Republic.[3] Pina does not have quite that level of consciousness, but there is little doubt about her views or sympathies. Even if she has little knowledge of Resistance activities, she is never cowed. She stands up defiantly to the Germans when they arrest her husband-to-be and pays the ultimate price when she reacts animatedly to his arrest. Pina's desperate attempt to save her fiancé as she breaks free of a cordon of soldiers and runs out into the street after the truck that is bearing men away for probable execution is senseless. Its utter instinctiveness is underscored when an unseen German machine gun brings a sudden end to her run and to her life. The manner of Pina's screen death, her 'precipitous removal from the narrative' left an eloquent void.[4] As Marcia Landy has observed, 'though visually absent later in the film, her presence continues in elegiac fashion to have an impact.'[5] Her repeated cry of her fiancé's name 'Francesco!' was the cry of all those women who had lost a husband, a brother or a son to Nazi or Fascist violence in the Italian civil war. It contributed to her becoming a symbol of lasting importance – of sacrifice, of humanity, of a new right to citizenship on the part of women. All this meant that Pina, unlike Giovanna in *Ossessione* (Luchino Visconti, 1943, see Chapter 6), who was still burdened with the conventional carapace of the femme fatale, was unambiguously a positive character who was well equipped to bear the hopes of a new era on her shoulders.

Pina was given a special charge by the performance of the actress who played her. Anna Magnani poured every possible dose of humanity into this figure whose personal tragedy turns her into an emblem of the suffering of ordinary Italians. Pina's scruffy dark mane, soulful eyes, stocky figure and husky Roman accent are Magnani's, as are her gentle manner, explosive temperament, good heart and biting sarcasm. Though not all Italian critics immediately grasped the greatness of Rossellini's film,[6] Magnani's special contribution to the emotional texture of a supremely moving drama was widely recognized. It was a contribution that determined in part the impact of the film and that profoundly marked Magnani's own image. It situated the actress in a realm in which cinema and actuality appeared to become unified, with the actress's performance, to cite Francesco Pitassio, being central to the 'merging [of] past events with their fictional representation'.[7] Her highly emotional style did not seem like acting at all, and this would ensure that Pina and Magnani became inseparable. For Landy, Pina constituted 'an unforgettable memory rooted deep in the culture of stardom and identified with a form of sacrality that [posed] an alternative to clichés inherited from the fascist era and that [was] slated to become a permanent attribute of Magnani's stardom'.[8] The way in which she was sacralized involved an inversion of the conventional distribution of gender roles. When Don Pietro gathers up and holds the dead Pina in his arms, he assumes the position of the Madonna in Michelangelo's Pietà, while Pina occupies the position of Christ. The critical mobilization of religious iconography, which was underscored in promotional posters that placed a faint crown of thorns alongside the shadowed face of Magnani, served, Landy observes, 'to metamorphose her figure from one of ordinariness and render it sacrosanct'. It fixed her firmly in cinematic memory and in the public imagination.

Anna Magnani was no newcomer to the screen. She had appeared in some seventeen films before *Roma città aperta*, always in supporting roles. Twice she had appeared alongside Aldo Fabrizi, who played the priest Don Pietro, in the Rome-set dialect comedies *Campo de' fiori* (The Peddlar and the Lady, Mario Bonnard, 1942) and *L'ultima carrozzella* (The Last Wagon, Mario Mattoli, 1943). In the former, she is a feisty flower seller who banters with Fabrizi across the market stalls, while in the second she is an actress who engages him to transport her in his horse-drawn carriage. In earlier films, including her small role as a cheeky servant girl in Mario Mattoli's madcap comedy *Tempo massimo* (Full Speed, 1936), which starred Vittorio De Sica, and this actor's directorial debut, the comedy-drama *Teresa Venerdi* (Doctor Beware, 1941), she had demonstrated an ability to steal the scene with little more than a cameo appearance. Though she was often cast as ordinary women, she had never previously taken a dramatic part. It was as a popular entertainer, a star of stage revues, that she was best known. Indeed, in both *L'ultima carrozzella* and *Teresa Venerdi*, she plays caricatures of variety performers, overdressed women of a theatrical bent who are worldly and cynical if also to some degree genuine and warm-heated. Magnani herself was an established theatrical personality who in these films was required to play women who were not dissimilar to the image she projected of herself to the public. In both films she was given an opportunity to showcase something of her talents as a performer of Roman popular songs.

Revues reached great popularity in the 1930s and 1940s and enjoyed a heyday in the period immediately following the liberation of Rome in June 1944. A show staged by the producers Garinei and Giovannini and directed by Mattoli, *Soffia so'*, was one of the most successful, mixing comedy, sketches, humour, song and satire.[9] Magnani engaged audiences with a repertoire of Roman *stornelli* that drew people to her and helped establish her special connection to the city of Rome. She won admirers by her habit of descending from the stage and moving among the audience as she sang. As Patrizia Carrano notes, this abolition of the distance between stage and stalls lent a particular inflection to her stardom and gave rise to an affectionate nickname. 'She had become Nannarella. She was the queen of that city which had survived the war almost untouched; she was the image of a brazen, rebellious, furious, disrespectful spirit; she was at one with the cynicism, the resentment, the couldn't-care-less attitude, the ambition, the fundamental nature and cowardice, the brusqueness and the affection of those people.'[10]

The film-makers who would give expression to Italian neorealism were drawn to Magnani, and the three most prominent of them, sooner or later, would all direct her. De Sica had worked with her in the theatre in the early 1930s, and he would cast her in *Teresa Venerdì* as the singer Maddalena Tentini, otherwise known as the artiste Loletta Prima. Rossellini succeeded in the face of some opposition in casting her as Pina and would direct her again in a film version of Jean Cocteau's one-act drama for a single actor, *La voix humaine*, as well as the short film *Il miracolo*, which were released together in 1948 with the umbrella title *L'amore* (Ways of Love). Visconti, who had wanted to cast her as the adulteress Giovanna in *Ossessione*, would eventually direct her in *Bellissima* (1952) and in an episode of the multi-author film *Siamo donne* (We, The Women, 1953).

What fascinated them about Magnani was her rich, larger-than-life personality, her ability to play women outside of the clichés of the cinema of the Fascist period and her capacity to inject emotional intensity into her performances in a way that made it seem as if she was emptying herself into them. She had a range of registers, which went from the exuberant to the intimate and could capture the attention at either end of this scale. For filmmakers who were seeking to find a new eloquence in the human face, she constituted a template that was different from that usually offered by professional actors. Her eyes and face became highly important signifiers of her persona. She was often shot in close-up, and her close-ups often featured on the posters advertising her films. For André Bazin, silent communication was crucial in conveying meaning in neorealist films. Dialogue was less important than belief – you had as a spectator to understand what was being said without words.[11] Jacques Aumont argues that this use of physiognomy changed the sense of beauty and laid down a mortal challenge to conventional facial aesthetics. From this moment, he argued, 'beauty will no longer be the cold, abstract one of the photogenic, or still less the manufactured and lying one of glamour, but an interior, personal beauty that truly reflected the soul.'[12]

Already in 1946 Magnani's face was thought of as a phenomenon. The photographer Federico Patellani offered readers of *Tempo* a close study of her in June of that year, which included eleven close-ups of her expressions.[13] He described her as 'extrovert, whimsical, impatient, quick-tempered and mad'; 'Anna is a great artist because she is profoundly spontaneous' and does not care about the judgement of others. 'Passionate in character', she 'builds up and exaggerates her sufferings, almost wilfully martyring and bringing humiliation on herself through them'.[14] 'Anna has perhaps never done her hair, in the normal way that is understood. The arrangement of her hair recalls days of gales and winds by the sea. Yet it would be quite wrong to think that she neglects her appearance.' In her, there were elements of art, tradition and instinct. 'Everything in her that is most natural is in fact the result of careful selection', Patellani continued. 'If she chooses to wear a tailored suit, it is not because she looks bad in other clothes, but simply because a suit is best adapted to her personality as an independent woman. However, Anna is a slave to coral; she loves it and has rings, bracelets and earrings made of it.'

Her taste for coral jewellery signalled her identity as a woman of lower-class southern parentage. Coral was not precious, like diamonds or other stones. Rather, it had a long-standing appeal to peasant and poorer women, especially in the centre-south of the country. The transformation of red coral into jewellery had been associated since the late eighteenth century with the town of Torre del Greco, which stands at the foot of Vesuvius. According to legend, coral was born from the petrification of the blood of the severed head of the Gorgon Medusa, while for Christians it symbolized the blood of Christ. It was invested with superstitions and was commonly held to ward off bad luck.

Magnani had not managed to make her mark in Fascist cinema, and in 1945 she was neither a recognized screen actress nor a box office draw.[15] Her irregular features, excessive gesticulation and lack of grace in movement restricted her to character parts.[16] There was, however, something intrinsically choral about her that interested cinema's reformers. Even though, as screenwriter Sergio Amidei recalled, the character of Pina 'was thought up and conceived for Magnani', the production company was dead set against her. It took the persuasive intervention of the influential producer Giuseppe Amato to change their view and win her the role.[17] After *Roma città aperta*, it would be very different, for suddenly she was in huge demand. A new cinema was born with the potential to transform conventional ideas of stardom and performance. From the important but supporting role of Pina, she was catapulted into a series of leading roles that would see her become one of the country's biggest box office attractions.

She began working intensively, mostly in films produced by Lux, and appeared in six titles released in 1945–46, of which three were lead roles and three were supporting ones. She maintained a punishing rhythm of work until 1948, after which she made one or two films per year until 1952. Of these roles, nearly all were conceived with Magnani in mind. Many of them combined elements of both the personae she had forged: the variety artiste and the woman of the people. The offers she received were not generally very artistic; they came from producers and directors who were seeking to breathe new life into popular cinema. *Abbasso la miseria!* (Down with Misery! Gennaro Righelli, 1945) saw her play Nannina, the ambitious wife of the less successful of a pair of black-marketeering chauffeurs. Much of the plot revolves around her relationship with a young orphaned boy (played by Vito Annicchiarico, her son Marcello in *Roma città aperta*), who her hapless husband – thinking he may be the father – brings home from his travels. Initially she rejects the boy, only to warm to him and face disappointment when his true father, who had been thought dead, returns to claim him. The film includes numerous gags, several of them centred on the boy, and features various real-life scenes of the streets of Rome, bombed buildings in Naples and even a picturesque panorama of the Bay of Naples. The aspirational Nannina, whose hilarious bad taste in clothes and furnishings signals her illicit wealth, is played engagingly by Magnani, who is afforded two opportunities to display her singing talents.

The following year, Righelli made a follow-up, *Abbasso la ricchezza!* (Peddlin' in Society, 1946). In the film, Magnani is no longer Nannina but Donna Gioconda Perfetti, a former grocer who has enriched herself thanks to the black market. Much of the comedy derives from her social pretensions. She lives in a house once owned by a count, which she has filled with false modern masters, adopts a snobbish manner and seeks to marry her younger sister to a humble American G.I., who they erroneously believe to be a mining millionaire. The film again revolves around Magnani and her eye-popping costumes. It includes set pieces scenes of her singing her trademark song 'Quanto sei bella Roma' and dancing the boogie woogie. As the impoverished count who seeks to tutor her in the ways of the world, De Sica provides her with the perfect foil. Both actors offer caricatures of themselves and previous roles as they reprise a double act established in moments of *Tempo massimo* and *Teresa Venerdì*. Nannina and Gioconda are both women of the present, immersed in the complex moral and material universe of postwar society. By the end of each film, they have seen their hopes dashed and have returned, chastened, to their regular status.

If Magnani became a key figure in postwar cinema – the single actor who, more than any other, embodied the period and its traumas and hopes – it was also because her characters explored the shadows and legacies of war and did so, due to the actress's histrionic performances, in ways that registered with audiences. To evoke a backstory was not, in her case, to raise the spectre of a compromised past. Max Neufeld's *Un uomo ritorna* (A Man Returns, 1946), which, like Camerini's *Due lettere anonime* (Two Anonymous Letters, 1945), was also scripted by Ivo Perilli, cast her as Adele, a widow who awaits the return of her son while meditating revenge against the family of the man who caused his capture. Her story constitutes a thread of a larger one in which her former neighbour (who hails from the same village as her), an engineer played by Gino Cervi, returns from war to find that his sister is a prostitute and his younger brother a street urchin and black-marketeer. Adele eventually discovers that her son is dead but abandons her plan for revenge and, with Cervi's character and his chastened siblings, leaves the moral quagmire of Rome for their home village. By leaving the city, they can purify themselves and somehow begin again. The film highlights the divisions of the civil war and the difficulties of overcoming them.

Carmine Gallone's *Avanti a lui tremava tutta Roma* (Before Him All Rome Trembled, 1946) was set, like *Roma città aperta*, during the Nazi occupation of Rome. It is the story of opera singers who rehearse and perform Puccini's *Tosca* while simultaneously seeking to aid the Resistance. Magnani is a diva (Ada) who consorts with the Nazi command and inadvertently betrays her lover when, thinking him unfaithful, she alerts a German officer to his suspicious actions. In fact, he has been engaged in hiding a British airman. Magnani's down-to-earth manner is displayed in her banter with waiters, and her temperament is evident in her character's jealousy, but her character is ambiguous and her playing is wilfully inauthentic. The film concludes after the liberation of Rome, but Ada's destiny is unclear. *Avanti a lui tremava tutta Roma* explicitly drew on melodrama to amplify and emphasize the emotional aspects of recent history. Catherine O'Rawe suggests that opera provided a narrative frame that rendered these events meaningful in terms of popular culture.[18]

In Lattuada's *Il bandito* (1946), however, which is further discussed in Chapter 10, melodrama is woven into the plot in a less obvious way to bolster what is ostensibly a crime story. There is still a contemporary concern at the core of the film (the plight of returning soldiers and the difficulty of their reintegration in society), but there are also stock characters and deliberate genre effects deriving from the gangster film. Magnani is a theatrical performer whose over-the-top costumes and ostentation recall Donna Gioconda. She is a seductive worldly woman who proves irresistible to Amedeo Nazzari's sex-starved demobilized soldier, Ernesto. But she is also the leader of a criminal band and undergoes the humiliation of having drink thrown in her face when Ernesto discovers the source of her wealth. She exits the film after tipping off the police about his whereabouts and betraying the members of her own gang.

For all the negativity of these characters, Pina resonated through them. Magnani embodied the redemptive charge of her sacrifice and ensured that her own genuineness and good heart overshadowed the transgressions and misdemeanours of her subsequent characters. Giuliana Minghelli has shown how this could be. There is, she argues, a sharp divide between the main female characters of *Ossessione* and *Roma città aperta*; while *Ossessione*'s dark heroine Giovanna was a 'symbol of national guilt', Pina became a 'symbol of national redemption'.[19] 'Giovanna is reborn in Pina', she asserts; 'her unborn child transformed into a partisan child that mourns the mother and is moved to action'. In terms of a critical discourse that accords special weight to these two films, seeing the latter as a continuation of the discourse of the former, this interpretation makes sense. Pina was, as has been shown here, an unusually powerful screen figure. But she was also different from many of Magnani's characters in terms of the entirely positive legacy of Christian sacrifice she left. What is striking about most of the actress's roles of this period is that they are complex and ambiguous. Yet, while such characters departed from the Pina type, the difference should not be exaggerated. In fact, all of Magnani's characters are imperfect; they are flawed to one degree or another and they make mistakes. Moreover, they all have pasts. Even Pina, who has none of the perfection of appearance or costume of the conventional female lead, is fatally impulsive. As a widow and a mother who is pregnant but unwed, she also has a complicated backstory.

Almost all Magnani's films include references to a troubled present even if they move in the direction of comedy or popular music. They also tend to feature set-piece scenes, which foreground some of her stock characteristics, be they a verbal conflict, a musical interlude, a public dispute or an excessive costume.[20] In *Molti sogni per le strade* (The Street Has Many Dreams, Mario Camerini, 1948), a picaresque comedy involving a stolen Fiat 1500 belonging to a rich man, there are two such set-piece scenes. The first involves Linda (Magnani), the disputatious wife of unemployed mechanic Paolo (Massimo Girotti), standing in front of the vehicle and refusing to budge while she loudly berates him for living it up and going after other women while failing to provide for his family. The crowd that is drawn by this altercation is treated, like the film's audience, to one of Magnani's signature explosions. The second such scene occurs when Linda and Paolo, both now aboard the stolen vehicle, come across a crowd that is taking part in a political rally. Unable to force their way through, they accidentally knock a man over. This arouses the anger of other members of the crowd, who, noticing their large car, accuse them of profiting from the black market. While Paolo descends to fist-icuffs, Linda mounts the bonnet and, gesticulating wildly, vocally defends herself and her husband from the charge. For her pains, her hat is rudely knocked off.

Magnani's characters have often been described as women of the people or, to use the Italian term, *popolane*. Such labels are almost never questioned for, as Landy observes, 'her star image resided in her identification with the Roman working-class and maternal figures she played in many of her films.'[21] This term has been explored by Sarah Culhane and Sergio Rigoletto;[22] however, its meaning needs to be further interrogated. It is generally taken to refer to members of the urban lower class, be they properly working class in the sense of being dependent labourers or members of a less stable and variegated underclass that lives by expedients. The notion in truth is more cultural than economic, since the idea of 'the people' evoked by the term is rooted in a sense of belonging forged through shared experiences and customs rather than a common economic position. Even the self-employed and the dependent petite bourgeoisie may merge into this lower class in certain circumstances, though they may also seek to distinguish themselves from it by means of the ownership of property or goods. The feminine term *popolana*, however, is more common than the masculine *popolano*, for it is not immediately associated with specific types of employment. Moreover, the *popolana* is associated with a richer iconography, having been more widely represented in art, poetry, songs and theatre. In the nineteenth century, the *popolana romana* was often located in a very specific neighbourhood such as Trastevere, which was considered to be the most picturesque and genuine of Roman districts, whose inhabitants claimed to be directly descended from the ancient Romans. In the drawings of an artist like Bartolomeo Pinelli, who was active in the first three decades of the nineteenth century and who found many of his models on the streets of Trastevere, the figure of the *popolana romana* was portrayed mainly as a young woman of attractive appearance who was intense, proud and dignified. She could be poor and shabby or – if better off – showy and ostentatious with elaborately coiffed hair. Until the interwar years, various folk rituals and festivals gave a platform to picturesque *popolane* and their traditional costumes. These waned under Mussolini, as the regime took over these exhibitions while investing its energies in an imperial idea of Rome and its people.

Magnani's *popolane* were influential because they were novel. While lively peasant women had been represented on the screen,[23] the figure of the urban woman of the people had only ever been a background figure in cinema until Magnani began to develop more complete roles with *Campo de' fiori*, in which she plays the argumentative stallholder Elide (see Figure 8.2), and Pina in *Roma città aperta*. For

Figure 8.2 Anna Magnani as the feisty market stallholder Elide in *Campo de' fiori* (Mario Bonnard, 1943), one of two pre-1945 films in which she acted opposite Aldo Fabrizi (screenshot by the author).

Giulio Cesare Castello, writing in 1957, *Roma città aperta* heralded the birth, alongside neorealism, of a great actress 'who was able to express, with an unprecedented searing truth and intensity, the passions and torments of a Roman *popolana*'.[24]

'In this way', he continued, 'the Magnani persona was born: brown-haired and not beautiful but with eyes of a deep, devouring, feverish vivacity shining above dark circles; with tufts of hair that were forever scruffy and uncontrolled, she was the emblem of common sense and combativeness, of the corrosive, acerbic humours and impulses of the people of Rome'. Her *popolane* were invariably mothers, often possessive ones, but they had nothing in common with the silent, suffering mothers and the dutifully prolific child-bearers that had been dear to Fascist propaganda.[25] They were strident, defiant, vulgar, and Magnani, standing proudly with her hands on her hips and tossing her dark hair, conveyed them with great intensity. Pina was not in any way a caricature or a stock figure; she was a dramatic invention of great originality, and Magnani's playing of her enhanced her impact. Having established the *popolana* persona, Magnani worked to develop it in drama and comedy, despite reservations voiced by critics sceptical of heterodoxy.

Magnani's Roman-ness is never questioned on account of the way she became, as Carrano notes,[26] a symbol of the city and its spirit as it emerged from occupation and war. Her strongly Roman accent completed an identification that became an integral part of the Magnani persona. But there is an issue of how Roman she was. She was not, for example, a *'romana de' Roma'* (Roman from Rome) – that is to say, she could not boast, like Aldo Fabrizi, that her family had been Roman for generations. Her mother was originally from Fano, near Pesaro, in the Marche region, while her father, who she never knew, was from the southern region of Calabria. This recent migration placed her in a broad current of population movement. Rome underwent considerable expansion after it became the Italian capital in 1870, and it grew further on account of the extension of the state, which occurred under Mussolini. Over these decades, tens of thousands of people moved to the capital from other regions of Italy. It has been pointed out that these outsiders were not treated as 'foreigners' in the way that they would have been in any other Italian city. 'All those who transferred here were immediately "adopted" by Rome without it being expected, even implicitly, that they would abandon or hide the habits and ways of life of their regions of origin', Emilio Colombo wrote in the preface to a 1970 volume dedicated to the non-Romans of Rome.[27] The city welcomed and adopted everyone, with the result that the passage from *'romani de fora'* (Romans from outside) to *'romani de Roma'* could occur within just one generation. However, for some years mystery surrounded the actress's birth, her family, her father's name (Magnani was her mother's surname) and other details.[28] For a period, she did not deny a rumour that she was born in Alexandria to an Egyptian father. This had the double advantage of endowing her with a measure of exoticism and diverting interest in her early life away from illegitimate origins, which she preferred to conceal. In fact, her mother moved to Egypt following her marriage to an Austrian, while Magnani herself was mainly raised by her grandmother and her aunts who lived in Rome between the Campidoglio and Palatino districts. Though neither of her parents was Roman, Magnani was accustomed to assert, once the Egyptian legend was laid to rest, that she was 'romana di Porta Pia' (Roman from the Porta Pia district).

While Magnani might have lacked a deep family identification with Rome, her Roman persona rested on a specific connection she forged over time with the

Figure 8.3 Anna Magnani at the inaugural Nasto d'argento (silver ribbon) ceremony in 1946, at which she received the award for best supporting actress for her role in *Roma città aperta* (Rome Open City, Roberto Rossellini, 1945) (author's own collection).

population. Her accent, her dialect-inflected speech and her use of a local musical culture assisted this and reinforced it. However, this connection arose in a theatrical context. As a performer, the Romanesco dialect provided her with a way of communicating with the public. It was a device that she adopted or set aside according to circumstance. When she appeared in court in Rome in 1953 accused of contravening rules governing the importation of foreign motor vehicles, it was reported that 'La Magnani made her deposition very calmly, in perfect Italian without any Romanesque inflections.'[29] This gave rise to scandalized comment because one of the chief characteristics of the Magnani persona as it was forged in the immediate postwar years was its ostensibly seamless blending of screen roles, the public personality of the actress and her personal experiences, including her background, emotional life and temperament. Millicent Marcus refers to this as her 'divistic myth of unity'.[30] Magnani herself at times encouraged the idea that there was a strong connection between herself and her screen characters; for example, by maintaining in real life the same artfully wild coiffures that marked her characters and by cultivating a reputation for loudness and irascibility. She did not renounce the glamour and wealth that came with fame and recognition, but nonetheless she gave out an impression of genuineness that transcended these (see Figure 8.3). 'She is not a star', Castello argued; 'rather she, like almost all the other great actresses of the screen, is the polar opposite of the processes of star manufacture, since she seeks and expresses with great frankness and immediacy a truth that is all the more universal for its being rooted in the world that spawned it'.[31] The problem was that by marking out a singular path that made her the unique interpreter of the unruly, untameable spirit of a type of Italian woman who was resourceful, spontaneous, traditional and yet somehow progressive, she became imprisoned in a cliché. 'Her very cantankerous, rebellious and biting nature turned her into a phenomenon that was also picturesque',[32] observed Castello.[33] Though original and apparently authentic, Magnani could also be perceived as prone to repetition and predictable.[34]

The originality of the *popolana* type that Magnani created derived from the specific disruptions that the circumstances of war and foreign occupation heralded. The humours, the attitudes and the type of interpersonal relations that prospered at a time in which community was undermined by individual and familial strategies of survival all contributed to the backdrop to her emergence. '*Roma città aperta*', Vittorio Spinazzola noted, 'brought to the screen a type of woman who had nothing in common either with the pale little misses and the naughty boarding school girls of the prewar era or with the classic Italian divas. She was a modern woman, free of prejudices and sexual slavery, aware of her own dignity but nonetheless feminine and susceptible to feelings'.[35] She was also mature, earthy, strong, defiant and a mother.[36] Her age also drew comment. Writing in *Tempo* magazine in 1946, Diego Calcagno in *Tempo* reflected on the mature women who aroused the sexual interest of men more than younger ones. The most appealing variety consisted of 'those women who are to be appreciated in the highly mysterious season in which youth is about to wane or those women, like Wanda Osiris or Anna Magnani, who stand on the edge of that delightful season'.[37] However, these circumstances were temporary, and the passage from reconstruction to growth meant that the conditions for the existence of this sort of screen character were undermined. The Magnani type would find a range of adaptations and re-propositions in cinema and other media, but these tended to bypass the actress herself as a new generation of younger performers emerged from postwar beauty contests.[38] At the same time, the traditions of the Roman lower class lost their organic character and ceased to be part of everyday life, though they persisted on certain occasions and continued to be evoked or revived in the theatre; for example, in the period-set musical comedy *Rugantino*, which debuted in Rome in 1962.

Roma città aperta was top at the box office in 1945–46, and the comedy *Abbasso la miseria* figured in eighth position, while three of her films – *Il bandito*, *Avanti a lui tremava tutta Roma* and *Abbasso la ricchezza* – featured among the top ten earners of 1946–47.[39] After that, most of her films did less well. She began to devote more time to theatre and the rhythm of her film work slowed. In 1947, just one film featuring her was released, while in 1948 four were. Then she made one or two per year until 1952. The fact that after 'the explosion of popularity of the immediate postwar years, she came to be seen as a negative influence at the box office'[40] has been attributed to the unchanging nature of her screen persona. Though her reputation as an actress and indeed her personal popularity remained high, her box office appeal declined. Magnani often lamented the fact that she had been abandoned by cinema (by which she meant directors and producers), but it is also true that the films constructed around her were quite quickly deserted by spectators. Spinazzola argues that Magnani suffered at the hands of directors who rendered her strikingly innovative persona conventional and amusing. So disruptive was such a figure in a country in which the question of female emancipation was only just beginning to be discussed that 'it was necessary to reduce her immediately to less challenging proportions'.[41] For Spinazzola, already Lattuada in *Il bandito* and Gallone in *Avanti a lui tremava tutta Roma* imposed a turn towards melodrama, but it was the 'descent to the level of comedy' that 'completely distorted the physiognomy of the character . . . suffocating it with jokes and laughter'. The result was 'the very widely-known image of an uncouth, dishevelled, loud Magnani with slippers on her feet and her skirt twisted: a histrionic caricature of the heroine of *Roma città aperta*'.[42] The actress was an active participant in this process and only realized too late, Spinazzola argued, 'the danger of becoming imprisoned in a facile stereotype'.[43] Contemporary critics tended to take a dim view of the low-budget quickies in which she starred, seeing them as unfortunate lapses in which the purity of Pina is tainted by commercial roles. Magnani rejected criticism of the more popular parts she played in the 1940s on the grounds that the characters were genuine, delightful and 'written especially for me'.[44] It did not bother her that some were comedies. She claimed that she needed believable characters 'well-formed characters without imbalance or falsity. True to life. True to life means characters taken from life' to whom she could dedicate herself sincerely.

There is a sense in which the disruptive character of Pina was tamed and domesticated in the films Magnani made after *Roma città aperta*. Her characters were forced into templates that reflected not only conventional fictional trajectories but also prevailing social values and gender roles. The difficulties that women encountered in their efforts to take their place in public life were documented at the time by the journalist and radio broadcaster Anna Garofalo.[45] The extension of the vote to women in 1946 unsettled the established male-dominated pattern of politics, but this did not mean that female candidates for election were not confined to lower places in party lists or obliged to play second fiddle to male politicians. The twenty-one women who were elected to the constituent assembly in 1946, many of whom had fought in the Resistance or been politically active before Fascism, were subjected to extraordinary public scrutiny in terms of their physical appearance, clothing, family situations and general demeanour.[46] The satirical press ridiculed them constantly as though they had no business straying outside the domestic realm.

One film that highlights both the opportunities that the Magnani persona brought filmmakers and the difficulty of going against social norms is Luigi Zampa's *L'Onorevole Angelina*. The story, like that of Pina, was based on a real one, which was spotted in the press by the writers Suso Cecchi d'Amico and Piero

Tellini. It concerned an ordinary woman from an outlying district of Rome who led a housing protest and for a brief period enjoyed great popularity. Angelina and her children are tempted by the opportunities for material and social advancement, which their prominence brings, and briefly become alienated from other campaigners before realizing the errors of their ways and reconnecting with their roots. The woman's husband (Nando Bruno, the sexton of *Roma città aperta*) is a policeman who is embarrassed by her role and angered by her neglect of her family. He reaches breaking point when she is imprisoned for her activities. In the end, she renounces any political role and returns to her traditional duties.

By this time, Magnani had evolved a way of working she found congenial. There was already an element of spontaneity to the films she made with Fabrizi in 1942–43. She appreciated Rossellini because he did not use rehearsals; instead he constructed contexts, gave instructions to his actors and expected them to give of their best. Magnani responded to this and sought as far as possible to immerse herself in the situations to be filmed. In more commercial films, she was also often given a measure of freedom to develop her character. In *L'Onorevole Angelina*, she worked closely with Zampa. The director later acknowledged that,

> we made Angelina together, we discussed many scenes, we chose the non-professional supporting cast together... No costume designers, make-up artists or special tricks were need for Magnani to get into a character. Anna was such an extraordinary actress that she worked out and found by herself all that was needed to improve it, without lots of tests and rehearsals.[47]

When they went together into the working-class district where the film was to be set, they were surrounded by women who recognized her, one of whom was wearing a dress she deemed perfect for Angelina. 'So we bought it for her, she had it washed at home, and when she appeared on set she was the perfect Angelina; she had got into the skin of Angelina and the poor women we met that day.'[48] The film was successful, reaching fourth position in the 1947–48 box office. However, it did not avoid the trap of repetition, even featuring a raid on a grocer's in the manner of *Roma città aperta*'s assault on the bakery. The director Franco Zeffirelli, as a young man, featured in the cast of *L'Onorevole Angelina*. After the actress's death in 1973, he claimed that 'it was decided to lock Anna down, to suffocate her with the cliché of the Roman suburbs.'[49]

The solution to the spiral of popular cinema, as mentioned above, was a new project with Rossellini. The pair had not worked together since 1945, though they had been engaged for some time in a personal relationship. The intention was to find a project that would be exclusively for her and would avoid the pitfalls of commercial formulas. They eventually settled on Cocteau's monologue *La voce umana*, which Magnani had performed at the theatre. Her former partner, the actor Massimo Serato, was worried by the collaboration, since he knew that people wanted humour.[50] There was also the problem that, though widely respected and much lauded abroad, the director's films after *Roma città aperta* had failed to draw audiences. The play, which involved a woman pleading on the phone with an unseen lover who is on the point of abandoning her, Rossellini claimed, was 'an opportunity to employ the movie camera as a microscope, with Anna Magnani as the phenomenon to be scrutinised'.[51] The aim was to highlight her art by means of a bravura single-handed performance. However, the result had none of Magnani's trademark vitality or choral quality. It was an experimental film that audiences 'refused resolutely to follow'.[52] It hardly helped that the monologue, on account of its brevity, had to be paired with another short film of a completely different nature, *Il miracolo* – together the two works were released as *L'amore* – in which a simple country woman who is seduced by a shepherd believes she has been impregnated by God.

The failure of the film was galling because Magnani was by this time a prominent public figure, the symbol of neorealism and of the transformed role of cinema in society. Though she did not align herself with any political party in the way that some did, her persona was unambiguously engaged. She was also a figure of female enfranchisement, since she was one of a small group of stars who were filmed by the Settimana Incom newsreel company as they prepared to go to the polls. In February 1949, she would be one of the leading figures at the Piazza del Popolo mass rally at which the film world called for action to protect the industry (see Figure 2.1, p. 43).[53] In consequence, she gradually became a prime target for vested interests. Furthermore, her high earnings caused resentment within the industry.[54] In March 1947, the trade publication *Araldo dello spettacolo* complained that she was demanding too much for her performances in theatre and cinema.[55] After the 1949 rally, a Christian Democrat deputy named Gabriele Semeraro, who represented cinema owners, criticized her in parliament.[56] Those hostile to her place in neorealism saw her as a factor in the increasing costs of film-making and therefore a contributor to the industry's difficulties rather than part of the solution to them. Her stardom was not a resource but an inconvenience.

The breakdown in her relationship with Rossellini further exposed her to public comment. She had lived with the director at the Excelsior Hotel in 1947–48, during their tumultuous affair. The couple had an artistic understanding, though this was strained by the failure of *L'amore*. Rossellini's burgeoning relationship with Ingrid Bergman – which is discussed in Chapter 16 – was a flagrant betrayal that turned her private life into public property. The spectacularization of the split in the form of the movie *Vulcano* (William Dieterle, 1950), which Magnani accepted to make at precisely the time when Rossellini and Bergman, on a nearby island, were filming *Stromboli* (1950), served to underline an inseparability of the professional and the personal.[57]

Magnani was much admired by the most prominent directors. Like Rossellini, they no longer saw her purely as an actress but as a phenomenon. They sought to harness the 'real' Magnani to their projects and encouraged extra-textual contaminations between characters and biography. Thus, far from overturning the commercial routinization of her persona, they contributed to her reification. When Visconti had sought to cast her in *Ossessione*, he was interested in the actress. By the time of *Bellissima* (1952) his focus was different; he declared that he was interested to see what relation would emerge 'between me and the "star" Magnani'.[58] His approach was not the authoritarian one that had made Calamai and Girotti tremble. It was more collaborative due to Magnani's ability to improvise. For Visconti, 'la Magnani has an acting style that is rich with popular instinct that has nothing to do with the professional theatre. She knows how to situate herself at the level of the others and somehow lift them to hers.'[59] 'I made recourse above all to this particular and extraordinary aspect of her personality', he said. Her character, Maddalena, is a simple working-class woman who wants to get her daughter into cinema because she thinks it will lead to fame and riches. However, as Millicent Marcus and others have shown, the Magnani persona impinges on the portrayal of a character who would herself like to have been an actress. The entire film, she argues, can be interpreted as 'a mirror of Magnani's stardom'.[60] It places her already mentioned 'divistic myth of unity' at service of a character who must learn to disassociate 'herself from her ideal mirror image, and from the daughter' on whom she has displaced her dreams of unattainable stardom'.[61] In the episode on her that he directed for the portmanteau film *Siamo donne* (We, the Women, 1953), Visconti explored the continuity between Magnani's private and public selves, as well as her 'genius for inventing and publicly presenting a powerful image of self'.[62]

The 'private' Magnani of the 1920s-set *Siamo donne* episode is a variety performer who hires a taxi to take her to the theatre. A dispute arises over whether she should pay extra for her lapdog. She is dressed smartly, with a fur stole, and carries her pet. When she finally reaches the theatre, she dresses down as a *popolana* and goes on stage as a flower seller to sing a popular song that had been associated with her since the 1930s,[63] against a painted backdrop of a typical Roman scene. The performer is shown to be a creation of the actress Magnani, who is in fact playing a character based on herself. The *popolana* therefore is a doubly staged construct who evokes an idea of Rome. Though actress and stage character are united by a single temperament and way of speaking, the work involved in creating a figure of ostensible realism is not in any way obscured. Indeed, it is shown to be a necessary precondition of its realization.

Recent studies have stressed the specific and original nature of Magnani's stardom. It was one in which 'authenticity and artistry, spontaneity and technique, nature and culture' were conflated.[64] This contrasted both with the formalized and controlled stardom of the Fascist period and the more overtly media-centred star discourses centred on feminine beauty and private life that developed in the postwar years.[65] She was sensual but without artful sex appeal, a well-known figure but not a celebrity. Magnani did not make a play of her personal life and, as a result, Mariapaola Pierini has found, she was not a consistent presence in illustrated magazines in the way that some other stars were.[66] When she appeared in the popular press, it was in performative rather than ostensibly real settings.[67] Though her body was a crucial element in her public image, she was better suited to moving rather than still images and this quality complemented a certain informal, unassuming demeanour. Even when she dressed up, she preserved a down-to-earth personality. Commenting on a gala at Rome's Grand Hotel, the magazine *Oggi* observed that, while she was wearing a striped satin evening gown, she was as 'unkempt as ever'.[68] 'A patina of glamour persists', Pierini observes, 'but it is a homely, approachable, lower-middle-class glamour.'[69]

Magnani was not averse to highlighting the two aspects of her life or the links between them. She never sought to make the public think that she was actually a working-class Roman woman. It was her ability to plausibly create such a character, to offer a representation of a type, that was the proof of her skill as an actress. While she could improvise, she also engaged seriously with scripts and prepared her parts meticulously, immersing herself intelligently in her craft. Her collaborations with directors extended to discussing shots, close-ups and aspects of the mise en scène. Far from being an untamed natural talent, she was, as Noa Steimatsky has observed, 'as professional as they get'.[70] Her ability to give her persona a variety of different inflections meant that she did not necessarily have to be cast as Roman. Beyond the Roman accent that most people associated with her, there was little or nothing in her manner or appearance in fact that marked her as specifically Roman. In terms of Italian popular culture, she might just as well have been Neapolitan, Sicilian, generically southern or even Emilian. Though her best known roles were Roman, not all her films were set in the capital, and her appeal to audiences was never limited mainly to one city or region in the way that was often the case with comic actors. Her melodramatic intensity and her fierce maternal attitude provided transcendent features of her persona that permitted her to connect with audiences from other regions and indeed other countries. In *Camice rosse* (Red Shirts, Goffredo Alessandrini, 1952), she played Garibaldi's Brazilian wife Anita, bringing to life a woman of temperament who, thanks to her role alongside the national hero, had herself become a national icon.

When she appeared in public, she dressed in fine gowns and wore furs and jewels. As newsreel footage testifies, she did not make an exception when she attended the premiere of *L'Onorevole Angelina* in the Pietralata district where the film was set. She liked to play up to her image and was content to provide the public with signature exhibitions, but behind this there was a woman who was jealous of her privacy and vulnerable. Though she was not consistently guided by a producer and her film roles followed no coherent pattern, she created a way of being that came to be associated with Italian cinema and that others would refine and develop. For two women journalists, she

> created in the postwar years, the myth of "Magnanismo". In those days, in order to be taken on, aspiring starlets mussed up their hair, put mascara on their eyes and said swear words. Anna Magnani, however, remained unique. Why? ... Before being the great actress we all know, Anna Magnani was someone who understood how to turn her struggles, her sufferings and her successes into rich humanity.[71]

This impression of authentic experience was a vital part of the perception of the actress and one she took pains to convey in all her roles.

Notes

1. In fact, Magnani won the Nastro d'argento award in 1946 for 'best supporting actress' for her role in the film.
2. M. Wood, 'Woman of Rome', in Sieglohr, *Heroines Without Heroes: Reconstructing Female and national Identities in European Cinema, 1945–51*, 153.
3. Gabrielli, 'La stagione delle scelte 1943–45', in Carrattieri and Flores, *La Resistenza in Italia: storia, memoria, storiografia*, 27.
4. Landy, *Stardom Italian Style: Screen Performance and Personality in Italian Cinema*, 100.
5. Ibid., 100.
6. On the film's early reception, see Forgacs, '"*Rome, Open City*: Before and After Neorealism"', 301–13.
7. Pitassio, 'Popular Culture, Performance, Persona: Between *Rome, Open City* and *The Rose Tattoo*', 375.
8. Landy, *Stardom Italian Style*, 100.
9. See Olivieri and Castellano, *Le stelle del varietà: rivista, avanspettacolo e cabaret Dal 1936 al 1966*, 72–76.
10. Carrano, *La Magnani*, 124.
11. Bazin, discussed in Schoonover, *Brutal Vision: The Neorealist Body in Postwar Italian Cinema*, 66-67.
12. Aumont, *Du visage au cinéma*.
13. F. Patellani, 'Anna e' in collera con dio', *Tempo*, 15 June 1946, pages unnumbered.
14. By 'her sufferings', Patellani was referring mainly to her attachment to her sick son.
15. Rigoletto, '(Un)dressing Authenticity: Neorealist Stardom and Anna Magnani in the Postwar era (1945–48)', 394.
16. Brunetta, *Cent'anni di cinema italiano*, 373.
17. Sergio Amidei, quoted in M. Fini, 'Chi era Anna Magnani', *L'Europeo*, 11 October 1973, 85.
18. O'Rawe, '*Avanti a lui tremava tutta Roma*: Opera, Melodrama and the Resistance', 185–96.
19. Landy, *Stardom Italian Style*, 100.
20. Pitassio, 'Popular Culture, Performance, Persona', reflects on Magnani in typical performance mode, while Rigoletto, '(Un)dressing Authenticity' addresses the question of costume, 395–401.
21. Landy, *Stardom Italian Style*, 92. For a rare discussion of the issue, see Culhane, 'Street Cries and Street Fights: Anna Magnani, Sophia Loren and the *popolana*', 254–62.
22. Culhane, 'Street Cries and Street Fights'; Rigoletto, '(Un)dressing Authenticity', 399–400.
23. For example, in Blasetti's rural drama *Madre terra* and Camerini's period adaptation *Il cappello a tre punte*, released respectively in 1931 and 1934.
24. Castello, *Il divismo: mitologia del cinema*, 420.
25. See De Grazia, *How Fascism Ruled Women: Italy, 1922–1945*, Chapter 3.
26. Carrano, *La Magnani*, 124.
27. E. Colombo, 'Prefazione', in G. and A. Padellaro, *I non romani e Roma: testimonianze e confessioni*, vii.
28. Carrano, *La Magnani*, 18–19.
29. Anon, 'Dive in tribunale', *La Settimana Incom*, 1953, 38.
30. Marcus, 'Visconti's *Bellissima*: The Diva, the Mirror and the Screen', 15.
31. Castello, *Il divismo*, 420–21.
32. Ibid., 421.

33. Ibid., 420.
34. The issue of Magnani's authenticity is closely explored in Rigoletto, '(Un)dressing Authenticity'. See also Bayman, *The Operatic and the Everyday in Post-war Italian Film Melodrama*, 84.
35. Spinazzola, *Cinema e pubblico: lo spettacolo filmico in Italia, 1945–65*, 81.
36. Wood, 'Woman of Rome', in Sieglohr, *Heroines Without Heroes*, 153.
37. D. Calcagno, 'Paradiso delle tardone', *Tempo*, 30 November 1946, 36.
38. The issue is implicit in the subtitle of Culhane, 'Street Cries and Street Fights'.
39. Spinazzola, *Cinema e pubblico*, 9–10.
40. Castello, *Il divismo*, 420.
41. Spinazzola, *Cinema e pubblico*, 81.
42. Ibid.
43. Ibid.
44. Quoted in Faldini and Fofi, *L'avventurosa storia del cinema italiano: raccontata dai suoi protagonisti, 1935–1959*, 125.
45. See Garofalo, *L'italiana in Italia*.
46. Gabrielli, *Il 1946, le donne, la Repubblica*.
47. Faldini and Fofi, *L'avventurosa storia*, 125. See also Carrano, *La Magnani*, 162.
48. Faldini and Fofi, *L'avventurosa storia*, 125. See also Carrano, *La Magnani*, 162.
49. Franco Zeffirelli, quoted in Fini, 'Chi era Anna Magnani', 92.
50. Carrano, *La Magnani*, 146.
51. Faldini and Fofi, *L'avventurosa storia*, 199.
52. Spinazzola, *Cinema e pubblico*, 27.
53. For an account of the rally, with photographs, see S. Pallavicini, 'Risolviamo la crisi del nostro cinema', *La Settimana Incom*, 26 February 1949, 6–7.
54. Faldini and Fofi, *L'avventurosa storia*, 94. See also Carrano, *La Magnani*, 119.
55. Anon., 'Libertà di scambio e misure prottettive', *Araldo dello spettacolo*, 15 March 1947, page unnumbered.
56. Semeraro, *Rassegna dello spettacolo*.
57. See Anile and Giannice, *La guerra dei vulcani: Rossellini, Magnani, Bergman – storia di cinema e d'amore* and Gundle, 'Saint Ingrid at the Stake: Stardom and Scandal in the Bergman-Rossellini Collaboration', 64–79.
58. Faldini and Fofi, *L'avventurosa storia*, 248.
59. Ibid.
60. Marcus, 'Visconti's *Bellissima*', 10.
61. Ibid., 15–16.
62. Ibid., 10.
63. Anile, *Totalmente Totò: vita e opera di un comico assoluto*, 108.
64. Pitassio, 'Popular Culture, Performance, Persona', 382.
65. Ibid., 378.
66. Pierini, 'Recitazione e rotocalchi, movimento e fissità: Anna Magnani – 1945-1948', 412.
67. Pitassio, 'Popular Culture, Performance, Persona', 383.
68. Anon., 'Gala delle stelle at Grand Hotel', *Oggi*, 18 January 1948, 12–13.
69. Pierini, 'Recitazione e rotocalchi', 411.
70. Steimatsky, *The Face On Film*, 181n.
71. M. Quirico and V. Metz, 'Una diva antidiva allevata da una nonna', *Amica*, 15 (1968), 61.

CHAPTER 9
Andrea Checchi
Shadows of Defeat

In Mario Camerini's fast-paced 1939 department store comedy, *I grandi magazzini* (The Big Store), the Tuscan actor Andrea Checchi played a commercial artist and window dresser. His character, Maurizio, is seen on the shop floor setting out the mannequins, in his laboratory and in the staff room, where he engages in banter with the shopgirls. There is nothing special about Maurizio, though two facts give the audience an insight into him. First, it is revealed that he is really a painter, who, instead of pursuing his artistic ambitions, has opted for steady employment. Like many educated middle-class young men of the period, he has had to sacrifice his ambitions to pragmatism, giving up his aspiration to be an artist for a settled life. Second, he has recently separated from his wife Emilia, who also works at the store, and has rented a room while Emilia shares their marital accommodation with a fellow shop assistant. Maurizio is not an unsympathetic character. He is assured in his manner and directs the employees under his authority with brisk confidence. He is not averse to a joke, as when, much to the amusement of the shopgirls, he produces a mannequin with the features of Bruno, a store van driver who has caught the eye of Emilia's room-mate Lauretta. But his world is small, and his story unfolds on the margins of the central plot, which is dominated by Bruno and Lauretta. In keeping with the ideology of the time, the couple's difficulties are overcome when Emilia discovers she is pregnant. Enthused by the prospect of becoming a father to a child he imagines will be a son, Maurizio announces that he will move back into their home and makes plans to raise him with his wife. He insists the child must be called Raffaello because he will surely grow up to become an artist. In the final scene, when he and Emilia, accompanied by the newly united Bruno and Lauretta, leave the store together, they pause for a moment to admire a banal illuminated window display that Maurizio tells them with pride is the result of three days' work.

The film was a star vehicle in which the roles of Lauretta and Bruno were played by Assia Noris and Vittorio De Sica. Maurizio is a minor character, who is presented in an entirely realistic way. Unlike the film's leads, he has little of the polish or performative artificiality that typified many comedies of the time, even those of Camerini, which were known for their treatment of commonplace people. Checchi suited the part; on screen, he looks ordinary, being neither tall nor short, having slightly curved shoulders, hollow cheeks, thin lips and an aquiline nose. His swept-back dark brown hair, baritone voice and strong jawline give him a certain presence, but it would be hard to describe him as either unusually handsome or as possessed of the charm of De Sica. His character is dressed with less care than the staff who wear uniforms or who occupy managerial functions. His creativity is signalled by the fact that the points of his shirt collar stick up and his jackets look worn.

These downbeat qualities brought him to the attention of those critics who were starting to call for more realism in Italian films. Giuseppe De Santis, who would cast him as a returning soldier turned bandit in his 1947 debut film *Caccia tragica* (Tragic Hunt), recalled that he and others in the *Cinema* group held Checchi in high estimation: 'we saw in him a realistic actor, even his physique connected him in our opinion with the great school of French cinema, which we all admired.'[1] He and others failed to convince Visconti to cast him as Gino in *Ossessione*, since the director preferred Girotti's undisputed 'angelic' beauty, whereas Checchi 'was realism for realism's sake, with a straightforward physical presence that did not allow for ambiguity or idealisation'. The latter, De Santis added, was seen as an actor like Elio Marcuzzo (who played *lo spagnolo* in *Ossessione*), 'who we identified as ideal for our realist approach to Italian cinema'.[2] Lizzani, who would also cast him in the postwar years, took a similar view: 'I liked him a lot; he had a face that transitioned into neorealist cinema without difficulty because it was a real face. Though it was in some way associated with the period of the white telephones, it was a face that fitted.'[3]

Checchi appealed on account of his understated presence and controlled performance style. Unlike the stars of the Fascist period, he had few mannerisms. 'A Tuscan by birth, he was an actor who did not "play the Tuscan"', it would later be observed. 'After getting into the cinema without passing through the theatre ... he immediately acquired that sobriety of gesture, that performative economy that has always distinguished the different phases of his career'.[4] For another commentator: 'Among the actors who came to the fore in the prewar years, in a short time winning public attention, Andrea Checchi, with his stony and frowning persona, perhaps more than any other, established the bases of an intimate and pared-down style of acting that would find fuller expression in the florid season of neorealism.'[5] His dark hair and features, inherited from his Calabrian mother, gave him a look that was in tune with the southernist aesthetic of the movement.

Checchi's passage from prewar to postwar cinema is worth examining closely because of the issues it raises about acting and performance, the changing requirements of stardom and the success or otherwise of efforts to reinvent Italian cinema. Checchi was not only an actor who was identified as a possible bearer of a new cinema. He was also a man who had situated himself in the anti-fascist current that was beginning to take shape in the film world. As the war came to an end, his moment appeared to have arrived. As men like De Santis and Lizzani passed from theory to practice, he was cast in a number of significant and leading roles. Ultimately, however, this prominence did not translate into stardom, even though there were certain preconditions for this to occur. This failure reveals something of the way neorealism was out of step with at least some of the expectations of the public. It also shows how possessing some but not all the qualities of a star was not enough in a context in which there were several alternatives. The actor's biggest problem was the way many of his characters remained caught up in wartime situations or legacies. His persona came to be marked by an air of national defeat and personal displacement. As the reconstruction reached an end, he seemed anchored to the recent past and its disappointments rather than the hopes it had engendered.

Checchi was a member of that generation of actors who were recruited, without significant experience of theatre, to the courses of the newly opened Centro sperimentale film school. It was there that he would be introduced to a series of individuals who would widen his cultural horizons and lead him towards critical, and ultimately anti-fascist, ideas: De Santis and Lizzani, of course, but also the future screenwriter and director Gianni Puccini and the teacher and admirer of Soviet cinema Umberto Barbaro. Like many of his fellow students, he was able to pass easily from the school to the set. At a moment in which the escapist comedy was entering its heyday, there was a need for handsome young leads to pair with the many girls and young women who were also winning roles. Checchi was of the same generation as the timid Roberto Villa and the more manly Rossano Brazzi, all three having been born in 1915–16. However, he lacked their intrinsic lightness and was more suited to drama than light comedy. His tormented air was exploited in many roles in which he was to one degree or another frustrated or defeated. His difference led to comparisons with his fellow Tuscan Fosco Giachetti and to growing attention on the part of those who would call for more depth in Italian films.

Checchi's roles were principally those of antagonist or counterfoil to a more prominent name. 'He was always an "anti" or a support', one observer noted.[6] He was cast in several of the best and most prestigious films of the period including historical drama *Ettore Fieramosca* (Alessandro Blasetti, 1938), Spanish civil war film *L'assedio dell'Alcazar* (The Siege of the Alcazar, Augusto Genina, 1940), the literary adaptation *Malombra* (Mario Soldati, 1942) and the everyday comedy *Avanti c'è posto* (Take Your Places, Mario Bonnard, 1942). His range was wide and his playing varied, something that may have contributed to his failure to rise to the status of male lead. He was a dependable actor who could add tone and quality to a film; an actor who never seemed to exaggerate or to be seeking to draw the limelight. This consistency won him respect and recognition from that category of spectators who followed closely the personalities of Italian cinema.

One of his most significant, if not large, roles was as Pedro, a Francoist soldier, in *L'assedio dell'Alcazar*. The cast was dominated by Fosco Giachetti, whose pre-eminence in military films had been established in the same director's colonial drama *Lo squadrone bianco* (The White Squadron, 1936). Giachetti embodied an idea of dutiful self-sacrifice that required a foil – that is, an example of flawed masculinity with whom his characters could be contrasted and to whom they could impart a lesson. Antonio Centa often played just such a type. On this occasion it fell to Checchi. In the besieged Alcazar of Toledo, Pedro encounters his former lover Carmen, a worldly woman who has come to understand that she must set aside frivolity and assist the wounded. He rekindles his love for her but is confronted with the fact that she now has her eye fixed on a superior example of masculinity, the much respected Captain Vela, played by Giachetti. Mortally wounded during a dangerous mission, Pedro overcomes his jealousy to reveal to Vela before expiring that Carmen has fallen for him. He urges him to take care of her. The interesting thing about Pedro is that he is not a weak man who needs an example to help him towards redemption. He has already repudiated his dissipated past when he spots Carmen. He is simply a more multifaceted man than Vela; he has a backstory, and he does not see life purely in terms of his military calling. He enjoys female company and wants to build a future. Vela, by contrast, never shows more than a passing interest in Carmen and is entirely committed to present and future ideological battles.

Checchi was sixteen years younger than Giachetti, but their common Tuscan origins and melancholic air contributed to comparisons. Though Giachetti's background was in theatre, the two actors had a number of features in common. Neither was particular handsome or physically impressive. Each wore his dark hair combed backwards off the face. Both had a preference for drama over comedy and were disinclined to levity and smiles. Their voices were precise and resonant, rendered rich and characterful through cigarette consumption. Both were deemed suitable representatives of Fascist style masculinity and military roles, though Checchi was forever the 'young' actor, the support, while Giachetti only ever played leading roles. Giachetti, moreover, had a pronounced star aura.[7] Though he never seriously challenged Nazzari in mass popularity, he was well-known and admired as one of the key male actors of the period. He worked with most directors and played opposite almost all the leading women of the day. He was nearly always introduced in a compelling way, his allure often being compounded by his gruff manner and remoteness. As a younger man, Checchi was less 'formed'; he is dutiful but is also alert to romance and to sex. He makes mistakes and can fail; at times he is obliged to draw consequences from errors. If his face is shadowed, it is not to render him mysterious and interesting, like Giachetti, but to reflect a turmoil that is rarely entirely interiorized. Both men could be passionate and jealous, but only Checchi systematically lost out in love rivalries.

The detachment that sometimes marked his roles, and the humanity of his characters, lent flexibility to Checchi. It did not seem improbable to cast him as a romantic lead, particularly if his counterpart was young. One such example is the schoolgirl comedy *Ore 9 lezione di chimica*, (9 O'Clock Chemistry Lesson, Mario Mattoli, 1941) in which he is Prof. Marini, the chemistry teacher who makes all the girls swoon. The script's efforts to build up interest around him are not subtle. Before he even appears, the enthusiasm of the girls is evident; when he explains chemistry, they are shown making sketches of him or writing admiring comments in their notebooks. When a staff member seizes the pupils' diaries and discovers the effect he has on them, he is called in for admonishment by the head teacher, who advises him that he should be stricter, since 'you are young, charming and well-dressed; you have all the qualities to turn the head of a girl.' The girls' spirited ringleader Anna (played by Alida Valli) also admirers him. In the course of a flirtatious conversation she strikes up with her teacher, which has chemistry as its pretext, she disarmingly reveals that she could not care less about the subject. Somewhat surprisingly, he confesses that he is of the same opinion.

The film is perhaps the only one in which Checchi gets the girl or vice versa (he and Anna announce their engagement in the concluding scene), though in the context of a boarding school his rivals are few and unappealing. Yet, despite the popularity of the film, Checchi was not entirely persuasive as far as some critics were concerned. Pietro Bianchi, writing in the magazine *Bertoldo*, found that he was an implausible heart-throb:

> In the hands of Mattoli, Andrea Checchi does not seem well suited to exciting violent passions. He has a spotted bow tie and wears a black hat. Now, my dear Mattoli, it is not customary for elegant young men to wear bow ties, and black hats are a mark of suburban elegance borrowed from old American gangster films. And it cannot be claimed that these sartorial choices are made ironically, since the girls who frequent a costly boarding school are perfectly up-to-date with men's fashions. Not only, but your teacher is too humble, dear Mattoli, and, psychologically, this too is a little mistake. Women don't like humble types who talk about inequalities in social conditions. This is a discourse suited to seamstresses, for heaven's sake, and not even the heroes of the dear departed [nineteenth-century popular French author] Georges Ohnet, do it.[8]

A further attempt to give Checchi a seductive air is apparent in *Avanti c'è posto*. In a Roman film centred on Aldo Fabrizi as the tram conductor Cesare, Checchi has a supporting role as Bruno, a tram driver. As a workmate of Cesare, he is soon shown to be a man of a certain superficial charm, who jests with colleagues and chats easily with women. He boasts to a girl who has lost her job as a domestic servant after being robbed on a tram, and who Fabrizi has befriended, that he has known 'grand hotels and fantastic women'. As chauffeur to 'one of the best Roman families', he once travelled widely in Italy and abroad. It is the war, he says, that has led to a reduction in his circumstances. In contrast to Cesare's romantic sentimentalism, Bruno woos Rosella overtly, even impressing her with a display of his physical agility in the tramworkers' after-work gymnasium. However, he reveals a cynical side when he seeks to lure Rosella to his home and seduce her. She reacts with outrage at this bold overture and slaps him. 'I have always had fun with women and have never taken them seriously', he responds, adding wistfully, 'but this time it was different.' Following his rejection, Bruno quits his job and enrols in the army: an unambiguous signal in Fascist Italy of his reformed character and a conversion that soon finds its reward. As he marches through the street with the troops who will depart first for Naples and then Africa, he is joined by Rosella, who embraces him and hopes for his safe return.

Checchi's characters often exhibit a detachment from the occupations or functions that the realities of life have forced them to play. If they are not redeemed, then they are anyway ripe for it. *I grandi magazzini*'s Maurizio is a painter *manqué*, who still sees himself as an artist. Prof. Marini, far from seeking to inspire his uninterested pupil, confesses that he does not care much for chemistry himself, adding that 'in life you cannot always do want you want.' The tram driver Bruno sees himself still as participating in the high life as a rich man's chauffeur. All the characters have an air of the unfulfilled dreamer about them.

The repeated motif of detachment recalls Jean-Paul Sartre's existentialist notion of 'bad faith', as developed in his philosophical text *Being and Nothingness*.[9] The person who is in bad faith is engaged not precisely in lying (that is, communicating something he knows to be false) but rather in concealing the truth from himself. Sartre offers the examples of the waiter who is acting at being a waiter, or the grocer, tailor or auctioneer who 'endeavours to persuade their clientele that they are nothing but a grocer, an auctioneer, a tailor'. Society expects people to limit themselves to their social roles, Sartre argued. So 'a grocer who dreams is offensive to the buyer, because such a grocer is not wholly a grocer.' He should behave 'just as the soldier at attention makes himself into a soldier-thing with a direct regard which does not see at all, which is no longer meant to see . . .'. The circumstances that imprisoned a man in his function were numerous, 'as if we lived in perpetual fear that he might escape from it, that he might break away and suddenly elude his condition'.[10] For Sartre, the waiter who acted the waiter was offering a 'representation' for others and for himself. The waiter was the person he had to be and yet was not.[11] The bad faith lay in consciousness of this fact, though this was not developed to the point at which the role was refused or abandoned.

Checchi's characters do not entirely deceive themselves, and their bad faith is usually made evident to the audience. In some respects, their air of detachment from the mundane roles they perform is a realistic version of the misunderstandings and misidentifications that were such a common feature of the light or 'white telephone' comedies of the period. The artist forced to work for a store or the driver of luxury vehicles obliged to drive a tram were reflections of a widespread state of underachievement of life goals afflicting the petty bourgeoisie and of the limited prospects offered by the Italian economy.

Checchi himself was the son of an artist who had been constrained by economic circumstances to abandon his studio in Florence in 1930 – when Andrea was aged fourteen – and move his family to Rome, where they could count on the support of influential relatives.[12] This shift of fortune and circumstance affected the youngster, then a high school student, and had the unintended consequence of starting him off on an acting career. After he tried to run away from home to join the merchant navy, his father decided to find something for him to do. Seeing a recruitment advertisement for the Centro sperimentale, and knowing his son's admiration for the Roman variety performer Ettore Petrolini, he enrolled him without his knowledge (see Figure 9.1). There he met the director Blasetti, who, despite the young man's initial lack of commitment, became his advisor and, later, friend. The ease with which he progressed grated, however. 'Probably for this reason, I don't particularly like my profession', he later confessed.[13] Checchi always felt he had become a film actor by chance. He nurtured his own ambition to be a painter and, throughout his adult life, he practised art. Massimo Girotti was one of many friends in the film world who owned some of his work. It is probable that the painting that Maurizio presents as a wedding present to a shopgirl in *I grandi magazzini* is one of his own.

Checchi liked to see himself as awkward and contrarian. While Giachetti made little of his Florentine origins, he boasted of them: 'Sure, I am argumentative, picky and stubborn; I am a true Florentine', he confessed in one interview. 'I pick fights and am difficult to get on with because, like all Tuscans, I speak my mind . . . I am not the sort to try to be nice at all costs, who loves praise or who is in search of publicity.'[14] It was this attitude that first brought him trouble with the authorities. He was inclined to speak out of turn, to make unwelcome jokes and generally fail to conform. Rarely were his gestures sufficiently serious to warrant sanction, but they won him a reputation that would do him no harm in the postwar years. Checchi would cite a number of episodes himself, but others rest on third-party testimonies. One which stands out concerns an incident in which the actor was introduced to Mussolini.[15] The occasion was a private view of the newly completed *L'assedio dell'Alcazar*, which all the male actors had been required to attend attired in a Fascist black shirt. Patting Checchi on the back, the Duce complemented him for his part. 'Well, Your Excellency', the actor replied, 'you would certainly have been better than me.' Surprised, Mussolini paused then smiled and walked on. As Starace, the secretary of the Fascist Party glared at him, Checchi realized that he had in effect reduced the dictator to the level of a mere performer. His vanity prevented him from realizing that Mussolini would simply have been astonished at the sheer stupidity of his remark.

Figure 9.1 Andrea Checchi, the young actor while still a student at the Centro sperimentale film school, 1938. His performance in *I grandi magazzini* (The Big Store, Mario Camerini, 1939) brought him to the attention of Giuseppe De Santis and others (author's own collection).

During the war years, Checchi, like his colleagues, worked exceptionally hard, making as many as ten films per year.[16] Though his films belonged to many genres, including more military dramas, he would acquire a reputation for failing to conform in the expected manner. While shooting the Medieval-set drama *Il re d'Inghilterra non paga* (The King of England Won't Pay, Giovacchino Forzano, 1941), at the director's Tirrenia studio, he commissioned a jeweller in nearby Livorno to make a tiepin on which was mounted a coffee bean. The gesture followed the reduction of the Christmas coffee ration due to each adult to a mere six beans. Such an impertinent gesture on the part of a public figure was soon noticed. Word reached the editor of the local newspaper, which was owned by the foreign minister Galeazzo Ciano. The story of the coffee bean led to an article in which he was sharply denounced as 'a defeatist imbecile and a filthy anti-Italian'.[17]

Such episodes ensured that Checchi soon fell from favour. With no one to protect him, he was compelled to work for reduced pay. 'To the delight of producers, this was the first move by the Fascist zealots after the coffee bean incident', he later reminisced.[18] He claimed that his reputation for dissent led to him being cast, in war films, as the misfit or antagonist. 'I was always the insubordinate and anti-fascist officer who redeemed himself at the last minute; who had lived a bad life but died a good death.'[19] This perception of him was confirmed by actress Doris Duranti, with whom he acted, taking the leading male role of Baldo Princivalli, in *La contessa di Castiglione* (The Countess of Castiglione, Flavio Calzavara, 1942). In her memoirs, Duranti, who was a keen Fascist and the lover of Minister of Propaganda Alessandro Pavolini, recalled that she tried to block his being cast opposite her. 'I felt an irredeemable dislike for this individual (he had the air of a resentful servant, of one who spits in his master's coffee ... he even took the liberty of making grimaces at the mention of Mussolini's name.' Nonetheless, she invited him to her home so that they might go over the script together.[20] The jealous Pavolini immediately suspected an amorous relationship. A report in the Central State Archives reveals that friends, probably as a joke, tipped off the political police. Swiftly informed of goings on, the minister had burst into the flat and forced Checchi, who was allegedly attired solely in his undergarments, to flee at speed.[21]

In general, the actor did not participate in the social circles of the regime and nor, despite his artistic background, did he relax, like Nazzari, for example, in the bohemian milieu around the artists' road Via Margutta. He mixed more commonly with intellectual friends and cultivated an unkempt demeanour that seemed to signal his detachment from Fascism. Duranti described him as 'a wiry, young actor, with angry eyes, who bit his dirty nails and dressed like an outcast'. He rolled his own cigarettes, a habit that he incorporated into a number of his screen interpretations. The incident with Duranti apart, he appears to have led a quiet private life. In 1938, he married a fellow student at the Centro sperimentale, the Hungarian Erika Schwarze, who gave up her own ambitions to support him.

The end of the regime did not, for Checchi, herald any concerns about his future career beyond those deriving from larger events. He could count on a network of influential friends, who provided him with assistance. During the period of the German occupation, he joined the cast of *I dieci comandamenti*, a Vatican-backed film, which many used as an excuse to turn down pressing invitations to the north to take part in Freddi's cinema project in Venice. Later, he took refuge on Capri with the writer and director Mario Soldati and others. By 1944, he was firmly in the frame as an actor with the potential to make a contribution to reborn cinema. His anti-conformism stood him in good stead when ideas for the rebirth of Italian cinema began to take concrete shape. In a two-part article evaluating Italy's screen actors published in the magazine *Star* in 1944, Antonio Pietrangeli singled Checchi out for praise. He was

> *a young actor whose commitment goes far beyond the scholastic and merely performative is Andrea Checchi, who for his intelligence and range (range that is greater than that of any other actor in Italy today can boast) has been revealing himself with a fine crescendo one of our most lively actors who we can always count on, with a sure heart.*[22]

With each role, Checchi had been able to create a memorable presence, to delineate a character and naturalize himself within a given social and physical environment. His characters were mostly petit bourgeois; he could be a schoolteacher, a soldier, an artist or a businessman. Occasionally, he played working class men or peasants but never an aristocrat.

In this context, it was no surprise that directors repeatedly turned to him in the postwar years. However, no one thought to remould or reconfigure him in the way that Visconti had done with Girotti. Though his roles were by no means all of the same type, there was a striking continuity between some of his prewar work, especially in military films, and the type of character he played afterwards. If he had found that, in some films, he was 'in demand for "bad guy" parts, bad guys, however, who in daily life had much tenderness in their hearts',[23] then it was because there was an abrasiveness to his persona that could not easily be expunged. Nonetheless, there were nuances and variations. In *Due lettere anonime* (Two Anonymous Letters, Mario Camerini, 1945), he is a jaded soldier returning from the Russian front who at first is interested only in putting the war behind him while others are planning resistance activities. He discovers that his fiancée, played by Clara Calamai (see Chapter 6), has not waited for him but got together with a fellow worker, with whom she now lives. Gradually, he overcomes his depression and contributes to the Resistance to the extent that he is imprisoned for his actions. In short, he redeems himself – in the new way that postwar circumstances would demand – but his character is not sympathetic or truly positive. The critic Pietro Bianchi dubbed him 'a little Italian who lets himself go because his sweetheart has dumped him'.[24] His character is far removed from the unambiguous heroism of Manfredi and Francesco in *Roma città aperta* (Rome Open City, Roberto Rossellini, 1945), figures of men who were equal to the drama unfolding around them. Nevertheless, he won a Nastro d'argento (Silver Ribbon) critics' award for his performance.

Checchi enjoyed a certain standing among filmgoers. A survey of readers that the magazine *Star* conducted at the end of 1945 revealed that Fosco Giachetti was the most popular Italian actor, while Checchi came seventh after Gino Cervi, Amedeo Nazzari, Carlo Ninchi, Massimo Girotti and Roldano Lupi.[25] The readers' comments that were published to accompany the poll suggested that the actor was identified with a model of masculinity that resonated with values endorsed by Fascism: 'I go crazy for Checchi because he is a truly "macho" type', wrote F. Marongin of Rome, while Orazio Strano of Catania asserted that Fosco Giachetti, Enzo Fieramonte and Andrea Checchi were 'types who are suited to all "oceanic" currents', deploying a term that had been regularly used to describe the crowds who were assembled for Fascist rallies.

This perception, which was shared by the film industry, would profoundly influence the way he would be used in the rest of the decade. Checchi was in demand mostly as a supporting actor. In 1946, he appeared in six films, and in 1947, five. At a time when the industry was struggling, this was a measure of his versatility. However, most of his roles were inflected with the past. His characters were men burdened in some measure by events – men who had chosen the wrong side or who were struggling to fit in. They carried an air of defeat about them, which was suggestive of a past that now carried little value. In the early 1940s, it was suggested on his death in 1974 that 'he was at risk of becoming a surrogate for Fosco Giachetti because they gave him parts that were unsympathetic or tormented and argumentative.'[26] His own talent, and the continuing popularity of the original, saved him from this fate. In the postwar years, he in effect became the vehicle through which the persona of Giachetti was inserted into different contexts and remodelled or displaced. This point requires some explanation because Giachetti himself was still active and would conserve his standing with the public until around 1950. The problem was that many new directors had no wish to work with an actor who, while respected for his craft, had forged a persona that was entirely in tune with Fascism and its wars. Giachetti was never detached about his acting, which he took extremely seriously; his characters, though in some respects varied, were always linear and intense. They were men of iron principle and inflexible devotion to their chosen cause or profession. If Nazzari was bypassed by the major figures of neorealism, then all the more so was Giachetti, despite the fact that the Florentine actor had never personally aligned himself with the regime.[27]

In the postwar years, he revealed his socialist sympathies and gave his support to the parties of the left. Checchi was more malleable. As a younger actor, with a sentimental side, whose characters had often changed or improved over time, he was more suited to the requirements of democratic film-makers. However, these qualities did not prevent him from being called upon to play abrasive, unlikeable characters. He was an actor appreciated by neorealism who would be given the task of playing angry or displaced individuals who had ended up on the wrong side of history.

In a number of instances, the anger of his characters was directed against women. In many of his interwar films, he played men who forged relationships with women only to lose them through their own errors or imperfections. Whether they are rough or debonair, they tend to be jealous and irascible. In postwar films, they react against female autonomy; they assert a proprietorial authority that is backward with respect to the female emancipation that was most visibly expressed in the extension of the franchise. As Patrizia Gabrielli has remarked, the participation of women in elections to the Constituent Assembly in June 1946 'undermined a concept of citizens' rights as masculine territory', a concept that organized the rights and obligations of men and women 'according to a hierarchical division'.[28] This democratic advance registered a backlash, which is evident in the possessiveness of the wastrel Roberto, who has set his sights on Valentina Cortese's enterprising schoolteacher in *Un Americano in vacanza* (An American on Holiday, Luigi Zampa, 1946), the jealous anger of Isa Miranda's former partner in *Au-delà des grilles* (The Walls of Malapaga, René Clément, 1949) when she falls for Jean Gabin, and the suicidal impulse of the man who has lost the woman he loves in *Roma città libera* (Rome, Free City, Marcello Pagliero, 1946), a film entirely constructed around the theme of suicide.

Checchi knew that while some considered him handsome he had the countenance of a tough guy, as Mino Doletti, editor of *Film*, had noted in 1942.[29] Though he never specialized in negative parts, like, say, Folco Lulli, whose burly physique and boxer's countenance limited his range, a negative current runs through many of his roles. For Checchi to have acquired star status in the later 1940s, he would have needed to overcome this, or at least to have balanced it with powerful parts with a more positive inflection. Another actor who risked becoming typecast in this way was Vittorio Gassman, who played the gangster Walter in *Riso amaro* (Bitter Rice, Giuseppe De Santis, 1949).[30] However, Gassman carried no baggage from the recent past and had a stage career to fall back on. Checchi, by contrast, ran the risk of forging an unappealing gallery of bullies, spies, gangsters and thugs. Moreover, the actor's characters often entered films with no fanfare or build-up. He enters casually, when the action is underway and without any special expectation. In *I grandi magazzini*, he enters the store's noisy staff room, but the camera follows his estranged wife as she hastily exits. In the rural melodrama *Tragica notte* (Tragic Night, Mario Soldati, 1942), his character Nanni appears in the first scene as one of four poachers plotting to capture and punish a burly gamekeeper who is responsible for them having spent time in prison. Though Soldati claimed that, in contrast to Delfino Cinelli's novel, Nanni, rather than the dutiful gamekeeper, was intended to be the hero of the story, critics found that none of the characters was truly appealing.[31] It is Checchi's character Nanni who carries out the cowardly beating – which the victim bears stoically – while the poacher's accomplices hold him down. Openings of this sort, devoid of diegetic fanfare, did not flatter him, and their persistence in the postwar years did not assist him in achieving the status of protagonist that his talents seemed to warrant.

The measure of his standing, probably unknown to him, was made apparent when Dino De Laurentiis rejected Alberto Lattuada's proposal to give him the lead role in *Il bandito* (The Bandit, 1946). The producer favoured Amedeo Nazzari, who he knew to have box office appeal.[32] To make his point, he led Lattuada into the street where he showed people two photographs, only one of which was universally recognized (see Chapter 9).

In 1946, Checchi was aged thirty and was still considered a young actor. He was well regarded and a recognized talent. But, aside from his cinematic past, there were other things that did not work in his favour. He seemed uninterested in the business of stardom. At a time when few Italian films were being released, actors took to the theatre, participated in the juries of beauty contests, played in charity football matches, made themselves available to the press or otherwise cultivated an aura of celebrity in the hope of better times to come. Checchi, by contrast, did nothing to enhance his standing with the public. There was also an issue around his physical presence. He inhabited all his roles intelligently and occupied the cinematic space with an economy and measure that stood as witness to his mastery of his art. However, his features bore evidence of hard times. His broad mouth and thin lips rarely broke into a smile. His hollowed cheeks and dark-rimmed eyes suggested hunger and suffering. His head dominated his wiry body and his screen presence. A man of average height and build, he did not cut an impressive figure or communicate a sense of strength. At a time when changing tastes and audience composition – in combination with competition from returned American stars – all worked in favour of a more immediately physical type of stardom in which sex appeal was central, he seemed to convey a cerebral idea of masculinity – expressed in interiority and self-containment – that derived from interwar French cinema and that, in the postwar years, would continue to be carried forward by an actor like Serge Reggiani.

In 1946, De Santis cast Checchi in his debut film *Caccia tragica*. Produced by Giorgio Agliani for the partisans' association ANPI, the film explored the difficulties of returning soldiers and the struggle of agricultural cooperatives to assert control over the land. The lead roles were taken by Massimo Girotti and Carla Del Poggio as newly-weds who are involved with the workers in their battle against the landowners' guards. Alberto (Checchi) is an unemployed former soldier who has thrown in his lot with a gang of outlaws led by a one-time collaborationist nicknamed Lili Marlene (Vivi Gioi), with whom he is conducting an affair. Alberto, who is known to Girotti and others, is not fundamentally evil, and he is given the chance to redeem himself after he kills Lili Marlene to prevent her from setting off land mines in the fields. After a workers' trial at which Girotti takes his defence, he is allowed to go free. As he walks away, the workers throw clumps of earth at him in a mock punishment that also serves to reintegrate him with nature. The ending anticipates a similar scene at the end of the director's next feature, *Riso amaro* (Bitter Rice, 1949), in which the rice workers throw fistfuls of rice over the dead body of a fellow worker who has betrayed them. Also in 1947, he renewed his partnership with Clara Calamai in the aviation drama *Ultimo amore* (Last Love, Luigi Chiarini). Once more, he is cast as a servant of the Fascist state who redeems himself by aligning himself with the King after 8 September 1943. For this honourable gesture, he pays with his life. His characters often change or reveal a double dimension that may take the form of the revelation of disappointed aspirations, the unveiling of a nature that is better than first appears, or the insertion within the narrative of a process of improvement or redemption. In *La primula bianca* (The White Primrose, Carlo Ludovico Bragaglia, 1947), he is introduced as a professional criminal, a safe-cracker, who turns out to be a policeman.

Checchi's contemporary films of the later 1940s and after provided him with occasional opportunities to free himself of roles inflected with the traumas of the recent past. *Il grido della terra* (The Earth Cries Out, Duilio Coletti, 1949), a Lux-produced drama about the founding of the state of Israel, saw him ally himself with the political aspirations of Zionism. He is a man who has suffered and who places himself at the service of those who have suffered more. In 1951, Lizzani gave him the part of the industrialist in *Achtung! Banditi!*, his cooperatively produced drama set in wartime Genoa. As a critic turned director, and member of the PCI, Lizzani was among those who had long had a high regard for Checchi as an actor and a physical type. The industrialist – or 'the engineer' as he is listed in the credits – is a bourgeois who needs to be persuaded by the workers in his factory of the need to take a stand against the occupying German forces, who want to dismantle and appropriate machinery (see Figure 9.2). The workers' leader Marco is played by Lamberto Maggiorani, the unemployed Antonio in *Ladri di biciclette* (Bicycle Thieves, Vittorio De Sica, 1948), which carried connotations of the positive hero deriving from his class origin and previous role. Marco and his fellows hide the machinery from the Germans, while the engineer turns a blind eye. Checchi gave a powerful performance as a man who must assume a responsibility that will ultimately lead to his death. His frown and melancholy are deployed to fine effect. Both he and Maggiorani's Marco are executed off-screen in the director's tribute

Figure 9.2 Andrea Checchi as a factory boss who lends support to the Resistance in *Achtung! Banditi!* (Carlo Lizzani, 1951) (screenshot by the author).

to those who gave their lives for the nation's freedom. However, the film, which was released six years after the end of the war, was a late example of Resistance drama. It cast Checchi back to the war period, even if it aligned him with the side of justice and freedom.

By this time, Checchi's commercial standing was low. Already in 1947 he had written to De Santis to inform him that, in Naples, *Caccia tragica* had had a low profile release and 'naturally my name [on the poster] was the last.'[33] Now publicity posters for *Achtung! Banditi!* were dominated by the face of a beauty queen turned actress who was just beginning to make her mark, Gina Lollobrigida, even though her role in the film was a small one. Moreover, her character is initially disengaged from the central action. On her very first appearance, she confesses that she cannot wait for the war to end so she can go once more to the beach at Portofino.

Checchi would continue to appear in a variety of period and contemporary films until the mid 1950s. But he failed to make himself an indispensable figure in postwar cinema. The utter marginality of his presence in the advertising for *Achtung! Banditi!* was not unusual. Even in the poster for 1942's *Avanti c'è posto*, alongside Aldo Fabrizi it is the character actor Virgilio Riento who provides the counterfoil. Though he ostensibly had the lead role in *Il grido della terra*, he was overshadowed on posters by his screen partner, Marina Berti. In *Caccia tragica*, Girotti and Del Poggio filled the space. The poster for *Roma città libera* is particularly telling. While a large portrait of Valentina Cortese occupies the central space, Checchi is barely more than a silhouette, a shadow presence that stands as a cipher for general crises and the displacement of others. For a man of reserve who cared little for the vanities of stardom, such matters were more an irritation than a major concern. Unfortunately, they were a harbinger of an effacement that would soon affect his very place in the film industry.

Notes

1. Gili and Grossi, *Alle origini del neorealismo: Giuseppe De Santis a colloquio con Jean A. Gili*, 49.
2. Ibid., 51. Marcuzzo, 'lo spagnolo' of *Ossessione*, had also studied at the Centro sperimentale and was known to his associates as an anti-fascist actor. He was killed by partisans in the Treviso area in the spring of 1945 after being mistaken for a Fascist spy. See Sciarra, *Quizario del cinema italiano*, 125–27.
3. C. Lizzani, 'A proposito di *Achtung! Banditi!*' extra content on DVD *Achtung! Banditi!* (Warner Brothers 'I classic del cinema italiano', 2010).
4. Anon., 'Un attore per tutte le stagioni', *Tempo*, 12 April 1974, 15.

5. L. Autera, 'L'attore Andrea Checchi stroncato da un morbo virale', *Corriere della sera*, 30 March 1974, 14.
6. Anon., 'Un attore per tutte le stagioni', 15.
7. See Gundle, *Mussolini's Dream Factory: Film Stardom in Fascist Italy*, Chapter 9.
8. Bianchi, *L'occhio di vetro: il cinema degli anni 1940–1943*, 102. The review was published on 5 December 1941.
9. Sartre, *Being and Nothingness*.
10. Ibid., 102.
11. Ibid., 103.
12. T. Torri, 'Adesso il suo amore è la pittura', *Settimana TV*, 23 February 1974, 22.
13. L. Alimandi, 'Prende il caffè bestemmiando il gentiluomo pittore della TV', *Settimana TV*, no. 20 1970, 37.
14. Ibid., 37.
15. Ibid., 37.
16. He made five in 1939, ten in 1940, five in 1941 and eight in 1942.
17. A. Checchi, 'Una bella ragazza in ascensore è stata la mia unica avventura', *Gente*, 6 November 1971, 48.
18. Ibid., 49.
19. Ibid., 49.
20. Duranti, *Il romanzo della mia vita*, 136–37.
21. Archivio Centrale dello Stato, Segretaria particolare del Duce, carteggio riservato, b.48, f. Pavolini Alessandro. A note dated 26 January 1942 reports Pavolini's fury on finding a partially dressed Checchi at Duranti's home.
22. A. Pietrangeli, 'Gli attori', *Star*, 30 September 1944, 13.
23. A.M.M., 'Un solo grande amore: la moglie Erika', *Stop*, 13 April 1974, 15–16.
24. P. Bianchi, '*Due lettere anonime*' (1946), in Bianchi, *L'occhio di vetro*, 26.
25. Anon., 'Alida Valli batte Clara Calamai', *Star*, 5 January 1946, 5.
26. Anon., 'Un attore per tutte le stagioni', *Tempo*, 12 April 1974, 15.
27. When Giachetti was rejected for a part in Visconti's *Vaghe stelle dell'Orsa* (*Sandra*, 1965), he reacted badly. In reply, Oscar Brazzi of the Vides production company told him bluntly: 'Mr Giachetti, the time for fierce faces – of the type to which you were accustomed – finished a while ago . . . The cinema of today, which is free, civil, artistic and professional, is not suited to you.' Archivio Centrale dello Stato, Folder 'Vaghe stelle dell'Orsa', letter from Brazzi to Giachetti, 26 September 1964.
28. Gabrielli, *Il 1946: le donne, la repubblica*, 153.
29. Checchi, 'Una bella ragazza in ascensore', 49.
30. See Ceratto, *Caterina Boratto: la donna che visse tre volte*, 198.
31. Morreale, *Mario Soldati: le carriere di un libertino*, 270–75.
32. Faldini and Fofi, *L'avventurosa storia del cinema italiano: raccontata dai suoi protagonisti, 1935–1959*, 116.
33. Centro sperimentale di cinematografia, Fondo Giuseppe De Santis, Corrispondenza 1944–1947, letter to Andrea Checchi and De Santis, 5 December 1947.

PART III

Popular Idols for New Times

This part of the book is concerned with the stars who achieved great popularity in the late 1940s and early 1950s. Two of them, Totò and Amedeo Nazzari, had been active since the 1930s or before. However, there was no simple continuity between their prewar and postwar work. The variety performer Totò only made a handful of films before 1943, which had not done well. With more sympathetic direction and a freedom to create his own unique screen presence, the films he made from 1948 would prove to be hugely successful. It is no exaggeration to state that the recovery and growth of the film industry from the late 1940s was largely powered by the box office bankability of this prolific star. Nazzari had established himself as the leading film star of the Fascist period. His re-emergence was an unexpected development. Still popular at the end of the war, he had migrated to Spain and then Argentina after offers of work at home declined. His return in a series of popular melodramas was indicative of a certain continuity in gender ideals and tastes. However, the Nazzari of the 1950s was a different star to that of the pre-1943 era. He worked exclusively in popular cinema and mainly in one genre instead of several.

The remaining three stars under consideration here all emerged in the postwar years and were products of the mixture of commercial and political impulses of the transition. Silvana Mangano became an overnight success thanks to her role as a sultry rice worker in De Santis's *Riso amaro* (Bitter Rice). Her subsequent career was planned by her producer-husband Dino De Laurentiis, who carefully moulded her into a key asset of the company he founded with Carlo Ponti and of the Italian film industry in general. Silvana Pampanini did not benefit from strategic guidance of this sort. After coming to prominence in the first Miss Italia contest in 1946, she appeared in a large number of popular, low-budget films, many of them musical in theme. The two Silvanas represented the different faces of the film industry, the first directed tendentially towards the international market and the second towards the rapidly expanding audience of the provinces and the south. The final chapter deals with Raf Vallone, a new male star, who, like Mangano and Pampanini, was not a trained actor. After making his debut alongside Mangano in *Riso amaro*, he went on to create a rough-hewn star persona that was combative and charismatic. A politically engaged actor, Vallone endeavoured also to embody progressive figures on screen. All five would contribute to the establishment of a new star system that would constitute one of the strengths of the film industry in the phase of its greatest expansion. They spoke to the dramas and desires of the Italians as postwar reconstruction came to an end and the country embarked on the path to economic growth. With their strongly physical presence and the lower-class connotations of most, they provided a means whereby once marginalized sectors of the population were represented and indeed granted dignity within the national culture.

CHAPTER 10

Totò
Jester of the Republic

No performer was more important to the recovery and expansion of Italian cinema in the postwar years than Totò, the stage name of Neapolitan comedian Antonio De Curtis. A master of both physical and verbal humour, De Curtis did not devote himself predominantly to cinema until 1950. Much, if not all, of his screen work, moreover, was informed by the repertoire he had built up over many years of performing on the stage in various types of popular theatre. Some films, including *Yvonne la nuit* (Giuseppe Amato, 1949), *I pompieri di Viggiù* (The Firemen of Viggiù, Mario Mattoli, 1949) and *Totò a colori* (Totò in Colour, Steno, 1952), situated him in a theatrical world in which he played either his established stage persona or characters loosely inspired by it. Many others incorporated gags and routines refined before live audiences. Yet the huge number of films he made between the late 1940s and the mid 1950s – the period that saw the rapid expansion of cinema as popular entertainment and its triumph over other forms of spectacle – ensured that he soon became best known as a screen performer. For many filmgoers with little or no previous experience of the medium, their whole experience of cinema was inseparable from the character of Totò.[1] The films were often top box office earners that remained in distribution in the provinces for years after their initial release.

Comedians are sometimes excluded from discussions of stars and stardom because they do not occupy the same place in collective and individual fantasies as the stars of genres like drama, adventure or romantic comedy. Spectators do not project themselves on to them or make them the object of erotic fantasies in the same way. Their personas, rarely configured as authentic, are often obvious constructs, which remain constant over time. As Douglas Riblet suggests, comedian comedy 'requires not only a recognisable star but also a consistent comic persona, with the comedy designed around and for this persona'.[2] Not only do comedians not usually conform to established canons of physical beauty; they may also possess a voice – indicated by Martin Shingler as 'the distinctive and defining feature of the star's persona' – which is itself a trigger of laughter.[3] However, there are numerous reference works on stars of comedy in international cinema, and to think of the Italian star system without comedians would be an absurdity.[4] Not only did comedy actors – starting with Aldo Fabrizi and including occasionally Totò – also take on dramatic or semi-dramatic roles. They possessed unrivalled power as box office attractions. Indeed, by this measure, comedians were among the most significant stars in postwar Italian cinema.

Totò, in particular, was such a guarantee of good box office earnings – especially in the second and third-run cinemas of the provinces and the south, where the entertainer found his most loyal fans – that producers competed to place him under contract. The fact that his name appears in the title of approximately one third of his films is indicative of his sure-fire appeal. Comedy expanded in the postwar years, challenging the well-established supremacy of musical genres and melodrama.[5] The regular employment of numerous male vaudeville performers, including the Neapolitans Nino Taranto and Peppino De Filippo, the Romans Aldo Fabrizi and Renato Rascel and the northerner Erminio Macario, testify that this expansion was star-driven. Fabrizi was the most versatile as well as the most successful in the years following his acclaimed performance in *Roma città aperta*. However, between the late 1940s and the mid 1950s, Totò established himself as the dominant figure in the genre and indeed as the pre-eminent entertainer in the country.

There have been several biographies and numerous studies of the Neapolitan comedian and his screen work.[6] Most of these date from the 1980s and after, when thanks to a rediscovery, which began a few years after his death in 1967, and to repeated television screenings of his films,[7] he acquired a new audience among the young. The declared aim of these studies and memoirs is to win recognition and respect for a performer who was often dismissed by critics in his lifetime. As a result, a great deal is known about the rich cultural heritage of Neapolitan popular theatre from which he emerged, and which formed his main source of inspiration, his rise to prominence in variety theatre and show revues in the interwar period, and an intense film career amounting to more than one hundred credits. The unique comic creativity of Totò has been amply explored, as well as the peculiarities of the person of his creator, Antonio De Curtis. The volume *Totò: l'uomo e la maschera*, co-authored by Goffredo Fofi and Franca Faldini, his companion for the last fifteen years of his life, first brought the private man fully into view. This body of work is of great assistance in seeking to identify his place in the star system and the production context of his films. For Totò's success said much about postwar culture and the film industry's efforts to win back the domestic market from Hollywood.

One problem facing anyone wishing to investigate the Totò phenomenon concerns the difficulty of identifying exactly who he is. At one level, Totò is an actor whose name appears in the credits of films like that of any other artist. But unlike, say, Fabrizi, Toto is also a character who bears a distant resemblance to Chaplin's little tramp. He is a puppet-like everyman who is identified by his baggy trousers and trademark derby bowler hat. In fact, Totò only appears on occasion in this costume, usually when he is performing a theatrical routine, as in the revue film *I pompieri di Viggiù*. The 'Totò' who features in films like *Tototarzan* (Mario Mattoli,

Figure 10.1 Totò played a living corpse or an automaton in some of his prewar performances. He toyed once more with the macabre in *Totò cerca casa* (Totò Seeks a Home, Steno and Monicelli, 1949) when his homeless family finds accommodation in a cemetery (screenshot by the author).

1950) and *Totò le Mokò* is not this Totò, though he exhibits the same physical attributes and capacity for disarticulated movement, as well as certain comic traits such as a strongly instinctive nature and an uncontainable attraction to beautiful women. Rather he is a film character, not by chance named Antonio (or its diminutive Totò), who is played by the actor Totò. In the former, he is a Tarzan type who has been raised in the jungle and, in the latter, a street musician turned tough-guy gangster. But Totò the actor can also be multiple screen characters, some of whom scarcely resemble at all the Totò character, as in *Totò terzo uomo* (Totò, the Third Man, Mario Mattoli, 1951) in which he plays three brothers, two of whom have some of the characteristics of Totò the character but only one of whom is actually called Totò (and who introduces himself – when brought into a chaotic courtroom in the midst of a dispute between the other brothers – with the phrase 'Sono Totò, il terzo uomo'). The public emergence of the man behind the mask in the postwar period led to further complications but never to the appearance of the name of Antonio De Curtis in the opening credits. The actor tried to keep his off-stage self and his performer self utterly distinct, but the inconsistent relationship between man and mask, character and actor, lent intrigue and complexity to a much-loved performer whose appeal in part lay in his predictability.

In the prewar years, Totò was mainly known for his stage work. His occasional forays into cinema were not regarded as successes. His fame was not that of great stage actors of the period like Ermete Zaccini, Ruggero Ruggeri and Armando Falconi. Rather, he enjoyed the popularity that was reserved to comics and song and dance performers. Straight men and chorus girls were his typical fellow cast members. He won acclaim for the way he was able to take on the characteristics of a puppet, a mannequin or a cadaver. With his long face and bent nose, he already had a distinctive look. The ability he displayed to move his arms, legs and neck in a disarticulated, robotic manner provoked amazement and hilarity. Not only could he lean his upper body forward in a way that appeared to defy gravity, he was able to extend his neck and apparently slide his head from side to side across his shoulders in an inhuman fashion. These qualities had led to him entering the theatrical world as an imitator of 'puppet comedian' Gustavo De Marco, a popular entertainer of the early twentieth century with a similar capacity for disarticulation.[8] But Totò was no mere contortionist or pale copy, and he quickly established his own stage personality.[9] He could sing and dance; he had a strong resonant voice, a sense of timing and a capacity for verbal invention and improvization that made him the equal of the best stage performers of the day.

Popular theatre in the interwar years took several forms: there were lavish revues, which catered to the well-to-do, stage shows of more limited ambition known as *avanspettacolo*, which preceded the showing of new films, and sketch-based variety entertainment, which reached a wider lower-class audience. All enjoyed a popular following, and the latter two even enjoyed a measure of intellectual credibility. Critics may have paid these spectacles little attention compared to prose theatre, but they possessed an energy and vitality that intrigued younger intellectuals, who approved of their anarchic verve and easy absorption of avant-garde influences. Naples in particular had been a significant centre of the Futurist movement, and the latter's openness to all the technical and communicative innovations of the period was exemplified by popular theatre's constant innovation. Totò was part of this milieu as a sort of automaton; not quite human, he was a living corpse or 'amusing phantom', to use Marco Ramperti's term (see Figure 10.1).[10]

For Alberto Anile, the suspension between life and death lent him a persistent macabre aspect that would find few echoes in the postwar years.[11] In the nineteenth century, Collodi had laid a precedent by representing the Italians of his time who had not yet been turned into conscious citizens as the wooden boy Pinocchio.[12] In the interwar period, Totò's embodiment of the dead, the semi-human or the quasi-human draws parallels with the somnambulist Cesare of Robert Wiene's *The Cabinet of Dr Caligari* (1919). While Cesare, who is manipulated to commit murder by his evil controller, was seen by the film's leftist writers as a symbol of the masses who had been sent to slaughter in World War I, Totò was the unwitting symbol of the masses of Italians who provided fodder for the choreographed rituals of Mussolini's regime and who would fight the dictator's wars.[13]

Born in 1898, Totò grew up as a street child in the poor Sanità quarter of Naples. Though his father boasted a noble lineage, he had not married Totò's lower-class mother and not did allow him to use his surname of De Curtis until he was already an adult. Poverty and hunger would be daily experiences that would shape the future entertainer and provide a source for his comedy. Through stage colleagues, he absorbed traits of both the *commedia dell'arte* and classical comedy, although the original Greek texts were probably not known to him. In discussions of Totò, the Neapolitan mask of Pulcinella is often mentioned, also because the latter was a stock character in Neapolitan puppetry. Though Totò did not share Pulcinella's chicken-like shape and pot belly, his chicken walk routine established an ideal link. A wily character who always ends up on the side of the winner, the mask is self-interested and often unctuous. He has a double nature, leaving others uncertain as to whether he is intelligent or ignorant. He is proud and sensual, a workshy sub-proletarian with an ability to adopt the mannerisms of different social classes. Critics have differed over the influence of Pulcinella on the Totò persona. For Goffredo Fofi, the comedian mingled with the actors who played the mask and first took to the stage in farces featuring him. 'He took from Pulcinella that which was essential', he asserts.[14] Anile, by contrast, prefers to widen the range of influences to include Harlequin as well as Pulcinella, not to mention the Neapolitan comedies of Eduardo Scarpetta and the contemporary actor-playwright Eduardo De Filippo, in addition to Gustavo De Marco, the Roman satirical actor Ettore Petrolini and the artistic avant-garde.[15]

Though he would not successfully take to cinema until the late 1940s, De Curtis began his career in the age of the movies, and the great silent comedians fascinated him.[16] The writers of stage comedy and revues sometimes explicitly referenced them in titles, songs and situations. Though some saw elements of Buster Keaton and Groucho Marx in Totò, he would mostly be compared to Chaplin, who achieved worldwide fame in the mid 1910s with the short films he made for the Essanay and Mutual companies. The two actors shared a background of poverty and hardship, and the personas of both were those of lower-class outsiders determined to survive despite their physical inferiority and lack of means. They both ran rings round their betters and were attracted to beautiful women. Totò's stock costume, moreover, bore some resemblance to that of Chaplin's little tramp, with his bowler hat, little jacket, baggy trousers, walking cane and clownish shoes. In his not entirely reliable autobiography, Chaplin claimed to have based his outfit on a real man he had observed, a down-and-out who was struggling to preserve a modicum of self-esteem.[17] Totò preferred to give the impression that his costume was the result of improvization. 'My wardrobe was very limited and I had to make do with whatever I could find: an over-sized tailcoat, a pair of trousers that were too short and ridiculous, which showed off some tacky coloured socks with stripes, and a bowler hat', he claimed. 'I was missing a tie', he went on, 'so I took a shoelace and knotted it around my shirt collar. That was an ingenious touch! The result was a hard-up but dignified "little man" who throws into crisis the "system" of which he is a part by the illogical and ridiculous use of the very elements that that very "system" has placed at his disposal'.[18]

Comparisons between the two comedians were invited by a one act show of 1930 entitled *Totò, Charlot per amore* (Totò, Charlie For the Sake of Love) in which

Totò impersonates one Pirolini, a comic actor and Chaplin imitator, in order to approach a great screen diva for whom he cultivates a passion. De Curtis plays Totò, who passes himself off as Pirolini taking off Chaplin, in a series of parodies and impersonations that resembled a comical set of Russian dolls.[19] The show was a farce that was lavishly populated with more than the usual quota of chorus girls, but the critics were most impressed with the bravura central performance. 'Totò has perfectly grasped the bitter irony of his great colleague of the screen. He has penetrated his spirit, persuasively imitated his makeup, and evoked perfectly gestures which have been consecrated by kilometres of film and are known the world over', noted one reviewer.[20]

However, the Chaplin association would not always work in his favour. In his first two films, *Fermo con le mani* (Keep Your Hands Off Me, Gero Zambuto, 1937) and *Animali pazzi* (Crazy animals, Carlo Ludovico Bragaglia, 1939), the Totò stage character is dropped into ostensibly humorous situations (a beauty parlour in the first, a mental hospital for animals in the second) without adaptation. While the gags are indisputably visual, they stand out as staged numbers. They are stiff and lack naturalness. His performance in the second film led to criticism that he was a 'poor man's Charlie', a provincial comedian lacking a personality of his own.[21]

In fact, there were other differences between the actors' personas. The sentimentalism or pathos that was an important part of the appeal of Chaplin was largely absent from Totò. He possessed little of the humanity that endeared 'Charlie' to millions. Chaplin's agility was remarkable, but much of his physical comedy was based on sight gags, ass kicks and animated objects. Totò's trademark movements of face and body were not just funny but astonishing in their gravity-defying contortions and variety. A human invertebrate, he was a spirited loser whose horizons were not the limitless ones of the New World but those of a country in which the powerful always got the better of the little man. He was not just ground down by circumstances and bad luck, like the little tramp, but by centuries of religious and temporal tyranny. He had, Mario Soldati would later note, 'the greatness of the humble, the instinctive, the disappointed and the beaten, like Keaton. This type of greatness has a particular vibration to it that is missing in the greatness of the arrogant, the aware, the self-satisfied and the victorious, like Chaplin'.[22]

Men like writer and editor Cesare Zavattini and the pro-Soviet Centro sperimentale lecturer Umberto Barbaro admired Totò's comic gifts and sought to develop more fruitful film projects for him. The central role in 'Totò il buono'

(Good-Hearted Totò), which would become De Sica's 1950 neorealist fable *Miracolo a Milano* (Miracle in Milan) was originally written with him in mind,[23] though when the film was finally made, in keeping with neorealist practice, a non-professional took the lead. However, it is unlikely that the actor would have found the role of the good-hearted Totò – an unworldly innocent born in a vegetable garden who only believes the best of people – more suitable than the others that cinema afforded him in the prewar period. In *San Giovanni decollato* (Saint John, the Beheaded, Amleto Palermi, 1940), the actor did play a simpleton, a cobbler devoted to a holy image of the saint. The play had been performed many times by the Sicilian comedian Angelo Musco, and only the latter's sudden death led to Totò taking the part. On this occasion, the character of Totò was subsumed in the screen character of the cobbler, to whom he brought a familiar physiognomy and certain trademark movements but little or nothing in the way of his usual self-seeking, individualistic personality.

Despite the critical and commercial failure of his early films, there was a widely shared conviction that Totò was destined for cinema and that sooner or later a character so distinctive and popular would find a suitable vehicle. That opportunity would come in the postwar years, when cinema was acquiring a wider audience and seeking new ways of entertaining it. The director of Totò in no fewer than twelve films between 1947 and 1954, Mario Mattoli understood that in order to replicate in cinema the success the comedian had in the theatre he needed to be able to exercise the same freedom that he did on stage.[24] The Neapolitan Mattoli was a man with a profound knowledge of theatre who had directed Totò's first film in 1934, and it was by developing an approach more sympathetic to the performer that he would finally succeed in turning the stage idol into a film star. As Valentina Ruffin has noted, he 'left room for improvisation, preserving the spontaneity and immediacy of the first takes, placing the camera at the service of the actor, privileging medium and full-figure shots which could capture a player's small unscripted movements in a way that more ambitious camera movements could not'.[25]

De Curtis played in the quickly forgotten *Il ratto della sabine* (The Rape of the Sabine Women, Mario Bonnard, 1945) before making *I due orfanelli* (Two Little Orphans, Mario Mattoli, 1947), a parody of the 1942 melodrama *Le due orfanelle* (Two Little Orphan Girls), in which Alida Valli and Maria Denis had been directed by Carmine Gallone. The story begins in an orphanage for girls in which Gasparre (Totò) and Battista (Carlo Campanini) are menial employees. While the director of the institution is away, the two men embark on an adventure that leads to the discovery that the humble Gasparre (rather than the self-regarding Battista) is in fact the long-lost descendant of a noble family. When the two men first enter the historic family seat, they observe a series of portraits of titled ancestors, all of whom resemble Toto, including the oldest, who is the carbon copy of the Ferocious Saladin, a much sought-after card belonging to the 'Four Musketeers' series, which fired a collecting mania in the late 1930s.[26] Set in nineteenth-century Paris, the film incorporated many revue tropes, including a bevy of attractive young women (ostensibly the inmates of the orphanage), and satire. In fact, it is full of direct and indirect references to Fascism and its rituals, which are mercilessly parodied.

The three films that would establish Totò as a major box office attraction were all made in 1948, when he was fifty, and directed by Mattoli. The films were: *Fifa e arena* (Fear and Sand), a parody inspired by the Hollywood bullfighting drama *Blood and Sand* (Rouben Mamoulian, 1941), *Totò al giro d'Italia* (Totò at the Giro d'Italia), a satirical encounter with the world of professional cycling, and *I pompieri di Viggiù* (The Firemen of Viggiù), which was centred on the theme of the stage revue. They marked the onset of a Totò craze that would last through the 1950s and beyond. 'People desperately needed some happiness and Totò's films provided the Italians of those years with relaxation', it was later noted.[27] Though Italians were 'poor, miserable and hungry', this was not, Ennio Di Nolfo argued, due to 'their own incapacity but rather because of undeserved misfortunes'.[28] Their willingness to work hard for modest reward, together with 'the resources of a constructive imagination', provided the impulses that would soon enable the country once more to stand on its own feet. Comedy was a release, a safety valve in some ways, as well as a means of exorcizing present and past woes.

The first comedian to provide a comical exploration of the preoccupations of the reconstruction period was Erminio Macario, a diminutive, round-faced song and dance man whose theatre company specialized in enormous, lavish sets that showcased his famously beautiful female dancers. Macario had made a handful of films before 1943, which he followed with *L'innocente Casimiro* (The Innocent Casimiro, Carlo Campogalliani), a boarding school comedy in pure 1930s style, which horrified critics, who expected the first films of the new era to express something of their time. His subsequent films, all directed by Carlo Borghesio, *L'eroe della strada* (Hero of the Street, 1948), *Come persi la guerra* (How I Lost the War, 1948) and *Come scopersi l'America* (How I Discovered America, 1949) were more topical, though their good-humoured buffoonery quickly dated.[29] By the end of the forties, he had returned to the stage and was only playing supporting film roles. Totò prospered when Macario declined, as his brand of humour blended physical comedy with fantasy, parody, social commentary and free-wheeling dialogue.

Comparisons with Chaplin would not be so frequent after the war, though the journalist Orio Vergani, who spent several hours with the comedian before and after a stage performance in 1948, noted that Totò had something of Chaplin's ability to impress himself on the collective imaginary. He observed that, after the curtain fell, 'our imagination follows him, as it would Charlie Chaplin or a great clown, and it makes him live in a way and in situations that apparently have nothing at all to do with the usual repertoire of that mask.'[30] 'His persona carries on living in memory and fantasy while he himself immediately turns back into Totò the man.'[31] Though the prewar Totò possessed some potential in this regard, the postwar work deliberately exploits it by keying into common sensibilities and creating, via a familiar cast of supporting actors and co-stars, memorable patterns and scenarios. There is also a marked self-referentiality, which is often expressed in diegetic uses of the Totò name and image as well as in the use of his name in film titles. Totò imitators prospered on the stage in the same way as had occurred with Chaplin, albeit on a smaller scale. Indeed, the comedy road film *Bellezze in bicicletta* (Beauties on Bicycles, Carlo Campogalliani, 1952), starring Silvana Pampanini and Delia Scala, is centred in the desire of two young women to find work as chorus girls with Totò's touring company. When they eventually catch up with the company, they find that the 'Totò' is a fake (in fact played by the real Totò's regular screen stand-in) who will shortly be exposed and humiliated.

It has been claimed that the postwar Totò differed from the prewar version by being more human. No longer the amusing phantom or living corpse, he evolved into something more realistic: a man with common worries who was sometimes endowed with a family and a job. The macabre aspect of his persona, though it did not disappear, was less prominent. In fact, the element of realism in three films of 1948, which were determinant in bringing him success, was rather modest, while the fantasy aspect remained important. The first of these,

Fifa e arena, begins with Totò working in a pharmacy. Street scenes establish that we are in Rome. Wartime bombardments have affected his nerves and made him timorous. Though, as always, he is ever ready to womanize, he is a poor specimen of masculinity. The story takes off when a newspaper accidently publishes his picture identifying him as a serial killer, causing him to flee to Spain disguised as an air hostess. Subsequent events lead to him becoming an improbable bullfighter. Written by a team of authors of great experience, the film amply drew on gags and situations that had been rehearsed in revues.

With a storyline about small-town firemen that served as a pretext, *I pompieri di Viggiù* was even more dependent on songs and sketches from the revues. In fact, it was no more than a compilation of sketches featuring some of the best-known acts of the time. It could be said that the film was in some respects a giant advertisement for a form of entertainment that was enjoying a last hurrah. The songs and sketches were not merely escapist fodder; they were shot through with references to the issues of the day: Americanization, the black market, censorship and repression, familism, nostalgia for belle époque Paris and so on. Totò performs a shop dummy sketch, conducts the orchestra in comic mode and leads the entire cast in a grand finale parade to the tune of the fanfare of the Bersaglieri regiment, repeating a well-known ritual of Rome's Quattro Fontane theatre. While in the wings, he mingles with English chorus girls and jokes with the firemen, who have come to persuade their chief's runaway daughter to return home and marry her childhood sweetheart. With its dynamic camera work and cutaways from stage to picturesque landscape, the film ultimately asserted the superiority of cinema.

Only *Totò al giro d'Italia* placed the comedian in a real context, albeit one that was centred on two highly mediatized spectacles of the time: the Miss Italia pageant and the Giro d'Italia cycle race. Tullio Masoni and Paolo Vecchi have referred to it as a 'multimedia farce' on account of its 'organizing a myriad of show business materials, even if ultimately founded on the "mother language" of revue theatre'.[32] Totò plays a teacher who falls in love with a fellow jury member at the beauty contest only to be rejected unless he can prove himself by winning the Giro d'Italia. In order to achieve this unlikely objective, he makes a Faustian pact with a devil and enters the race. One of the film's great attractions was the participation of many professional cyclists, who the public only knew from radio commentary. Indeed, Masoni and Vecchi describe it as a 'sort of radiophonic film'.[33] Audiences were offered not only Totò and a real Miss Italia, the 1948 winner Fulvia Franco, but also the idols Fausto Coppi and Gino Bartali and even the motor-racing champion Tazio Nuvolari. Alongside scenes shot in the studio were many shot on location in Stresa, Milan, Bologna and other parts of the peninsula. Mattoli had tackled a sporting theme in his first film *Tempo Massimo* (Full-Speed, 1934), and on this occasion he repeated the comical device of inserting a person unsuited to sport in a competitive environment.[34] A mixture of parody, picaresque adventure, newsreel feature, theatrical farce and meta-cinematic palimpsest, the film heralded cinema's supplanting of theatre as the dominant medium of parody and synthesis. Released in January 1949, it perfectly illustrated how far the devastation of the war had been consigned to the past, and a mass culture of popular spectacles and shared rituals was providing the Italians with a new shared identity based on leisure and consumption.

Mattoli, alongside Carlo Ludovico Bragaglia, who also directed Totò five times in this period, would contribute decisively to his explosion as a phenomenon of cinema. He saw that the rapid expansion of cinema in the south and the provinces provided an opportunity to make comics of proven popularity even more widely known as well as to recycle material from a variety of theatrical sources. Anile has identified many instances of sketches and gags from revues that resurfaced in films, probably as a result of joint decisions by producers, directors and writers.[35] This is not to say that Mattoli and Totò had a close relationship. In fact, the director would later deplore 'the almost complete lack of professionalism of this *monstre sacré* of our showbusiness'.[36] Schooled in popular theatre and still attached to its working practices, he often failed to even read a script, hated being made-up and, accustomed to the nocturnal lifestyle of a stage actor, refused to begin work before 2.00 PM. On the set of *Totò al giro d'Italia*, he allegedly kept Coppi and Bartali waiting for hours. Though he found all this frustrating, Mattoli worked out that it was cinema that had to adapt to the requirements of the actor, and not vice versa, if the best were to be extracted from a born entertainer. 'He was born to make people laugh', he observed. 'There was no need to teach him anything; he was an instinctive performer and his instinct did not usually let him down.' The director's task was to provide him with as much autonomy as possible:

> Those marionette gags, those clown-like grimaces, who could teach him things that were inseparable from his persona? Sometimes, so as not to interrupt his improvisations, that were true theatrical inventions, so as not to have to ask him to repeat the same scene a hundred times in different ways – as you do in the cinema – I just let him freewheel, with four movie cameras trained on him from different angles.[37]

To describe Totò as 'director of himself', as Blasetti did on the comic's death, would not be quite accurate, but it contained a kernel of truth.[38]

If the postwar Totò assumed a more human, everyday guise, then this was also due to a certain contamination with neorealist cinema. Younger directors, sometimes at the behest of producers, sought to bring him into realistic milieux that were either familiar or intriguing. Luigi Comencini directed him in *L'imperatore di Capri* (The Emperor of Capri, 1949), a satire of the eccentricities of the bohemian elite who vacationed on the famous island, while Steno (Stefano Vanzina) and Mario Monicelli did so in *Totò cerca casa* (Totò Seeks a Home, 1949) and *Guardie e ladri* (Cops and Robbers, 1951), comical takes – respectively on homelessness and the law and its enforcers – that required a measure of social observation. *Totò cerca casa* was dominated by a preoccupation with the unresolved problem of those living in temporary accommodation. Totò, a government clerk, and his family are still living in a high school some years after the end of the war. In the course of the film, they are rehoused in a cemetery, occupy an artist's studio, are tricked by bogus apartment salesmen and are eventually transferred to a lunatic asylum (see Figure 10.1). Each episode gives rise to comical situations and relationships in which a theatrical template is evident, but there is no easy solution, and the conclusion is a bitter one. The same pessimism marked *Dov'è la libertà* (Where is Freedom, 1954). Directed, apparently with some reluctance, by Roberto Rossellini, the film cast Totò as a jailbird who prefers to return to prison after undergoing a series of negative experiences following his release on completing a long sentence.

Despite the return of censorship in the late 1940s, the nonconformist verve of his comedy was never eliminated. Totò and the writers of his films worked on the assumption of a shared baggage of experiences and attitudes towards the powerful. References back to Fascism reflected not so much a critical attitude towards the dictatorship as towards official uncertainty over how to relate to the past. In *Totò cerca casa*, the actor is a clerk whose job is to register births. He kindly informs one new father of a boy that certain names are inadvisable. Those he mentions are Franco (the Spanish dictator), Umberto (the former king, who was assassinated in 1900) and Tito (the Yugoslav ruler). There is no need for him to mention Mussolini's first name, Benito, but it is as though he had. In the course of the film, he serially humiliates a pompous politician – in the final instance, by crashing into a monument to the Reconstruction that he is in the process of inaugurating. His character in the film claims he is 'social democrat, monarchist, republican', an odd mixture of the old-fashioned and the mildly progressive, not dissimilar to the views that the comedian occasionally espoused.[39] In later films, including *Gli onorevoli* (The Members of Parliament, Sergio Corbucci, 1963), he would adopt a nostalgic outlook for Umbertine Italy, but in the politically divided period of the early Cold War, he positioned himself in opposition to all representatives of power and authority. Totò was an everyman who perhaps could be seen in relation to the masses of people who in 1946 voted for the Uomo Qualunque (Anyman Movement) led by his friend, the Neapolitan playwright Guglielmo Giannini. First a weekly published in Rome from December 1944, the Uomo Qualunque was characterized by hostility towards politicians of all stripes ('Abbasso tutti' or 'Down With Them All' was the headline in the first issue) and a desire for the ordinary man to be left alone.[40] In 1948, the party would disappear as the Christian Democrats mopped up the votes of its supporters. Nonetheless, De Curtis continued to position himself on the side of the little man. In a ghosted text first published in 1952, he counterposed ordinary 'men' to the overbearing 'corporals' who bullied and intimidated them.[41] The book would inspire a film, *Siamo uomini o caporali* (Are We Men or Corporals? Camillo Mastrocinque, 1955), in which Totò is repeatedly obstructed or humiliated by a bully who is impersonated on each occasion by the same stone-faced actor (Paolo Stoppa).

Totò was a nonconformist and an iconoclast who, like many artists, refrained from endorsing any political party. Yet his contribution to the common culture of the republic was considerable. At one level, he helped undermine the residual patriotic patrimony, which had been taken over and amply exploited by Fascism in the interwar years. Efforts to revive this in the postwar years would enjoy some success, though only insofar as it was absorbed by the new official doctrine of anti-fascism.[42] Both the Catholics and the left subscribed to this, though the parties of the left did so more insistently. However, it was more through shared patterns of leisure and cultural consumption that a new common culture would be formed. In the view of Mario Soldati, the high-minded ideals of the Risorgimento were displaced in the formative texture of media-sustained mass culture not by the institutionalization of the Resistance but rather by 'the only surviving myth of the 1930s... eroticism'.[43] The judgement is debatable, but, despite censorship, the twin influences of the liberalization of customs during the liberation and the frankness of the news and entertainment media produced a diffusion of erotic appeals centred on the female body. The Totò character was integral to this; he was always accompanied by soubrettes and beautiful supporting players. In film after film, he eyed-up, kissed, hugged and squeezed Isa Barzizza, Silvana Pampanini and numerous screen socialites and showgirls, though not usually in quite such an unrestrained way as in the spoof Tarzan movie *Tototarzan* (see Figure 10.2).

Figure 10.2 Totò with the showgirl Isa Barzizza, who appeared alongside him in numerous stage shows and several films (author's own collection).

Totò spoke to his audiences from a particular vantage point, that of a Neapolitan rooted in a specifically southern culture of entertainment, which, following the incorporation of picturesque southern imagery into the iconography of the nation in the post-unification period, came to form the basis of a culture that was seen to be national. In the postwar years, this would prove to be a resource for both the film and music industries in their efforts to compete with American products. Totò was a proud Neapolitan who deplored what he saw as the calumny perpetrated by Curzio Malaparte in his graphic novel of the occupation, *La pelle*.[44] But he was no dialect comedian. Though he spoke with a strong Neapolitan accent, his Italian was perfectly comprehensible to everyone. Often loquacious, his linguistic contortions and inventions contributed as much to his popularity as his physical ones. In his linguistic history of united Italy, published in 1963, Tullio De Mauro highlighted the contribution of the actor's trademark manipulations of official Italian to a language that was finally becoming widely spoken in the peninsula.[45] As Mario Isnenghi has more recently noted, one his best-known catchphrases *'a prescindere'* (literally, 'notwithstanding' or 'leaving aside'), used when he was seeking inappropriately to adopt an elevated tone, and sometimes without reference to any particular object, caught on because it encapsulated something of the reticence relating to past and present issues in the dominant political discourse.[46] Totò's linguistic humour, seasoned as it was with colourful expressions and double entendres, constituted a proudly particularist response to old and new social hierarchies, foreign languages and modern innovations.

Though born and raised poor, De Curtis was aware that his father had an aristocratic lineage. The pursuit of his right to adopt noble titles became an intense personal concern, which, over time, would come to be incorporated into his star persona. Totò the clown was determined to establish a second identity that was utterly removed from his profession. After a ruling of the civil court of Naples in 1946 confirmed his right to be called Antonio De Curtis Griffo Focas Comneno Gagliardi, Prince of Byzantium, he began to behave in a way that reflected his new-found status. When the critic Gian Luigi Rondi was invited to visit him in early 1949, he was warned by Mattoli that he should be prepared to address him as 'Prince'.[47] Though he initially bridled, Rondi complied and was surprised to find that, outside of the set, De Curtis was composed and ceremonial. His manner reminded him of 'many patricians with titles and coats of arms dating from the Kingdom of the Two Sicilies'. The actor played the part well, affecting persuasive attitudes of paternalistic grace. He behaved with consummate generosity towards fellow actors, technicians and extras and invariably responded positively to the appeals for financial assistance that he, along with many other stars, was accustomed to receive.[48] He provided a striking public demonstration of old-fashioned chivalry in July 1950 when he authored a newspaper article in defence of a lady who had been verbally abused for her immodest dress in a Roman restaurant by a zealous young Christian Democrat deputy (and future president of the republic), Oscar Luigi Scalfaro. On learning of the incident, her husband had challenged Scalfaro to a duel, a practice that, though not widespread, was still in vogue at the time.[49] The politician, however, rejected the challenge on the grounds that duelling was un-Christian. In his article, Totò chastised Scalfaro for invoking religious principles to get out of his time-honoured duty as a gentleman, when those very principles 'should have impeded you and your friends from making comments in a public place about a perfectly respectable lady'.[50]

In 1952, the newly recognized prince moved to a ten-room apartment in the chic Parioli district, whose period furnishings were described in detail in a feature in the illustrated magazine *Oggi*.[51] Unusually for a successful actor, the dwelling was devoid of all artefacts and souvenirs of a show business career. Instead, on the walls there were aristocratic symbols and old portraits (acquired, it was freely admitted, in antique shops, on the basis of a supposed physical resemblance),[52] in the manner of the historic family seat in *I due orfanelli*. In his home, he was said to rarely laugh or smile. 'When I am talking or listening to amusing stories', he told one journalist, 'I only smile a little, to be polite and also so as not to look too much like Totò. The character has not taken me over; I am still a distinguished gentleman by the name of Antonio De Curtis' (see Figure 10.3).[53] In keeping with this reserve, his tailor was instructed to make his suits in a sober, classical style without concessions to fashion.[54] His aim was to be elegant without being showy. Fans of the actor were kept firmly at bay: 'to get access to him you had to get past the obstructions of the porter's lodge, the secretary and the domestic staff', it was remarked.[55] Yet, at the same time, he embraced some features of the ostentatious life of a star. He holidayed on Capri and the French Riviera and was not averse to exhibiting the wealth that came with success.[56] 'He competed with [frequent co-star] Peppino De Filippo to see who had the longest and flashiest American automobiles', revealed Mattoli; 'and in 1958, when Dino De Laurentiis, another Neapolitan with a fixation for Cadillacs, signed them up for *Totò, Peppino e le fanatiche*, the set was like a Detroit car park on the day of a beauty pageant for automobiles.'[57]

Figure 10.3 Prince Antonio De Curtis (Totò) at home. The actor sought to draw a sharp distinction between his public and private personae but was not always consistent in doing so (author's own collection).

The question of the relationship between De Curtis and Totò inevitably came up after he brought his aristocratic prerogatives into the public realm. When a journalist suggested to him in 1949 that they were one and the same person, he became irritated.[58] 'Let's not muddle things up that should be kept properly distinct', he told him. Later, he explained that 'Totò is still me, but I am also a displaced gentleman who, to earn his living, has to do strange things: jump, paint his face, wear a funny costume.'[59] 'I love my work like a drug, but it is still a job. At home, among these dear old, well-loved possessions, I feel happy and calm, once more a gentleman. At such times, how can I love my other self, the puppet?' He saw Totò as a rough and uncouth individual who waved his arms about, made rude gestures and winked. His clothes were ridiculous; they were props that derived from the old Neapolitan world of the café chantant.[60] In fact, the distinctions were not so clear-cut. De Curtis deployed his different identities as and when it suited him. In particular, there was a realm of ambiguity between Antonio De Curtis and the public figure Totò. To distinguish between the prince and the comic character was easy; between the prince and the actor less so. For example, when Mattoli treated him with disrespect, he was ordered to address him as 'prince',[61] while De Sica, his director in *L'oro di Napoli* (The Gold of Naples), when he asked whether he should call him 'prince' or 'Totò', was invited to use his stage name. Moreover, it was as Totò not as De Curtis that he signed his article deploring Scalfaro and listed his name as author of *Siamo uomini o caporali?* (the subtitle was 'Semi-serious Diary of Antonio De Curtis'). It may be suggested that the nobleman persona provided De Curtis with a refuge from the obligation always to inhabit Totò, gratifying his desire for social dignity and providing some consolation for the moral and emotional privations of his hard upbringing. Yet Totò was a multiform persona who was difficult to confine or contain. Between the Toto character (the equivalent of Chaplin's 'little tramp'), the actor (the Totò of film credits) and the public figure (the film star, the author), the slippages were numerous: for instance, Totò the public figure dressed like the prince, while the actor sometimes played noblemen with absurd titles resembling his own. To complete a complex picture, the nobleman was no less a performative identity than the character. It was an assumed persona, even if its authenticity had been established by a court, and even if it provided a congenial refuge from the various roles and identities of Totò. If Totò was 'the equivalent of a worker's overalls', as he told Franca Faldini, the actress who became his companion in 1953,[62] the prince was not so much the essential man as the suit he reserved for Sunday best.

The comedian was a box office phenomenon. In the two seasons between 1948 and 1950, ten of his films figured in the top ten box office earners, while at least one of his films enjoyed similar fortune in every season up to 1956.[63] The fact that his films fared best in second and third-run cinemas in the centre and south,[64] leading to comments that he was a 'poor folks' star', makes these figures all the more striking, since ticket prices were lower in these categories. By 1950, he was one of only three names who could make a difference at the box office (the others were Silvana Magnano and Amedeo Nazzari).[65] Yet he never featured among the top stars in the annual polls of the *Hollywood*, a fan magazine with a mainly northern and middle-class readership. For producers, his films offered a guarantee of box office returns that proved to be crucial to the recovery and growth of Italian cinema. Both Carlo Ponti and Dino De Laurentiis founded their careers as independent producers on him, with the latter making *I pompieri di Viggiù* when Lux boss Gualino at first turned it down, and the former winning the actor's agreement to make *L'imperatore di Capri*, since the shoot would take place on his favourite island.[66] Ponti also produced *Totò cerca casa* under the auspices of a company called ATA. For Ponti and De Laurentiis, his films were second-order products: parodies and spin-offs, often quickly made using existing sets. They were cash cows on which they founded larger ambitions. With the Lit.150 million Ponti earned from *Totò cerca casa*, he was able to set up their joint company.[67] When the pair took over two small companies, Golden Film and Humanitas Film in 1951, they acquired a contract with the actor that allowed them to establish an exclusive relationship that would last for five years.[68] The profits they generated from intense commercial exploitation enabled them to become major players in the national and international markets.

De Curtis was resentful at the intense exploitation to which he was subjected. He often complained that he was treated badly by producers. He yearned for opportunities to tackle more challenging fare and to escape from the routine quickies that constituted the bulk of his film work. Only when the writer-turned-director Pier Paolo Pasolini took him up in the 1960s, towards the end of his career, would he find fulfilment. Though he turned down many more proposals than he accepted,[69] he was certainly complicit in the exploitation of his box office appeal for he did not allow anyone to represent him or manage his commitments. In the film industry, as in other sectors of Italian show business, it was standard practice to seek to extract maximum gain from a success, to milk it for all it was worth before the audience tired of it. The extraordinary workload he took on reflected a belief that his screen success was no more than a passing fad. In fact, he would establish himself as a significantly more durable and bankable name with the public than two other stars of variety who turned successfully to cinema. But his artistic satisfactions were more meagre. Aldo Fabrizi established himself as an author and director, taking on a wide range of comic and dramatic roles, while Anna Magnani would rise above her variety origins to acquire a reputation as a great actress with a worldwide reputation. Magnani and Totò had worked together in revues, but a project reuniting them failed to materialize because of the different positions the pair occupied in the film industry. Only in 1960 would they feature together, respectively as a film extra and a petty thief, in *Risate di gioia* (Joyous Laughter) under the direction of Monicelli. With Fabrizi, however, Totò would make one of his most rewarding films. Steno's *Guardie e ladri* (Cops and Robbers, 1951) would encounter problems with the censors on account of its depiction of the law, but the pairing of two of the most popular actors produced bravura performances from both in their respective roles as policeman and thief.[70] The stout Roman and the wiry Neapolitan provided a physical contrast that acted as a springboard to a comic pairing of great efficacy. Writing in *L'Eco del cinema*, Gaetano Carancini noted that the comedy and pathos of the film had a Chaplinesque flavour, while the director had simultaneously managed to restrain Fabrizi and find a new humanity for Totò amid the desolate periphery of the capital.[71] It provided confirmation of the aristocratic comedian's unique ability to portray the artful wiles of outsiders and society's rejects.

Notes

1. On Totò's place in popular memory, see Continanza, *Totò dopo Totò: il ricxordo dell'attore nella memoria collettiva dei napoletani*.
2. See King, *Film Comedy*, 36.
3. Shingler, *Star Studies*, 80.
4. See, for example, Quinlan, *Quinlan's Illustrated Directory of Film Comedy Stars*, and Finkelstein, *Jewish Comedy Stars: Classic to Cutting Edge*.
5. Spinazzola, *Cinema e pubblico: lo spettacolo filmico in Italia 1945–1965*, 10.
6. Faldini and Fofi, *Totò: l'uomo e la maschera*; Governi, *Vita di Totò: principe napoletano e grande attore*; Totò, *Siamo uomini o caporali? Diario semiserio di Antonio De Curtis*; Bispuri, *Vita di Totò*. Among several volumes by Alberto Anile are: *I film di Totò (1946–1967): la maschera tradita*; *Totò proibito*; and *Totalmente Totò: vita e opera di un comico assoluto*.
7. G. Fofi, 'Prefazione', 7–8 and Fofi, 'Perche Totò', 109–10 in Faldini and Fofi, *Totò: l'uomo e la maschera Totò*.
8. See Rodolfo De Angelis testimony in De Matteis et al., *Follie del varietà: vicende, memorie, personaggi 1890–1970*, 101.
9. Totò testimony in Ibid., 102.
10. Ramperti, quoted in Anile, *Totalmente Totò*, 30.
11. Anile, *Totalmente Totò*, 30.

12. Stewart-Steinberg, *The Pinocchio Effect: On Making Italians, 1860–1890*, 22.
13. On Fascism and its crowds, see Schnapp and Tiews, *Crowds*.
14. Fofi, 'Perche Totò', in Faldini and Fofi, *Totò: l'uomo e la maschera*, 117.
15. Anile, *Totalmente Totò*, 49. See also Vergani, 'Il più popolare' in Caldiron, *C'era una volta il '48*, 172.
16. Fofi, 'Perche Totò', 115.
17. Chaplin, *My Autobiography*.
18. Quoted in Governi, *Vita di Totò*, 62–63.
19. Anile, *Totalmente Totò*, 74.
20. Taken from a news clipping reproduced in http://www.tototruffa2002.it/il-teatro/1932-toto-charlot-per-amore.html. Consulted 7 September 2018.
21. Anile, *Totalmente Totò*, 94.
22. Soldati, 'Totò' (1967), in Soldati, *Cinematografo*, 407.
23. Anile, *Totalmente Totò*, 104–5.
24. A point first made in Spinazzola, *Cinema e pubblico*, 84–101.
25. Ruffin, 'Totò al massimo', 270.
26. For details, see Gundle, *Mussolini's Dream Factory: Film Stardom in Fascist Italy*, 104–6.
27. G. Cavallotti, 'Il principe triste che donava sorrisi', *Gente* 12, 1967, 76–79.
28. Di Nolfo, *Le paure e le speranze degli italiani (1943–1953)*, 153.
29. Macario, *Macario un comico caduto dalla luna*, 221–22.
30. O. Vergani, 'Il più popolare', in Caldiron, *C'era una volta il '48*, 167–68.
31. Ibid., 169.
32. Masoni and Vecchi, 'Totò al giro d'Italia di Mario Mattoli', 53.
33. Ibid., 54.
34. Della Casa, *Mario Mattoli*, 61.
35. Anile, *Totalmente Totò*, 155–85.
36. R. Barneschi, 'Soltanto per me Sofia scese nulla nell'acqua', *Oggi illustrato*, 19 April 1976, 97.
37. G.L. Rondi, 'Mattoli: difendo i telefoni bianchi', *Il Tempo*, 9 July 1978, 16. More testimonies of the actor's working methods are contained in Faldini and Fofi, *L'avventurosa storia del cinema italiano: raccontata dai suoi protagonisti, 1935–1959*, 289–95.
38. Quoted in Soldati, 'Totò', in Soldati, *Cinematografo*, 406.
39. See Faldini, 'Quindici anni con Antonio De Curtis', in Faldini and Fofi, *Totò: l'uomo e la maschera*, 69.
40. Setta, *L'uomo qualunque, 1944–1948*, 3–4.
41. Totò, *Siamo uomini o caporali?*.
42. See Schwarz, *Tu mi devi seppellir: riti funebri e culto nazionale alle origini della Repubblica*, Chapter 2.
43. Soldati, 'Totò', in Soldati, *Cinematografo*, 404.
44. Totò, *Siamo uomini o caporali?*, 21.
45. See Aronica et al., *Totò: linguaggi e maschere del comico*, 131.
46. Isnenghi, *Storia d'Italia: i fatti e le percezioni dal Risorgimento alla societa' dello spettacolo*, 562–63.
47. Rondi, *Le mie vite allo specchio: diari 1947–1997*, 70–71.
48. 'His personal wealth would amount to millions if he had not given much of it away in acts of charity in which his name was never mentioned, helped needy fellow artists or made loans that no one would ever pay back.' Cavallotti, 'Il principe triste che donava sorrisi', 76.
49. See Hughes, 'Duelling After the Duce: Postwar Conflicts of Honour in Italy', 615–26.

50. The incident is recounted in detail in Olivieri, *Totò, Scalfaro e la ... "malafemmina"*. Totò's article (reproduced on pp. 12–13) was published in *L'Avantì*, 23 November 1950.
51. Anon., 'Entriamo nelle case delle celebrità', *Oggi*, 11 February 1954, 24–27.
52. See A. Porro, 'Gli telefonarono: "sei imperatore"', *Grazia*, 26 January 1958, 22–23, and M. Chierici, 'Il principe De Curtis oddia Totò', *Oggi illustrato*, 13 January 1966, 31–34.
53. Chierici, 'Il principe De Curtis', 32.
54. Ibid.
55. Anon., 'Entriamo nelle case', 24–27.
56. One summer, he caught sight of Chaplin while vacationing in St Tropez. He refused to introduce himself, convinced that the great comedian would not even know who he was. Instead he observed, with a touch of pride, that he had to resort to a fake moustache and a little hat to make his features funny, while in his own case to make people laugh it was sufficient to move the features with which he had been endowed by nature. Faldini, *Roma, Hollywood, Roma: Totò, ma non soltanto*, 163.
57. Barneschi, 'Soltanto per me Sofia scese nulla nell'acqua', 97.
58. E. Emanuelli, 'L'uomo che non ride alle recite di Totò', *L'Europeo*, 3 March 1949, 176.
59. Ibid.
60. Ibid.
61. Faldini, *Roma, Hollywood, Roma*, 159.
62. Totò, quoted in Faldini, 'Quindici anni con Antonio De Curtis', 63.
63. Ruffin, 'Totò al massimo', 268.
64. A. Ferraù, 'Rapporto tra gli incassi delle prime visioni di 16 citta capozona e il resto del mercato nazionale', *Cinepsettacolo*, January 1956, 22.
65. Anon., 'I film italiani nel mercato interno', *Cinespettacolo*, 14 February 1953, 6.
66. Ibid., 142, 173.
67. Ibid., 143.
68. Ibid., 173.
69. Anile, *Totalmente Totò*, 141.
70. For a discussion of many aspects of the film and its place in Totò's film career, see Anile, *Guardie e ladri*.
71. *L'Eco del Cinema*, 15 January 1952. Cited in Lancia and Melelli, *I film di Aldo Fabrizi*, 74.

CHAPTER 11

Silvana Mangano
Beauty and Stardom

Silvana Mangano was the first new actor of the postwar years to become a star with genuine box office appeal. Aged only eighteen when she made her debut in a major role, she brought an unfamiliar, ostensibly natural sex appeal to Italian screens. With her undoubted beauty and relaxed, unpolished demeanour, she asserted a physical presence that owed something to both the emancipatory impulses of the period and the new culture of female spectacle that accompanied the Allied occupation. *Riso amaro* (Bitter Rice, Giuseppe De Santis, 1949) was one of the first films deriving directly from the milieu of neorealism to be produced by Lux, the leading production company. Filming on location in Vercelli was supervised by one of the company's executive producers, Dino De Laurentiis, who mapped out a professional trajectory for Mangano that would see her become one of the biggest stars of Italian cinema. This status was not achieved by the usual method of frenetic participation in as many films as possible. She made only six features and one episode between 1948 and 1954, all of them titles that would win a place in popular memory or Italian film history.[1] Mangano was not a star who was possessed of steely professionalism or a strong sense of ambition. Indeed, she seemed remarkably detached for a woman who had begun her ascent to fame in the cut-throat world of beauty contests and open auditions. It was De Laurentiis who was limitlessly ambitious, and all of her films were carefully planned to build and exploit a star image that was soon made to evolve from that of sexy starlet to fully-fledged international diva.

One of the most controversial films of the later 1940s, *Riso amaro* was a working-class melodrama that was conceived as an exploration of the world of the female seasonal workers, who, each spring for six weeks, planted and weeded the rice in the northern provinces of the country. While most of the workers were country women, the demand for labour was such that some were also recruited from nearby towns and cities. De Santis was a member of the Italian Communist Party, and he and his collaborators were committed to a cinema that explored the social and political tensions of the period by bringing the experiences of the lower classes to the screen. The rice workers had a reputation for militancy that dated back to the early twentieth century, when the first battles to restrict the working day to eight hours were fought and won. The director and his team researched the milieu and then constructed a story, which drew on established cinematic conventions of narrative and character in order to give the film popular appeal. *Riso amaro*'s central characters are two women who meet and clash while working in the rice fields: Francesca is a petty thief's troubled companion who hides among the workers and is eventually redeemed by her immersion in proletarian life; the other is a dreamy girl named Silvana, whose love of American music and comic-book fantasies leaves her defenceless before the blandishments of the fascinating thief.

De Santis's first film, *Caccia tragica* (Tragic Hunt, 1947), had been produced outside of conventional channels, and filming had been interrupted several times on economic grounds.[2] The Lux company gave his new project its backing and ensured that it had an adequate budget. Despite the defeat of the left in the 1948 election and the blow this constituted to those who had been seeking to carry forward the neorealist discourse, Lux boss Riccardo Gualino and De Laurentiis saw the commercial potential in a story that was infused with drama, violence and sex appeal. Irritated by suggestions that the film might be vitiated by left-wing propaganda due to the director's known political affiliation, the company stressed that 'Lux wants a spectacular film and has chosen the setting of the rice fields because it is new and unexploited.'[3] The attribution of the part of Francesca to Hollywood exile Doris Dowling was intended to bolster the film's international appeal. The biggest challenge lay in casting the role of the restless Silvana. De Laurentiis told De Santis that, if they got it wrong, then the whole film would be ruined.[4]

There are a number of versions of how Silvana Mangano, then a young model and former holder of the Miss Rome title with a couple of small bit parts to her name, came to be awarded the role. De Santis considered many possible candidates, rejecting along the way several who would go on to screen careers. The 1947 Miss Italia, Lucia Bosè, was either discarded or declined the role on the grounds that she refused to dye her hair blonde. Mangano herself, who worked near the Via Veneto for the Atelier Muscetti, had also been passed over despite having the support of some members of the director's team. Though she had attracted some attention as an anonymous tousle-haired beauty on a poster urging Italians to exercise their right to vote, the polished look she had put on for the audition – which was the same as that she adopted for various beauty contests – had put off a director who was seeking unvarnished genuineness (see Figure 11.1). De Santis would later recount that it was when he chanced to see her again, walking on the Via Veneto in the rain, dressed simply in a raincoat with her hair soaking wet and a flower in her hand, that he realized he had been mistaken. 'It was like a bolt of lightning to see her again like that, beautiful and unassuming, authentic in her true state of a not very well-off young woman ... I did the screen test again, that turned out magnificently, and I signed her up for the role', he revealed.[5] De Santis at this juncture had not yet acquired a reputation as a discoverer of female screen talent, so he had to convince De Laurentiis of the wisdom of giving the part to an unknown. The producer not only took a keen interest in casting; he actively followed every step of the film's production for Lux and was often present on set.[6]

Figure 11.1 An elegant young Silvana Mangano, a contestant at the Miss Lazio pageant, 1947. It is likely that she presented herself in a similar way at the audition for *Riso amaro* (Bitter Rice, Giuseppe De Santis, 1949) (author's own collection).

The part, in reality, was ideally suited to a newcomer, a young woman who could be seen as representative of the social tensions and aspirations of the postwar years. These had seen American cultural influence infiltrate the collective consciousness, of young people above all, with new images and suggestions.[7] As a result, ideas and practices of the self were changing.[8] The character of Silvana was meant to 'resemble a Rita Hayworth of the Italian periphery', De Santis later asserted.⁹ Hayworth was one of the biggest Hollywood stars of the time, whose 1945 film *Gilda* had startled Italian audiences with its glamour and compelling love-hate dynamic.¹⁰ Silvana is a siren too in her own small way. She is an unsettled, indolent girl whose head is filled with dance music, Hollywood movies and photoromance magazines. She is aware that men look at her, and this makes her think that she can use her beauty to escape from drudgery. Though she attracts the attention of an honest army sergeant who is about to return to civilian life, she is unable to resist the promise of excitement and luxury that Walter, a callous thief on the run, seems to offer her. Indeed, there is an immediate electric attraction between them as soon as they catch each other's eye. Silvana betrays her fellow workers, and even though she is proclaimed the winner of the 'Miss Mondina' (Miss Rice Weeder) beauty contest on the final evening of the planting season, she knows that she no longer belongs among them. Full of shame and remorse, she spectacularly commits suicide by throwing herself from a watchtower. In a moving concluding scene of the film, her fellow workers make a symbolic gesture of reconciliation; as they prepare to return home, each casts a handful of rice over her covered body.¹¹ She may have made mistakes, but she was still seen by the women as one of them.

On paper, the character of Silvana was a supporting role to the two male characters, played by the stage actor Vittorio Gassman as the thief and another screen newcomer, Raf Vallone, as the sergeant, and the positive female character of Francesca. But Mangano's extraordinary embodiment of the part lent it a significance that went well beyond what the writers had intended. Though she had very little experience of cinema, she struck everyone who visited the set with her presence. A reporter for *La Stampa* wrote that 'she looks like Rita Hayworth. Seeing her, she seems to be perfectly in her element and she moves lazily, wiggling her hips like a diva.'¹² The writer Italo Calvino, at the time a 26-year-old journalist on the Communist daily *L'Unità*, was equally bowled over:

> Silvana Mangano ... is, on my honour, the most beautiful girl I have ever seen ... She is Roman, she is 18 years old, and she has the face and hair of Botticelli's Venus but an expression that is at once proud and remissive, with dark eyes and fair hair and a clear complexion. Her shoulders open out on to a décolletage worthy of a cameo and her upper body is harmoniously triumphant and shapely. Her waist is like a slim stem amid an amazing rhythm of full curves and long limbs.¹³

Such was her personal magnetism that he felt that 'no photograph can ever do her full justice'.

For Carlo Lizzani, who contributed to the script, Mangano's magical presence suggested 'a relationship between nature and the human body that was not present in the screenplay, or that was barely hinted at'.[14] In this relationship, in which 'nature is seen as a great container not only of water, rice, grasses, sky or trees, but also of human bodies', the actress was 'offered up to view as a prodigy of nature, like a beautiful animal or a beautiful tree'. The connection that would be established in this film between the female body and the landscape would acquire much significance over time. It informed the 'rebirth' that was so frequently invoked in the period of reconstruction and that from 1945 had been associated with female imagery.[15] *Riso amaro* was the first of several films that, to use Giovanna Grignaffini's words, identified the earth as 'the place of the mother or more generally of the feminine'.[16] This was aided, she argues, by neorealism's absorption of the tradition

Figure 11.2 Silvana Mangano dances the boogie woogie in her breakthrough role as a misguided rice worker in *Riso amaro* (Bitter Rice, Giuseppe De Santis, 1949) (screenshot by the author).

of corporeal recitation that had long been a feature of popular theatre, embracing the notion that 'face and body are language'.[17] There was a widespread assumption – which was manifested in public discussion as well as press photography, beauty contests and cinema – that the female body was the imaginary site of the rebirth of the nation.[18]

This argument has become widely accepted and is often repeated even in contemporary criticism. It is time it was closely examined and deconstructed. The ready connection that was established in the postwar media between the nation and young women, whether beauties anointed at pageants or simply girls photographed in the street, corresponded to several needs: for a new peaceful imagery that marked a break with Fascism's cult of war and masculinity, for new faces that looked optimistically to the future and for images that could be connected with the reconstruction and impulses towards material improvement. The predominance of female imagery in American mass culture was a model and example here, but it was also a reflex response, a throwback to old perceptions. Feminine beauty had long been a significant aspect of Italian identity, while the whole modern preoccupation with feminine beauty as a national banner was a product of culture in which women, denied the status of citizens, provided a range of allegorical images, including ones relating to the nation.[19] The upheavals of war, foreign occupation and political transition provoked reassessments and a renewal of its role.[20] The problem was that this idea of the female image as a national resource bypassed the dramatic changes in women's condition that derived from their contribution to the Resistance and their conquest in 1946 of the vote.[21] That observations like those of Calvino and Lizzani should have emerged from the most progressive sector of opinion was evidence of a cultural lag that also affected the left and that would shape much of the female representation in Italian cinema. The female characters of the screen would for many years bear greater witness to the persistence of social customs and gender inequalities before the law than they would to the political emancipation of women. The young women of the movies could be sassy and strongheaded, loud and assertive, but rarely were they citizens or social actors, even if they were immersed in the world of work.

De Santis did not fall into this cultural trap from the outset. Backward perceptions may have infiltrated the film, but his intention was to explore the experiences of the women who every year took on the back-breaking and insanitary seasonal work of rice-weeding. He was not interested in providing a picturesque vision of Italy's natural environment or an idealistic depiction of nature's subordination to society's needs. Nor did he seek to furnish images of women in the landscape that had the simplicity and staticity of nineteenth-century paintings of peasant women. The origins of some of the workers are announced in the radio commentary at the outset of the film and are elaborated further in some of their individual stories. In homage to the rebellious traditions of the rice weeders, especially in the Vercelli area, emphasis is placed on the role of trade unions. Reference is also made to the impact of modern consumer goods and practices on the women. But undoubtedly there is a sense of the moral and universal value of the land and a validation of the value of feminine beauty. Doris Dowling's wayward Francesca is redeemed not only by her contact with the working women but also by honest work on the land. Silvana's reabsorption after death into the community shows a maternal indulgence that derives not only from the women but from the land itself. Moreover, the simplicity of the peasant, though not a characteristic of the film's protagonists, or indeed of most of its secondary female characters, persists in the choral presence of the many ordinary women who fill out the background, few of whom appear to have had any contact with urban culture prior to Silvana's arrival with her record player and boogie woogie moves. Modern commercial goods are a novel, contaminating influence.

The alignment of the character of Silvana with a national template of images of women and the land was a retrograde step that occurred on set during filming. It was the product of various factors including the unexpected screen presence of Mangano herself. What has been called her 'taking power', above all at the expense of Dowling, led to a series of adjustments to the way she was featured in the drama.[22] These did not take place at the 'dynamic-narrative' level – which led to the reformed Francesca (Dowling's character) emerging at the end, together with Vallone's noble sergeant, as the positive figures to whom the future belonged. Rather they occurred at the more specifically visual 'static-contemplative' level that Grignaffini describes as that of the 'scenic event'.[23] 'It is the appearances of Silvana which assert themselves as events and which silence the narration while capturing the gaze', she argues. Silvana, in other words, is the visual centrepiece of the film; at several junctures, including two dance sequences, some moments of rest, and the round of hostile choral singing, which she instigates against irregular, non-unionized workers, she is overtly constituted as visual spectacle. The camera closely tracks a body 'that breathes in time with the surrounding landscape while at the same time going beyond it, bearing its hallmarks and giving it meaning'.[24]

In fact, more than 'going beyond it', Silvana is positioned against it. Only for the male intellectuals who took an interest in the film did she bear the landscape's hallmarks or give it meaning. As a creation, she was a multifaceted, contemporary figure, who, at the level of image, drew not so much on the typologies of nineteenth-century painting as on a recent female iconography, which included the pin-up, the Hollywood vamp, the heroine of photoromances, the beauty queen and the ordinary, everyday girl.[25] In this sense, she was internal to the media developments of the moment, and she embodied the controversial impact of American-style mass culture on the collective imaginary. Grignaffini argued that her body was a representational paradox: on the one hand it stood for 'all of the positive values of the community that has elected her queen' while at the same time being 'an effective self-signifier' of her subservience to 'New World glamor and romance'.[26] Her beauty title Miss Mondina 'comes to signify treachery, sterility and greed when she betrays her co-workers by facilitating the theft of rice and jeopardises future harvests by flooding the fields'.[27]

Literary realism's association of raw sexuality with the countryside, as for example in Verga's tale *The She-Wolf*, was an influence here, though De Santis liked to attribute the strongly erotic atmosphere of *Riso amaro* to his own uninhibited upbringing in rural Lazio. More recently, the director had worked with Visconti on *Ossessione*, and it was through that film that he had learned how to blend sexual tension and violence. The presentation of Silvana is certainly informed by the first shots of Calamai in the part of the careworn innkeeper's wife, Giovanna, in Visconti's film. Both portrayals start from the feet and legs. While the spectator hears Giovanna singing to herself in the kitchen before she appears on the screen, and then sees her legs swinging as she sits on the table, Silvana is announced by the sounds of boogie woogie and is then seen from a distance dancing barefoot. Silvana is significantly younger than Giovanna, and her presentation is more carnal and immediate. The camera slowly pans up her body, finishing with a close-up of her radiant face. However, it is not just Giovanna whose portrayal informs the character of Silvana. In her taste for the finer things, which leads her to treachery, she is also a successor of *Roma città aperta*'s drug-addled Marina, the rejected lover of Resistance hero Manfredi who inadvertently betrays him.[28] Unlike Giovanna and Marina, however, Silvana is not inserted into a pattern of social or economic mobility; she is at the aspirational stage, a naive girl who grasps at the chance of some excitement in her life.

Her costumes provide confirmation of this. She is never dressed up; on the evening of the end-of-season party, she wears a simple dress. Her only accessory is the stolen necklace that the thief Walter has given her, which turns out to be fake. For most of the film, she is seen in jumpers or blouses, which she wears with a skirt or shorts. The film's costume designer, Anna Gobbi, started from the premise that Silvana is poor, but then quickly moved on to the need for her to be eroticized. Therefore, though she wears torn thigh-high stockings, these are the cheaper black ones rather than the more expensive grey variety. Her costumes are more revealing and close-fitting than those even of other younger workers, and, for this reason, they would be criticized as inauthentic in the lively discussions that followed the film's release.[29] Nevertheless, they successfully communicate what is supposed to be her unstudied allure. Her skimpy clothes are meant to look like something the character has assembled herself to show off her attributes. They amply expose her legs and arms while revealing the outline of her bust, thus creating the necessary premise for the camera to capture her in profile shots, construct her as body in landscape, and move in for close-ups of her restless eyes and full lips. In short, everything is done to stage the character and highlight the actress's compelling indexical qualities and endow her with some of the features of the pin-up, though not the latter's usual intrinsic, uncomplicated cheerfulness. Though popular, Silvana is moody and irritable.

De Laurentiis was a regular visitor to the set near Vercelli, where, in keeping with his American-style image, he would arrive in his Buick Roadmaster convertible.[30] He took a keen personal interest in Mangano after he noted that she had the unusual ability to draw all eyes and involve strangers in her personality, a quality that Hollywood talent scouts regarded as 'buried gold'.[31] To promote the film, he commissioned paintings from Renato Guttuso, which would adorn the lavish pressbook. The Spanish Civil War photographer Robert Capa was also invited to the set. His image of Silvana standing thigh-deep in water dressed in a tight blouse and shorts, above thigh-high, torn black stockings would arouse worldwide interest in the film months before its release.

Mangano was different to most would-be starlets, and this explains to some degree the extraordinary effect she had on male observers. Though she was assimilated instantly by Calvino and others into an Italian tradition of feminine beauty, she was in fact only half-Italian. She was born and raised in Rome to a Sicilian father and an English mother, who hailed from Croydon. Though the family was not well-off – her father was a railway employee – she had taken acting and dancing lessons and these had inculcated in her a certain refinement. Like the fictional lead characters of Madame de Stael's *Corinne, ou de l'Italie* and George Meredith's *Vittoria*,[32] she had both Italian and English facets. Though she did not look foreign in the way that some of the prewar stars of foreign or mixed background did, she had an aloof, almost regal bearing that conferred distinction on her. Her fair complexion and light brown hair set her apart from most of the other women who passed from beauty pageants to cinema.

Even before *Riso amaro* was released, De Laurentiis set to work for Lux on a new project to consolidate quickly the acclaim he expected her to receive. This time the role assigned to his protégée was unambiguously the leading one. Steno and Mario Monicelli were hired to lead the scriptwriting team, while the direction was entrusted to the experienced Duilio Coletti. *Il lupo della Sila* (The Wolf of the Sila) would be another story of passion and violence, though this time the setting was rural Calabira, a region that had scarcely ever appeared on screen before and that was remote from the modern tensions of *Riso amaro*'s Piedmontese setting. The collective dimension and the leftist engagement with contemporary cultural conflicts were this time excluded. The aim was evidently to build Mangano's appeal in the south and ensure that she would not become typecast as a northern woman. She was cast as Rosaria, a beautiful young woman who is determined to wreak vengeance on Rocco, the landowner who she holds responsible for the death, years before, of her older brother, who had been conducting a secret liaison with his sister. The film was to confirm her as an erotic siren; Rosaria was envisaged as a southern version of Silvana who is enmeshed in a social order dominated by patriarchy and honour. She takes on a femme fatale persona by deliberately instigating a deadly love rivalry between Rocco and his son in her pursuit of revenge.

De Laurentiis persuaded Amedeo Nazzari to return to Italy from Argentina to play the part of Rocco. As a gesture of courtesy, Mangano went to Rome's Ciampino airport to greet him. It was there that the actor, Italy's biggest star of the Fascist period, first caught sight of his next screen partner:

> *Right from when I disembarked from the plane, the splendid exuberance of her figure struck me and, contrary to my usual custom, I started to give vocal vent to my appreciation in terms that were not precisely "orthodox". Fortunately, a friend gave me a nudge to make me realise that I should change my tune. Later he explained to me that Silvana Mangano was the official girlfriend of the producer Dino De Laurentiis.*[33]

The long-awaited launch of *Riso amaro* occurred in a context in which the political tensions in the country continued to grow in the months following the 1948 election. Though defeated, the left remained powerful and determined to enhance its influence in society and culture, while the Christian Democrats were equally determined to undermine it.[34] Among conservatives, there were fears that the film would give succour to Communist propaganda and, for this reason, it was excluded from the Venice film festival. In fact, though the film gave rise to firm Catholic and conservative opposition when it came out in September, there was some relief that De Santis's 'politico-social intentions' had not been realized. As the moderate weekly *Oggi* noted, '*Riso amaro*, as it is, is not at all a left-wing film, and if any pro-communist meanings were initially there, these have evidently got lost along the way. What has happened is that a Communist director, Giuseppe De Santis, has tried to make a propaganda film but has failed first of all to achieve even this objective.'[35] For one right-wing observer, it was a strange hybrid, 'the first social-erotic film, the birth of the proletarian photoromance'.[36] Some leftist critics took a similar view and voiced objections that centred mainly on the role of sex and violence, the implausibility of the melodramatic storyline and the inauthenticity of some of the costumes and situations.[37] While its choral nature and depiction of working women won praise, the suggestion that a working-class girl like Silvana would chew gum and dance to American music was rejected. Between the late 1940s and the mid 1950 there was a growing firmness on the part of critics, who expected left-wing film directors to pursue the neorealist agenda rigorously. Concessions to American fads and techniques were seen as dangerous and damaging. Criticism of De Santis only subsided when the PCI leader Palmiro Togliatti personally intervened to support him.[38] Though he endorsed a more rigid cultural policy as the battles of the Cold War intensified, Togliatti differed from some critics in maintaining that his party should connect with the customs and tastes of working class people as they were. He never objected, for example, to the activities of the Communist illustrated weekly *Vie Nuove*, which even organized its own beauty contests.

De Santis argued that Mangano's beauty and the strong passions that are unleashed around her character were important factors in ensuring that the film reached a popular audience.[39] Melodrama was not a deviation, in his view, but a necessity. He claimed that the huge instant impact registered by her went beyond anything that could have been conceived or planned by a production company. It began with the response her character received from workers on the set. 'I saw the birth of a spontaneous stardom, because Mangano was loved and elected a *diva* by the rice weeders that she represented. It was in the paddy fields that Mangano became a star, spontaneously, not artificially created by publicity.'[40] The workers recognized her as a young woman of the postwar years like themselves. They took her to heart, and some even modelled their outfits on her. Despite her character's fate, she lent them an image that was both more forceful and more feminine than that of a category of humble seasonal workers toiling in harsh conditions. For De Santis, she was proof that, while the star phenomenon was impossible to eliminate, it could be reappropriated for progressive ends.[41] This was something that his critics could not accept and that would be a source of reflection and dispute within left-wing cultural circles for years to come.

Riso amaro was the fifth biggest grossing film in Italy in the 1949–50 season, but its impact was also huge in foreign markets. In the United States, the film's explicit treatment of sex provoked a stern reaction from the Motion Picture Code Association, whose chief, Joseph Breen, was horrified by its blatant indecency. 'This association, in the first instance, was started with the purpose – among other things – to put an end to the exhibition in this country of pictures of this type', he thundered.[42] Despite his opposition, the film was released first with subtitles and later in a dubbed version. For the latter, in September 1950, a 25ft high image of Silvana in the rice fields was erected in Manhattan. The film would attract great interest from those, like the *New York Times* critic Bosley Crowther, who appreciated the adult feel of Italian films. 'A competent actress, Silvana Mangano is especially noteworthy for having introduced to the world Italy's own brand of unvarnished, unself-conscious cinematic sex', he argued. 'It is a product that exists without Hollywood-style trappings of glamour. It needs no speech coaches, protein diets or plastic surgeons. It thrives on tattered clothes, unkempt tresses and squalid settings.'[43] Crowther and others admired Italian cinema's rejection of suggestive artifice and studied flirtatiousness; they regarded its approach to sex as direct rather than coy or furtive in the Hollywood manner.

Riso amaro marked the starting point of international recognition of what came to be perceived as a new Italian take on American sex appeal. Silvana's 'attractiveness is truly pulchritude', commented one observer; 'there is nothing sophisticated about her and her presence alone draws attention.'[44] This directness struck Americans particularly, precisely because it dispensed with all the well-established studio procedures for elaborating images that turned sex into glamour. For Italian men, the character of Silvana – sexualized, slothful and materialistic – evoked a type that they associated with the brothel,[45] a state-licensed institution present throughout the peninsula that would only be abolished in 1958, following a vigorous campaign led by the socialist senator Lina Merlin. Silvana's death interrupts a trajectory that would most likely have led to prostitution, a phenomenon that was amply evoked in postwar cinema though, as Danielle Hipkins has shown, brothels were usually only represented indirectly.[46] Censorship and euphemism combined to transmute commercial sex into cinematic sex appeal.

Regardless of the reservations of some critics, Mangano became an instant star. Her breakthrough was dramatic and immediate, just as the production team had hoped. *Il lupo della Sila*, released just three months after *Riso amaro*, in December 1949, brought further impulse to her burgeoning stardom. The film repeated the melodramatic formula of her debut film, presenting a drama that is played out against an unforgiving mountainous landscape. Mangano's character Rosaria is even more disruptive and troubling a force than Silvana; she is a force of nature set on revenge. Her costumes mostly consist of a black underskirt, a figure-hugging top and simple workwear. During a local festival, at which men are driven to fight over her, she is dressed in a beautiful traditional costume. With her long, thick light brown hair, full lips and womanly body, she is the central focus of the entire film.

De Laurentiis and Mangano married in Campidoglio in July 1949, thereby setting the seal on a partnership that would last for more than thirty years. As Gianni Puccini would lament, Mangano did not 'extend the realistic meaning of her first character';[47] instead her 'unprecedented personal success' would be subjected to 'commercial exploitation'. As a major new cinematic property, she was a great asset to De Laurentiis and his associate Carlo Ponti after they left Lux to found their own company. Both men had an understanding of popular entertainment and were aware of the commercial importance of star names.

The actress's third film *Il brigante Musolino* (The Brigand Musolino, Mario Camerini, 1950) was, on the face of it, a rather similar film to *Il lupo della Sila*. Once again, the setting was rural Calabria and the story was one involving passion, rivalry and murder. The decision not to return her to the north reflected a determination to free her of the inconvenient political associations of her first role. There was also a shift of period away from the controversies of the present. This time the setting was the early twentieth century, and the main events were inspired by the life of a real outlaw, who had spent more than forty years in gaol for a crime he did not commit, namely the killing of a prominent member of the local mafia. It has been described as a 'Southern' in the sense that it transposes to the Italian South some of the features of the American Western.⁴⁸ Once more the male lead was played by Nazzari. Mangano's role was that of Musolino's love interest Mara. Though Nazzari was some twenty-three years her senior, he did not look out of place as the turbulent but virile Musolino and nor did Mangano as the feisty woman who leaves her disapproving father to join him in his quest for natural justice. Location work confirmed the growing provincial passion for cinema. The screenwriter Steno recalled how 'the population went crazy for the two stars, it was overflowing with enthusiasm for cinema, perhaps because it brought excitement to a life that cannot have been among the most pleasant.'⁴⁹ The film was shot just a few months after Mangano had given birth to her daughter Veronica in January. For the first time, there is no focus on her body; instead it is her face that is repeatedly shown in close-up. It is a proud, distinctive face that had been deemed worthy of close scrutiny even in *Riso amaro*. In this, her third film, its 'immaculate beauty' was beginning to become a cinematic icon, though it had not yet gone 'cool', to use Noa Steimatsky's expression describing her appearance in *Le streghe* (The Witches, Luchino Visconti and others, 1967).⁵⁰ It was a measure of her international impact that a film that, in Pauline Small's view,⁵¹ accorded centrality to the role of the male star, was for the American market retitled *Outlaw Girl* and launched with the slogan 'Don't Tangle With Mangano'.

The striking thing about Mangano was that marriage and pregnancy did not come after she was a well-established star but coincided with her affirmation. In contrast to Italian cinema's fixation with the female body as erotic lure, she cultivated a personal image that increasingly placed the accent on her family life. The birth of her daughter in January 1950 was national news; she was interviewed on the radio three days after the birth while still in the clinic.⁵² She was not a star who worked hard or made large numbers of films. Indeed, when her first pregnancy was announced,⁵³ in coincidence with the release of *Il lupo della Sila*, she even expressed the wish to abandon cinema. Her pregnancy was immediately linked in the press with that of Rita Hayworth, to whom she had earlier been compared. The Cannes wedding of the Hollywood star to the playboy Aly Khan, heir to the Aga Khan, leader of the Ismaili Muslims, had been a major media event and had also been accompanied by a declared desire to cease making films.⁵⁴ However, in the world of the postwar illustrated magazines, marriage, motherhood, family and domestic life were aspects of a famous woman's life that had a high commercial value.⁵⁵ Mangano was often photographed with her growing baby and, in later years, subsequent three children.

De Laurentiis knew that his wife's new status did not sit comfortably with her starlet appeal. As the consort of the most enterprising and dynamic of Italian producers, she belonged to the elite of the Roman film world even when she was not making films. She was at her husband's side in the official social scene that revolved around award ceremonies and receptions, and the more informal one that the producer orchestrated to assert his place at the centre of the film business and its creative milieu.⁵⁶ Far from being a regular young mother, she occupied a unique position and led a highly enviable lifestyle. As one magazine journalist wrote:

> *Silvana Mangano is truly glamorous; she is rich, she is popular and she even has in the family a producer who can satisfy all her desires and all her whims as an actress. She lives on the Via Appia Antica in a villa that is situated in enormous grounds and which has the inevitable swimming pool and all the Hollywood-style lavish decoration that we know from so many films.*⁵⁷

The extraordinary transformation in her life was accompanied, indeed was marked, by a steady occlusion of the attributes that had most contributed to her popular success. The focus on motherhood and family was a way of bridging the gap between an original image and present reality, a means of asserting a regular dimension with which women could identify. She gave the impression in magazine spreads and accompanying interviews that she was content in her family life and had little interest in nurturing her screen career.⁵⁸ In 1953, *Festival* ran a feature on her in its 'Album di famiglia' series – which highlighted, alongside her screen roles, her family life as a mother, and her 'simple, domestic tastes'.⁵⁹ She was, as *Amica* entitled an article a few years later, 'Molto mamma poco diva' (More Mum than star).⁶⁰ It was as a Mamma not as an actress that she ostensibly preferred to be seen.⁶¹

It is commonly assumed that the replacement of her sexy image, which she had not chosen, with a more refined one that she found more congenial was a sign of her taking charge of her own body. The decade-long transformation of the actress from teenage seductress to elegant bourgeois beauty has been attributed by feminist critics to the actress's growing agency,⁶² especially, it is implied, in relation to De Laurentiis. Adrienne McLean's work on Hayworth, who is often considered to be the archetypal manufactured star, reveals that a surprising degree of agency may be exercised even by those who appear to have minimal control over their own destinies.[63] Yet, it is difficult to exclude De Laurentiis from the equation, at least as far as the early 1950s are concerned. The producer was deeply involved in modifying Mangano's image from starlet with pin-up appeal to something more appropriate to her new public and private status. He was also aware that starlets had a short shelf life; modifications were required if she was to conserve her value over time. Her films may have been few, but none of them was routine; each was planned with an eye to the development of her screen personality. The same was probably true of her wider image. Her co-star Nazzari became convinced that the change was the product of a well-concealed strategy. Looking back in the mid 1960s at his experience of working with her fifteen or so years earlier, he commented: 'I suspect that her silence in those days, her reserve, her wish to be as detached as possible, rather than a genuine timidity, as I thought then, were expressions of a very precise "plan" which has led to her becoming today a sophisticated woman and the complete and complex actress that we all know.'[64]

The film *Anna* (Alberto Lattuada, 1951) was a watershed. It was conceived by De Laurentiis and Ponti as a film in the style of Raffaello Matarazzo's hugely successful *Catene* (Chains, 1950), which was produced by the rival company Titanus. It was a melodrama that brought together erotic and spiritual elements to function as a star vehicle for Mangano. The film relates the story of a novice nun, working as a nurse in a Milan hospital, who chose to give up her job as a nightclub singer to devote herself to God after her one-time fiancé killed a love rival. Much of the narrative is told in flashback after Anna's former fiancé is brought to the hospital for treatment following a serious road accident. The audience was offered two Manganos for the price of one – the nun and zealous nurse in the present, and the seductive entertainer in suggestive flashbacks. The film, moreover, recreated the passionate triangle of *Riso amaro*, with Raf Vallone cast as the honest but dull – though this time wealthy – fiancé Andrea and Vittorio Gassman as the insidious and seductive barman Vittorio. The De Laurentiis villa would feature in the film as the home of the industrialist Andrea. The director Lattuada described the film as above all 'a production operation' that was 'cynical-pharmaceutical' in its intentions. It began, he said, from the premise: 'We have got la Mangano, let's see if, by stripping her down and dressing her up as a nun, making her do bad and do good, we can ...'.[65] A tearjerker on a grand scale – 'an erotic-religious pudding' for Spinazzola,[66] an 'urban remake' of her first film for Cimmino and Masi[67] – the film suggests that, even in her nunly garb, Anna is still capable of arousing Andrea, though in the end she opts not to flee with him. Her conscience strikes when a railway accident means that she is needed at the hospital. Ever intense, her choices are total and uncompromising.

Anna was released in Italy in December 1951 and became the second top box office film of the 1951–52 season. It was important in terms of the refinement and development of Mangano's image in that it marked a significant step in the normalization of her persona aimed at rendering her a less explosive and erotic presence.[68] Instead, she emerged as a multifaceted actress capable of conveying both the physical and the spiritual. Although the extraordinarily close identification in the public mind between Mangano and her first screen character informs her characterization, her sensual persona is restricted to flashbacks and consigned to memory. The intended adjustment of her image is underscored by a physical change; her cheeks have hollowed out and she has a 'new face' in which her long, full but rarely smiling lips are more evident and her aquiline nose emerges, 'presenting certain problems to cinematographers'.[69] The 'aristocratic' trait that marked her from the beginning,[70] a quality she shared with another beauty contest winner, Lucia Bosè, permitted a transformation that might otherwise have been improbable. Her eyes, above all, stand out, and their melancholic expressiveness is magnetic. As her body receded, her face emerged as her key trademark.

Writers and intellectuals approved of this change, and they began to write about her flawless face, whose deep-set eyes and full lips marked it as Mediterranean as opposed to the Nordic severity of Greta Garbo in her prime. For Vasco Pratolini, she had a capacity to interpret a feminine ideal that had been distorted by the trite effort to turn her into a cinematic vamp, a voyeur's delight.[71] It was her dark eyes, her long neck and her white complexion that were seen to encapsulate the essence of her femininity. For the Armenian, Milan-based portrait painter Gregorio Sciltian, her face was a Renaissance one that, however, bore an expression that had something 'eternal, indescribable' about it.[72] Moreover, her personality became increasingly remote. Physical refinement was aligned with an attitude that became at once aloof and timid. Though the process of transformation would not be completed until 1966, when the weekly magazine *Oggi* invited a selection of professional image-makers to comment on her beauty,[73] its origins can be dated from the period following *Il lupo della Sila*. Acute observers, alert to her English parentage, identified her appearance as a combination of northern and southern elements. In the new image, the English elements came for the first time to the fore.

Anna's huge international success consolidated the actress's status as the leading star of Italian cinema. It would not mark the start of a popular series; rather it was a stepping stone to greater things. Mangano's next films formed part of De Laurentiis's plans for the conquest of the international market by means of collaborations with Hollywood and films that were conceived and made on an international scale. Though both *Mambo* (Robert Rossen, 1954) and *Ulisse* (Ulysses, Mario Camerini, 1954) were made in Italy, the first involved the participation of Paramount, while the second was the first Italian film to feature a major American star, Kirk Douglas, as the male lead. The films again gave the actress a chance to play out a change of persona or, in the case of the latter, to play two roles once again, that of the stoical, patient queen Penelope, awaiting the return of her long-absent husband, and 'seductive, smouldering Circe, against the spell of whose beauty no man is armed'.[74] Without leaving her home country, Mangano was positioned as an international star with multiple facets to her screen persona.

In the same year, she also appeared in an episode of *L'Oro di Napoli* (The Gold of Naples, Vittorio De Sica, 1954). Mangano played Teresa, a prostitute originally from Rome who is wooed and married by a handsome, wealthy man whom she soon discovers has wed her because he is seeking to expiate the guilt he feels for the suicide of his one-time sweetheart. It was a role that called for more engaged acting from Mangano to convey the emotional rollercoaster of her character. No one was better qualified to assist her in the development than De Sica, who had helped non-professionals play leading roles and who would also coach other young female stars, including Sophia Loren. But the extent of De Laurentiis's involvement in her presentation can be gauged from the fact that he sent the troupe back to Naples to reshoot the ending when he found it unsatisfactory.[75] No expense was to be spared in ensuring that her episode was perfect. For Silvana, it signalled the start of a transition to more bourgeois parts for, like many fictional prostitutes, Teresa is entirely capable of carrying off the role of bourgeois spouse. The association with sex is still there, but it is embedded in the backstory of the character rather than marked through emphasis on the actress's physical person. Only the Romanesque inflection to the actress's screen voice betrays Teresa's lower-class origin. Indeed, she is elegant and poised. For the journalist and radio broadcaster Anna Garofalo, she had 'that bloodless and sophisticated air of a *Vogue* cover girl or of a well-bred girl who studies languages at Oxford'.[76]

The efforts to displace her first film in the popular imagination would continue for many years. 'Unfortunately, a good part of the public is stuck with the impression of Silvana Mangano from the time of *Riso amaro* and perhaps still goes to see my films with the sole expectation of seeing my legs exposed', she lamented.[77] This type of attention caused her to recoil from some aspects of stardom. As an actress who had never struggled to win attention and who had no need to engage in the unseemly battle for publicity, she could afford to remain aloof. Beyond her identity as a mother, she never revealed much of herself to the public or enjoyed engaging with fans. In interviews, she never spoke of her privileges and often appeared detached. She defended her privacy: 'If a photographer has an interest, almost a duty to photograph a famous person, I think that the individual also has the right not to be photographed. I do not think of myself as a national monument, nor as a landscape. And I do not think that I provide such an original gallery of attitudes as to merit being photographed almost every day.'[78] 'I am jealous of my private life', she complained, 'just like anyone who does not want to expose the intimacy of their existence in public. What's more, I do not consider myself to be a "sensation" actress. I do not wish to go around exhibiting myself in public with the attitudes of a "diva"'.[79] She disliked the adulation that her success brought. 'When I appear in public, my admirers give me no peace even if my reaction offers them no encouragement. I make an effort to be kind, but I try to avoid requests for autographs and escape from conversations as quickly as possible. It is fear of the public and of interviews, which perhaps is unjustified, that leads me to such extremes' (see Figure 11.3).[80]

Mangano lacked the film star's sense of obligation to her fans because of the way fame came to her. But she also lacked the conviction that she had achieved her position through her own labour.[81] She was notoriously unsure of herself as a screen performer, not least because she was dubbed by a voice actress in all her films.[82] Despite the significant on-the-spot guidance she received from De Sica, she was self-deprecating. 'As an actress, I just improvised', she confessed. 'I have never studied acting and so I have always been afraid of falling short. Mixed with pride, this fear often made me freeze.' In truth, Mangano's screen performances do not betray any amateurishness or woodenness. Though she had minimal training, she occupies the scene convincingly, in line with the shift towards corporeal recitation that became such a key feature of postwar cinema. In relation to Nazzari or Gassman, she may have felt inadequate, but she learned fast and her directors gave her support.

Figure 11.3 Silvana Mangano signing autographs at the 1952 Venice film festival. Meeting fans and satisfying their requests for autographs were among her least favourite activities (author's own collection).

Her social position, if anything, heightened her timidity. Her fame and her privileged existence isolated her from the real world and trapped her in a golden cage in which a certain capriciousness, perhaps unsurprisingly, flourished.[83] Although she developed a fashionable, more sophisticated persona, she only superficially became like one of Truman Capote's elegant super-rich 'swans', who included Fiat heir Gianni Agnelli's elegant wife Marella.[84] She does not appear to have been interested in exercising the sort of aesthetic power that Annette Tapert attributes to high society wives who engaged in individual and personalized acts of self-fashioning.[85] 'I am half English and half Sicilian – a permanent contradiction' she said. 'When you are like that, it is difficult to have strong self-esteem, to accept yourself as you are.'[86] Despite her diffidence towards film-making and the public, her world remained the cinematic one she shared with her husband, and it was in that milieu that she felt most at ease. Mangano's reserve contrasted with the excess of her initial persona and endeared her to colleagues and public alike. Amid the bright lights and clamour of postwar stardom, it conferred on her a quasi-regal aura. Her detachment fed into a refinement that would leave her early image far behind while maintaining the emphasis on beauty. Over time, it lent her a sphinx-like quality that observers would find increasingly fascinating, as they had in the prewar era with Garbo. The close collaboration between the actress and De Laurentiis was vital to the construction and transformation of her star persona, though there were also tensions that would later undermine, and finally break, first their partnership and then their marriage.

Notes

1. In U. Lisi, 'Le paghe degli attori', *Cinema Nuovo*, March 1955, 177–84, 177. Mangano's cachet per film, the highest in Italy, was estimated at Lit. 60m, while, by contrast, Silvana Pampanini's was Lit. 30m.
2. See the exhibition catalogue by Gundle et al., *Dream makers: come i produttori hanno fatto grande il cinema italiano.*
3. Anon., 'Un film sulle mondine', *Stampasera*, 3 July 1948, 3.
4. Kezich and Levantesi, *Dino: De Laurentiis, la vita e i film*, 71.
5. Quoted in Faldini and Fofi, *L'avventurosa storia del cinema italiano: raccontata dai suoi protagonisti, 1935–1959*, 154.
6. Kezich and Levantesi, *Dino*, 74–75.
7. See M. Wood, 'From Bust to Boom: Women and Representations of Prosperity in Italian Cinema of the Late 1940s and 1950s', in Morris, *Women in Italy, 1945–1960: An Interdisciplinary Study*, 52, 55.
8. See Forgacs and Gundle, *Mass Culture and Italian Society from Fascism to the Cold War*, 73–91.

9. Faldini and Fofi, *L'avventurosa storia*, 154.
10. See Gundle, *Bellissima: Feminine Beauty and the Idea of Italy*, 108–12.
11. The rice workers were partly paid in kind, receiving 1kg of rice for each day worked. Before they travel home, each woman takes a fistful of rice from her sack to cast over Silvana's body.
12. Anon., 'Un film sulle mondine', 3.
13. I. Calvino, 'Tra i pioppi della risaia la "cinecittà" delle mondine' (1948), in Calvino, *Saggi 1945–1985*, 1882–87. Originally published in *L'Unità* (Piedmont edition), 14 July 1948.
14. Lizzani, *Riso amaro*, 97.
15. See Cigognetti and Servetti, '"On Her Side": Female Images in Italian Cinema and the Popular Press, 1945–1955', 55–63.
16. G. Grignaffini, 'Il femminile nel cinema italiano: racconti di rinascita', in Brunetta, *Identità italiana e identità europea nel cinema italiano dal 1945 al miracolo economico*, 358. Among the other films that made use of this identification are *Non c'è pace tra gli ulivi* (No Peace under the Olive Tree, Giuseppe De Santis, 1950), *La donna del fiume* (Woman of the River, Mario Soldati, 1954) and *La risaia* (Rice Girl, Raffaello Matarazzo, 1956). The latter two films were star vehicles respectively for Sophia Loren and Elsa Martinelli.
17. Grignaffini, 'Verità e poesia: ancora di Silvana e del cinema italiano', 43. The phrase is italicized in the original.
18. See Cigognetti and Servetti, '"On Her Side" and, for a recent discussion, Carman, 'Mapping the Body: Female Film Stars and the Reconstruction of Postwar Italian National Identity', 322–35.
19. See Landes, *Visualizing the Nation: Gender, Representation and Revolution in Eighteenth Century France*.
20. See Gundle, *Bellissima*, Chapters 5 and 6.
21. See Gabrielli, *1946, le donne, la repubblica*.
22. Grignaffini, 'Verità e poesia', 45.
23. Ibid., 45.
24. Ibid., 45.
25. See Gundle, *Bellissima*, 145–46.
26. M. Marcus, 'The Italian Body Politic is a Woman: Feminized National Identity in Postwar Italian Film', in Stewart and Cornish, *Sparks and Seeds: Medieval Literature and Its Afterlife*, 338.
27. Ibid., 338.
28. On Marina, see Holdaway and Missero, 'Re-reading Marina: Sexuality, Materialism and the Construction of Italy', 348–58.
29. See S. Gundle, 'Il PCI e la campagna contro Hollywood (1948–1958)', in Ellwood and Brunetta, *Hollywood in Europa: industria, politica, pubblico del cinema 1945–1960*, 121–22.
30. Kezich and Levantesi, *Dino*, 74–75.
31. Davis, *The Glamour Factory: Inside Hollywood's Big Studio System*, 83.
32. Mme de Stael, *Corinne, or Italy*, and Meredith, *Vittoria*.
33. A. Nazzari, 'Ho un sospetto sui silenzi di Silvana', *Oggi*, 2 June 1966, 74.
34. See Gundle, *Between Hollywood and Moscow: The Italian Communists and the Challenge of Mass Culture, 1943–1991*.
35. A. Solmi, 'Le colpe di Riso amaro', *Oggi* 42 (1949), 37.
36. Quarantotto, *Il cinema, la carne e il diavolo*, 166.
37. Gundle, 'Il PCI e la campagna contro Hollywood', 121–22.
38. See Gundle, *Between Hollywood and Moscow*, 67 and 230n. Togliatti's letter was published in *Vie Nuove*, 13 November 1949, 15.

39. Gili and Grossi, *Alle origini del neorealismo: Giuseppe De Santis a colloquio con Jean A. Gili*, 123.
40. A. Costa, 'Conversazione con Giuseppe De Santis', *Cinema & Cinema* 9(30) (1982), 68–69.
41. Renzi, *Gina Lollobrigida*, 26.
42. AAMPAS, MPAA PCA, *Riso amaro*. Memorandum of Joseph Breen to Gordon White.
43. *66*, issue no.15 (undated, approximately 1957), 10–13.
44. Anon., 'Le celebrità prese di petto', *Stampasera*, 10 January 1950, 3.
45. For a nostalgic evocation of the imaginary of the brothel, see Fusco, *Quando l'Italia tollerava*. On the linkages between materialism and prostitution in postwar films, see Wood, 'From Bust to Boom', in Morris, *Women in Italy, 1945–1960*, 56–57.
46. Hipkins, *Italy's Other Women: Gender and Prostitution in Italian Cinema, 1940–1965*, 204.
47. G. Puccini, 'Il fenomeno Mangano' (1954), in Aristarco, *Il mito dell'attore: come l'industria della star produce il sex symbol*, 279.
48. Germani, *Mario Camerini*, 110–11. On the theme of the 'Southern', see also Farassino, *Mario Camerini*, 182–83.
49. Steno, cited in Faldini and Fofi, *L'avventurosa storia*, 173.
50. Steimatsky, *The Face on Film*, 187.
51. P. Small, 'The *Maggiorata* or Sweater Girl of the 1950s', in Bondanella, *The Italian Cinema Book*, 121.
52. Cimmino and Masi, *Silvana Mangano: il teorema della bellezza*, 35.
53. See, for example, the cover of *La Settimana Incom*, 10 December 1949 'Anche la Mangano aspetta un bambino' and text on p. 2.
54. See Gundle, *Glamour: A History*, 205–7.
55. See Buckley, 'Marriage, Motherhood and the Italian Film Stars of the 1950s', in Morris, *Women in Italy*, 35–49.
56. Kezich and Levantesi, *Dino*, 96–97.
57. V. Ciuffa, 'Molto mamma poco diva', *Amica*, 27 May 1962, 17.
58. S. Mangano De Laurentiis, 'Scusatemi ma non sono una diva', *Oggi* 44 (1957), 34.
59. *Festival*, 17 January 1953, 9–11.
60. Ciuffa, 'Molto mamma poco diva', 15–19.
61. F. Patellani, 'Silvana Mangano: due terzi mamma e un terzo attrice', *Tempo*, August 1952 (n. 34), 43–45. Buckley observes that it is difficult to know entirely how far this was by her own choice. See Buckley, 'Marriage, Motherhood ...', in Morris, *Women in Italy*, 46.
62. The metamorphosis of her appearance from sexy starlet to elegant actress and diva occurred over time. It is the single most important element in the development of her star persona and, it might be added, a watershed in the configuration of the postwar female star system. Though it was specifically related to changes in Mangano's life, it coincided with the process of modernization in society, which would lead to the ascendancy of different ideals of feminine beauty that were more youthful, urban, bourgeois and ethereal. In the actress's case, the conventional view is that by altering her image she reasserted control over her body and its representation against the imposed sexualization that marked her screen image from the moment she was cast as Silvana. She distanced herself from her former image and thus paved the way for the autonomy that she would assert in the later 1960s, when she made Pasolini's *Teorema* without the consent of De Laurentiis. See Detassis, 'Corpi recuperati per il proprio sguardo', 24–31, and Carman, 'Mapping the Body', 332.
63. McLean, *Being Rita Hayworth: Labor, Identity and Hollywood Stardom*.
64. Nazzari, 'Ho un sospetto sui silenzi di Silvana', 74.

65. Lattuada, cited in Faldini and Fofi, *L'avventurosa storia*, 173.
66. Spinazzola, *Cinema e pubblico: lo spettacolo filmico in Italia, 1945–1965*, 29. The critics of the time were not kind. Franco Valobra, for example, judged the film to be incoherent, both in the ways the characters were drawn and in the situations in which they were placed. See 'Vocazioni sbagliate', *Rassegna del film* 1(1), February 1952.
67. Cimmino and Masi, *Silvana Mangano*, 37.
68. Spinazzola, *Cinema e pubblico*, 82.
69. Cimmino and Masi, *Silvana Mangano*, 38 and 41.
70. Fofi, *Più stelle che in cielo*, 133.
71. V. Pratolini, 'Silvana Mangano', in Prono, *Le sirene immaginarie: dive raccontate da scrittori*, 116.
72. G. Sciltian, 'Bellezza rinascimentale ma con gambe troppo corte', *Oggi*, 2 June 1966, 75.
73. A.M. Mori and S. Mazzocchi, 'Esaminiamo e giudichiamo le donne più belle: iniziamo da Silvana Mangano', *Oggi* 2 June 1966.
74. 'Notes on the Ponti-De Laurentiis Production *Ulysses*'. Folder *Ulysses*, Kirk Douglas papers, University of Madison at Wisconsin.
75. See Marotta, *Al cinema non fa freddo*, 47–52. De Laurentiis demanded a decisive ending in favour of the ambiguity of the original tale and De Sica and Zavattini's first version.
76. A. Garofalo, 'Maggiorate offese' (1955), in Aristraco, *Il mito dell'attore*, 264.
77. Ibid., 34.
78. Mangano De Laurentiis, 'Scusatemi ma non sono una diva', 32–37.
79. Ibid., 32.
80. Ibid., 35.
81. Tapert, *The Power of Glamour*.
82. In all her early films, her voice is that of Lidia Simoneschi.
83. See Irene Brin's first-hand account of the actress's behaviour during a promotional trip to the USA in Brin, *L'Italia esplode: diario dell'anno 1952*, 139, 144.
84. Capote socialized with a number of high society women in New York, until he was ostracized after he broke their confidences in his short story 'La Côte Basque, 1965'. On Marella Agnelli, see Agnelli and Caracciolo Chia, *Marella Agnelli: The Last Swan*.
85. Tapert and Edkins, *The Power of Style*.
86. Mangano De Laurentiis, 'Scusatemi ma non sono una diva', 36.

CHAPTER 12
Amedeo Nazzari
The Hero Domesticated

Over the period between 1938, when he starred in the defining film of his career, the aviation drama *Luciano Serra pilota* (Luciano Serra Pilot, Goffredo Alessandrini), and the fall of Mussolini in July 1943, Amedeo Nazzari was indisputably the most prominent film star in Italy. He starred in some thirty-two films, which included some of the most prestigious titles of those years. For the regime, he was proof that Italian cinema could produce stars equal in stature to the idols of Hollywood. The leading Fascist official in the cinema sector, Luigi Freddi, claimed part of the merit for building him up.[1] Nazzari also showed that cinema could serve the interests of Fascism by offering examples of courage and dutiful endeavour, patriotism and self-sacrifice. Though he made light comedies and costume dramas as well as some propaganda films, he was so aligned with the imaginative universe of the regime that some critics have seen him as a cinematic alter ego of the dictator himself. Gian Piero Brunetta argues that the actor was seen as 'the Mussolinian hero par excellence' (albeit 'unjustly'),[2] while Giuseppe Gubitosi has discussed the 'complementary nature – within the collective imagination – of the myth of Mussolini and the personality of Nazzari'.[3] The air of authority and patriotism that was a hallmark of all the star's characters – and a frequent feature of the plot of many of his contemporary and modern historical films – bolstered the Fascists' palingenetic project of collective national re-foundation.

However, Nazzari was not only a tool of the regime. While there were undoubtedly areas of overlap between the physical and moral qualities that were associated with his persona and the idea of the nation and its people that was endorsed by Fascism, some of this was due to the way in which the regime took over ideas and values that predated its inception and that were embedded in the Risorgimento tradition. His generosity of spirit, nobility, sense of justice, respect for tradition and loyalty were qualities that had been associated with Italian nationalism long before the rise of Fascism. His sturdy presence and the unflinching character of the men he played seemed to belong to an old order of society in which the land and inherited roles dominated. Nazzari, it has been said, was the ideal bearer of national virtues; he was an Italian as 'the Italians would have liked to be'.[4] If he was also an example of the Italian that the Fascists wanted to create, this was because they sought to appropriate national traditions for their own divisive ends.[5]

These qualities mean that Nazzari was not so bound up with Fascism that any major postwar role was barred to him. On the contrary, he stood for values that still had some currency and that a wide range of forces wished to inherit. Though it was not at all clear how or in what forms they would feed into the political and cultural texture of a democratic Italy, they belonged to a current of Italian nationalism that was associated with the founding of the modern state more than the recently deposed dictatorship. The film industry faced particular challenges in finding ways of rebuilding the confidence of audiences and engaging with the process of democratization in the country. How it would choose to employ its most prominent star was a conundrum (see Figure 12.1). As American films took the lion's share of Italian screens and threatened to push national films to the margins of the market, it became an issue that the industry could not ignore.

On a personal level, Nazzari could not be subjected to much reproval. He had avoided any overt engagement with the regime, though several of his films contained instances of anti-American or anti-British attitudes, and his patriotic impulses were harnessed to military-themed films.[6] The actor had been called up to serve in the army, though he was stationed in Rome and benefited from certain privileges that derived both from his star status and from his being the sole male child of a widowed mother. 'I was a soldier to some degree after my own style and I enjoyed a certain freedom that was granted to me for my work as an actor', he later commented. 'My uniform, rather out of the ordinary and with silk shirts, was looked at askance by some of my superiors.'[7] He had not gone to Venice with Freddi and even tried to save his friends, Osvaldo Valenti and Luisa Ferida, who had not only travelled north but had lent their support to the Italian Social Republic. After the liberation of Rome in 1944, realizing that they were getting themselves into a dangerous situation, he decided to act. With the film director Aldo Vergano, he went one day to the offices of the Committee for National Liberation in Via Po and offered to be parachuted behind the line that separated northern from southern Italy to film the war events of the moment.[8] His true objective, however, was to rescue the two actors. After a wait of several weeks, he was told that he was too well known to accomplish the mission. In April 1945, he would learn that his friends had been executed by partisans.

Nazzari only recounted this episode in a magazine interview in 1964. The picture it gives suggests that a certain confusion had entered his mind between his screen roles and his real capabilities. However, if he ever thought that nothing was beyond his powers, this conviction would not last for long after the war. Though he was renowned for his professionalism and consequently enjoyed a positive reputation among producers and many directors (some, however, resented his habit of interfering with the organization of a shoot and having his lines rewritten when he felt they could be improved),[9] it was not at all clear what place, if any, he might find in the postwar film industry. The critics and film-makers who were engaged in plotting a new course for Italian cinema took a dim view of most of the actors who had been active during the later years of the regime. They objected to the very idea of the film star and where possible were concerned to abolish the notion of the professional screen actor as this had been hitherto configured. None of the pioneers of the new wave in postwar cinema – Rossellini, De Sica and Visconti – would ever cast him in one of their films. They uniformly sought new figures and types to interpret the themes and issues that they held dear.

Yet Nazzari was not without friends or resources. Established directors including Blasetti and Camerini held him in esteem, and there was no reason to suppose that he did not still exercise some appeal for audiences.[10] However, the question remained as to how he could be used, and this was presented most pressingly in the period in which Italian production was quantitatively small and the country's screens were filled with foreign, mainly American imports. Taking the period 1945–53, it is possible to divide Nazzari's postwar trajectory into three reasonably distinct phases. The first is marked by an attempt at reconfiguration. Nazzari's patriotic persona was given a new dimension by inserting him in the context of the civil war and the reconstruction. This brought him into contact with the prevailing democratic mood and positioned him to some degree in such a way that, in principle, he might have been able to find a place in the most interesting current in Italian cinema. The second phase began when this failed to happen and he entered a period of crisis. At this time, he emigrated first to Spain and then to Argentina, where he made a number of films, none of which would ever be released in Italy. Finally, there is his re-emergence in a context that saw conservative forces triumph over impulses to social reform as well as the re-establishment of the film industry and rapid growth of the exhibition sector in the provinces and the south. This shift in the general climate and in film production enabled him to emerge once more – against the background of the ebbing of the neorealist current – as Italian cinema's biggest box office draw. It is notable that, over this whole period, the light comedy roles that Nazzari had taken in films including *Centomila dollari* (One Hundred Thousand Dollars, Mario Camerini, 1939) and *Dopo divorzieremo* (Afterwards We Will Divorce, Nunzio Malasomma, 1940) dried up entirely with the disappearance of the genre that had given rise to them. The Nazzari of the 1950s was not simply a more mature version of his earlier persona; he was a narrower figure who functioned only in two genres and whose appeal was strongest among the lower classes and in the provinces. First-run audiences in the north and centre of the country showed little interest in him.

His first postwar role was in a film produced by the Catholic production company Orbis and directed by Blasetti. Set almost entirely in a convent, though largely filmed in the studio in Rome, *Un giorno nella vita* (One Day in Life, 1946) explores the cordial relationships that are gradually established between a community of unworldly nuns and a band of partisans who seek their help as they hide from German soldiers. There is a strong gender aspect to the film, since the female space of the convent is violated by both the partisans and the Germans, the difference between the two being that the former are generally respectful and form a series of connections with the nuns. A choral work that was shot on a shoestring, the film featured several stars, including Nazzari, Massimo Girotti, Elisa Cegani and Mariella Lotti. All concerned appear to have been aware that the film offered an opportunity to take their distance from the cinema of the Fascist era. The mood and performance style is notably subdued. The film engages directly with war events and ends in tragedy when the nuns are shot for harbouring the partisans.

For Nazzari, to embrace the role of a former soldier – a captain – turned partisan chief was a bold move, although care was taken not to accord his character the sort of heroic status he would have had in the past. For Piero Pruzzo, the actor seemed to be trying to adopt a lower profile: 'He knew full well that the period of three or four years that separated this film from the seasons of his full employment at Cinecittà and the apex of his personal star appeal was as long as a century, that cinema needed to turn over a new leaf. And he began again humbly, just like many others.'[11] The names of the protagonists appear, without star billing, in alphabetical order in the opening credits, and he is introduced without ceremony or glamour. As befits his role, he is unshaven, dishevelled and downbeat.

He has a nasty cold and blows his nose into a large, dirty handkerchief. When he smokes, he grasps his cigarette claw-like between his fingers. He delivers his lines without emphasis, in understated fashion. But he gradually emerges as a figure of stature in a band that includes boys, jokers, a former Fascist and one seriously wounded fighter. The nuns see that, to his fellow fighters, he is 'like the mother superior is for us' and note that he is respectful towards them. There is a hint of his handsome presence in a scene in which a group of nuns seek to reassure each other that they did not allow their gaze to fall on him when the partisans briefly joined them in the chapel. Their hollow denials serve to underline his charisma. He demonstrates comprehension for all, giving practical shape to a new idea of the nation that grants space to different views and experiences. Sister Bianca, a novice played by Lotti, begins to wonder if she would not be more useful in the wider world; she converses with him and makes to leave the convent with the men. Nazzari sends her back with the promise that he will return; after the massacre, he lifts her lifeless head in affectionate tribute before he exits in haste to rejoin the battle.

The film was released in Italy in May 1946 and was presented at Cannes. In both contexts, it received a positive response. Noting similarities with the ecumenical approach of *Roma città aperta*, critics praised the ability with which Blasetti tackled the theme of the Resistance and the encounter between a varied band of partisans and a community of nuns. Writing in *Hollywood*, Adriano Baracco reserved praise for the actors, who, he said, 'had never worked so well as in *Un giorno nella vita*'.[12] Only Eugenio Ferdinando Palmieri in *Film* condemned the work as 'a star-studded film; not a drama of anonymous faces but of celluloid glamour. Not people but actors: la Cegani remains la Cegani, Nazzari is still Nazzari and so on'.[13] For Carlo Trabucco, writing in the Christian Democrat daily *Il Popolo*, this did not present a problem. He was pleased to see that the partisan chief played by Nazzari was 'a brusque character, unalloyed and likeable', a comment that blended the actor's screen persona and the character of the soldier-turned-partisan into one.[14] However, the film did not please everyone, and a group of Roman university students even wrote to Blasetti to protest against the film's 'banal and monotonous realization' and 'down-beat and disengaged acting'.[15]

Little is known of the actor's personal attitude towards political events as the war drew to a conclusion, beyond the fact that he refused to join Freddi in Venice and took part in the Vatican-sponsored film *I dieci comandamenti* (The Ten Commandments, Giorgio Chili, 1945) during the German occupation of Rome.[16] But

Figure 12.1 A polished Amedeo Nazzari on the cover of *Cine illustrato*, 15 February 1948 (author's own collection).

his habit of jealously protecting the integrity of his screen persona meant that he will have taken care over the roles he accepted as the country adjusted to peace. All Italians carried baggage, and Nazzari's task was to inhabit characters who embodied an awareness of this as they struggled to move forward with dignity. Two of the five roles he played in 1946–47 were prestigious, high-profile ones produced by Dino De Laurentiis for the Lux company. The first of these was Alberto Lattuada's *Il bandito* (The Bandit, 1946) in which a returning soldier finds that his family and moral world has been destroyed. Lattuada had originally thought of Andrea Checchi for the part of the soldier turned bandit, thinking him 'more suited, better prepared' for the part, but De Laurentiis sent him out onto the street to test the actor's name recognition.[17] After drawing a blank, he found that when Nazzari's name was mentioned 'everyone knew him and remembered him very well'. The producer encouraged him to think of his film as a popular spectacle. 'You must make a popular film: Magnani, Nazzari!', he proclaimed to him, brushing aside Lattuada's fears that propaganda films had compromised the latter's name if not his marketability.[18]

With Italian cinema's most prominent stars in the leading roles, the film's treatment of the devastation wrought by civil war on Italy's social fabric offered several appeals. Shot partly on location amid war-damaged buildings, it was infused with an air of reality that was complemented by the depiction of the devastation that events had wrought on Nazzari's character Ernesto's family and their home. But it also bore the hallmarks of genre cinema. *Il bandito* more or less turns into a gangster movie in the second half. After learning that his sister has become a prostitute, Nazzari's character goes on the rampage and kills the man who has pimped her and then murdered her. To escape capture, he is forced to join a criminal gang headed by Magnani's character, the seductive Lydia. He is eventually killed by the Carabinieri in a shoot-out. However, this outcome occurs after he has redeemed himself by saving the baby daughter of one of his former comrades-in-arms from danger. The film reflected some of the real dramas that had been experienced in Italy and gave Nazzari the chance to reassert his persona as a man alone, albeit, for those who recalled his earlier roles, 'unusually contained, unusually self-controlled.'[19]

Ruth Ben-Ghiat has highlighted the added value that star casting could bring. 'The handsome and physically imposing Nazzari brought a sense of glamour as well as danger to his role, giving [*Il bandito*] its libidinal charge and its commercial viability', she argues, even though 'his popularity came in part from having starred in fascist military films.'[20] Alluding to this ideological aspect of his persona, she concludes that, 'the sorry fate he meets ... as an unredeemable example of militarised masculinity ... has a performative meaning in several senses.' While all films belonging, broadly speaking, to the current of neorealism sought to set out a vision of the nation that was pluralist and democratic in contrast to the totalitarian one of Nazism and Fascism, Ben-Ghiat suggests that star casting 'opens up for public view and discussion an Italian manhood in crisis, as personified in the returned soldier-prisoner, who stood for both the hard heart of fascism and for the ignominy of its defeat'.[21] *Il bandito*, in her view, 'draws parallels between injuries to national prestige and injuries to Italian manhood' and appears to locate solutions to both types of wound in the re-establishment of the family as the locus of responsible male roles.[22] Reflecting on the poor critical reception the film received, she suggests, taking the viewpoint of one contemporary reviewer, that it aimed not to speak to critics but directly to spectators, in recognition that the work of reconstructing Italian masculinity in a new context would necessarily be a collective one.[23]

Nazzari was certainly a prominent enough actor for collective discourses to revolve around him. Lattuada's film (which was written by the director and a team of collaborators including Tullio Pinelli and Piero Tellini) was an important one. But the issue of how far the questions it raised could be aired through him depends not only on this film but also on the other films he made in the postwar period. The second film he made for Lux was less immediately relevant. Indeed, it was a classic film of the type in which he had excelled in the prewar period. Directed by Mario Camerini, *La figlia del capitano* (The Captain's Daughter, 1947) was a product of great professionalism, which was screened at Cannes. A costume drama filmed on a grand scale, it was a project that reflected the ambitions of De Laurentiis as well as a disenchanted faith in traditional film spectacle. Adapted from a Pushkin story, it presented a romantic narrative unfolding against the background of the Cossack rebellion against Empress Catherine II. After making a low-key entrance as an anonymous figure found wandering in the snow, Nazzari's character is revealed as the Cossack leader Pugacev, the self-styled Tsar Peter III. Almost unrecognizable beneath a bushy beard and exaggerated eyebrows, it is his distinctive voice that signals to spectators the star's presence. As so often in the past, his character's authority is not institutional but derives from an ascendancy over his fellows. Attired in skins and heavily tattooed, this peasant chief offers his followers an example of cruelty and bravery; primitive in his rude attitudes and uncontrolled laughter, yet honourable in his behaviour towards an imperial soldier who offered him disinterested help, he is at once dignified and repulsive. For sure, no one could say that Pugacev's masculinity was anything but unreconstructed. The film won Nazzari plaudits, with *Il Messaggero*'s critic claiming that 'for the first time Nazzari participates intimately in the nature of his character.'[24] His most telling scene comes when he receives the visit of Catherine II in his condemned cell. Reflective and soft-spoken, Pugacev asserts his traditional Russian identity against the Prussian-born empress, who has come to discover whether the officer who once assisted him is guilty of treason. In the final scene of the film, his slow final walk down a long corridor that leads through two massive doors to the appointed site of his execution establishes the rustic rebel's honour and resignation.

In 1947–48, Nazzari was once more working to an intense rhythm, appearing in three further films. But all were routine productions devoid of any meaningful innovation. None of them built on the credit the actor had acquired though his first postwar films or offered any significant indication of how his persona might be further redefined in a new context. The first, *Il cavaliere del sogno* (Life of Donizetti, Camillo Mastrocinque, 1946), was a costume drama based on an episode from the private life of the composer Donizetti. It is likely that the film appealed to Nazzari on account of its patriotic theme – it is set during the Risorgimento and features a nationalist plot against the Austrian occupation of northern Italy – and the quality of those involved. He had previously worked with Mastrocinque, while the sets and costumes were designed by the highly regarded Vittorio Nino Novarese, and the love interest, Luisa di Cerchiara, was to be played by Mariella Lotti, the headstrong nun from *Un giorno nella vita*, with whom he had co-starred on four previous occasions. However, despite a certain fidelity of detail (the composer's own house in Bergamo is employed for some scenes) and the artful combination of romance and patriotism, the film was clearly made on a budget. Though Donizetti (and with him Nazzari) is associated with the noblest and most democratic of nationalist strains,[25] the plot lacks dynamism and even interest. A great deal is made to depend on close-ups of the familiar features of the fair and suitably glamorized Lotti and the rugged Nazzari, which in the latter case only serves to highlight a fault that the critic of *L'Illustrazione italiana* identified: 'That character on the screen is too Nazzari to look a bit like Donizetti.'[26]

The second and third films, *Malacarne* (For the Love of Mariastella, Pino Mercanti, 1947) and *Fatalità* (Fate, Giorgio Bianchi, 1947), saw him take what were little more than supporting roles in minor contemporary dramas. In the first, a melodrama set among the fishing community of the Aeolian Islands, he plays uncle to Mariella Lotti rather than her lover, while the male lead is played by Otello Toso, a prolific but not very prominent actor who had played many small supporting roles since 1938. *Fatalità*, which is discussed in Chapter 5, returned him to the role of romantic lead, albeit one whose physical appeal and human qualities are contrasted with those of Massimo Girotti. Nazzari's character Renato, a worldly seaman, fascinates Girotti's wife Paola (Maria Michi), a restless young woman to whom he is attracted; he has a wealth of experience of life, and there is a mystery about him that is entirely lacking to her mediocre, if good-looking, husband. The difference between the two men is established by reference to water: Girotti's Vincenzo loves the river; he was born close to it and it is central to his work and his life. Renato, by contrast, is a man of the sea.[27] A former sailor, he has been to Japan and South America. His horizons are broader, and he has no time for trivial diversions (in one curious meta-cinematic scene, he rejects an invitation to go and see a movie on precisely these grounds). Nazzari projects a rich and intense humanity; by contrast Girotti seems insubstantial. Yet there is little depth to Renato; it is as if Nazzari were playing his screen persona, as he had in *Giorni felici* (Happy Days, Gianni Franciolini, 1942) and, more explicitly, in *Apparizione* (Apparition, Jean de Limur 1943), rather than the sort of nuanced, introspective characters that he had brought to the screen in *Un giorno nella vita* and *Il bandito*.

In these postwar films, Nazzari oscillates between innovation and repetition. The actor is cast in roles that producers and directors knew he could handle with ease and that, in the case of costume films, perhaps no one else could fill with such authority. At the same time, encouraged by directors who were keen to harness his proven appeal as well as his talents to films that dealt with the recent and continuing traumas that were besetting the country, he introduced elements of reflection and critical revision into his portrayals. These contrasting impulses were supported or, in some cases, undercut by casting, which was either traditional or alert to novelty. For example, in Blasetti's para-realist film, Nazzari's innovative portrayal occurs in a context in which the cast is composed entirely of actors who became established names before the fall of Fascism. In *Fatalità* by contrast, in which the degree of innovation is much reduced, he co-stars with one actor who had been reconfigured by Visconti (Girotti) and another (Michi) who had been consecrated by Rossellini in *Roma città aperta* (1945) and *Paisà* (1946). The cast of *La figlia del capitano* includes Irasema Dilian, familiar to audiences of the schoolgirl comedies that were popular in the early 1940s, and, in the part of a treacherous coward, Vittorio Gassman, a stage actor who had made his screen debut the previous year. The recurrence of Lotti in the cast of his postwar films suggests that both actors were deemed to have sufficient appeal to weather the transition. In fact, Lotti would soon be consigned to minor films and would give up her screen career altogether in 1952.

In this regard, a closer look at the pairing of Nazzari and Magnani, the first new star of the period, in the only film they made together is instructive.[28] In *Il bandito*, the two actors appear to share a certain chemistry deriving from the earthiness and depth that was a feature of each. The sexual attraction of their two characters lacks the veil of paternal restraint that sometimes marked Nazzari's relations with his earlier girlish co-stars. Both play people who have been damaged, who have suffered and become cynical. Their relations in consequence are unambiguous. During filming, the two actors established a rapport, though the force with which Nazzari threw a glass of vodka in Lydia's face riled Magnani.[29] Nazzari won a Nastro d'argento (Silver Ribbon award) for his performance, which critics noted was 'unusually contained, unusually controlled'.[30] Evidently, he was making an effort to modify his performance mode. It is noteworthy that, despite the box office success of the film, the pairing was not to be repeated. Undoubtedly, there was an asymmetry between Magnani's improvisational technique and Nazzari's more traditional theatrical approach to his craft. It is almost impossible to imagine the latter working with non-professionals, for example, and Magnani is more contained in *Il bandito* than she is in her other roles of the period. He remained a traditional figure in many respects, while she was associated with reform and change.

Nazzari's decision to accept invitations to go first to Spain and then Argentina is indicative of the difficulties besetting the film industry. In a situation in which both the political context and cinema remained in flux and, indeed, were marked by increasing tensions at the onset of the Cold War, resulting in the break-up of the postwar coalition of parties and conflicts over attitudes towards domestic and imported films, the future looked uncertain. The prospects for an actor who was accustomed to regular prestigious work looked bleak. 'Crisis is a big word, but if in mid-1947 Nazzari agreed to make three films in Barcelona for an Italo-Spanish combination – and what Spanish cinema at that time amounted to is easy to imagine – it means that it was truly a dark moment for him', comments Piero Pruzzo.[31] He was one of several actors to go to Spain. Thanks to the close relations between Mussolini's and Franco's regimes, many Italian films of the prewar and war periods had been distributed in the latter country, and Nazzari's popularity was established. His films had also done well in Argentina, where a large emigrant community provided a ready audience. Certainly, none of the films did anything to enhance his reputation; the first, *Quando gli angeli dormono* (When Angels Sleep, Ricardo Gascon, 1947), which saw him play a heartless social climber who only realizes when it is too late that he has wasted his life, was briskly liquidated by Italian critics despite the presence in the cast of Clara Calamai. The second and the third fared even worse. The swashbuckler *Il ribelle di Castiglia* (The Rebel of Castiglia, Ricardo Gascon, 1947), in which Nazzari was the only Italian member of the cast, was only distributed in Italy several years later, while the hotel drama *Conflicto inesperado* (Unexpected Conflict, Ricardo Gascon, 1948) was never released in the actor's home country.[32]

The actor then moved to Argentina, which in Italy was perceived as a rich country and a destination for emigration. The out-of-work airman Luciano Serra had migrated there in the eponymous film of 1938. Nazzari's Argentinian interlude was not intended to be a short one, since he was contracted to make between four and six films. However, when he saw that the screenplay of the first one would have involved him playing a corrupt and clownish Italian, he broke the contract – just as Serra threatened to do when a gaggle of diminutive Argentinian businessmen had tried to coax him into undertaking a flight to Italy for publicity reasons. Patriotic pride, combined with his protective attitude towards the screen persona that had always served him well,[33] led him to this clamorous act, which caused great controversy in Argentina. Eventually, after being received by Evita Peron in person, he agreed to make a film on another subject. The resulting work, *Volver a la vida* (Carlos Borcosque, 1948), would not be screened until three years later and received no Italian release.

If Nazzari returned to Italy and within a short time re-established himself as an asset to an industry that, following the adoption of the Andreotti law in 1949, was finally able to count on the sort of state support that had prevailed under Fascism, it was due to two of the most dynamic producers of the period: De Laurentiis and Goffredo Lombardo, who had taken over the reins of the Titanus company from his father.[34] The former tempted him back from South America with a leading role in a rustic melodrama set in the mountains of the southern region of Calabria (see Figure 12.2).[35] Influenced by neorealism's preoccupation with the south, *Il lupo della Sila* (The Wolf of the Sila, Duilio Coletti, 1949), which is discussed in Chapter 12, presented a story of honour, betrayal and revenge set against a background of rural labour and a family-run lumber business. The film offered few concessions to the

Figure 12.2 Amedeo Nazzari returns from Argentina to take the lead male role opposite Silvana Mangano in *Il lupo della Sila* (The Wolf of the Sila, Duilio Coletti, 1949), *La Settimana Incom*, April 1949 (author's own collection).

picturesque in its visual composition while using folk music and customs to establish a sense of place. The film was conceived as a star vehicle, with Nazzari featuring alongside Gassman and De Laurentiis's recently wed wife, Silvana Mangano, both of whom, not long before, had scored an enormous success with *Riso amaro* (Bitter Rice, Giuseppe De Santis, 1949). The French actor Jacques Sernas, who in Italy had already made *Gioventù perduta* (Lost Youth, Pietro Germi, 1947) and *Il mulino del Po* (The Mill on the Po, Alberto Lattuada, 1949) completed a star-studded cast

Nazzari's role is that of Don Rocco, a widowed landowner and businessman who enjoys high regard in the rural community. Rocco is a proud family man whose determination to avoid scandal at all costs first leads to two tragedies: the death in a shoot-out of his sister's secret lover Pietro and, many years later, his own death when his sister kills him to prevent him from turning his rifle on his own son Salvatore and a beautiful servant girl played by Mangano. For the first time, Nazzari played a vigorous, if middle-aged, man who loses out to a younger man, his own son. Though physically far larger and ostensibly more powerful than the lean Sernas, he loses a tree-felling contest before also losing Mangano to him. In a melodrama shaped by old-fashioned values of honour and shame, he is a strong character with a weak side: he is too rigid, he rides roughshod over the feelings of his sister and son and he struggles to come to terms with the waning of his own powers.

More frequently than in the period up to 1943, Nazzari played family men, honest and dependable breadwinners who take for granted their ascendancy over female and younger male family members. There was a substantial continuity of his persona with the prewar years in that his characters were generally upright, instinctive and untroubled by doubt. Like Jean Gabin, the symbol of French cinema and the 'représentation du Français *au masculin*' for Ginette Vincendeau,[36] he stood within a conventional gender pattern. Though he was a very different figure to the prewar proletarian Gabin, both actors shared an identification with the land while their characters possessed an artisanal practicality.[37] The measure of introspection that had become a norm for many male screen characters did not undermine his clear sense of right and wrong. The film that would consecrate him as a major postwar star and that would remain for decades lodged in the popular imagination was the melodrama *Catene* (Chains, Raffaello Matarazzo, 1949). The film was the first example of what would come to be known as 'popular neorealism'; instead of blending elements of melodrama into a realist mix (as *Roma città aperta* and other films had done), it substantially merged a melodramatic plot with lower class, quotidian settings and characters. Produced by the Titanus company, which had been founded in Naples and had first established itself in the silent era with a series of melodramas, it was aimed squarely at a mass popular audience, including an acknowledged female component, which had not existed in the prewar years.[38]

A woman-centred story, it featured an actress of Franco-Greek origin, Yvonne Sanson, who had been discovered by Lattuada and given a small part in *Il delitto di Giovanni Episcopo* (Flesh Will Surrender, 1947). She takes the role of a wife and mother whose happy ménage is fatally threatened by the unexpected reappearance of a man to whom she was once engaged. His efforts to court her and then blackmail her lead to a tragic sequence of events involving misunderstandings and murder, a flight abroad from justice, a false confession of adultery and much suffering before the family is happily reunited. In the role of the husband, who believes his wife has betrayed him, Nazzari undergoes an emotional calvary, which is centred on the issue of honour and which leaves no space for comprehension or trust. His character, sustained by his elderly mother, believes what he sees and is quick to judge. The fact that his conduct in ejecting his wife from the family home and killing her presumed lover is utterly in line with a conventional code of honour signalled an alignment with the value system of southern audiences, which were becoming a significant force within a fast-growing cinema-going public.

Catene was an enormous success; it topped the box office hit parade for 1949–50 and gave rise to a series of films. Nazzari starred in eight of them in total, and in seven he was paired with Sanson, a dark-haired, full-figured actress born in 1925 who corresponded to the director's personal ideal of feminine beauty.[39] He does not seem to have been alone in his appreciation, if the selection of letters to her published in the magazine *Cinema Nuovo* is anything to go by.[40] Though she was some eighteen years younger than Nazzari, who by 1949 was 42, her look was maternal and even mature rather than youthful. She was sensual and attractive rather than brazenly sexy in the manner of the starlets who were coming to the fore through beauty pageants. Her familiar, accessible appeal was an important factor in the emotional charge that these tearjerkers delivered; audience members could easily imagine themselves in her shoes. Maggie Günsberg notes that the male figure in these dramas is usually the 'dynamic agent', but, as Spinazzola argues, female desire is nevertheless a compelling and disruptive force.[41] *Catene* was followed by *Tormento* (Torment, Raffaello Matarazzo, 1950) and *I figli di nessuno* (Nobody's Children, Raffaello Matarazzo, 1951), which together formed a trilogy.

Further titles followed, with the last, *Malinconico autunno* (Melancholic Autumn), being released in 1958. The films were a phenomenon that delighted audiences and made the fortune of Titanus. The melodramas proved to be a winning card in the Italian industry's battle with Hollywood.[42] However, they dismayed critics, especially those on the left, who struggled to understand why audiences preferred them to the films to which they gave their seal of approval. An article written by the director in 1955 for the Communist daily *L'Unità*, in which he defended his work, gave rise to an extended debate.[43]

Though the content of the films appeared to have little to do with the contemporary preoccupations of the country – history is utterly absent from them and there is no sign even in scenes shot on location of war damage or of the endeavours of the reconstruction – they connected up with postwar developments in the media scene and spoke to needs and experiences that did not figure prominently in public debate. They placed Nazzari at the centre of a 'vast multimedial network that included, beyond cinema, comics, photoromances and romantic literature'.[44] The films offered spectators – female spectators first and foremost – a type of experience that matched and was informed by the boom in illustrated story magazines and photoromances. The first and most popular of these, the weekly *Grand Hôtel*, founded in June 1946 by the Del Duca brothers of the Edizioni Universo company, offered readers compelling and melodramatic stories in instalments, as the French feuilletons of the nineteenth century had once done.[45] However, with its highly coloured covers and protagonists whose looks were modelled on those of current Hollywood stars, it catered also to precisely the desires and dreams that were bound up with American cinema. The films generally avoided wealthy and aristocratic milieux that were such a key feature of the magazine stories, and which the writer Aldo De Benedetti had often evoked in his many scripts for pre-war 'white telephone' films, and concentrated instead on the lower middle class as the ideal of realized status. Stability and respectability rather than riches are key aspirations that are perennially under threat from fate and misfortune. The absence of subplots, descriptive elements and aesthetic flourishes rendered the films direct in their appeal.

In Matarazzo, Nazzari is always a father, consolidating a paternal strain within his persona that had first emerged in *Luciano Serra pilota*. The insertion of his characters in a network of familial and blood ties served to situate him squarely within a patriotic framework. As Alberto Banti has shown, the concept of the nation as a 'community of descendants (ancestors, mothers and fathers, present generations composed of brothers, sisters, friends, and future generations)' conferred 'a decisive bio-political substance to the national community'.[46] This removed it from the realm of abstract ideas and made it readily understandable. Nazzari's paternal aura owed nothing to the actor's personal biography (he did not become a father until 1958), but it became the main way in which his persona was endowed with leadership, authority and patriotism. In the postwar era, the sense of the nation as a brotherhood that had been elaborated from the Risorgimento through both Fascism and the Resistance waned in favour of a stronger focus on the family. This reflected the ascendancy of the Church and its political allies. The family of the films was hierarchical and patriarchal with Nazzari as the defender of honour and integrity.

The films contained no references whatsoever to recent or contemporary national events. In itself, this was not unusual. Even many neorealist films made after 1946 made only oblique or indirect reference to Fascism or the war. Though allusions were not uncommon, a mixture of reticence and censorship removed these themes from cinema for more than a decade. But it meant that the backstories of screen characters could only be guessed at. On which side in the civil war had Pietro, the mechanic and garage owner of *Catene*, fought? What sort of business had Carlo, the wrongly imprisoned fiancé of *Tormento*, been engaged in under Fascism? What was the political affiliation of Guido, the owner of a marble business in *I figli di nessuno*, whose liaison with the daughter of one of his employees is truncated by his disapproving mother? That many spectators had no desire themselves to face questions like this justified the curious conjunction between the format of the nineteenth-century popular melodrama and the 'presentism' of narratives that occluded the recent past. However, it may be said that the prominence of Nazzari within the films meant that anyone wishing to imagine the past of these characters could do so via his persona. Those who did not were not presented with any compulsion to do so.

The films Nazzari made for Titanus with Matarazzo would prove to be a straightjacket. The head of the company, Goffredo Lombardo, was primarily responsible for harnessing the director and his actors to this type of story, even though they would have preferred to diversify.[47] But they contributed decisively to returning Nazzari to a position of great popularity. In the annual readers' poll of *Hollywood* magazine, he had scored poorly in 1948 and 1949, but in 1950, thanks to *Il lupo della Sila* and *Catene*, he beat Vittorio Gassman to the top position.[48] *Catene* and its successors consolidated – or established – his following among audiences in the provinces and the south. For Giulio Cesare Castello, the actor 'managed over a period of twenty years, to correspond to the tastes of the most minor Italian public; he became a sort of Clark Gable of the "backward regions"'. 'He was an eminently popular personality in his transparency and refusal of compromise, in the fundamental, constitutional "health" of a man who was often better than his destiny.'[49] For his daughter Evelina, the Matarazzo films ended up eclipsing the rest of his work, even though they were, in her view, 'among the least good'.[50] Nazzari himself also had some doubts at first; however, he overcame them because 'they were pure relaxation and Matarazzo was a serious professional.'[51]

Between 1949 and 1952, the actor worked no less hard than he had done in the early 1940s. He made no fewer than twenty films, an average of more than six per year. It is striking how often his characters were outlaws or bandits. Many of them were southern. After *Il lupo della Sila*, he was an outlaw in *Alina* (Giorgio Pastina, 1950), *Donne e briganti* (Women and Brigands, Mario Soldati, 1950) and *Il brigante Musolino* (The Brigand Musolino, Mario Camerini, 1950). He could also be a police officer or government official, battling the drug traffic as in *Barriera a settentrione* (Barrier to the North, Luis Trenker, 1950) and *Lebbra bianca* (White Plague, Enzo Trapani, 1951) or pursuing a bandit as in *Il brigante di Tacca di lupo* (The Brigand of Tacca di Lupo, Pietro Germi, 1952). Though occasionally he might don the garb of an earlier period, such as the late eighteenth century of *Donne e briganti*, most of his films were set between the mid nineteenth and mid twentieth centuries. A number had patriotic themes. In *Donne e briganti*, he is a bandit known as Fra' Diavolo who organizes guerrilla activity in support of King Ferdinand IV of Naples. In Clemente Fracassi's Risorgimento drama *Romanticismo* (Romanticism, 1951), set in 1848 in the Austrian-occupied Lombardy and Veneto, he is an aristocrat who is executed for his nationalist sympathies. All, however, were eclipsed in popularity by the Matarazzo series.

Nazzari was not a star who cultivated publicity. Like many older stars of the period, he disliked any invasion of his private life. Yet he was increasingly drawn into a media context that placed new demands on stars. Though he was cast alongside long-standing screen partners like Mariella Lotti, Irasema Dilian, Elisa Cegani and Alida Valli, with whom he made three films between 1951 and 1953, he was also paired with new stars, whose relationship to the world of publicity was more calculated and consistent. He was cast a second time with Mangano in *Il brigante Musolino*, with Gina Lollobrigida in *Alina*, Eleonora Rossi Drago in *Sensualità* (Barefoot Savage, Clemente Fracassi, 1952) and *La fiammata* (The Flame,

Alessandro Blasetti, 1952), and Silvana Pampanini in *Processo alla città* (The City Stands Trial, Luigi Zampa, 1952) and *Un marito per Anna Zaccheo* (A Husband for Anna Zaccheo, Giuseppe De Santis, 1953). His directors included old hands like Blasetti and Fracassi as well as postwar newcomers.

Nazzari had lived the lifestyle of a film star since the late 1930s. In the period of his postwar success, magazine readers would be given insights into his home, hobbies and working methods. A bachelor until 1957, he was forever seen as a man alone, unencumbered by lasting attachments. He lived ostentatiously and treated friends and acquaintances with generosity. The director Mario Mattoli saw him 'like a prince from times past' who laid on the most lavish New Year's Eve parties in the film world, 'with the style of a Renaissance gentleman or an Oriental nabob'.[52] However, there was a secret anxiety that informed his staging of himself, a fear that his great popularity was not as solid as it appeared. 'There was a taxi outside the main entrance for each one of his guests, with mountains of caviar and rivers of champagne for everyone inside', Mattoli continued; 'yes, because if Nazzari suspected that the guests were less numerous than expected, he used to send the taxis around the city to gather up volunteers for his parties.' The self-assured screen persona was not the same as the other-directed actor, who required constant approval from peers and public alike.

Notes

1. Freddi, *Il cinema*, 425.
2. Brunetta, *Cent'anni di cinema italiano*, 212.
3. Gubitosi, *Amedeo Nazzari*, 71.
4. F. Di Giammatteo, 'Nazzari, eroe per tutti', *Radiocorriere*, 26 July 1958, page unnumbered.
5. On the Fascist appropriation of the Risorgimento, see Banti, *Sublime madre nostra: la nazione italiana dal Risorgimento al fascismo* and Baioni, *Risorgimento in camicia nera: studi, istituzioni, musei nell'Italia fascista*. See also Duggan, *The Force of Destiny: A History of Italy Since 1796*.
6. See Gundle, *Mussolini's Dream Factory: Film Stardom in Fascist Italy*, 197.
7. Nazzari's own writings, cited in Buffa, *Amedeo Buffa Nazzari*, 88.
8. A. Libonati, 'I digiuni allungano la mia giovinezza', *Gente* 28 (1964), 34. On the deaths of Valenti and Ferida, see Bracalini, *Celebri e dannati: vita di Osvaldo Valenti e Luisa Ferida*. The episode is explored in dramatic form in Marco Tullio Giordana's film *Vincere* (2009). On Nazzari's relationship with Valenti, see Gundle, *Mussolini's Dream Factory*.
9. See, for example, Freda, *Divoratori di celluloide: 50 anni di memorie cinematografiche e non*, 104–5, 108–9.
10. The release after the liberation of *Apparizione* (Apparition, Jean de Limur, 1943), in which the actor played himself, while Alida Valli is a young fan whose overtures he tries to discourage, was

quite successful. It showed that, as far as some of the audience was concerned, they were still the king and queen of the screen. V. Lilli, 'Dive in prima linea', *Star*, 14 October 1944, 7.
11. Pruzzo and Lancia, *Amedeo Nazzari*, 96.
12. A. Baracco, 'Un giorno nella vita', *Hollywood*, 20 May 1946. Extracts from this and the reviews cited in notes 13 and 14 are reproduced in Pruzzo and Lancia, *Amedeo Nazzari*, 96.
13. F. Palmieri, 'Un giorno nella vita', *Film*, 1 June 1946.
14. C. Trabucco, *Il Popolo*, 7 April 1946.
15. Anon., 'Banco ... e Nero', *Hollywood*, 17 June 1946, 7.
16. Nazzari's episode was the tenth commandment, 'Thou shalt not covet thy neighbour's wife'.
17. Faldini and Fofi, *L'avventurosa storia del cinema italiano: raccontata dai suoi protagonisti, 1935–1959*, 116.
18. Ibid., 116.
19. C.A. Felice, 'Il bandito', *Film*, 16 November 1946.
20. R. Ben-Ghiat, 'Unmaking the Fascist Man: Masculinity, Film and the Transition from Dictatorship', 355.
21. Ibid., 355.
22. Ibid., 356.
23. Ibid., 359.
24. A. Orecchio, '*La figlia del capitano*', *Il Messaggero*, 12 October 1947.
25. Gubitosi, *Amedeo Nazzari*, 84–85.
26. V. Guarnaccia, 'Il cavaliere del sogno', *L'Illustrazione italiana*, 15 December 1946.
27. In real life, it was Girotti who was a man of the sea, as he had grown up near the coast in the Marche region and always recalled the smell of the sea when asked about his youth. P. De Luca, '30 e più domande a Massimo Girotti', *Bolero*, 13 June 1971, 44–45.
28. Magnani had in fact had a very small part as a singer in Nazzari's first major film, *Cavalleria* (Goffredo Alessandrini, 1936).
29. Carrano, *La Magnani*, 47–48.
30. Felice, *Film*, 16 November 1946.
31. Pruzzo and Lancia, *Amedeo Nazzari*, 103.
32. Brief details of three films are listed in ibid., 102–4.
33. 'But I have always played Nazzari, you know? I have always maintained a coherent persona', he told Francesco Savio. See Savio, *Cinecittà anni trenta*, 824.
34. See Germani et al., *Titanus: cronaca familiare del cinema italiano*.
35. Kezich and Levantesi, *Dino: De Laurentiis, la vita e i film*, 75.
36. G. Vincendeau, 'Gabin unique: le pouvoir réconciliateur du mythe', in Gauteur and Vincendeau, *Jean Gabin: anatomie d'un mythe*, 96.
37. Ibid., 114.
38. See Günsberg, *Italian Cinema: Gender and Genre*, 20–21. The whole of Chapter 1 is devoted to popular melodrama.
39. Testimony of Liana Ferri, quoted in Faldini and Fofi, *L'avventurosa storia*, 170.
40. S. Martini, 'Mia leggiadrissima Yvonne (quattro lettere a una diva)' (1957), in Aristarco, *Il mito dell'attore: come l'industria della star produce il sex symbol*, 315–19.
41. Günsberg, *Italian Cinema*, 27–28. See also Spinazzola, *Cinema e pubblico: lo spettacolo filmico in Italia, 1945–1965*, 83.
42. On Titanus and the Italian film market, see the essays in Zagarrio, *Dietro lo schermo: ragionamenti sui modi di produzione cinematografici in Italia*.

43. See 'Trentasette milioni di spettatori hanno visto i miei film', *L'Unità*, 18 December 1955, 3. See Gundle, *I comunisti italiani tra Hollywood e Mosca: la sfida della cultura di massa (1943–1991)*, 11–12.
44. Gubitosi, *Amedeo Nazzari*, 96.
45. On the various literary and mediatic influences on the Matarazzo films, see Spinazzola, *Cinema e pubblico*, 73–79. On *Grand Hotel*, see Ventrone, 'Tra propaganda e passione: "Grand Hotel" e l'Italia degli anni 50', 603–31.
46. Banti, *Sublime madre nostra*, 60–61.
47. Nazzari testimony in Faldini and Fofi, *L'avventurosa storia*, 171.
48. *Hollywood*, 28 October 1950, 12.
49. Castello, *Il divismo: mitologia del cinema*, 408.
50. S. Casavecchia, '"Mio padre è alto, ha i baffi e con un pugno spacca tutto!": conversazione con Evelina Nazzari', in Casavecchia, *Amedeo Nazzari: il divo, l'uomo, j'attore*, 30.
51. Cited in Faldini and Fofi, *L'avventurosa storia*, 171.
52. Mattoli, quoted in R. Barneschi, 'Soltanto per me Sofia scese nulla nell'acqua', *Oggi illustrato*, 19 April 1976, 97.

CHAPTER 13

Silvana Pampanini
Dream Girl of the Masses

On the surface, the early careers of Silvana Pampanini and Silvana Mangano may seem similar. Both first came to public attention via beauty contests, both were the object of considerable attention on account of what was regarded as their 'natural' sex appeal, and both would become stars with a national and international following. Moreover, both of them came from Roman families that were less poor than the frequent description of them as lower-class beauties might imply. Finally, each had a talent (dance for Mangano, music for Pampanini) that would form a key element of their screen persona. Abroad, the two were often linked, especially in press and publicity material that placed the accent on the stream of beauties that were emerging from postwar Italy.[1] The fact that the two shared a first name only served to facilitate the association. However, the differences between them were considerable. In an interview, Pampanini recalled saying at the outset of her career, 'One day I will be so famous that they will simply call me Silvana', adding 'and so it has been.'[2] 'Alright', she conceded, 'there is another Silvana, the one from *Riso amaro* (Bitter Rice, Giuseppe De Santis, 1949), but when anyone speaks of her they say "La Mangano". I am the one every Italian knows simply as Silvana.' Pampanini underlined the universal affection with which she was regarded, but she also admitted that the other Silvana had achieved a higher measure of success. In fact, Pampanini became a huge success in a strand of popular cinema that had little to do with the great innovations in filmic language developed by Italian cinema. Of the up to eight films per year that she was making in her heyday in the early 1950s, only a few would make a lasting impression.

Pampanini first achieved renown at the first Miss Italia contest in 1946. The pageant was a focal point in the debate about the nature of Italian feminine beauty in the postwar era. It was established by a prominent figure in Italian advertising, Dino Villani, as an updated version of the 'One Thousand Lire for a Smile' contest, which he had invented for the Chlorodont toothpaste company before the war. Sponsored by the illustrated weekly magazine *Tempo* and the film weekly *Film d'oggi* in addition to the toothpaste company, the pageant was meant to provide an uncontroversial diversion from the pressing tasks of the reconstruction and a platform for the reassertion of feminine beauty as a banner of national identity.[3] In the event, the final, held in September 1946 in the Piedmontese resort town of Stresa, would prove highly controversial in terms of the outcome it produced. The jury, which included representatives of the film world (Vittorio De Sica, Cesare Zavattini, Luchino Visconti and Isa Miranda), variety theatre (Macario), fashion (Brunetta, Lucio Ridenti), art (Carlo Carrà), literature and journalism (Giuseppe Marotta, Arrigo Benedetti) poetry (Alfonso Gatto) and advertising (Villani himself) was tasked with selecting a young woman who evoked the type of beauty rendered world famous by the great Italian artists of the Renaissance. At the same time, however, they were required to take account of the opinion of the audience present at the event, which was invited to express its preferences via a ballot box. While the latter voted overwhelmingly for Pampanini, a twenty-year old Roman with the confident, cheerful demeanour of a pin-up, half the jury was inclined to back a contestant from Tuscany named Rossana Martini, whose classic features fulfilled the criteria Villani had laid down. Acutely aware of the need to protect the respectability of his pageant, Villani steered his fellow jurors towards Martini, telling the men present that they should imagine they were selecting an ideal future wife for their son. However, when the radio announcer reported that the jury was divided, the public, which sided with the Roman candidate, began to protest loudly. Pampanini herself would later recount that a controversy ensued in which she was labelled an example of a 'glamour girl' of the American type, while Martini, with her Renaissance-style oval face and reserved disposition, was judged to be a more traditional example of Italian beauty.[4] 'The public', she continued,

> was not interested in the Renaissance and such fine distinctions. While a well-known lawyer from Brussels shouted curses in French at the Marquis Visconti [owner of the company which produced Chlorodont], two young men from Milan decided, before the very eyes of my horrified mother, to establish my material victory by hoisting me on their shoulders and carrying me around the room.[5]

With the jury intent on crowning Martini, a tumultuous response broke out among the well-dressed crowd that risked turning into a full-scale riot. The whistles only subsided when it was announced that the title would be awarded *ex aequo* to both candidates.[6]

In the aftermath of the controversial outcome, the debate continued in the press. Martini attracted approval on account of her medium brown hair and the 'virtuous look in her eye'. For one female observer, she had 'a gentle grace' and a 'Madonna beauty'.[7] Her photograph, with her eyes timidly cast down, was published in *Tempo* surrounded by several iconic Renaissance female portraits including the Mona Lisa.[8] Pampanini, by contrast, was seen as sophisticated, polished and glamorous.[9] It was her picture that *Tempo* opted to use for its cover. The photograph shows her from the waist up, attired in a black, figure-hugging tailored suit. Her head is turned as she casts a knowing smile over her shoulder. The image is a mixture of the sort of street shot of attractive, unknown young women that the magazines were starting to use regularly, also for symbolic moments such as the declaration of the republic in June 1946,[10] and the more contrived photographs of Hollywood starlets that figured in the film magazines. Although she was not as worldly as many assumed, Pampanini already had an assured manner about her; she had a pleasantly proportioned, round face and long legs that recalled those of the dancers and showgirls who were such a prominent attraction of the theatrical revues of the time, as well as a generous bust. She had precisely the qualities of an American-style pin-up that, up to that point, had been the prerogative of the half-German actress Elli Parvo, a screen vamp who had been dubbed 'the number one pin-up of Italian screens' and 'the glamour actress of Italian cinema'.[11]

The controversy was a mark of recognition that brought her public sympathy. As she later recalled:

> *Everywhere we went on our travels, first to the Island of the Fishermen [on Lake Maggiore], then to Milan, I had the sense that everyone was interested in me, as they would be in the "victim" of an unjust sentence. It is difficult to convey my impressions of those days. I, who had never been to a party in my whole life, and whose experience of life was limited to the nuns, school and the academy of music, should have found myself overwhelmed. Instead I recall immediately feeling a strange calm, even as I was raised onto the shoulders of the admirers who bore me round in triumph. I felt in charge of myself and the world; I had no hesitations; I understood that a new chapter of my life was beginning. All the other contestants were more emancipated than me; they went to the hairdresser's, they smoked with a long cigarette holder, they knew the latest modern*

dances. But I don't think I handled myself any worse than them or that I committed any more faux pas than they did.[12]

Though she was born and raised in Rome, Pampanini was never identified as strongly with the lower-class life of the capital as Anna Magnani or Aldo Fabrizi. This was not only because her family originally hailed from the north-eastern Veneto region (after all, Magnani was also the child of immigrants); it was because she did not live in the colourful districts of Campo de' fiori or Trastevere but in a comfortable residential area. Although no less feisty than Magnani, she did not speak with a pronounced Roman accent and was never unruly or uncouth. Her father, who had once been a boxer, was the manager of a printing works that was responsible for producing one of the capital's newspapers. Additionally, she was a niece of the celebrated soprano Rosetta Pampanini, famed for her Puccini roles, and she had already sung on the radio.[13] Though middle class, it would later be said that she had the physical exuberance and breezy manner of a lower-class woman of the people.[14]

Pampanini's acclaim at Miss Italia marked a step on the way to a redefinition of the idea of Italian feminine beauty that would become embedded in postwar popular culture. This has been identified with the eclipse of a traditional pictorial beauty centred on the face by an emphasis on body, and in particular the breasts. This shift would be consecrated by the entry into common usage of the term *maggiorata fisica* to refer to the leading female stars of the 1950s. It was first employed in an episode of the 1952 film *Altri tempi* (Olden Times, Alessandro Blasetti) in which a beautiful murderess played by Gina Lollobrigida is acquitted of her crime by a court on the grounds not of mental incapacity but on account of her 'physical super-capacity'.[15] More significant than this, however, was the evolution that occurred within the photographic realm from the artificial to the natural. Liz Conor has remarked that, in the modern age, it was not enough 'to be beautiful in the common acceptance of the term'; 'in the modern sense it was more important to be photogenic.'[16] The photographic glamour of the prewar stars had been heavily constructed in the studio by Elio Luxardo, Arturo Ghergo and other society photographers.[17] It was assumed that it was the job of these men and cinematographers to give actors the best appearance possible. The postwar stars were more likely to be shot by news photographers like Federico Patellani, in outdoor settings that made their photogenic qualities seem entirely natural. The placing of them

Figure 13.1 Silvana Pampanini in period costume on the cover of *Le Ore* magazine. The actress was one of the most popular cover girls of the late 1940s and early 1950s. Many of her films had a feel of belle époque Paris (author's own collection).

in streets, fields and by the sea gave them a meaning as community symbols that film actors had not had before.

Though her curvaceous figure was widely remarked upon, Pampanini was more of an Italian version of the wartime pin-up girl than the postwar 'sweater girls'.[18] Although she would not have won such general approval had it not been for the influence of American ideas of beauty and glamour during the liberation, she was never just a local adaptation of these. Close examination of her screen roles and the specific iconography associated with her reveals that her physical appeal was centred on the legs, with the bust coming a distinct second. The female leg was a key icon of the liberation. The arrival of the Americans in the peninsula heralded a proliferation of female images deriving from Hollywood. These included photographs of film stars and starlets, illustrated pin-ups, film posters, advertising, calendars and cigarette cards. Italians were presented with innumerable polished images of physically flawless, smiling young women often attired in swimsuits or bikinis. Nylon stockings, like chewing gum and boogie woogie, were signifiers of a prosperous way of life. Pin-ups were morale boosters for troops fighting overseas and a reminder of the future wives waiting for them at home.[19] In the climate of war, men were less interested in the elaborate European-influenced eroticism of Garbo and Dietrich; instead they wanted something that was more straightforwardly arousing, as well as utterly American. The 'pin-up girl', it has been observed, was typically 'the healthy, American, cheerleader type – button-nosed, wide-eyed, long-legged, ample hips and breasts, and above all with the open, friendly smiles that disclose perfect, even, white teeth'.[20] Such images were not wholly unfamiliar in Italy. The illustrator Boccasile had created in the late 1930s a cover girl for the magazine *Le Grandi Firme*. His 'Signorina *Grandi Firme*' was an urban young woman with a job who was depicted engaging in a variety of mostly outdoor leisure activities.[21] She was dynamic, cheerful and tantalizingly flirtatious. Boccasile emphasized his creation's legs,[22] not least because this enabled him to communicate an idea of modernity and movement. As Michel Beynet has argued, the focus on the leg had nothing to do with classical ideas of beauty; it was American and a product of the aesthetics of the mass age that lacked individuality and expressiveness.[23] Nonetheless, women seemed to appreciate a focus that was remote from reproductive sexuality and that implied a certain freedom of movement and behaviour. It carried an emancipatory thrust that keyed in with the efforts of women to take on new responsibilities and to maintain a pattern of unity even in the face of political division.[24]

However, the proliferation of images reflecting the American taste for standardized beauty did not go down well with all. 'Italy is full of legs: news kiosks are covered with them, certain theatres bustle with them', lamented the bourgeois weekly La Domenica del Corriere; 'but we don't want to believe that feminine beauty has finished up in the extremities. It shines above all in the face.'[25] Through 1945 and 1946, the magazine insisted that 'beauty belongs in the face' and repudiated the current emphasis on legs.[26] This stance was bound up with a rejection of the swimsuit as an appropriate vehicle for the presentation and appreciation of beauty. Italian beauty was free of 'frills and distillations'; it was 'devoid of ambiguous mischievousness'.[27] The allure of the Italian female face, it was claimed, sprang from the 'sense of intimate goodness' of the woman it belonged to, not from the 'super-modern "perverse glamour" of the cover girl'.[28] This stance was not just a matter of face or leg but of a resistance to professional beauty and the spread of commercial culture.

Italian variations on American sex appeal were plentiful in the mid forties. Screen actresses adapted to the climate by posing for magazines in swimming costumes with their legs dangling in the water. The lavish theatrical revues that prospered in the reconstruction period made much of female appeal. Like American revues of the early twentieth century, they turned feminine beauty into 'a form of aesthetic spectacle'.[29] Like these, they also offered a combination of beauty and comedy, or 'girls and laughter', which would also be exploited by cinema. However, the lines of dancers who populated the lavish theatrical revues that were enjoying a boom, as well as those who worked in lesser touring companies, presented a spectacle of legs that rarely met the exacting standards of impresarios like Florenz Ziegfeld, who had pioneered female entertainment in the United States.[30] The Italian ideal was still more 'real' and less astutely manufactured.[31] A short-lived men's magazine called Sette featured a cover girl who was evidently a re-edition of Boccasile's Signorina.[32] She did not appear in every issue but alternated with American illustrations. What is noteworthy about her is her imperfection. Despite her hourglass figure and shapely legs, she lacks polish and has an everyday manner. For the Italians of the postwar years, there was still a sense that sex appeal was something that could not be divorced from sex.[33] While the Americans had perfected the art of distilling the essence of sexual allure such that it could be reproduced as an inoffensive quality to enhance the saleability of commodities, in Europe the two remained more closely linked. The huge expansion in prostitution in Italy during the Allied occupation, which extended an already institutionalized, long-standing system of state-licensed brothels, only confirmed the idea that any form of female display was a sign of sexual availability, usually in exchange for money or goods in kind. The coarse invitations from a predominantly young male crowd to raise skirts and reveal legs – that were often heard at provincial beauty pageants – were an instinctive response to the institutionalization of the display of women's bodies on the part of those who were accustomed to seeing sex offered for sale.[34] For this reason, the organizers of these contests were intensely concerned to maintain a high tone by connecting them to a national artistic tradition in order to neutralize accusations of immorality that emanated from the Church and Catholic lay associations.

Pampanini's screen sex appeal was constructed in ways that incorporated American, European and Italian elements. The national was unquestionably dominant. Indeed, despite the conviction at Stresa that she represented 'glamour beauty', or stood for the American current in popular culture, she was quickly embraced as an example of Italian beauty and was universally praised for her pleasing screen presence. It is significant that she did not make her debut in a neorealist film or indeed feature in any film related to this current until 1953, when she starred in Giuseppe De Santis's melodrama *Un marito per Anna Zaccheo* (A Husband for Anna Zaccheo).[35] It was rather in popular cinema of a conventional type that she made her mark. All her early directors were men who had been working in the film industry since before the war: Camillo Mastrocinque, Mario Mattoli, Carlo Bragaglia, Carmine Gallone and Guido Brignone were seasoned professionals – all of them born between 1885 and 1901 – who were well versed in the genres of the musical film, the screwball comedy and the costume drama. In the postwar years, they adapted these where necessary and invented some new genres, such as the film revue and the picaresque road movie. With her background, Pampanini had the right qualifications to step into one or more of the variants on the musical film, including the opera film, the musical comedy, the comedy with songs and the variety film. In her first two films, *Il segreto di Don Giovanni* (When Love Calls, Camillo Mastrocinque, 1947) and *Arrivederci, papà* (Be Seeing You, Father, Camillo Mastrocinque, 1948), she partnered the baritone Gino Bechi, who was best known for his Verdi roles. More handsome than Beniamo Gigli, who had crossed over from opera to popular film in the 1930s, Bechi had already made four films in which the female protagonist was played by demure starlets like Adriana Benetti and Irasema Dilian. With her vocal talent and more imposing screen presence, Pampanini quickly established herself as a box office attraction. *Arrivederci, papà* saw her get the better of Mariella Lotti, a renowned star of fascist cinema who would ultimately fail to make a successful career in the postwar film industry. Pampanini was an exuberant, cheerful presence in the cinema of the late 1940s who spoke directly to the needs and tastes of audiences of those years.

Both the films mentioned above had period settings and were elaborately costumed. Pampanini's height enabled her to wear exaggerated hats with broad brims and gigantic feathers with panache, while long gloves, parasols and accessorized gowns gave her an ostentatiously ladylike appearance. These outfits recalled ones that Clara Calamai had worn in one of her best-known femme fatale roles, as the seductress who steals the heart of a naïve student from his seamstress sweetheart in *Addio, giovinezza!* (Goodbye to Youth, Ferdinando Maria Poggioli, 1940). But at this stage in her career, Pampanini was not cast as a femme fatale. Her characters were not calculating or destructive. Rather, they were determined, sunny in disposition, sometimes impatient and fundamentally sincere. They always attracted male attentions and sometimes used this capacity to obtain what they wanted, while keeping ardent admirers at arm's length and unceremoniously repelling would-be seducers.

Her first director, Mastrocinque, understood that it would be a mistake to seek to channel Pampanini's natural qualities into a conventional dramatic performance.[36] For her to have the maximum effect on screen, it was necessary to preserve a certain spontaneity, to allow her to go over the top and go inject something of her real personality into her parts. The experienced professionals who followed him did not depart from this practice, and only with her more melodramatic roles of the 1950s, for which she was dubbed, would her performances lose their rough edges. It was as a natural brown-haired Italian beauty, a girl who was devoid of artifice but who knew only too well what effect she had on men, that she established her screen presence. In this respect, she had something of the feel of the protagonists of neorealist films, though her singing talent was uncommon. She was an entertainer rather than an actress, who offered audiences a female spectacle that was completed, when required, with songs and dance.

The expansion of cinema at the expense of other forms of popular entertainment saw a wholesale migration from popular theatre to the medium. It was as a partner to the leading names of variety theatre as they increasingly focused on cinema that Pampanini would impose herself. Her first big success was in the first of many revue films, *I pompieri di Viggiù* (The Firemen of Viggiù, Mario Mattoli, 1949). A multi-protagonist film starring such luminaries as Totò, Nino Taranto,

Carlo Campanini, Wanda Osiris and Isa Barzizza, it presented a flimsy – if interestingly meta-cinematic – basic storyline about a company of firemen from Viggiù in the province of Milan who travel to the big city to interrupt the performance of a show entitled *I pompieri di Viggiù* on the grounds that they prefer to be known by the more high-sounding term *'vigili'* (officers) rather than *'pompieri'* (firemen). The trip also appeals to the men because it will give them the chance to ogle some beautiful girls – an experience denied to them in their small home town. The plot is a pretext for a series of sketches and songs featuring the film's stars, some of them in their original stage setting. Pampanini plays the daughter of the chief fire officer (Campanini), who is also performing in the revue. Her most notable costumes were a two-piece swimsuit (for a sketch entitled 'Censorship and the Bikini', which had originally been performed in the revue 'Nuvole') and a black bodysuit, which closely models the contours of her figure. The film was the third biggest earner in the 1949–50 season. Though it left much to be desired as a film of substance, it provided filmgoers of second and third-run cinemas with a taste of popular theatre and its stars.

Though she had none of the stage experience of showgirls like Delia Scala and Isa Barzizza, who would also work regularly in cinema, Pampanini had more of the qualities that were appreciated by fast-growing film audiences. In cinema, greater naturalness was required than in theatre, especially in the films that were designed to cater to the tastes of vast new provincial audiences of the centre and south.[37] Over the next four years, she would star in some thirty films and play regularly opposite all the male stars of *I pompieri di Viggiù*, as well as Walter Chiari (*L'inafferabile 12*, The Elusive 12, Mario Mattoli, 1950), Peppino De Filippo (*La bisarca*, The Transporter, Giorgio Simonelli, 1950) Aldo Fabrizi (*Antonio di Padova*, Anthony of Padua, Pietro Francisi, 1951), Renato Rascel (*Io sono il capataz*, I'm The Capataz, Giorgio Simonelli, 1951) and a long list of other variety names. In these films, she played a range of roles, many of which involved her removing her outer clothing or sporting costumes, which ensured that spectators were given an eyeful of her legs, arms, shoulders, neck and the top of her breasts. Popular theatre was historically the home of female spectacle, and few understood better than the directors and producers of these film vehicles for variety performers how much revenue depended on having a beautiful soubrette and chorus.

Pampanini was an uncomplicated presence, a dream girl that men could imagine they might actually meet, a hyperbolic female whose beauty, because it was perceived as natural rather than manufactured, did not overshadow her down-to-earth, unpretentious manner. Though women might feel wary of her, they could be sure that she would never wittingly steal a husband or boyfriend. The poet Vincenzo Cardarelli memorably affirmed that 'her beauty is of that exuberant florid type that is typically Italian and which banishes from the minds of spectators any type of reflection and militates against any form of critical activity of the spirit or reasoning; but it is a beauty that entirely satisfies the vision of it by proclaiming itself to be ... utterly relaxing.'[38] The point was confirmed by a journalist. 'Silvana Pampanini is the most popular', he wrote.

> *On her own she makes more films than all the others put together ... People rush to see her because she is the image of abundance, the cornucopia of sex. After so many years of herring types, pale, skinny and boney actresses who recalled the war, bread rationing and the impossibility to finding a bottle of oil, at last we have a woman built without economising, rounded, firm and full. Silvana's success is the product of old appetites, of tightened belts, of darned clothes. Now, finally, all this is behind us and we don't want to hear mention of it again. Hard times are over and there is no lack either of cured hams or beautiful legs.*[39]

One of her most successful films was *Bellezze in bicicletta* (Beauties on Bicycles, Carlo Campogalliani, 1951), in which she starred with the delicate fair-haired soubrette Delia Scala. The film recounts the misadventures of two young dancers from Rome – who are given the actresses' real names of Delia and Silvana – who want to win work with Totò's touring theatre company, which is currently based in Milan. They set off on their journey by coach but are forced to resort to other means of transport when the driver goes on strike. Eventually, the women enter a cycle race, which terminates in Milan. With some unauthorized help, they win the race and are awarded prize money and a trousseau. The film ends with them planning to marry the men who have been courting them from the start. Silvana immediately establishes her superior appeal to the popular Delia when a dashing gentleman in a sports car offers them a lift. While she is invited to take the passenger seat, Delia is obliged to squeeze uncomfortably into the back. The film demonstrates the extraordinary capacity of the postwar film comedy to incorporate a little of everything: sport, catchy songs, jokes and sketches, feminine beauty, the battle of the sexes, topical issues (there are fleeting references to the bandit Salvatore Giuliano) and self-referentiality. Silvana and Delia are taken on by what turns out to be a fake Totò company and are obliged to flee the theatre dressed only in basques. At one point, they cross-dress as soldiers and are drawn into a line of men awaiting medical inspection. The threat of Silvana having to open her shirt for the doctor to listen to her heart provides the impulse to a gag. However, it is the girls' legs that provide the focus of their sex appeal. They are constantly on the move; they walk, they run, they cycle. The film's title song was a hymn of praise to *'le gambe snelle, tornite e belle'* (slim, shapely and beautiful legs), which *'m'hanno già messo la passione dentro al cor'* (have already set my heart racing). The scrapes the pair get into are of the cartoonish type visualized by Boccasile for his Signorina Grandi Firme. The film was deemed by critics to provide sparkling entertainment of the most untaxing kind. For the *Corriere della sera*, it was 'one of many that offer a combination of male comedy and female legs in accordance with a formula that is not worthy of any sort of aesthetic evaluation. To expect films like this to convey ideas is on a par with expecting a cat to roar'.[40]

Pampanini was herself a popular cover girl (see Figure 13.1). The illustrated press increasingly opted for full colour female images as it developed the formula that would allow magazines like *Oggi*, *Epoca* and *L'Europeo* to reach circulations of hundreds of thousands. Domestic and foreign stars provided the ideal sort of upbeat iconography that tuned in with the onset of economic growth and the increasing integration between the different media. Silvana was a special favourite of *Tempo*, the magazine that had given her her first cover and for which she functioned as a lure, first of all on the newsstands for the magazine in question but also for the prosperous way of life that was propagated in the illustrated press and that was increasingly coming to occupy the Italian imagination. Though Pampanini claimed that she never entered into a battle with other stars to achieve the most covers, she was a prime 'camera celebrity' whose image easily graced all the visual media.

In some respects, the Pampanini persona was constructed with great astuteness. This especially concerned the original synthesis of her sex appeal. Edmund Wilson commented in 1923 on the Ziegfeld girl, noting that they had 'not only the Anglo-Saxon straightness – straight backs, straight brows and straight noses – but also the peculiar frigidity and purity, the frank high-school-girlishness which Americans like'. 'He [Ziegfeld] does not aim to make them, from the moment they appear, as sexually attractive as possible, as the Folies Bergère, for example, does', Wilson continued. 'He appeals to American idealism, and then, when the male is intent on his chaste and dewy-eyed vision, he gratifies him on this plane by discreetly disrobing his goddess.' The balance between an image that was simultaneously unthreatening and infused with excess and hedonism was difficult to achieve, and it was one that Ziegfeld perfected by means of a process of selection, standardization and limitation.

Pampanini too offered a synthesis of titillation, hyperbole and innocence. The last quality was guaranteed by her father Francesco, who kept surveillance over her, acting as her agent and protector. In the absence of a system of agents, stars had to make their own arrangements, which were not always based on any expertise in the sector. According to the cinematographer Aldo Tonti, he 'read all the screenplays, he gave his approval, he was always there in the studio'.[41] These cinematic parents, Tonti continued, 'threw themselves into cinema with the spirit with which they had thrown themselves into beauty contests. In short, they believed in the beauty of their daughters more than they did in their expressive abilities, as if cinema were a photographic competition'. It must therefore be partly blamed on her father if Pampanini accepted so many roles of a similar type with what appeared to be little discrimination. Giulio Cesare Castello would deal with her summarily in his 1957 study of stardom as an actress who was of 'exuberant and cordial temperament, mainly employed in low-level productions, concerned above all to display her generous forms'.[42] Though she was not a star who was forced by a studio into an industrial rhythm of work, she worked relentlessly. There does not seem to have been any awareness of the risks of repetition or overexposure.

Pampanini was unusual in maintaining a fundamental screen image of purity that derived from the strict adherence of her characters to a conventional moral code. She was the object of heterosexual carnal desire who was only interested in the honest love of a nobly intentioned partner. At the same time, she provided a textbook case of the male gaze as any number of pretexts were deployed to partially reveal her body or to constitute through dialogue or situation an imagined vision of its exposure. Typically, this was achieved by drawing her into a showbusiness context or a period setting (or both) in which skimpy dress was justified. The erotic aura was often created by incorporating Parisian atmospheres imbued with a spirit of *galanterie* and pleasure reminiscent of the belle époque. As Jeanette Basinger has observed, cinema offered moments in which beauty could be ogled through the use of plot or scenic devices to expose the bodies of actresses.[43] Pampanini's *nudités* were presented by costumes that revealed her arms, her shoulders or her legs. Screens, towels and bubble or milk baths were all employed to conceal (while also suggesting) naked forms. In *L'inafferrabile 12*, she was obliged to preserve her modesty by covering her breasts with her hands – giving rise to a daring shot that would be widely reproduced in many contexts, including on the cover of the risqué French pin-up magazine *Folies de Paris et de Hollywood*.[44] Over time, she embraced a studied repertoire of Parisian motifs, elaborate period dress, staged exposures and suggestive songs. Many of her films are set in the late nineteenth or early twentieth centuries and a significant number in France or some environment in which there is a Parisian vaudeville atmosphere. In this specific context, her characters often manifest some of, but not all, the hallmarks of the cocotte.

Pampanini was saucy and titillating in the manner of a British seaside postcard. It was not uncommon for her screen characters temporarily to embrace a showbusiness persona, as for example in an episode of *Amori di mezzo secolo* (Mid-Century Loves, 1954) in which she plays Susanna, the wife of a provincial Fascist squad member who has his eye on enjoying the night life of the capital. After she follows him into a nightclub and overhears him disparaging her ordinariness to a hostess, she proves that she is no less versed in the arts of seduction by performing a number as Salomé in the club's stage show. As Glenn remarks, King Herod's daughter Salomé, who famously demanded the head of John the Baptist, was, for modern culture, the classic vamp, 'a powerfully transgressive symbol of women's desires, passions and powers'.[45] The faithful but indignant Susanna wins her revenge by temporarily taking on the guise of 'a sexual seductress who makes her allure the cause of male destruction'.[46]

Pampanini performed a similar masquerade in an episode of *Un giorno in pretura* (Steno, 1953), a courtroom film in which she plays an elderly vagrant who was once a great stage star known as Gloriana. A flashback to World War I shows her seductively entertaining the troops, one of whom, an inoffensive junior officer played by Peppino De Filippo (who will become the judge she faces decades later), is chosen to give up his room for her when it turns out that no overnight accommodation has been reserved. The officers gossip about Gloriana taking a new lover every night and deride De Filippo when he fails to seduce her in his room. She overhears and invites him back with the sole aim of saving his manly pride. The pair do not in fact sleep together, but the soldier's superiors are satisfied both that he has done his duty and that the chanteuse has confirmed a sexualized reputation that bears no connection to her true nature.

Only when she is fully immersed in a period French setting do Pampanini's characters lose their essential respectability. In *La presidentessa* (Mademoiselle Gobette, 1952), Pietro Germi's screen adaptation of the French pochade 'La présidente', she again plays a stage entertainer, a chanteuse named Gobette, whose exhibitions have interested the justice system. Gobette is a seductress in the Parisian mould, who without compunction debauches the magistrate sent to gather evidence against her. Situated in a French context, her Italian modesty could be substituted with the brazen immorality of the true cocotte.

French audiences took Pampanini to heart. She cheerily embraced the nickname of Nini Pampan that she was given by the *Le Figaro* newspaper. Indeed, in the Cold War comedy *L'incantevole nemica* (The Enchanting Enemy, Claudio Gora, 1953), in which she plays an industrialist's daughter, she sings the self-referential song 'Nini Pampan' as she sunbathes by a pool. Her popularity was international, but nowhere was it greater than in France. 'Silvana Pampanini is by now a Parisian – and more generally a French – beauty. She has conquered Paris and its people like no other foreign actress', remarked the anonymous author of a pamphlet about the beautiful women of international cinema.[47]

In 1952–53 Pampanini would complicate her light comedy personality with a series of dramatic roles in which her sunny image would be shadowed by melodrama (see Figure 13.2). She had the looks and the screen presence to play convincingly the part of the dark lady, and there can be little doubt that these films constitute some of her best work. The swashbuckler *Le avventure di Mandrin* (Don Juan's Night of Love, Mario Soldati, 1952) and the noir *Bufere* (Their Last Night, Guido Brignone, 1953) were French co-productions, reflecting the popularity she enjoyed across the Alps. In this period, as a necessary condition of playing in more demanding, adult films, she set aside her purity of body if not spirit. Her characters are often drawn into messy sexual situations as lovers and victims of exploitation.

She would finally get the chance to work with directors who had in different ways contributed to the engaged reputation of postwar Italian cinema. Luigi Zampa's *Processo alla città* (The City Stands Trial, 1952), co-written by Francesco Rosi, was a hard-hitting indictment of the struggle of the Camorra to control the city in the early twentieth century. Opposite Amedeo Nazzari's inflexible magistrate, Pampanini played a prostitute and lover of a *camorrista*. In Giuseppe De Santis *Un marito per Anna Zaccheo* (A Husband for Anna, 1953), she would take the title role, starring once more with Nazzari. The film has a contemporary setting and takes as its theme the challenges faced by a beautiful woman in her efforts to make her way in the world. For De Santis, the film was an exploration of the world of work and the problems women faced in winning a job without being the object of unwanted attentions. 'La Pampanini was one of my fixations', the director revealed, 'because to get actresses like Pampanini, who were so far removed from reality and the qualities of a certain type of cinema, to have realistic experiences

Figure 13.2 After becoming a mother out of wedlock in *La schiava del peccato* (Slave of Sin, Raffaello Matarazzo, 1954), Silvana Pampanini is obliged to earn her living as a factory worker (screenshot by the author).

was a real challenge'.[48] De Santis worked to rid her of 'certain vices deriving from a given way of performing that she had grown accustomed to' in order for her 'true lower-class nature' to emerge. The actress was pleased that her 'genuine recitation' was appreciated and did not object when De Santis urged her to tone down her delivery to achieve a more nuanced effect.[49] *Un marito per Anna Zaccheo* was perhaps Pampanini's most complete performance, a sign of what might have been had she had more opportunities to work with the leading postwar innovators. Otherwise, the films of the early 1950s did not signal a genuine progression. Though she was a convincing dark lady from a visual point of view, she was often dubbed by the deeper-voiced Lydia Simoneschi (even her singing voice was dubbed by the popular singer Nilla Pizzi in *Processo alla città*) and something of her cordial persona was missing. Before long, she had reverted to musical films, co-starring in the critically disparaged, but highly successful, colour film *Canzoni, canzoni, canzoni* (Songs, Songs, Songs, Domenico Paolella, 1953).

Pampanini conducted a high-profile film star lifestyle. She frequented the rich and famous, wore mink, drove a red Ferrari and travelled widely. She was a keen practitioner of several sports including swimming, horse riding and fencing. But she was also very private and intensely conservative. In fact, she lived with her parents on the Via Flaminia until they died in the 1970s.[50] When the journalist Alessandro Porro visited her at home, he found a drawing room furnished with a grand piano, golden-backed couches, curtains and tapestries, numerous ornaments and dull late nineteenth-century paintings. Though many of her films had period settings, he was surprised to find that a woman barely into her thirties had absorbed so completely the tastes of her parents' generation.[51] The interior decoration was wholly unaffected by trends in modern design, a field in which Italy had excelled since the 1920s.

A devout Catholic, she was an old-fashioned girl in matters of the heart too. Though she was assumed to drive men into a frenzy of desire, she was also known for the parsimony with which she distributed her favours. She proudly asserted her reputation as 'the lily of Italian cinema' (white, moreover, was her favourite colour).[52] The weekly magazine *L'Europeo* commented in 1956 that, 'since she became a film actress, some ten years ago, Silvana Pampanini has been the woman without love of Italian cinema. Her colleagues get engaged, marry, divorce, fall in love. La Pampanini, by contrast, has no affairs to remember or to blot out. The man who is most frequently beside her is her father. As a woman, La Pampanini has been, and is, a woman alone.'[53] In later years, the still unmarried actress would talk freely only of the declarations of love that she had received from the comic actor Totò, who she rejected, saying she thought of him as a father figure.[54] In acknowledgement of the contradictory nature of her image, she entitled her autobiography *Scandalosamente perbene* (Scandalously Respectable).

One relationship that was intense and continuous was that with her many fans. Reka Buckley argues that the investment she made in them 'was part of the reason for her phenomenal following in the early 1950s'.[55] She understood that fans regarded her as a friend and therefore that she had to act accordingly towards them. To maintain the illusion of accessibility, she devoted much time to her fan mail and responded quickly to letters. When a Milanese factory worker wrote to her to ask if she could have the wedding dress she had worn for the film *Un marito per Anna Zaccheo* for her own wedding, the actress personally delivered the garment, ensuring that a photographer was on hand to record the moment.[56] She knew that she was a popular idol and committed herself to the work of being a film star. The publicity of *Un giorno in pretura* promised a Pampanini *'uguale per tutti'* (a reference to the legend found in all Italian courtrooms that 'all are equal before the law'), and her appeal was not in any way sectoral. Though she was always pleased to find herself in the company of the rich and the titled, she was perfectly aware that 'it was the lower classes who most easily got excited over me.'[57] She made a point of being as devoid of artificiality as possible. Her own personality heavily informed the way she presented herself; at the start of her career, she had rejected suggestions that she should adopt a shorter surname for cinema. Though her background was more refined than that of other female stars, she was a precursor, and in some respects a trailblazer, for others. She was 'the first Italian actress of the new type, the first "mass" diva'.[58] She lived up to her image, allowing quotes to be attributed to her by her press agent, such as when she affirmed that 'Flattening the bosom in the way that Dior decreed is as absurd an idea as trying to hide the Colosseum.' She knew how to stimulate the fantasy of admirers and keep herself in their thoughts, playing up to expectations of her persona. Unlike some stars, she was always polite and friendly with journalists, knowing that they helped maintain her public image.[59]

Fans besieged her with letters and gifts. In an article for a weekly, published in 1953, she wrote about this phenomenon.[60] She received around one hundred or so letters every day, as well as around twenty poems per month in which she was equated to Venus or otherwise elevated to the status of goddess. Many admirers aspired to meet her in person, offering to make great sacrifices in exchange: 'one writes that he will travel the entire distance (73km) from his village to Rome on foot; another promises that, if I agree to meet him, he will shave his hair off, while a third will kiss my photograph every morning on getting up.' In addition to requests for autographed photographs or a reply to a letter, there were many requests for a lock of her hair or a cutting from a garment she had worn (her mother helped her satisfy these requests). Provincial fans sent her baskets of grapes, salami, bottles of wine or other typical local products. More romantic gifts of flowers, rare books and antiques also reached her, as well as unusual items from abroad including a brightly coloured poncho from Mexico that drew much comment when she wore it around Rome. She had created, she claimed, a small personal museum containing photographs, artworks, dried flowers, ties and badges as well as such treasures as a pair of moustaches, which an admirer from Calabria had cut off after losing a bet over her, and a fragment of a plate that a wife had broken over the head of her husband after he had expressed his ardent appreciation of the actress. There were offers of marriage, which included promises to separate immediately from a current spouse in the event of acceptance. No mention is made of letters she received from women, confirming that she was primarily a figure of male fantasy.

The actress treasured this mass of material and sometimes argued with her father when he took the initiative and threw some of it away. 'I would like to make a collection of this avalanche of post, not out of vanity', she explained, 'but because I am sure that it would constitute a fascinating correspondence, an insight into people's behaviour that few would be able to put together'.[61] In this she was surely right for, in the period up to the early 1950s, there was no other female star who entered the dream life of the nation in the same way or who encountered such sustained enthusiasm from the consumers of popular cinema and perhaps even the public at large.

Notes

1. See, for example, the British-published magazine 66, issue no.15 (undated, approximately 1957), which offered '66 photographs of Silvana – Mangano Pampanini'.
2. A. Pensotti, 'Con il mio primo bacio misi nei guai la troupe', *Oggi*, 19 December 1984, 26.
3. See Villani, *Come sono nate undici Miss Italia*, 42–44, and Monza and Scaroni, *Cinquantanni di Miss Italia*, 18–19.
4. For Pampanini's account of this event, see S. Pampanini, 'A Stresa il pubblico mi volle Miss Italia', *La settimana Incom*, 14 November 1953, 26–28. She gave a further account in Pensotti, 'Con il mio primo bacio', 24–29. The debate over the two different models of beauty was reported in *Tempo*, 21 September 1946, 25. See also Villani, *Come sono nate undici Mis Italia*, 55–72.
5. Pampanini, 'A Stresa il pubblico mi volle Miss Italia', 28. See also L. Cavicchioli, '"Quando mi spogliavo era il caos"', *Domenica* 12 (1975), 46.
6. In fact, in the annals of the contest, Rossana Martini would go down as the first winner.
7. G.D., 'La più bella', *Tempo*, 21 September 1946, 25–27.
8. Picture spread, *Tempo*, 28 September 1946, 28–29.
9. G.D., 'La più bella', 25–27.
10. Cigognetti and Servetti, '"On Her Side": Female Images in Italian Cinema and the Popular Press, 1945-1955', 55–63.
11. The cover of the issue of 29 September 1946 featured no tag line and did not name Pampanini. Details of the contest were given on internal pages.
12. Pampanini, 'A Stresa il pubblico mi volle Miss Italia', 26–28.
13. Ibid., 28.
14. Cavicchioli, '"Quando mi spogliavo era il caos"', 45.
15. See Gundle, *Bellissima: Feminine Beauty and the Idea of Italy*, 149–50.
16. Conor, *The Spectacular Modern Woman: Feminine Visibility in the 1920s*, 140.
17. See Gundle, *Mussolini's Dream Factory: Film Stardom in Fascist Italy*, 82–84.

18. The original 'sweater girl' (a publicity term that followed labels like 'the goddess of love' Rita Hayworth and 'the sarong girl' Dorothy Lamour) was Lana Turner.
19. See A. Bazin, 'Entomology of the Pinup Girl', in Bazin, *What is Cinema?*, 158–61.
20. Hess, 'Pinup and Icon', in Hess and Nochlin, *Woman as Sex Object: Studies in Erotic Art, 1730–1970*, 227.
21. For a fuller discussion of this figure, see Gundle, *Bellissima*, 89–92. See also Biribanti, *Boccasile*.
22. O. Vergani, 'Introduzione', in Villani, *Come sono nate undici Miss Italia*, 8.
23. See Arvidsson, *Marketing Modernity: Italian Advertising from Fascism to Postmodernity*, 22–25.
24. Gabrielli, *La pace e la mimosa: l'Unione delle donne italiane e la costruzione della politica della memoria (1944–1955)*, 29.
25. *La Domenica degli italiani*, 18 November 1945, 3.
26. *La Domenica degli italiani*, 9 December 1945, 6.
27. *La Domenica degli italiani*, 30 December 1945, 6.
28. *La Domenica degli italiani*, 23 December 1945, 5.
29. Glenn, *Female Spectacle: The Theatrical Roots of Modern Feminism*, 48.
30. On postwar popular theatre, see De Matteis et al., *Follie del varietà: vicende, memorie, personaggi, 1890–1970*. On Ziegfeld, see Mizejewski, *Ziegfeld Girl: Image and Icon in Culture and Cinema*.
31. 'The bodies of our actresses and starlets did not have the sugary smoothness of the American-made products; they were exuberant in a more casual way, or in other words they were more lewd in that they were furnished with an innocent but unsubtle naturalness', Spinazzola, *Cinema e pubblico: lo spettacolo filmico in Italia 1945–1965*, 101.
32. Gundle, *Bellissima*, 111–12.
33. S. Guarnieri, 'Campioni e dive', in Aristarco, *Il mito dell'attore: come l'industria della star produce il sex symbol*, 49–50.
34. See, for example, the account of the crowd's boisterous demand to see more of the contestants' legs at the Miss *Vie Nuove* contest for the Marche region, held in Ancona in September 1951. *Vie Nuove*, 16 September 1951, page unnumbered.
35. In the same year, she starred in Antonio Leonviola's *Noi cannibali* (We Cannibals), which had a lower-class setting.
36. Brunetta, *Cent'anni di cinema italiano*, 380.
37. Vittorio Spinazzola notes that 'of the innumerable actresses who appeared alongside male leads [in revue films] not a single name has survived – with the exception of Silvana Pampanini. They were interchangeable figures.' *Cinema e pubblico*, 101.
38. Quoted in Castello, *Il divismo: mitologia del cinema*, 424.
39. Quarantotto, *Il cinema, la carne e il diavolo*, 172–73.
40. Lan (Arturo Lanocita), 'Bellezze in bicicletta', *Corriere della sera*, 3 March 1951, 17.
41. Aldo Tonti testimony in Faldini and Fofi, *L'avventurosa storia del cinema italiano: raccontata dai suoi protagonisti, 1935–1959*, 271.
42. Castello, *Il divismo*, 423.
43. Basinger, *A Woman's View: How Hollywood Spoke to Women 1930–1960*, 138.
44. The film underwent various cuts at the insistence of the government censor's office – including a scene in which Pampanini's character is given a spanking by Walter Chiari, another in which the pair roll around in an evidently sexual manner and a final one in which she adjusts her dressing gown after locking him in a wardrobe. Istituto Luigi Sturzo, Archivio Andreotti, Serie Cinema, Sottoserie censura 1948–2001, b. 1073. Letter from Industrie Cinematografiche Sociali to Ufficio Censura, 8 September 1950.

45. Glenn, *Female Spectacle*, 96.
46. Ibid., 97.
47. Anon. c.1953. 'Silvana Pampanini: la conquistatrice di Parigi' in *Le più belle donne del mondo*, Milan: Biscione, page unnumbered.
48. De Santis testimony, Faldini and Fofi, *L'avventurosa storia*, 318. The director wrote to Pampanini as follows:
    Anna Zaccheo ... is a poor girl like many you meet in the street of any city, in the tram, in the offices, in the residential quarters, in the cinemas; it is the first time, I believe, that you change roles and attitudes in a film. Here you are not the usual woman who, maybe cynically or with bad intentions, commercialises her beauty disturbing men and breaking up families. Anna Zaccheo is the exact opposite in the sense that not only is it the others who spoil and seek to corrupt her but also because she is good, loyal and confident that life will turn out well for her. She struggles to assert her rights as a woman to a normal, honest life, just as millions and millions of other women like her do. In brief, this is a new character for you.
    Centro sperimentale di cinematografia, Fondo Giuseppe De Santis, Corrispondenza 1952–1953, b.29. Letter of De Santis to Pampanini, 2 November 1952.
49. Pampanini testimony, Faldini and Fofi, *L'avventurosa storia*, 319.
50. The journalist Camilla Cederna commented that, uniquely in the world of cinema, there was no gossip about Pampanini. 'Silvana's appearance is in contradiction with her life. In fact, the "sex bomb" lives at home with her mother and father and, when she travels, one of them always accompanies her'. 'Venere educanda', *L'Europeo*, 17 October 1954, 22.
51. A. Porro, 'Pampanini fuori tempo', *Grazia*, 30 July 1961, 24–28.
52. Faldini and Fofi, *L'avventurosa storia*, 274–75.
53. Anon., 'La coppia Jean Gabin-Silvana Pampanini', *La Settimana Incom*, 7 February 1953, 17.
54. Pampanini, *Scandalosamente perbene*, 15–24.
55. Buckley, 'Italian Female Stars and their Fans in the 1950s and 1960s', in Burke, *A Companion to Italian Cinema*, 166–67.
56. See *Annabella*, 27 September 1953, 29.
57. Pampanini, *Scandalosamente perbene*, 74.
58. Cavicchioli, '"Quando mi spogliavo era il caos"', 45.
59. Roberto Paolella, who interviewed her for *Cinema*, found her courteous and generous. See 'Un marito per Anna Zaccheo', *Cinema*, 15 February 1953, 68–70.
60. Pampanini, 'Venti poesie al mese e cento lettere al giorno', *La Settimana Incom*, 28 November 1953, 18–20.
61. Ibid. In fact, the first and only such collection would be published by Claudia Cardinale. See Grazzini, *Cara Claudia....: lettere dei fans alla Cardinale*.

CHAPTER 14

Raf Vallone
The Physiognomy of Fame

More than any other star of the postwar years, Raf Vallone found himself repeatedly at the centre of dramas that explicitly engaged with the disputes and conflicts of the period. This is not to say that his was a persona that was ambiguous, tormented or inadequate. Rather he stood tall and strong when others proved weak. As soldier, returning soldier or prisoner of war, involuntary bandit or migrant worker, he nearly always played men who stood for justice and for good. However, circumstances often conspired against him, obliging him to take up cudgels to defend himself or others against bullies, thieves and the badly intentioned. In difficult times – when authority was sometimes unreliable, partial or absent – the just were often put on the defensive. Vallone almost always played men of the people, often of peasant extraction. With his square head, broad shoulders and curly dark hair, he did not have the appearance of a bourgeois; indeed, he looked like the southerner he was by family origin, something that worked to his advantage in the postwar years as cinema broadened the range of physical types from which it drew its recruits.

Vallone had a nobility about him that was reflected not only in the natural leadership qualities of his characters but also in the causes they embraced. Whenever he was obliged to fight an opponent, as he often was, he was bound to win. His agility and strength were important, but more so was the fact that he was always in the right while invariably his adversaries were not. Virtue aided his cause and ensured narrative resolution worked in his favour. Even if his adversaries had the advantage of a weapon such as a knife or gun, they inevitably found themselves on the losing side. He drew women to him, although his characters rarely indulged in any form of wooing, and his manner was brusque. Rather, he won them by a mixture of sympathy and vulnerability. Yet he could also lose women to men who were found to be more fascinating; his goodness and simplicity sometimes suggested a certain stolidity and even dullness. Thus, he was a warrior for right and for justice who often emerged victorious from the battles into which he was pitched but who could also suffer setbacks and disappointment.

Vallone first won recognition in the role of the army sergeant Marco in Giuseppe De Santis's neorealist melodrama *Riso amaro* (Bitter Rice, 1949). His character was the last of the four protagonists to be introduced. Whereas Walter, Francesca and Silvana are all first encountered in the context of the melodramatic vignette that follows the documentaristic opening of the film, Marco is first seen writing on the wall of the barracks he is about to vacate for the female rice weeders, who are arriving to begin the season's work. The words spell out the following jaundiced message: *'Vivo morendo in caserma non in tempo di guerra ma in tempo di vita'* (I am undergoing a living death in a barracks, not in a time of war but of peace). He pauses to contemplate what is evidently a heartfelt expression before resuming his packing and engaging in banter with Francesca and Silvana. Almost instantly, his gloomy mood is lightened by the laughter of the women as a suitcase falls from an upper bunk bed onto his head. Physically, Marco is robust and powerful. The first frontal medium shot of him highlights his broad shoulders, the hairy chest beneath a half-unbuttoned shirt, strong arms and thick neck. He is also an innocent; he holds the handkerchief containing the necklace stolen by Walter and kept by Francesca in his hand and assumes simply that it must contain wedding favours.

Marco is world-weary and worn down. He confesses he has been in the army for ten years, sleeping only in barracks. He is awaiting demobilization but has few illusions. Throughout the film, he is constantly about to leave. When asked where he is from, he claims to be from Lombardy, but his speech is unaccented. Yet he is not spoiled; he has a winning smile and a ready laugh. Love is something that he says he still believes in as he seeks to cancel a vulgar graffito from the wall. He is quick to seek to plant a kiss on Silvana's unwilling lips, while Francesca is immediately attracted to him. Later, when the troops he is leading on an exercise stumble across a fight between unionized and non-unionized weeders, he immediately acts as the voice of reason, ordering the women to cease their violence and stop shouting. He tells the angry unionized women that they should understand the need of others to work and come to an agreement. This they do, accepting the good sense of the sergeant. After he spots Silvana, he expresses surprise that she was involved in the commotion, which she in fact instigated.

Marco has a clear sense of morality, which is independent of authority. When Silvana and Francesca argue over the stolen necklace, which the younger woman has surreptitiously taken, he intervenes again, refusing to judge Francesca or agree to report her to the police. He is not interested in the object, which he instructs Silvana to return, or its value. Honest and upright, he expects others to be so too but does not impose himself on them. 'I am no-one's spy. It is up to you to decide', he says when Francesca asks him what she should do. When prison is mentioned, he is dismissive of its redemptive benefits. However, he is not a very good judge of character, for he mistakenly concludes that Silvana must share his values for the simple reason that he desires her. He judges people on the basis of what he sees, and for this reason he takes Silvana's beauty to be a sign of her intrinsic goodness. By the same token, he refuses to report Francesca. When Silvana asks him about his understanding of people, he remarks, 'You see, Silvana, it is always a question of face', playfully slapping his own, while claiming that, since he has travelled the world and been in uniform, he has seen many thousands of them and of all different races. Everyone's destiny is written on their face, he believes.

Marco's outlook is rooted in the Platonic alignment of good with beauty.[1] For this reason, he misjudges Silvana, while, for her part, she misunderstands him. When he expounds his theory of faces, she mistakes him for a fortune teller and proffers her hand so that he can read her palm. He declines and claims not to be able to read anyone's future. Marco in fact is more interested in character than destiny and in faces more than beauty in general. He shares Aristotle's view that the face was a particularly suitable part of the body to indicate mental character. Yet Silvana's shift to palmistry is not as quirky as it might appear. As Anthony Synott has argued, 'the rise of astrology in the fourteenth century resulted in a new contribution to physiognomics as astrologers described faces according to seven planetary types, and detail the influence of the 12 constellations by the markings on the face. Not only was a new cosmic principle added to the "science" of physiognomy, but physiognomy also became predictive rather than "merely" descriptive.'[2] Silvana equates Marco's face-ism, which is unfamiliar to her, with the more popular predictive practice of palmistry, which she knows. As Synnott notes, palmistry flourished as astrology's credibility declined in the seventeenth century.[3]

None of this is known to Marco, whose firm convictions are simply a version of popular wisdom. His belief in physiognomy has reached him through the diffusion in the late nineteenth century of the ideas of the Italian positivist physician Cesare Lombroso, whose anthropological criminology presumed that criminal tendencies were evidenced in physical defects. In short, you could tell a criminal type from his face. Lombroso drew on physiognomy and social Darwinism, as well as other currents, to formulate a theory, which was later elaborated by Guglielmo Ferrero to include social factors and to interpret typologies of beauty.[4] These ideas circulated widely and gained much currency beyond the scientific community because they corresponded to commonplace assumptions about the meanings of physical characteristics.

Riso amaro endowed Vallone with precise connotations.[5] He is the moral core in the film, the one who is positive from beginning to end, an expression of the northern proletariat who acts to some degree as the voice of the director. His correct Italian devoid of dialect inflections marked him out as a national figure, an Italian of the future. He was not uprooted or displaced from a region so much as above regional specificities. He was a man of the people, good and strong. De Santis denied that his characters were always precisely drawn, without ambiguity, citing the case of Silvana. But he admitted to wanting to make a cinema that was 'very simple, very elementary, with the precise aim of directly reaching the heart of the spectator whether lower class or intellectual ... I am a man like that, who prefers clear, stark things to ambiguity and subtleties'.[6] Though probably not familiar with the theories of Bela Balàzs, who attributed a role to physiognomy in his theory of film,[7] he understood its place in conveying meaning in cinema. Marco, while disenchanted, fitted this design, and Vallone was plausible in the role.

Vallone had an unusual background for a novice film star. A former professional footballer, he was also a university graduate, who, in the late 1940s, was working on the cultural pages of the Turin edition of the Communist newspaper *L'Unità*. Born in Tropea, Calabria, to a Turinese father and a Calabrian mother, he had enjoyed a relatively privileged upbringing. His father was a lawyer, while his mother's family was of noble extraction and wealthy enough to permit her to travel once a year with her friends to Paris. Almost uniquely among the screen actors of the period, Vallone maintained a range of cultural and literary interests.[8] It was this intellectual dimension that struck the director.[9] He had joined the liberal anti-fascists of 'Justice and Liberty', participated in the Resistance and even been captured and tortured before making an escape during transportation to a German prison camp by throwing himself into the icy waters of Lake Como.[10] At the suggestion of one-time Fascist journalist – now turned Communist – Davide Lajolo, he had been taken on to assist Lizzani and others with their location scouting.[11] In the course of this, he got to know Lizzani, Puccini and De Santis.

One evening, he recited for them the testament of Woyzeck from the eponymous play by Büchner. A simple soldier, Woyzeck assumes the stature of greatness, as, foreseeing his own death, he informs a fellow soldier what he should do with his few significant belongings.[12] One of the most performed plays in the history of the German theatre, *Woyzeck* deals with the dehumanizing effects of military life on a young man. The play is often seen as a proletarian tragedy. Impressed, De Santis thought Vallone might be able to play the sergeant Marco and summoned him to Rome for a screen test. He accepted light-heartedly and, the record states, suddenly found that he had become a screen actor from one day to the next.[13] In fact, a year before, while he was working as a journalist and film critic, Alberto Lattuada had asked him if he has considered becoming an actor. On that occasion, after some reflection, he declined the offer.[14] It took De Santis and his leftist colleagues to persuade him that he could further his progressive ideals through cinema.

Despite his bourgeois extraction, Vallone had the look of an unusually fit and eye-catching southern Italian labourer, his light-coloured eyes adding a touch of the angelic. His face was seen to represent a handsome ideal.[15] Even before he got involved with De Santis and Lizzani, his ideal qualities had been harnessed to the left. The Communist cultural official Antonello Trombadori had persuaded him to join Lizzani's German fiancée and a child in posing for an election poster in 1948. He was selected not because he was famous but because 'he was just a handsome young Italian, manly and serious.'[16] The poster pictured the family group against a background of agricultural workers. The wedding ring was missing from the hand of the woman, which curled round the child in the foreground of the image. However, despite fears that this would be a gift to the left's Catholic adversaries, no one appears to have noticed.

Vallone's character in *Riso amaro* is clearly a man of the left and thus it is to him that a key part of the film's message is attributed. When Silvana asserts her fascination for North America, where she has heard that everything is electric, he swiftly corrects her. 'Yes, even the chair is electric', he responds, disenchanted. Soon, he begins to realize that her dreams are different from his and that perhaps she is lost to the progressive cause. 'Boogie woogie, novels, *Grand Hotel*! You don't know how to look at anything else!' he exclaims. In the closing scene of the film, after Silvana's tragic suicide, Francesca and Marco stand side by side ready to depart. Low angle shots of them walking away are intercut with images of the open fields and the dispersing women. The couple is rendered heroic and exemplary by this visual framing. However, it is Marco – who Francesca glances at with quiet triumph and admiration – who emerges as the untainted positive hero of the saga.

Vallone was an engaged actor rather than a hired hand, one who expected to make a contribution to a film project and to believe in the character he played. This led him to reject roles of a standardized type (for example, in which he would simply play a seducer) and to directors and producers excluding him from consideration for many parts. He was at his happiest in productions in which there was a sense of common purpose. The great success of *Riso amaro* set him on a screen career. He would work under De Santis' direction on two further films: *Non c'è pace tra gli ulivi* (No Peace under the Olive Tree) the following year and, then, in 1951, *Roma ore 11* (Rome, 11 O'Clock). Though he would work on many films, his standing in postwar cinema would rest on his performances in barely more than a handful of films. These were the first two he made with De Santis, two further films he made in 1949, Luigi Zampa's *Cuori senza frontiere* (The White Line) and Pietro Germi's *Il cammino della speranza* (Path of Hope), and Lattuada's *Anna*, which employed the three lead actors from *Riso amaro* in a revisitation of the former film's melodramatic love triangle. In addition, in this period, he made one film of considerable artistic but little commercial interest, *Il Cristo proibito* (The Forbidden Christ), the only film directed by the writer and polemicist Curzio Malaparte, and a number of genre films of variable quality, including, most notably, the French-set historical adventure movie *Le avventure di Mandrin* (Don Juan's Night of Love) in 1951 and the football film *Gli eroi della domenica* (Sunday Heroes), directed by the veteran Mario Camerini in 1952. By the mid 1950s, his career as a film actor was in decline. Although he would continue to work occasionally with Carlo Lizzani and Alberto Lattuada, for whom he played a Communist mayor in the provincial scandal drama *La spiaggia* (The Boarder, 1954), he made a small number of films with minor directors before pursuing his career mainly in French cinema and, later, in Hollywood productions. From the late 1950s, he focused much of his attention on the theatre, notably with a production in French of Arthur Miller's Brooklyn-set *A View From the Bridge* (which would be filmed by Sidney Lumet in 1962, with Vallone in the lead role of Italian emigrant Eddie Carbone).

Non c'è pace tra gli ulivi was another leftist project that arose within the film industry; like *Riso amaro*, it was produced by Lux. Smarting from the criticism levelled at his previous film by the left, De Santis sought to make a more orthodox film. As left-wing critics expected him to set things right, the new film was in some respects a remake, stripped of the elements of American film noir that had so antagonized them. The petty criminal of *Riso amaro* is replaced as the main negative character by a landowner – that is to say, a class enemy. Vallone is a shepherd, Francesco, who returns to the Ciociaria region from a prisoner of war camp to find that his sheep have been taken by the landowner Agostino (see Figure 14.1). Not only is the latter now engaged to his former girlfriend Lucia, whose parents he has impressed with his wealth; he also rapes Francesco's sister Maria and then takes her in as a servant before killing her. Played by Folco Lulli, Agostino is melodramatically drawn as a villain, while the peasants, who are at first fearful and divided, develop a class consciousness and come together to rebel against their boss. The characters are roughly drawn in the manner of Soviet propaganda, while the message of the film is delivered through emphatic cinematography and theatrical speeches to camera. Mangano, who was pregnant and therefore unavailable for the film, was substituted by Lucia Bosè in the role of the peasant love interest. Her folk dance offers the same key to character as Silvana's boogie woogie. Vallone's Francesco is a victim, who seeks revenge and becomes the symbol of a demand for justice and equality. He is turned into a sort of revolutionary leader of the oppressed. The ending is happy, in tune with socialist realism. Francesco and Lucia are reunited, and the new world beckons. Though the visual style of the film owed something to Soviet cinema's preference for statuesque human figures and especially Eisenstein's stark iconography, it also bore a debt to the Hollywood Western's taste for unambiguous characters and drew on neorealism's investment in the landscape. Though derivative, the film offered a complex and striking choreography of glances, bodies and landscapes. *L'Unità*, however, remained dissatisfied; 'the characters are still too much like De Santis wants them to be', wrote the paper's reviewer.

> We don't know if the shepherds of the Ciociaria will see themselves in those of Non c'è pace tra gli ulivi any more than the rice-weeders saw themselves in Riso amaro. Anyway, it is obvious that the director imagines his characters before he sees them in the reality of the fields; he makes the act and feel according to a preconceived idea and not as they really are outside of his head. In brief, they are not living people, they are performers.[17]

In the film, Vallone is winning and charismatic. He is robust and solid, and he wears a broad smile, but he is not sunny in disposition. Francesco is someone who has been through experiences that have tested him; he is used to coping on his

Figure 14.1 Raf Vallone as wronged farmer Francesco in *Non c'è pace tra gli ulivi* (No Peace under the Olive Tree, Giuseppe De Santis, 1950) (screenshot by the author).

own and he is tough. His hairiness – of chest and arms – gives him a down-to-earth, lower-class feel. Though he is clean-shaven, he often sports the shadow of beard. The role marked him out, to adopt Emiliano Morreale's suggestive label, as 'a left-wing Nazzari'.[18] He lacked the versatility of the older actor; he could neither play comedy nor easily take roles of the bourgeois or the squire. However, he has not just a sense of justice but also a cause that connects his individual trajectory to the collective. He is attracted by beauty, be it Silvana in *Riso amaro* or Lucia in this film. Moreover, his moral impulse is platonically underlined by the fact that he is normally the most handsome man on the screen.

Vallone's two other key films were *Cuori senza frontiere*, which was released in September 1950, the same month as *Non c'è pace tra gli ulivi*, and *Il cammino della speranza*, which opened two months later, in November 1950. The first-mentioned film again sees him play a returned soldier. Domenico is a former prisoner of war in Russia, who, after escaping, is somehow making his way back to Italy. Members of his family were killed in the American bombing of Rome in 1943, while others were executed by the Germans, leaving him alone. We encounter him, wounded, in a village on the border between Italy and Yugoslavia. He is taken in and cared for by the daughter of a peasant farmer, Donata, played by a young Gina Lollobrigida, who becomes his reason for living. The action takes place in 1947, when a barrier dividing the two states is erected through the middle of the village. The inhabitants are given a few hours to decide which side they will choose. The tragic consequences of this development are explored in relation to a group of children, who, after playing happily together, become enemies. However, after a while, they opt to rebel against the division, uproot one of the border signs and resume playing. Domenico is counterposed throughout to Donata's long-standing boyfriend, Stefano, who chooses the Yugoslav side for ideological reasons and persuades her father to join him. Domenico intervenes to take Donata back to Italy. Tensions explode following the children's removal of the sign, and he and Stefano are fighting when news comes that little Pasqualino, Donata's young brother, has been shot. At this point, Donata's whole family are allowed to return to Italy so Pasqualino can be taken to hospital, where he dies. The film did not do very well, tackling a theme that was no longer topical by the time of its release. The message, that adults have much to learn from children, was vapid at best. The filming was problematic as the local population, goaded by the Titoist press, protested noisily at the lack of roles for the Slovene minority (although Stefano was in fact played by the Slovene actor Erno Gisa). These protests unsettled Vallone, who was close to the PCI but known for his unorthodox views.[19]

Il cammino della speranza was a film of greater ambition and success. It followed the fortunes of a group of Sicilian sulphur miners, who after learning that their mine will close opt to emigrate to France in search of a better future. They encounter many obstacles in their bid. At the outset, they are tricked by a shady figure, who dazzles them with the prospect of emigration and then abandons them at Termini station in Rome. The police intervene to round them up and send them back to Sicily. After they manage to avoid this and proceed north, they become embroiled in a local labour dispute near Parma after a landowner takes them on for a week to replace his striking labourers. A situation similar to the conflict between unionized and non-unionized workers in *Riso amaro* develops. Eventually some, who have become demoralized, return to Sicily, while for the others there is a happy end in sight at the conclusion of their epic journey. As they reach Val d'Aosta, after weathering a mountain snow storm, they are allowed to cross by a surprisingly indulgent French border policeman, who is won over by the smile of a child. Vallone is Saro, the effective leader of the migrants, while his antagonist is a local criminal, Vanni, who has mingled with the group and who is linked to a woman named Barbara, who has been ostracized in home village on account of her irregular personal life. Played by Elena Varzi, Barbara reveals her nobility when she ignores Vanni in order to help a girl who has been injured in an altercation with the striking workers. Vanni correctly suspects a growing sympathy between Barbara and Saro and challenges the latter to a duel – a knife fight against the dramatic backdrop of the Alps – in which he is killed. The film is not at all measured; it contains melodrama, folkloric elements, simplistic characters and sentimental appeals. But it is powerful and rich, a true drama. For these qualities it was awarded the Silver Bear prize at Berlin film festival, but it did not feature among the top twenty biggest grossers of the season in Italy. Nevertheless, its poetry and stress on human solidarity won the approval of the Catholic Cinematographic Centre. Initial ministerial objections to showing Italy as a country of poor emigrants were rescinded when it was appreciated that the film's expression of solidarity towards poor workers who seek a better future was not so much class-based, or of leftist inspiration, as sentimental.[20]

Il Cristo proibito, released in March 1951, was another film that did not trouble the box office, despite being nominated for prizes at Berlin and Cannes and a cast that included Gino Cervi, Alain Cuny and Serge Reggiani. The film once more accords Vallone the role of a returning soldier, Bruno, who has been a prisoner of war in Russia. He returns to his home village in Tuscany determined to avenge his dead brother Guido, who has been shot by a German firing squad after being given away by a resident of the village. Everyone knows the identity of the traitor, including the men's mother, but they refuse to tell Bruno for fear of unleashing further bloodshed and tragedy. He carries within him the burden of defeat and of a devastated country. An outsider, he finds a kindred spirit only in the prostitute Nella. He believes in individual justice and is not talked out of his vengeful intentions by those who realize that, by 1950, things have changed. The Christ-like carpenter Antonio confesses to the betrayal – even though he is not the guilty party – in order to bring an end to the persistence of hatred. Bruno duly kills him, but his quest continues after he is inadvertently informed that Guido's actual betrayer was a fellow partisan named Pinin, who was jealous of his relationship with the pretty villager Maria. Once more, as in the earlier films, there is a face off or duel. Pinin believes Bruno will kill him as he leads him away out of the village and pleads remorsefully for him to do so. However, as the villagers gather fearfully above to observe, Bruno just slaps him and abandons him to his pathetic self-recrimination. After this act of renunciation, normal life can resume, although the film ends with Bruno raging against the isolated house where Antonio's dead body lies. He deplores the innocent need to pay for the crimes of the guilty.

The film was a programmatic one, in which Malaparte presented an odd mix of Marxism and Christological notions of forgiveness and atonement. For the writer, it was always the innocent who suffered, and he wanted to make a statement against the principle of individual sacrifice for the good of the collectivity. A complex film, it stands in relation to Malaparte's belief that a 'razza marxista' (Marxist human type) had been formed by the concentration camps and widespread suffering. 'So', Luigi Martellini writes, 'for his heroes he sought faces that expressed that "Marxist type" that was the same, he claimed, as the Fascist and Nazi type; it was the totalitarian type, whether of right or left. In the film Bruno embodies this breed of totalitarians. Antonio counterposes to him the Christian type.'[21]

The writer-director was determined to find two 'Marxist faces' for the lead roles of Bruno and Nella. Vallone was immediately signed up, while Elena Varzi, with whom the actor became romantically linked after they worked together on the Germi film, was engaged after he set up a casual meeting between her and Malaparte.[22] Given Vallone's previous roles, it is not surprising that Malaparte should have chosen him for the role of Bruno. But it is worth reflecting on what he meant precisely by a 'Marxist face' and what this was supposed to convey. Although anthropologists recognize that 'the body communicates information for and from the social system in which it is a part' and see it as 'mediating the social situation' by acting as a site for the construction of meaning,[23] the communicative possibilities of particular actors are often taken for granted and rarely explicated. Age and sex are the primary limiting factors, but many others may intervene to determine the range of types a given actor can play. Like Aristotle, Malaparte had very precise notions about faces, which in his case expressed social types and periods. His remarks in *Kaputt* on national faces began a reflection that he continued in his 1947 Paris diary (which was not published until 1966), where he first elaborated his idea of the Marxist type – that is, 'the type that is taking shape in Europe, the European type'; this was, he said, very different from the type of his own generation – that which had fought in World War I. What struck him was the fact that it was cross national:

It is the same young, nervous, better-looking type, which is more delicate and more healthy at the same time, that can be found in the democratic countries as well as those that were fascist until yesterday. The same type is found in Moscow, Berlin, Rome, Paris and London. I would call this the "Marxist type" since it is the product not so much of cross-breeding as of better nutrition, sport, widespread hygiene, the gradual evolution of social ideas and of feelings, since ideas and feelings influence the physical to the same extent as sport, hygiene and nutrition. A 20-year old youth in Moscow, Kiev, Berlin, Prague or Rome shares distinctive characteristics with the young people of every other country in the matter of feelings, appearance, and that attitude towards life which distinguishes periods, races, generations and peoples ... It is a more cynical, cold, diffident type perhaps and maybe less brave, less moral in the bourgeois sense of the term, with a morality of its own that can repel anyone who is not aware of the profound transformation that the human race is undergoing in this period, in this century.[24]

The type was a reflection of the diffusion among the working class of habits and values that, before the war, had been solely bourgeois: a certain optimism and sense of entitlement based on good health and individual aspiration. This phenomenon of embourgeoisement would be attributed by Edgar Morin more specifically to the social impact of cinema on the individual's desire for realization.[25]

Vallone and Varzi, to Malaparte's mind, had faces that were proletarian in two respects; they were roughly hewn, stark and simple; they bore traces of suffering and endurance, of being on the side of the losers. However, they were Marxist in the sense that their austere beauty, which was decidedly not bourgeois, suggested a positiveness, a hope for the future despite the suffering and humiliation that had been experienced. This positivity was ideological; it was similar to that of Soviet statuary and propaganda posters. It was the same feature, as far as Vallone was concerned, that had led him to be selected as the face of the future in the 1948 election poster. Their faces were in this sense contemporary and modern but not commodified, glamorous faces. They conveyed, to draw on Jacques Aumont's reflections,[26] the recovery of the natural beauty of the face against the film industry's preoccupation with the photogenic; this recovery, which derived from neorealism, testified to the revival of humanist values and even of humanity itself in the aftermath of the war.

Vallone later recalled that he thought Malaparte's dialogue too literary; he also found the ending too rhetorical: 'on that account, I had a huge argument with Malaparte while we were doing the dubbing. In the end I did not dub the film *Il Cristo proibito*; there is another voice in place of mine.'[27] Vallone, evidently, was not an easy actor to work with. He was not just the bearer of a handsome countenance but an intellectual who demanded a voice. He expected to collaborate with a director rather than obey orders. There are several testimonies – some of them his own – that signal his refusal to go along with decisions he disagreed with. Often rows resulted in him being dubbed by another actor. One such example was *Camicie rosse* (Anita Garibaldi, Goffredo Alessandrini, 1952), which recounted the story of Giuseppe Garibaldi and his Brazilian wife Anita in the aftermath of the fall of the Roman Republic in 1849, when they refused to surrender to the French and left Rome to continue the struggle for Italian independence. The film was constructed around Magnani in the role of the feisty Anita, and the actress insisted on taking over some of the scenes that historically had been attributed to Garibaldi. Vallone lost his temper when he learned that a scene had been re-shot with Anita reviewing the troops instead of his Garibaldi. After clashes with Magnani, Alessandrini was replaced first by Visconti and then by Francesco Rosi (though the film is attributed to Alessandrini).[28] According to the actor, 'it was not easy to get me to dress up again in Garibaldi's poncho after this; I recall that it took an intervention from the Honourable Andreotti, who at the time was under-secretary in the prime minister's office.' Without his voice and barely recognizable beneath fair hair and beard, Vallone brought little to the role beyond his customary presence. Reviewers were not impressed; Vallone 'gives us a stock Garibaldi' commented Morandini.[29] Not even Magnani came out of the experience well, though some critics appreciated the passion with which she played the suffering and dying Anita.

Vallone's characters were simple and positive, and his physical presence was similarly unambiguous. Lacking formal training as a screen actor, he developed his own approach to film work. Though he had some of the rough authenticity of the postwar non-professionals, he was called on to play roles that were sometimes challenging. As a former footballer, who had played with the Torino reserves between 1935 and 1938 and for the first team in 1938–39, he had a special resource on which to draw. His approach to acting, he would later say, was drawn largely from sport, and football remained 'the backbone' of his life. Girotti too had been a sportsman, but it was team sport that inspired Vallone. 'As an actor', he stated,

I owe a lot to football: the familiarity with the public, control of the emotions, fair play in competitive contexts, personal discipline, acceptance and contemplation of human experience in all its various components: among them, dreams and the destruction of dreams, from which, however, is reborn ever victorious and vital the desire to improve and to repeat that myth of childhood in all its purity, that is to say, to charge life with its most precious substance.[30]

He claimed to have a 'double nature': 'a very contemplative nature and a nature consisting of internal dynamism'.[31] On screen, the latter manifests itself in his readiness to tackle matters or obstacles physically. He was able to endow roles with warmth and passion, bringing to them a concrete humanity. The former is evident in silences and moments of reflection, which, for his characters, are more often matters of morality or the fruit of experience than intellectual exercises.

The actor's political commitment, which saw him align himself closely with the PCI, though not actually join the party, informed his choices of roles. He believed intensely in the drive to reform and change after Fascism and war and brought this to his film work. 'I played in those engaged films with enthusiasm and idealistic passion. It seemed as though I was continuing the Resistance struggle and contributing to the improvement of mankind ... I felt profoundly integrated into the reality of our country', he said.[32] He showed this by lending his name to Communist appeals for peace, and he sent Lit. 20,000 to an appeal for Epiphany presents for the poor, organized by *L'Unità* in 1949, 1950 and 1951.[33] Unfortunately, a gap opened up between his beliefs and the direction that was taken by the film industry in the early 1950s. Changes in the cultural and political situation and the decline of neorealism affected the nature of the films that were made and left him with fewer options. The four films he made in 1952 would be the last ones of significance in this period. Each offered him less than he felt he had to offer.

In the Mangano vehicle, *Anna*, he once again took the part of the noble hero against Vittorio Gassman's villainous charmer. His character Andrea is good and strong like Sergeant Marco, but he is a bore and bourgeois. He is not inserted in any social context or endowed with any purpose. *Roma ore 11* saw him once more work with De Santis, though in a supporting role. The film explores the stories of several of the young women, who, while queuing for a job interview, lose their lives or suffer injury due to the collapse of a staircase. Vallone is a penniless artist whose bourgeois girlfriend, played by Lucia Bosè, is among the jobseekers. He is regarded by her family as unworthy, and out of indignant pride he gives her up. *Gli eroi della domenica* provided him with a rare chance to bring his football experience directly to a role (see Figure 14.2). In the film, he is Gino Bardi, the veteran centre forward of a small team who must beat AC Milan if they are to remain in Serie A. As expected, Bardi does what is required to save the day, but he is not a strong character. Though in his thirties, he lives with his mother, who reminds him to wear a vest. Moreover, his girlfriend is a woman with expensive taste and unsavoury connections, who turns his head with the offer of a bribe to throw the game. A typical Vallone character would have dismissed such overtures in an instant. Bardi, by contrast, takes his time before coming round and doing the right thing.

The Italian-French co-production *Le avventure di Mandrin* was a costly period production set at the time of Louis XIV. It was a star vehicle for Vallone, in which he plays an arrogant but charming army deserter who helps traders and contrabanders cross from France into Piedmont. In time, his teasing of the French authorities turns him into a famous bandit, a popular hero who is admired by men

Figure 14.2 The one-time professional footballer Raf Vallone returned to the game in the popular drama *Gli eroi della domenica* (Sunday Heroes, Mario Camerini, 1953) (screenshot by the author).

and loved even by ladies of the court. He is vain and confident, a man with a big personality and a sense of humour. Vallone's good looks and vigour are contrasted with courtly government officials, who are older, ugly, short or comical. The role is one that might have been played in earlier times by Amedeo Nazzari or, in an American production, by Errol Flynn. The casting of Vallone testified to his popularity in France but also to an irresistible slide towards genre productions. Mandrin was a stock Robin Hood type of cartoonish simplicity.

Vallone's appeal was evident to a director like De Santis, who used physical beauty 'to create an immediate rapport with the audience'.[34] In his view, this was necessary to 'a cinema that wanted to radicate itself firmly in the heart of the great lower-class public'. In the case of Vallone, there was a feeling that he was a leftist version of the noble hero that Nazzari had so often played. He was a 'solid protagonist' with 'light-coloured and ingenuous eyes'.[35] The actor was undoubtedly a sex symbol. He was powerfully built, with the robust solidity of a wardrobe. His face was wide and flat, and his hair dark and curly. His physical beauty was identifiably Mediterranean, save for his clear blue eyes. There was something earthy and authentic about him that was underlined by psychological intensity and clear inner-direction. Yet there was something that did not entirely work. Giulio Cesare Castello noted that postwar cinema's failure to create adequate male personalities became ever more evident when compared to the rich variety of female stars. 'The heavy, opaque Vallone, with the physique of a former athlete', he commented, did not resonate as forcefully as would have been desirable.[36] In December 1951, *Hollywood* lamented the lack of male actors in Italian cinema beyond comedians and those who were by now too mature.[37] Vallone was deemed to be too wooden and not suited to a wide enough range of roles. Yet some saw potential. A year later, the trade magazine *Cinespettacolo* hailed him as the only new male star to emerge since 1946, the only possible replacement for Nazzari and Girotti.[38] As an actor who emerged in the context of neorealism, he was better at conflict than intimacy. If he got involved in physical conflicts, it was not because of any issue of honour but because that was how his proletarian characters resolved matters. His rugged individualism gave him a romantic aura, but he lacked the film star glamour of Nazzari.

Vallone and his future wife, Elena Varzi, were a prominent left-wing celebrity couple. Together they attended events such as the Turin fashion show that was organized by the Communist women's magazine *Noi Donne*. *L'Unità* announced that 'Raf' and 'Elena' would be there 'with their commonplace faces'.[39] Though they endeavoured to keep their wedding a secret by holding it at 6.00AM, it became public knowledge after the priest published the announcement. Reporters and photographers mobbed them as they left the church and then followed them on scooters. They were a couple who shared a political outlook, a sort of Italian Yves Montand and Simone Signoret. They led a film star lifestyle, with magazine readers being treated to photographic spreads of their apartment in Rome's Parioli district.[40] Vallone developed a passion for sports cars and was pictured at the wheel of a Lancia cabriolet and later a Ferrari. Yet they maintained a certain cultural profile. Despite his lower-class image, Vallone counted Pavese, Camus, Salvador Dali and Picasso among his friends. At the villa they built at Sperlonga, 120km from Rome, where they were often photographed, and in later years with their three children, the couple often hosted intellectuals and celebrities. After interesting opportunities in Italian cinema dried up, they spent much time in France and later in the United States, where Vallone occasionally taught Italian at UCLA while taking supporting and cameo roles in numerous films, culminating in *The Godfather Part III* in 1990.

Notes

1. Synnott, 'Truth and Goodness, Mirrors and Masks – Part 1: A Sociology of Beauty and the Face', 611.
2. Ibid., 614–15.
3. Ibid., 615.
4. Lombroso's most famous work was *L'uomo delinquente* (1876), while Ferrero's ideas on beauty are contained in *L'Europa giovane*, which was published posthumously in 1946.
5. Reich and O'Rawe, *Divi: la mascolinità nel cinema italiano*, 88.
6. Faldini and Fofi, *L'avventurosa storia del cinema italiano: raccontata dai suoi protagonisti, 1935–1959*, 154.
7. See Koch and Hansen, 'Bèla Bàlazs: The Physiognomy of Things', 167–77.
8. Almost uniquely because Girotti too had been a student and cultivated cultural interests.
9. Faldini and Fofi, *L'avventurosa storia*, 154.
10. Vallone, *Alfabeto della memoria*, 72–75.
11. Lizzani, *Il mio lungo viaggio nel secolo breve*, 86. Lajolo, unlike others, was quite open about his conversion from Fascism to Communism, which he would allude to in the very title of his 1962 autobiographical novel *Il voltagabbana*. The title translates as 'The Turncoat'.
12. Vallone, *Alfabeto*, 102.
13. Anon., 'I nostri artisti: Raf Vallone', *Corriere canadese*, 5 July 1955, 7.
14. Obiettivo, '"Chi?" "Vallone?" "E' un buono"', *La Stampa*, 5 September 1954, 15.
15. For interesting reflections on Vallone as an example of masculine beauty, see Reich and O'Rawe, *Divi*, 87–88.

16. Lizzani, *Il mio lungo viaggio*, 84.
17. V., 'Non c'è pace tra gli ulivi', *L'Unità* (Piedmont), 13 October 1950, 5.
18. Morreale, *Così piangevamo il cinema melò nell'italia degli anni cinquanta*, 137.
19. The critic Tullio Kezich, who was on set and witnessed events, describes him as 'the then Communist Raf Vallone, was embarrassed by the intemperate behaviour of the comrades in the square.' 'Io, la Lollo, quel ciak al confine', *Corriere della sera*, 24 October 2004, reproduced in Pezzotta, *Ridere civilmente: il cinema di Luigi Zampa*, 236–37. Vallone had previously told Togliatti that he was not enrolled in the PCI because of the erasure of Trotsky from the history of the Russian revolution.
20. Spinazzola, *Cinema e pubblico: lo spettacolo filmico in Italia 1945-1965*, 30.
21. Martellini, *Il "Cristo proibito" di Malaparte*, 18.
22. Ibid., 26-27.
23. Douglas, in Polhemus, *Social Aspects of the Human Body*, 296.
24. Malaparte, *Diario di uno straniero a Parigi*, 40-41.
25. Morin, *L'esprit du temps*.
26. Aumont, *Du visage au cinéma*, 117-21.
27. Vallone, *Alfabeto*, 22-23.
28. See Hochkofler, *Anna Magnani*, 100.
29. Morandini, *Il Morandini: dizionario del film 2000*, 203.
30. Vallone, *Alfabeto*, 25.
31. Ibid., 62.
32. Ibid., 102-3.
33. Anon., 'Una fitta pioggia di doni è caduta fino a poco fa', *L'Unità*, 6 January 1951, 8.
34. Gili and Grossi, *Alle origini del Neorealismo: Giuseppe De Santis a colloquio con Jean A. Gili*, 123.
35. A. Scagnetti, 'Un duello rusticano tra le nevi delle Alpi', *L'Unità*, 26 February 1950, 8.
36. Castello, *Il divismo: mitologia del cinema*, 411.
37. De' R., 'Giovani bella presenza cercasi', *Hollywood*, 29 December 1951, 3.
38. Anon. 'Le attrici famose ci sono, ma gli attori?', *Cinespettacolo*, 20 December 1952, 5.
39. L.S., 'Una grande festa per voi nelle sale di Palazzo Madama', *L'Unità* (Piedmont), 14 December 1950, 5.
40. F. Vasquez, 'Serata in casa di Raf Vallone', *Hollywood*, 2 February 1952, 8-9.

PART IV

Reconfigurations of Stardom

CHAPTER 15

The Non-professional Actor and Low-Definition Stardom

Men, women and children who were not professional actors appeared extensively in postwar Italian films, most famously but by no means exclusively in neorealist classics such as *Paisà* (Roberto Rossellini, 1946), *Ladri di biciclette* (Bicycle Thieves, Vittorio De Sica, 1948), *La terra trema* (The Earth Trembles, Luchino Visconti, 1948), *Sotto il sole di Roma* (Renato Castellani, 1948), *Domenica d'agosto* (Sunday in August, Luciano Emmer, 1950), *Due soldi di speranza* (Two Cents Worth of Hope, Renato Castellani, 1951) and *Umberto D* (Vittorio De Sica, 1952). The close association between neorealism and the use of non-professional actors has meant that most discussions of the phenomenon have taken place in the context of analyses of the neorealist current, its purposes and its impact on Italian and international cinema. This focus has helped to identify some of the specific features and innovations of neorealism as it broke with certain practices and figures of the cinema of the Fascist period. What has been left out is a series of issues that have to do with the broader transformations that were occurring in cinema after the war. This chapter seeks to situate the experience of non-professional actors in relation not only to the cinematic innovations of neorealism but also to demands and expectations that were placed on cinema, to impulses towards renewal of the star system and to the growth of the industry.

All directors presumed, and some insisted, that non-professionals were engaged in a unique temporary experience that would see them return to their regular everyday lives at the conclusion of filming. This was sometimes stipulated at the outset as a condition of their employment. However, it proved difficult to implement. The idea that cinema could be demystified to the extent that it should be possible simply to resume ordinary life after acting in a film was a pipedream. Most non-professionals may have played people very like themselves, but this does not mean that there was a seamless passage from life to screen and back again. In the first place, it contrasted with the actual expectations of those involved. Many non-professionals became infected with the desire to stay in an environment that had given them rich experience and brought them great gratification for limited effort. Some developed a sense of entitlement, while others were convinced that they possessed the talent to continue. Even where this was not the case, the practices of cinema unavoidably conferred a certain notoriety on them. They were invited to film premieres, made festival appearances, gave magazine interviews and were occasionally the subject of foreign media interest. In their own communities at least, fame would linger around them for some time.

The postwar era witnessed pressures towards visibility as well as political influence on the part of the newly enfranchised masses. The enthusiasm for cinema reflected a demand for participation that was connected to aspirations for material improvement. The phenomenon of the non-professional actor was part of a wider process in which the film industry was seeking new faces and personalities. It was one channel among several, with beauty contests, magazine competitions and blanket scouting providing others. Though the non-professionals were unusual in being recruited from outside performative environments, they were not as remote from the culture of stardom as is often assumed. As anti-stars, they were also, in their own way, stars; they were the protagonists of what Giovanna Grignaffini has referred to as 'low definition' stardom[1] – that is, the spread of opportunities and demands for celebrity into new areas as a consequence of the democratic impulses of the period.

Non-professional Casting and Performance

The French critic André Bazin argued that the Italians were, 'like the Russians, the most naturally theatrical of people'.[2] 'In Italy', he argued, 'any little street urchin is the equal of a Jackie Coogan and life is a perpetual *commedia dell'arte*.' Though he was reluctant to ascribe this natural acting ability to an ethnic characteristic, he hypothesized that the urban Italian had 'a special gift for spontaneous histrionics' and this was the reason why De Sica and Visconti had been able to achieve 'such a superbly high level of acting' with the casts of their films. However, writing of *Ladri di biciclette*, the critic conceded that, ultimately, it was not 'the unique excellence of this workman and this child that guarantees the quality of their performance, but the whole aesthetic scheme into which they are fitted'.[3] In other words, non-professional performers were not required to adapt to all the practices of commercial film-making; rather, the whole surrounding context in which they were utilized was changed to throw their originality into relief and allow them to give of their best. As actors, they were called upon to *be* before all else; expression and performance came a distant second.

Neorealists did not invent the casting of non-professionals. In the late Fascist period there was a certain recourse to this casting practice, especially in military films in which the propaganda element was essential. Francesco De Robertis is generally credited with having made extensive use of them and also for having sought to amalgamate professionals and non-professionals.[4] Rossellini pursued the same strategy in his Fascist trilogy and in *Paisà* and his other films of the period. The purpose was to inject an element of authenticity into proceedings by having real soldiers or sailors play men like themselves. In the changed context of the postwar period, it was no longer a case of simply rendering military films more immediate and apparently genuine; there was a broader intention to challenge the conventions of fiction cinema by fashioning works that were neither plot-driven nor star-driven but which instead explored real-life issues and the experiences of real people. As Stefania Parigi notes, the desire to take the camera out into the street to engage with the hopes and travails of the social body led to the demand for new protagonists. 'It is in going out into the city streets, trodden by many of the protagonists of neorealist films, that directors sought the physiognomies, gestures, and experiences that were to be organised in a story that was also proposed as a slice of life.'[5] There was a need for a balance between figure and context, which led to a demand for 'figures capable of harmoniously blending in to the background as a natural feature'.

Some film-makers, particularly those belonging to the *Cinema* group during the war years, were perfectly aware of precursors in Soviet cinema, where Vertov and Eisenstein had both practised and theorized the use of non-professional actors. But there were aspects that were specific to the situation in Italy. Even film-makers who had nothing against the many actors who had played in Italian films during the industry's period of productivity in the early 1940s knew that it was not possible to make a new cinema without changes of personnel. The directors who were at the forefront of efforts to effect a sharp break with the cinematic production of the period before the end of the war were instrumental in the rise of the non-professional. 'The cult of the man "taken from the street" which was recurrent, for example, in the reflections of Zavattini', Parigi argues, 'suggests an attention to the human diffuse in postwar culture, as a point of departure for cinematic modernity'.[6]

The ideal of the non-professional actor could not have been realized on anything more than an occasional basis without recourse to practices that to some degree standardized the process of recruitment. There were three main ways in which people without previous experience were cast in postwar films: through being spotted on the street, through open auditions and by means of competitions of one sort or another. The first and last practices were long-established, though they expanded considerably after the war. The second was a practice instituted by directors seeking to see large numbers of candidates in person in a short time. Each one of these practices gave rise to its own mythology and legends, though certain overlaps also occurred. The first method, for obvious reasons, was a predominantly – though not exclusively – Roman phenomenon. Open auditions, too, were mostly held in the capital though they drew people from far and wide. They were an example of the way in which cinema sought to embrace the democratizing currents of the postwar period, since any individual who vaguely fitted the advertised requisites of a part could present themselves for consideration. Competitions took several forms, though typically they were organized by film companies and were sponsored by magazines or newspapers.

Rossellini claimed that he preferred to work with non-professionals because they 'do not have pre-conceptions'.[7] In other words, he found it easier to make the sort of films he wanted to with performers who lacked a professional outlook. De Sica's commitment to non-professionals was more categorical: 'I believe that the faces for the characters of a film must be sought, at all costs, outside the ranks of professional actors.'[8] Many selections did not occur through auditions as such but on the margins of them. For example, Lamberto Maggiorani, the worker Antonio in *Ladri di biciclette*, was recruited after his wife took their son to an audition for the part of the boy. De Sica rejected the son but was intrigued by the photograph of Maggiorani that the woman showed him.[9] Carlo Battisti, the university professor who played the title role in *Umberto D*, was spotted on the street by De Sica after he and his collaborators had spent a year looking for the right person to play the character created by Zavattini. When Battisti was noticed, he was with his own dog and De Sica sought to recreate for the camera the dynamic of a relationship he had observed in life. Brunella Bovo, a member of the cast of *Miracolo a Milano* (Miracle in Milan, 1951), was noticed by De Sica in a bar a few days before she began an acting course at the Centro sperimentale film school. In any event, the process was never rushed. Zavattini revealed that De Sica 'finds characters slowly, with calm, and he gets to like them like a father'.[10]

An example of his painstaking approach was the search for two young people to play Natale and Luisa, the protagonists of *Il tetto* (The Roof, 1956).[11] A drama about the housing crisis, it would be his last film with non-actors. A press article gave a sense of what was involved:

> *A selection conducted among thousands of girls and men, thirty screen tests, ten million lire spent; this is the considerable balance of the long search, which at last reached a good outcome, conducted by Vittorio De Sica and his collaborators to find the leading actors for* Il tetto, *that is to say the builder Natale and the servant girl Luisa. De Sica began to look for Luisa when he was in Sorrento acting in* Pane, amore e... *under the direction of Dino Risi. That was four months ago. He continued his search in Terracina where, one morning, on the walls of the houses posters appeared that caused alarm among boyfriends and fearful mothers. Then it moved to Latina and, finally, Rome. Over five hundred girls, almost all of them lower class, responded to this last appeal by the director, which was announced in the press.*[12]

De Sica had in mind a physical type for each character. Luisa was petite, thin, dark haired, of humble origins, strong in character and determined. She was to be from central Italy. Natale was to be tall and strong, shy but spontaneous and energetic. He was to be from the Veneto and to have fair hair and blue eyes. In the end, he chose for Luisa a girl who was middle class and pretty. For the part of Natale, he selected an unemployed 21-year-old named Sergio Listuzzi, who did not conform to any ideal. Indeed, 'he was the least beautiful of them all, but I chose him for this very reason, for the human sympathy that his face transmits.'[13] 'He is a simple, humble, modest being, with great potential for acting', De Sica said. 'His great lack of experience constitutes the basic appeal of the character; it makes him original. Listuzzi is not commonplace; he is fresh and unconventional.'

The young man's plainness of appearance was relatively unusual, as no neorealist director risked renouncing personal aesthetics altogether. In *Paisà*, Rossellini consciously sought to avoid established notions of the photogenic – entrusting roles in several episodes to men and women who evidently lacked any cinematic patina – though when it came to choosing an American soldier to play Joe the GI, who, in the first episode, interacts with local girl Carmela in the tower, 'naturally, the choice fell on the tallest and most blonde of them all, Robert Van Loon, who came from New Jersey and who, when he had to do a long shot lasting four minutes... managed it very well.'[14] De Sica did not hesitate to substitute the two shoeshines who informed him about their lives while he was preparing *Sciuscià* and whose nicknames were Cappellone (Long Hair) and Scimmietta (Little Monkey). As he later said, the originals were 'too ugly, almost deformed'.[15] While working on *Il tetto*, he admitted that 'a degree of beauty is unfortunately indispensable in cinema if the public is to like a character (the protagonist).'

As an actor himself, De Sica invested considerable energy in schooling his handpicked performers. Rossellini was concerned that a person plucked from everyday life lost their naturalness and tried to perform when placed in front of a camera. 'My job is to recover his true nature, to reconstruct it, to teach him once more his usual gestures', he said.[16] By contrast, De Sica was exceptionally successful at securing naturalistic performances from children, notably Rinaldo Smordoni (Giuseppe) and Franco Interlenghi (Pasquale) in *Sciuscià* and Enzo Staiola as Bruno in *Ladri di biciclette*. Adults were less malleable than children, but a variety of strategies could be employed to offset limitations and produce a result that was not out of keeping with the professional confection of the films. De Sica worked extensively with Maggiorani and surrounded him with professional character actors as well as some newcomers. His voice, however, like that of most non-professionals, was dubbed by an experienced actor.

The custom of combining non-professional and professional performers was widely adopted. In *Umberto D*, Carlo Battisti was flanked not only by the non-professional Maria Pia Casilio as the servant girl Maria but by a professional supporting cast, which included even his dog Flike. Battisti, like others, was selected because his face by itself transmitted the plight of his character. All the non-actors brought to the screen an authentic personal presence that was unaltered by the demands of storytelling: their physical 'flagrancy' formed the basis of 'the Zavattinian design to eliminate the barrier between reality and fiction'.[17] There was no spectacular enhancement of the regular rhythms of reality and thus no expectation of performative virtuosity. An essential ordinariness was fundamental to the achievement of the new cinematic aesthetic.

Non-professional actors brought their own specificity and biography to a role, complementing authentic settings with details like missing teeth or an imperfect gait, which were not found usually in professionals engaged in conscious imitation.[18] Maggiorani's careworn face was integral to Antonio. As Giuliana Minghelli has observed, 'Rome and Maggiorani's countenance, a face bearing the deep imprint of a sorrow going well beyond this anguished day, tell the story of this deeper stratum of history.'[19] His downbeat dignity formed the core of his character's persona. If, as Karl Schoonover has argued, the 'suffering body' is a key neorealist trope, then that suffering was manifested in a range of expressive modes.[20] The physical manifestation of the actual experience of class oppression transmitted by the face of Maggiorani or the feeling of offended but selfish dignity characterizing the 70-year-old Battisti were significant contributions. They communicated the human suffering arising from social conditions, such as the unemployed or impoverished pensioners, which was more prosaic than the general suffering arising immediately from the war and the occupation. In popular films that employed mainly non-professional casts, such as Luciano Emmer's *Domenica d'agosto* and Renato Castellani's *Sotto il sole di Roma*, the presence of amateurs served a different purpose.[21] The aim was to capture a certain vitalistic verve and a youthful spontaneity. If suffering could be conveyed through indexical qualities, then so too could other conditions, such as class and regional difference, energy and ambition. In the post-reconstruction period, this would be increasingly important in the continuing use of non-professional casting after the demise of neorealism.

Problems and Trajectories

Though some of the people who were chosen for parts were utterly ignorant of cinema and its ways, others had a clear, if not necessarily accurate, perception of what cinema could do for them. The tendency to 'perform', which Rossellini sought to expunge, went hand in hand with certain vanities. 'Italy is the land of the most extravagant improvisations', asserted one contributor to the magazine *Festival*; 'therefore the person who becomes an actor from one day to the next has, within a few days, taken on all the defects and snobbery of the actor.'[22] The magazine reported that, after a few days on set, the professor Carlo Battisti, who had to be persuaded by colleagues to accept the title role of the impoverished pensioner in *Umberto D*, asked De Sica if he should not consider surgical intervention to reduce the double chin that was surely diminishing his photogenic appeal.[23] 'Even the austere professor did not take too long to get contaminated by the germ of the star system', commented the article's author.

The illustrated press, especially if hostile to neorealism, pointed out contrasts between the supposed idealism of film-makers and the pragmatism of their protégés. The stories of non-professionals were laced with similar delusions. Maggiorani was convinced that the success of the *Ladri di biciclette*, beyond the merits of De Sica, depended on his ability as an actor.[24] 'Those of us who have promise, because we are workers we have a difficult time among the professionals', he lamented. Agnese Gemmona, who, at the age of fourteen, played the part of Lucia, the sister of a fisherman in *La terra trema*, went with other cast members to the film's presentation at the Venice film festival. 'I was photographed, interviewed, sought after by directors. I dreamed of becoming an actress', she recalled.[25] 'However, someone convinced my parents that the cinema was a sinful monster and the dream ended', she added. Francesco Golisano, who appeared in *Due soldi di speranza* and went on to take the role of Totò in *Miracolo a Milano* (Miracle in Milan, Vittorio De Sica, 1951), saw himself as a film actor even after he went into the wholesale soap business.[26]

Examples like this were covered in such a way either to show the unrealistic self-perceptions of the people concerned, or to convey the idea that they had been tricked into thinking that they were on a path to fame and wealth. Absorbed momentarily into the film world, non-actors, even if efforts had been made to disabuse them of misconceptions, were inclined to see themselves as actual or potential stars. They were not entirely mistaken in this. Although there was a great difference between them and the big established names, the non-professional in reality was intimately bound up with the star that he or she was supposed to replace. The star, as opposed simply to the actor, brought a pre-existing personality to a film and was always recognizable as him or herself. A character was merely a cloak beneath which the famous performer was clearly discernible. Non-professionals had no ready-formed screen identity or persona, but they possessed some of the same characteristics of typicality of the star.[27] They kept faith with their actual personality and were identifiably the everyday man or woman who had been selected to represent a particular type or category. Maurizio Grande has argued that neorealism's non-actors were called on to embody a new stardom based on physiognomy, on the correspondence between corporeal presence and exemplarity of the everyday man, capable of presenting themselves 'as effigies of a segment of humanity as image of the world'.[28] The difference with respect to the star lies in the fact that the non-actor neither benefited from a build-up during which time the public became interested in the true person, nor was inserted into a career pattern that was projected into the future. Even a transfer from one film to another was highly problematic. Grignaffini has referred to their celebrity as being '(if it does not sound paradoxical) "neutral in orientation" or in any case of low definition'.[29] This helped spread the idea of cinema as easily accessible to ordinary people and despite the insistence of directors led to some returns to screen work in similar or related roles.

Low-definition stardom was an inevitable reflection of the great desire of people to break into cinema and share in its rewards. As was shown in Chapter 4, widespread hopes for personal affirmation were directed at the industry. By the early 1950s, production companies were submerged with letters from aspirant actors. One magazine observed that:

> *Young men and women presenting themselves at the gates (of Cinecittà) were not after money but success above all. They were dreaming of seeing their names in big letters on posters, villas with swimming pools, sports cars, loads of admirers. Every girl tried to look like a star who was already famous and some resorted to the most naïve or absurd expedients to draw attention and to gain entry.*[30]

The announcement of a mass audition was often the catalyst of dreams and expectations. Yet they were often demoralizing affairs for all concerned. Zavattini wrote in his diary of his experience at an audition to find the two protagonists of the episode of *Siamo donne* (Of Life and Love, 1953) dedicated to young hopefuls.[31] He recalled the long addresses of the competitors, which suggested their humble backgrounds (Via Ugento, Lotto 8, scala M, int. 11, Quarticciolo, Rome). There was a girl who wanted to be the first to do the screen test because she had to leave in a hurry to have her tonsils out; the candidate who said to him, 'I come from Latina, I am not beautiful but I know what to do and I have all the right papers, including those of the trade union'; and one 'with bovine eyes like Bette Davis's', who confessed that she first became obsessed with acting as a child. Her passion was so strong that her parents took her to see doctors, one of whom told her 'that she would only get better by truly becoming an actress'.[32] What remained with him most though was the crestfallen air of the 150 girls who survived the first selection when they went into Theatre No.1, where lunch was laid out. 'They realised how numerous they were and almost all of them good looking', he noted; 'their hopes began to decline sharply. In vain a band tried to keep their spirits up. It seemed like the orchestra on the Titanic'.

For those who succeeded in being selected and who ended up working on a film, the eventual let-down was often even greater. The question of the destiny of film amateurs was a difficult one that from time to time was raised as an accusation against neorealists. They were accused of uprooting people from their environments and creating a category of misfits, some of whom would never recover from their brush with cinema.[33] Because they had no interest in developing talent or building screen personas, the neorealists unwittingly inflicted suffering on their performers. For every Carlo Battisti, who returned to his usual life while not excluding totally a possible return to the screen,[34] there were tens of others whose lives never returned to normal and whose existences were blighted by their brief encounter with cinema.

One trajectory of displacement and disappointment was that of Lamberto Maggiorani. The huge international acclaim the *Ladri di biciclette* received brought him fame but little fortune. In December 1949, the weekly *La Settimana Incom* sent a correspondent to find him working on a building site (see Figure 15.1). Though he had returned to his job as a mechanic at the Breda factory in Rome, as had been stipulated by De Sica,[35] he had been made redundant and was taking temporary employment.[36] With the Lit. 600,000 he had received, he had furnished his dining room, which, the reporter found, was decorated with autographed photographs of himself with De Sica. Yet he longed for another leading role and was encouraged when American journalists came to find him and were amazed to learn that he was not working regularly in cinema. A proposal that he should go to the USA to make a film about the New York police chief Joe Petrosino, a pioneer in the fight against organized crime, came to nothing after he appeared with his family on the cover of a Communist magazine. Maggiorani would appeal to De Sica for help and was taken on as a worker on a film troupe. Zavattini even considered making a film about his troubles, but nothing came of it.[37] He would make a handful of further screen appearances, including a small supporting role as a workers' leader in Lizzani's Resistance drama *Achtung! Banditi* (1951).

The tales of the afterlives of the non-professional actors appeared periodically in the press. The young cast members of Castellani's *Sotto il sole di Roma* and *Due soldi di speranza* offered further examples of disappointment. Francesco Golisano, who went on to take the role of Totò in *Miracolo a Milano* (Miracle in Milan, Vittorio De Sica, 1951), set up a soap business, while Oscar Blando opened a greengrocer's shop with his earnings.[38] Both still yearned for the cinema. Others fared worse. Vincenzo Musolino from *Due soldi di speranza* featured in the press when

Figure 15.1 After playing the unemployed worker Antonio in *Ladri di biciclette* (Bicycle Thieves, Vittorio De Sica, 1948), Lamberto Maggiorani lost his regular job and became a builder's labourer (author's own collection).

he was arrested for failing to return a car he borrowed. He was never reconciled to his former simple life. The saddest case of all was that of Carmela Sazio, who played the village girl Carmela in the first episode of *Paisà*. Unable to return to her life in a fishing community, she had begged in vain to be allowed to leave with the troupe. Later she reportedly turned to prostitution and was never heard of again.[39] Cases such as these induced Alfredo Guarini to write to Zavattini asking him if it 'was it not a mistake to choose "faces" – in so many films – without taking the trouble to turn them into actors?'.[40] He argued that, with some training and assistance, some displaced non-actors might have been able to continue and their suffering could have been avoided.

Only a small number of them did succeed in winning a toehold in the industry and in very specific circumstances. Their chances were greater if their type was reproducible or if their original role had not been so prominent as to identify them permanently in the public mind with one film. Maria Fiore, who made her debut at the age of seventeen in *Due soldi di speranza*, went on to appear in many light comedies through the 1950s and 1960s, often in roles that differed little from the leading one she took in her debut film.[41] The abattoir worker Gastone Renzetti, who was selected by Anna Magnani to play her husband Spartaco in *Bellissima*, was one of few adult non-professionals to speak with his own voice. Well-built and handsome, he too would continue to appear in supporting and character roles. *Umberto D*'s Maria Pia Casilio took many small roles through the 1950s, including in the first two films in the popular *Pane, amore . . .* series. Anna Garofalo noted that in postwar films the servant girl was becoming a character no longer confined to brief announcements of this or that event followed by deferential retreats: 'the symbol of these country girls, arrived in hostile city, could be represented by Maria Pia Casilio, the little servant girl of *Umberto D*.'[42]

The most successful example was Franco Interlenghi. When he took the part of Pasquale in *Sciuscià*, he was aged fourteen and a high school student. By the early 1950s, his career had taken off. He made eight films in 1952, seven in 1953 and would continue to work in many genres – light comedy, romantic comedy and drama – over several decades. However, initially, his destiny was not dissimilar to that of Maggiorani, as one magazine reported: 'He began to make fabulous plans for the future.

> "You'll see" – he said at home – "journalists will come to interview me; photographers too: Mamma mia, you won't be able to protect me from the photogra-

Figure 15.2 Carlo Battisti (right), in the title role, and Maria Pia Casilio (left) were the two main non-professionals to be cast in *Umberto D* (Vittorio De Sica, 1952) (screenshot by the author).

phers. They will follow me in the street. My photo will be in all the papers, like that of Gary Cooper". Gary Cooper was his favourite actor, his idol ... But no journalists rang the doorbell, no-one thought to take photographs of him and still less to publish them. "Not even in a small local newspaper – says Interlenghi – "What a disappointment!"[43]

However, the matter did not finish there. He went back to school and did some work in the theatre. Gradually, he was called for more film work. He appeared in *Fabiola* in 1948, then in *Domenica d'agosto* in 1950 and Emmer's subsequent film *Parigi è sempre Parigi* (Paris Will Always Be Paris) in 1951. After this, further work followed.

It was against this general background that directors began to seek to remove rose-tinted spectacles from the eyes of the public. When Visconti inserted in *Bellissima* a vignette in which Liliana Mancini is seen working at the moviola at Cinecittà and is identified by Maddalena Cecconi (Anna Magnani) as the character Iris from *Sotto il sole di Roma*, his intention was to reinforce the film's general warning about the illusory nature of the cinematic dream. The failure of *Bellissima* at the box office, along with that of other films that purported to expose popular illusions, such as Antonioni's *L'amorosa menzogna* (The Amorous Lie, 1949) and *La signora senza camelie* (The Lady Without Camelias, 1953), Fellini's *Lo sciecco bianco* (The White Sheik, 1952) and Dino Risi's *Viale della Speranza* (Boulevard of Hope, 1953) highlighted the lack of receptiveness to this message.

Impact on Stardom and Industry

Non-professional actors helped bring about a transition in the star system. They were part of a series of innovations in casting and performance, which, in a short time, effectively ended the close relationship that had existed between cinema and the mainstream theatre and even put an end to the more recent practice of casting students and graduates of the Centro sperimentale film school. The determination to register a break with the past prepared the ground for the development of further channels of recruitment. Before 1945, no one would have envisaged that beauty contests would become a source of screen talent. Such competitions often aligned themselves closely with cinema by offering screen tests as prizes or claiming that their purpose was to find 'new faces for Italian cinema'. Even the annual contest run by the Communist illustrated weekly *Vie Nuove* in the 1950s engaged in this practice, despite its organizers' claim that they wished to combat the unrealistic dreams peddled by commercial pageants.[44] Of course, there was a difference between the young person spotted in their normal environment and a woman noticed at a beauty pageant. While the former was presumed to harbour no cinematic ambitions, the latter was already part of a performative sphere. Moreover, beauty contest participants were not simply ordinary girls-next-door, whatever the image of them that was cultivated by organizers and the media. They were the best-looking members of their communities, who had benefited from some preselection on the basis of their physical appearance.

While the non-professionals who were cast in neorealist films were actively discouraged from cultivating aspirations of further work, the beauty queens who, with little or no artistic training or preparation, were cast in films faced no such conditions. The ambition to break into cinema was often what had led them to take part in pageants in the first place and thus the offer of a part necessarily opened up the prospect of further roles. In this case, aspirations were often encouraged by producers and not quashed by directors. Thus, while Maggiorani and Silvana Mangano ostensibly shared a casting experience, they were in fact poles apart. Maggiorani had never sought to enter cinema, while Mangano was an experienced participant in beauty pageants (she had been Miss Roma), who had already taken very small parts and attended auditions when she was spotted on the Via Veneto by Giuseppe De Santis.

The practice of street scouting was not confined to ordinary examples of humanity. It extended to young women of great beauty. A director with no sympathy for neorealism, Riccardo Freda spotted Gianna Maria Canale, then working as a typist, on the street in Rome. Unbeknown to him, she had won the title of Miss Calabria and was about to take part in Miss Italia 1947. He 'turned her into his muse, the protagonist of all his films from 1948 to 1953, the years of their love story'.[45] Lucia Bosè, who would win Miss Italia 1947 before embarking on a film career, was first noticed by Visconti working in a Milan patisserie, while Elena Varzi caught the eye of the producer Sandro Ghenzi at Ostia. In this instance, the producer had to overcome her initial disinterest and then persuade both her and her father of his seriousness. Stories such as these testify to a determination not to abolish screen stardom but to reinvent it on the basis of discoveries made directly among the people. It coincided with the recovery of the industry and the transition from the 'corpo popolare' (commonplace body) to the 'corpo divistico' (star body).[46] This saw a return of qualities that had been traditionally prized in cinema, such as beauty, physical harmony, health and sex appeal, as well as the photogenic.

The widespread use of screen performers with no training or experience was greeted with hostility in some quarters. Many in the film industry remained unpersuaded of the contribution of non-professionals. Blasetti thought that they were best suited to a type of film that dealt with the tragedy of war. For *Prima comunione*, the director only held auditions for the part of the little girl. All other roles were entrusted to professionals even though he later admitted that he could equally have used non-professionals for the supporting cast. The fact that he chose not to is testimony to his long-held commitment to the idea of an Italian film industry that was robust and professional in all its aspects. Freda, too, was always hostile. 'They only lasted a short while because they don't function at all as actors, they waste a huge amount of time and they take up energy and film stock', he stated.[47] The same thing, of course, was said of the beauties who migrated to cinema and whose performative talent was not always remarkable. 'We lack a genuine sense of quality in acting', lamented *Cinema nuovo* in 1955, echoing the remarks of American star Anthony Quinn.[48] 'The reason has to do with the way actors, and especially actresses, were recruited. The larger production companies need to create acting schools', it concluded.[49]

Though non-professionals were commonly accompanied by professionals, they were often inserted into real-life settings in which background non-speaking roles were filled by people recruited on the spot. These were people deemed able to offer the special 'mixture of anonymity and essential humanity' that was so important to postwar cinema.[50] Neorealism's preoccupation with 'real people' profoundly affected the traditional categories of secondary-part professionals and extras. So desperate did the members of these categories become, *Festival* reported, that when they heard that De Sica would be seeking to recruit ordinary men and women at the Termini station in Rome, they headed there in numbers disguised as simple folk. 'This is the ploy of the old "tradesmen", of the rejected "specialists in minor parts", of the derided representatives of the cinema world's "extra-pile"', the magazine reported. 'Disguised as "ordinary people", they pretended to be waiting for a train, or to have "just arrived", or to be accompanying friends and relatives, or even to be pickpockets who were hoping to conclude some business in those parts.'[51]

With the return of the industry, there was a greater self-awareness of professional dignity. Actors, too, were also hostile to amateurs, and in 1953 they formed an association to protest against both the increasing use of foreign actors in Italian cinema and untrained newcomers.[52] Even though only an estimated 10 per cent of films used non-professionals, and these only in films with a realistic theme, there was a conviction that work was being lost. Further protests arose three years later during De Sica's filming of *Il tetto*. Over four hundred screen actors banded together to create a new association. A communiqué was issued that read as follows:

> The widespread use in all sectors of the Italian entertainment business of improvised actors and other elements, the absence of any protection of our noble profession, tax burdens, the lack of an effective system of insurance and healthcare, the state of subjugation in which many of us are held by very expensive

agents. These and many other evils that afflict our category have induced us to identify the most effective means to affirm the value of our labour and defend our rights.

The reference to agents reflected a recent development in the management of talent in Italian cinema that was a consequence of both the hiring of foreign actors and the growth of the industry. The statement went on to denounce the 'deplorable custom' of 'making recourse to the man in the street'. It was proposed to institute a professional register that would act as gatekeeper. They found little support. In *La Settimana Incom*, the journalist Lamberto Sechi denounced the professionals for wanting to block new entries to the sector and to ensure ever higher earnings for themselves, despite the fact that they were not always very good. Indeed, while neorealist films were not cheap to make, the pay of non-professionals was hugely inferior to that of actors and especially star names.[53] 'There are actresses whose performances are non-existent and who should be sent back to school, actresses who earn enough to buy themselves apartments in the Parioli district and massive American cars in which they risk their lives and those of others. We have got the point: they want a yacht too.'[54] 'When the professionals demand so much that they will surely send a film's budget into deficit, then producers and directors are right to entrust the parts to people who improvise', he argued. *Cinema nuovo* found it surprising that among the founders was Raf Vallone, who had begun his career as a non-professional. The real issue, it was claimed, was the need to provide amateurs with schools and workshops through which they could better themselves and their performances to make more than one film. A director can choose his actors where he wishes, the magazine asserted; there are some films that require professional actors and others that do not. Post-war Italian cinema is rich with examples of fine non-professional contributions, and 'the balance is not in favour of the professionals', it concluded. In 1956, the periodical returned to this theme, with a series of interviews with directors, writers and actors, some of them non-professional.[55] The hostility to the 'non-actor' remained strong. It was not widely understood that the recourse to the non-professional was a consequence of the break that parts of Italian cinema wished to make with the past. Directors had sought the human material most suited to achieve that representation of reality that they sought at a time of a far-reaching process of social and political change in the country.

Notes

1. G. Grignaffini, 'Lo stato dell'unione: appunti sull'industria cinematografica italiana, 1945–1949', in Farassino, *Neorealismo: cinema italiano 1945-1949*, 44.
2. A. Bazin, 'Bicycle Thieves' (1949), in Cardullo, *André Bazin and Italian Neorealism*, 68–69.
3. Ibid., 69.
4. Parigi, *Neorealismo: il nuovo cinema del dopoguerra*, 41.
5. Ibid., 73.
6. Noto and Pitassio, *Il cinema neorealista*, 31–32.
7. Rossellini, quoted in Faldini and Fofi, *L'avventurosa storia del cinema italiano: raccontata dai suoi protagonisti, 1935-1959*, 145.
8. Ibid., 145.
9. Lamberto Maggiorani, cited in P. Cristofani, 'Processo al non attore', *Cinema nuovo*, 25 March 1956, 178.
10. Zavattini, *Diario cinematografico*, 186.
11. On the film and its making, see Gandin, *Il tetto di Vittorio De Sica*. For a recent interpretation, see Schoonover, *Brutal Vision: The Neorealist Body in Postwar Italian Cinema*, 172–82.
12. S. Martini, 'Natale e Luisa', *Cinema nuovo*, 25 November 1955, 378.
13. Ibid.
14. A. Farassino, 'Gli attori neorealisti', in Cosulich, *Storia del cinema italiano*, Vol. VII 1945–1948, 340.
15. Vittorio De Sica in Faldini and Fofi, *L'avventurosa storia*, 113.
16. Rossellini in ibid., 145.
17. Parigi, *Neorealismo*, 74.
18. Schoonover, *Brutal Vision*, 44–45.
19. Minghelli, *Landscape and Memory in Post-fascist Italian Film: Cinema Year Zero*, 109.
20. Schoonover, *Brutal Vision*, 161 on Maggiorani's bodily input to the character of Antonio.
21. Cited in Cristofani, 'Processo al non attore', 176.
22. P. Crisanti, 'Quando le stelle non brillavano ancora', *Festival*, 14 March 1953, 3.
23. Ibid.
24. A. Tasca, 'Il cinema ha rovinato Maggiorani', *La Settimana Incom*, 31 December 1949, 27.
25. Cited in M. Amorosi, 'La terra trema ancora 45 anni dopo', *Gente*, 13 December 1993, 129.
26. Rondi, *Le mie vite allo specchio: diari 1947-1997*, 65–66.
27. Parigi, *Neorealismo*, 75.
28. M. Grande, 'Attore' in Moneti, *Lessico zavattiniano: parole e idee su cinema e dintorni*, 75.
29. Grignaffini, 'Lo stato dell'unione', in Farassino, *Neorealismo*, 44.
30. V. Schiraldi, 'Le comparse arrivano in spider', *Oggi*, 31 August 1967, 37.
31. Zavattini, *Diario cinematografico*, 112–13.
32. Ibid.
33. Biondi, *Sottobosco del cinema*, 60–62.
34. Battisti stated in 1956 that he would be willing to return to the screen but only for a film of similar quality to *Umberto D* and for a part that drew in the same way on his personal experience. Cited in Cristofani, 'Processo al non attore', 175.
35. De Sica evoked this agreement in 1956; cited in Cristofani, 'Processo al non attore', 175.
36. Anon., 'Fame Mocks A Movie Star', *Life*, 13 February 1950, 44–45.
37. Zavattini, *Diario cinematografico*, 129–32. It was planned to make a film about his life after *Ladri di biciclette*, called *Tu Maggiorani* (You Maggiorani) or *Il grande inganno* (The Big Dupe). The

Hungarian director Geza von Radvanyi planned to make it with a script by Zavattini. He was supposed to attempt suicide by throwing himself in the Tiber. After emerging from the river, having had second thoughts, he was to meet De Sica and reject the invitation to make another film. Maggiorani, cited in Faldini and Fofi, *L'aventurosa storia*, 146. See also Parigi, *Neorealismo*, 176.

38. Rondi, *Le mie vite allo specchio*, 65–66.
39. Parigi, *Neorealismo*, 76n.
40. Zavattini, *Diario cinematografico*, 137.
41. Biondi, *Sottobosco del cinema*, 60.
42. A. Garofalo, 'Un nuovo personaggio', *Cinema nuovo*, 25 October 1954, 359.
43. E. Granzotto, 'Sarà geometra il piccolo sciuscià', *La Settimana Incom*, 25 April 1953, 24–25. Though Rinaldo Smordoni was 'better looking' as well as 'amazingly good', he did not continue for long in cinema. Vittorio De Sica in Faldini and Fofi, *L'avventurosa storia*, 113.
44. The controversies around Miss *Vie Nuove* are discussed in Gundle, *Bellissima: Feminine Beauty and the Idea of Italy*, 137–41.
45. S. Masi, 'Destini diversi dell'attore: l'ascesa del divismo femminile', in Cosulich, *Storia del cinema italiano*, Vol. VII 1945–1948, 340.
46. Parigi, *Neorealismo*, 72.
47. Freda, *Divoratori di celluloide: 50 anni di memorie cinematografiche e non*, 147.
48. C. Jubanico, 'Bellezza e talento', *Cinema nuovo*, 25 November 1955, 366.
49. Anon., 'L'albo degli attori', *Cinema nuovo*, 25 November 1955, 367.
50. Aumont, *Du visage au cinéma*, 121.
51. V. Talaricco, '"Presi dalla vita"', *Festival*, 10 January 1953, 3–4. Ever curious about street phenomena, Zavattini even had the idea of making a film about them, as he had about Maggiorani's misfortunes. In the course of his investigation, he found that typically they were recruited at Termini station. Whereas, once, they all hailed from the Quadraro district, near Cinecittà, now they came from all over the city. They were well organized, sometimes even as gangs, so that the required number and type could be supplied at short notice. Group heads were responsible to production directors for their punctuality, discipline, the return of costumes and so on. 'Naturally there are also those who try, in this way, to get into the world of cinema, by legitimate or secondary channels', he observed; 'but the milieu itself discourages all ambitions of this type.' L. Sechi, 'Gli attori protestano', *La Settimana Incom*, 25 April 1953, 39.
52. Already in April 1952, the actors of De Santis's film *Roma ore 11* (Rome 11 O'Clock) had protested to Nicola Pirro, Director-General of Entertainment, about the exclusion of the film from the Italian entry to Cannes. One of them wrote that

    We actors have a special reason to be saddened by this exclusion. Our cinema has almost always been represented – and has often won recognition – at these international festivals with films belonging to the neorealist current featuring non-professional actors. The example of "Roma ore 11" which, for the first time, brings together a good number of professional actors in a film of this very artistic current, seems to us to be particularly important in terms of winning recognition abroad for the potential of our category.

    Centro sperimentale di cinematografia (CSC), Fondo Giuseppe De Santis (FDS), Corrispondenza 1944–1947, Letter of 'gli attori di "Roma ore 11"' to Nicola De Pirro, 2 April 1952. Fourteen actors signed the letter. De Santis had deliberately cast so many popular actors in his film 'in open polemic with those who support the false line of a naturalistic approach and believe that the bits of real life in cinema can and must be played solely by improvised actors recruited on

the street'. CSC, FDS, Manoscritti e dattiloscritti 1936–1984, cartella 'Dattiloscritti di articoli pubblicati fra il 1954 e 1957 su *Cinema Nuovo*, Cinema e *Il Contemporaneo*.
53. A. Farassino, 'Il costo dei panni sporchi: note sul "modo di produzione" neorealista', in Zagarrio, *Dietro lo schermo: ragionamenti sui modi di produzione cinematografici in Italia*, 140–41.
54. Sechi, 'Gli attori protestano', 39.
55. Cristofani, 'Processo al non attore', 175.

CHAPTER 16

Co-productions and International Stardom

Italian cinema had, from its origins in the 1910s, operated in an international context. The years after 1945 witnessed the reproposition in modified form of some of the practices that had been adopted in the Fascist period. These included international co-productions, state involvement in film exports, some degree of international movement of actors, directors and other personnel, and an interest in foreign subject matter. The postwar situation, however, was different in important respects. The end of dictatorship and the incorporation of Italy into the western alliance under American leadership heralded a phase of unprecedented US involvement in all aspects of the film industry. It marked the end of political and cultural nationalism and the development of new policies founded on free trade, cooperation and a growing sense of a European industry, which would expand in the 1950s and 1960s.

The two most significant factors bearing on the transfer of stars between different cinemas were, first, the development of a pattern of European co-productions that was dominated by the formation of a special relationship with France and, second, the desire of the American industry to profit from a situation in which Italian cinema was offering a series of qualities and features that were of interest to international audiences. European cooperation was founded on the need to form a solid basis from which to compete with Hollywood. But, at the same time, Hollywood remained a model and a lure that producers, as well as individual actors, found irresistible. French stars began to appear in Italian-led co-productions from the late 1940s, while Italian stars, in lesser numbers, featured in French ones. Some Italian stars were also recruited by Hollywood producers, who resumed the prewar practice of cherry-picking the best European talent. Generally speaking, transfers to Hollywood were less successful than those to Paris, though they were surrounded with greater pomp and ceremony. The arrival of American stars in the peninsula was greeted with an enthusiasm that testified to the special appeal of Hollywood and its unique ability to capture the public imagination.

This chapter considers the international context of the film business in the postwar period, taking account of the various ways in which stars travelled across borders, and especially the Alps. The final two sections are dedicated respectively to the Italian stars who accepted offers to go to Hollywood and to the US stars, who, for shorter or longer periods, lived and worked in Italy in the 1940s and early 1950s.

Co-production and International Competition

Co-production, Mark Betz has noted, 'is a broad term that may apply to any form of co-financing or financial, creative, and technical collaboration in the production of a film'.[1] 'European countries especially', he continues, 'have used co-production as a strategy for making films with relatively high budgets and greater access to more markets'. It is a way that countries with small industries can pool their resources to compete in the international market with larger ones, notably Hollywood. The first effort in this direction was the Film Europe project in the 1920s. Cooperation between the leading European film industries helped limit the fast-expanding influence of Hollywood by producing films with budgets that exceeded what any single industry could expect to recoup from domestic distribution alone. The coming of sound led to a variety of government initiatives to restrict imports and safeguard national cultures. In response, industries collaborated to produce multilingual versions of films that could figure as national in more than one market. At the same time, American studios, which had engaged in occasional location productions, such as the 1926 version of *Ben Hur* in Rome, started to invest in the European film industry. The recruitment of Europeans to Hollywood was one aspect of a larger effort to compete with foreign films in the domestic American market and in Europe itself that included the establishment of production centres in Europe and the gradual replacement – mainly on grounds of cost but also in response to governmental requirements – of American-made multi-language versions of films with locally dubbed versions of a single product.

After World War II, the protectionism that many western European countries had practised between the wars proved less viable as a strategy. American hegemony ensured that the doctrine of free trade was widely adhered to and that, where it was not, pressure was brought to bear to impose it. Founded in 1945, the Motion Picture Export Association of America (MPEAA) was the industry's diplomatic arm that negotiated with governments and represented the interests of Hollywood around the world. Such diplomacy was necessary because the principle of international free trade in films came under repeated threat from nations whose film industries and wider economies were threatened by the invasion of American product. In some instances, a conflict of interest arose between Hollywood's desire to maximize profits and the US government's declared commitment to rebuilding European economies with the aim of spreading prosperity to secure political stability. The result was a variety of ostensibly voluntary quota systems, obligations to reinvest earnings from Hollywood films in local economies, indirect subsidies to national industries, and assistance in distributing European films in the US market – all of which formally respected the free trade dogma.

While film consumption in the United States began to decline in the late 1940s, in many European countries it was expanding. Thus, Europe became a more important market than ever before for Hollywood. Italy enjoyed a great deal of attention because of the size of its film market, the long-standing appetite of the population for Hollywood films, the qualitative level the industry had reached in the later Fascist years and the great acclaim that critics bestowed on the first neorealist films. However, the Italian industry had no intention of finding itself crushed or subordinated by the major Hollywood companies. The international reception of neorealism stood as proof that there was a demand for films that spoke specifically of the Italian experience. The first co-production accord with France, with which there had been a pattern of collaboration in the 1930s,[2] was signed in 1946. This signalled a rapprochement between the two countries, which, for an experimental period of one year, allowed approved co-produced films to benefit in both countries from national privileges and subsidies to the same extent as fully national films. It was extended and institutionalized in the agreement of February1949 (the details were published the following October), which accorded priority to films deemed to be of quality.[3] This slowly gave rise to a wave of films in whose production French and Italian companies cooperated. Though both countries were supposed to benefit equally, in fact more films were made in Rome, and the agreement ultimately worked in Italy's favour.[4] In the first year, nine of the ten films that were supposed to be made in Italy had been completed, while none of those assigned to France had been.[5]

At a time when American companies were about to embark on the long season of runaway productions and Italian collaborations that would go under the name of Hollywood on the Tiber, the accords with France gave the Italian industry a means of facing up to American competition directly. As Betz argues, 'Co-production treaties between nations were established as a means for maintaining standards of financing and participation for each nation's film industry (in order to qualify for state subsidies) while at the same time allowing for increased resources and budgets available for film production (in order to expand potential markets).'[6] Italy wished to overcome the negative image it had acquired under Mussolini and attract international film-making to its studios in Rome. The close ties of Christian Democrat governments to the USA and conservative hostility to progressive currents within Italian cinema meant that Italy did not impose the sort of limitations on the circulation of foreign films that were adopted in France (opting only for a dubbing tax). This stance provided producers with a strong incentive to forge their own competitive strategies. Though it has been argued that co-production would 'quickly degenerate from the line, that was at the basis of the accords, of a real collaboration between the forces of production (from producers to actors and technicians) to present itself as pure financial speculation designed to obtain contributions from the state in more than one country (there would even be tripartite co-productions)',[7] the phenomenon witnessed some significant achievements both artistically and industrially. In the intentions of their promoters, co-productions were supposed to be works of prestige that would function as ambassadors for the countries that produced them.[8] Culturally, this would only rarely be the case, but industrially it was more so. The phenomenon served to build close relations between France and Italy and to make a statement as to the vitality of the respective industries.

The Dynamics of the Multinational Cast

In Italy, the Universalia company of the producer Salvo D'Angelo is acknowledged to have been the postwar pioneer of the Italian-French co-production, to the extent that he anticipated the practice of cooperation that would be enshrined in the treaty. His most high-profile film was the Biblical epic *Fabiola*, based on the 1854 novel by Cardinal Nicholas Wiseman and directed in 1948 by Blasetti, which starred Michèle Morgan, Michel Simon and Henri Vidal (see Figure 16.1). The Italian cast included Massimo Girotti as the Roman soldier and future saint Sebastian, Gino Cervi, Carlo Ninchi and others. Shot in Rome, with an entirely Italian artistic and technical team, the film rendered its international nature visible through its

Figure 16.1 Glamorous French stars Michèle Morgan and Henri Vidal were engaged by producer Salvo D'Angelo to take lead roles in the epic film *Fabiola* (Alessandro Blasetti, 1949) (screenshot by the author).

cast. By telling a story of the struggles of early Christianity, it had a universal theme, to which critics felt the director and his writers had sought to add a modern relevance. However, the film's primary identity was as a flagship for Italian cinema and its capacity to make films on a Hollywood-style scale. The first spectacular film to be made in the reopened Cinecittà studios, the extensive publicity campaign built high expectations. The advertising techniques were certainly exceptional. Describing it as 'the first colossal of postwar Italian cinema', the critic Gian Luigi Rondi observed that Universalia was creating 'an "American-style" atmosphere around the film', 'with the arrivals of the great stars that play in it announced with fanfares and the opportunities to meet them engineered with a series of tricks devised deliberately to make an impact'.[9] When the actress Michèle Morgan arrived in Rome in January 1948 to begin filming, two aeroplanes with her name flew over the city and dropped little parachutes with advertising booklets. In September of the same year, during the Venice festival, a full-size third-century cargo ship built for Universalia and baptized Fabiola, with extras on board attired in praetorian costumes, dropped anchor in the port. Meanwhile at the Caffe Florian, the cloth backs of the armchairs were replaced by ones bearing the names of the film's players. There were countless visits by journalists to the set, which achieved 'the indirect effect of drawing attention to the [newly reopened] studios of Cinecittà'.[10]

A better balance in terms of the national affiliation of the various technical and creative personnel was achieved with *Gli ultimi giorni di Pompei* (The Last Days of Pompeii, Marcel l'Herbier, 1950), which was also produced by Universalia in collaboration with the French, this time under the provisions of the 1949 accord. However, once again the leading actors were French (Micheline Presle, Georges Marchal and Marcel Herrand), while secondary and supporting roles were played by Italians. D'Angelo opted for this pattern of casting because the greater continuity in French cinema between prewar and postwar, and France's experience of the war, meant that its stars carried greater weight in the international market. While Michèle Morgan had debuted in a major role in 1937 and scored a hit opposite Jean Gabin in Marcel Carné's *Quai des brumes* the following year, she did not suffer the postwar decline of Italy's leading female star of the 1930s, Isa Miranda. Indeed, while the latter was obliged by the war to interrupt her sojourn in Hollywood, Morgan began her brief American career in 1941 and only returned to France at the end of the conflict. She won the best actress award at the 1946 Cannes film festival for her first postwar role in Jean Delannoy's *Symphonie pastorale*. Thus, she was a star of international standing, even if she had not previously worked in Italy.

The success of *Fabiola* in particular, which was the top box office hit of the year in Italy, validated D'Angelo's casting decisions and encouraged him to continue to engage French stars. Italian directors were not all of the same mind about them, however. Blasetti found Morgan cold and aloof, while Riccardo Freda admired their high professional standards.[11] The French, for their part, did not have the reservations about some older Italian actors that the Italians did. Miranda, for example, did not interest Italy's postwar producers and directors, even though she had worked in European as well as American cinema. Despite the efforts of some directors to Italianize her, her appearance and star persona, which had been modelled on Marlene Dietrich and Greta Garbo, seemed dated.[12] It would be the French who would save her from an undeserved limbo by approving her taking the lead role of one of the first co-productions.[13] René Clément's *Au-delà des grilles* (in Italian *Le mura di Malapaga*, in English *The Walls of Malapaga*), scripted by Zavattini, Suso Cecchi d'Amico and Guarini, with inputs from two French writers, was a curious blend of interwar French realism and Italian neorealism. It starred Jean Gabin as an outlaw on the run who winds up in Genoa, where he falls in love with a local waitress, played by Miranda. Though ostensibly French, the character played by Gabin quickly acquires flawless Italian (thanks to dubbing).¹⁴ The film's reception highlighted the difficulty of achieving a successful co-production formula. It was widely praised in France, where it won awards at Cannes for best director and best actress. It also won the honorary Oscar for best foreign language film. In Italy, despite much publicity, it fared poorly and flopped at the box office.

French critics and cineastes were greatly interested in neorealism and its major directors. They baptized the current and played a fundamental role in constructing its international reputation.¹⁵ This interest would help raise the profile in France of some Italian stars and endow them with box office appeal in that country. Aldo Fabrizi and Anna Magnani would both feature in co-productions, though with different results. In 1950, Fabrizi starred opposite the experienced Gaby Morlay in Blasetti's Rome-set comedy *Prima comunione* (Father's Dilemma), which was produced by Universalia and the French company Franco-London Films. The film helped bring Fabrizi's established comedy persona into relief in France and balance the dramatic persona of *Roma città aperta*'s Don Pietro. Magnani starred in Jean Renoir's eighteenth-century set film *La carrosse d'or* (The Golden Coach, 1953), adapted from Mérimée's story of an Italian theatrical troupe on tour in South America, whose leading lady (Magnani) unleashes a jealous rivalry among the various men who compete for her favours. By this time, Magnani's box office appeal in Italy was in sharp decline, but her standing in international cinema was undiminished. Renoir was fixated with the idea of making a film with her; he saw her as 'the quintessence of Italy' but also as the 'absolute personification of the theatre'.¹⁶ Thus, he wanted to immerse her in the world of the *commedia dell'arte*. Shot in colour and endowed with the aura of prestige that, in the intentions, was due to co-productions, the film did nothing to revive her fortunes.

For the casting of French-Italian co-productions to work well, there needed to be some balance between the respective star systems of the two countries. In the 1940s, the relative continuity of the French system contrasted with the complex situation in Italy. It was only when a postwar Italian star system began to take proper shape that a balance of casting could be achieved. But there remained a problem that would create a structural imbalance. The almost universal use of dubbing in postwar Italian cinema meant that French and other foreign actors could easily be turned into Italian screen characters. While their physical presence, professionalism and star cachet brought lustre to films, their voices were replaced by those of Italian actors specialized in the dubbing process. One of the best-known examples of this was the casting of the comedy actor Fernandel in the role of the priest in the highly successful Don Camillo series, which was also directed by a Frenchman, Jean Duvivier. The use of live sound recording in France meant that the opposite was not the case. Consequently, many more French actors would make films in Italy than vice versa. The Italians who went to France were cast in Italian roles that justified their accented French. As Aprà has observed, exchanges were a business matter. There was little attempt to construct cross-border stories, with the result that 'only rarely did loans influence the narratives of films'.[17] Lux boss Riccardo Gualino had established Lux Compagnie cinématographique de France in 1934, the same year as the Italian company, with the result that it was able in effect to co-produce in house with France.[18] While several companies, smaller and larger, worked with France, others were more interested in the USA. Lux's ambitious executive producers Ponti and De Laurentiis would look to the United States and its larger market rather than Europe.

The rise of a new generation of Italian female stars would provide producers with a resource for planning the casting of co-productions. France would prove receptive to the charms of the beauty queens turned actresses, even if they lacked the professionalism of the French stars. The first of their number to win a significant following was Silvana Pampanini. However, between 1947 and 1953, she only made three co-productions (*Le avventure di Mandrin*, Mario Soldati, 1951; *Koenigsmark*, Solange Térac, 1952; *La tour de Nesle*, Abel Gance, 1954), of which the last two, both historical dramas, were French-led. Her fame in France would be surpassed by Gina Lollobrigida, whose well received starring role alongside Gérard Phillipe in the co-produced costume romp *Fanfan la tulipe* (Christian-Jacque, 1952) would greatly enhance her standing on both sides of the Alps.[19]

The Italian Star in Hollywood

A number of Italian stars of the prewar and war years would accept offers to work in foreign cinemas after 1945. Female stars of the white telephone films including Irasema Dilian, Mariella Lotti, Miria San Servolo and others who faced unemployment at home migrated temporarily to Spain and South America, as did the biggest star of the period, Amedeo Nazzari. A fortunate few received offers to go to Hollywood. Though Isa Miranda's experience had been less than fulfilling, Hollywood remained the Mecca of cinema, and the prospect of working there was flattering. It was in this context that David O. Selznick, as well as Paramount and Twentieth Century Fox, sought to cherry-pick the best talent and intervene to shape the production even of films belonging to the neorealist current. In their volume on European screen actors in the United States, Alastair Phillips and Ginette Vincendeau identify two main motivations for emigrating: on the one hand political or economic unease, and on the other ambition – that is, the desire to embrace a personal career progression that promised global fame and success.[20] Not all the Italians who accepted offers of contracts fall into one of these categories. Those who were politically tarnished were few, and in any case such people were not attractive to the Americans. With the end of dictatorship, no one was driven to flee violence or discrimination. Unemployment was an issue in the immediate postwar years but not a serious worry for most of those who went to Hollywood. A combination of circumstances including, in some cases, ambition led them to accept offers that appeared to open up the prospect of global stardom.

The most prestigious, if reluctant, émigré was Alida Valli, the brightest star in the firmament of the early 1940s, who, after the war, worked exclusively with established directors in genres of proven appeal.[21] Though her talent and beauty were universally acknowledged, she did not interest those directors who were keen to take Italian cinema in a new direction. Of northern extraction and partly of central European family background, she possessed a poise and polish that could not easily have found deployment in the gritty, realistic films that were becoming the hallmark of Italian cinema. Though her films of the early 1940s had occasionally taken her out of the studio, she was the product of a type of cinema that in Italy was no longer in vogue among more innovative film-makers. Valli was the most prominent of several Italians who aroused Selznick's interest. Throughout the interwar period, Hollywood had recruited talent from all over the globe in its relentless drive for hegemony in the international market. The industry was convinced that it could develop and present talent more completely than smaller foreign industries. With American involvement in western Europe having been established during the war of liberation, there were closer links than ever before between Washington and national capitals as well as between economies, elites and imaginary worlds. In the field of cinema, American commercial forces were eager to assert their influence and shape the development of local industries.[22]

Valli was brought to Selznick's attention by his representatives in Italy, who described her as a potential 'new Dietrich or Garbo'.[23] Not only was she a veteran screen performer of proven appeal who was still aged only 25 in 1946, she had attended film screenings staged by the American soldiers' publication *The Stars and Stripes*, and it was known that her jazz musician husband, Oscar De Mejo, was an Americanophile.[24] However, there were some issues that needed to be resolved before she could be brought to the United States. First, she was the object of a sustained campaign of denigration that accused her of having been the lover of Mussolini, his son Bruno and a Fascist minister.[25] Though they were advanced only in anonymous letters, such accusations were damaging and an obstacle to the actress being granted a visa. Her role in a small number of Fascist propaganda films also aroused official suspicions. Much to be actress's indignation, she was subjected to close questioning by the US vice-consul in Rome and faced considerable delays before eventually receiving her visa.[26] Second, there was the matter of her suitability for screen work in the United States. Her English was rudimentary and she was deemed to be overweight. These were pressing issues as Selznick had no intention of allowing her a period of acclimatization. Within twenty-four hours of arriving in California in January 1947, she found herself before the cameras of Hitchcock's courtroom melodrama, *The Paradine Case*, which also starred Gregory Peck, Louis Jourdan and Charles Laughton.

According to Phillips and Vincendeau, foreign actors in Hollywood faced four challenges that did not affect homegrown talent.[27] The first was the question of language. In the sound era, a poor command of English was a major drawback insofar as audience appreciation of a film was dependent on understanding what actors were saying. For the actors themselves, performing in a foreign language was not always a comfortable experience. Second, the sheer size of the Hollywood studios and the utter efficiency of their movie-making contrasted with the smaller scale, more familiar habits of most European film industries. This contrast could be disorientating. Third, the studios were accustomed to standardizing stars, fitting personalities to types and drawing on an actor's whole life in order to fashion an appealing public image. For those who preferred to keep at least some part of their lives private, this was a shock. Fourth, there was the issue of values and ideology. While foreign actors might typically be called on to represent alternatives to normative types (femmes fatales, villains and so on), they were expected also, and in a number of ways, to endorse the superiority of the American political and economic system at home and abroad. In the period of the onset of the Cold War, an actor like Valli was required to join in with the general effort to persuade the Italians that their best option for a prosperous future was to align themselves with the West and the political forces that had American approval.

Valli was professional in her dedication to mastering English and to reducing her weight but diffident, if not hostile, towards the standardizing processes to which she was subjected. Selznick had very clear ideas about how she should be presented. He saw her as a successor to Garbo and Ingrid Bergman – that is, as a star capable of operating at the highest level of cinema. Great efforts were made to glamorize her – that is, to turn her into a 'superlatively well-packaged' product in which realism would 'mingle with illusion and fantasy'.[28] His press chief, Paul Macnamara, came up with a variety of personality traits to fasten onto her, which included 'famous hostess', 'well-known do-gooder' and 'famous best-dressed woman'.[29] Selznick himself decided that she should be known solely as Valli and personally supervised the way in which she was photographed on set.[30] In *The Paradine Case*, she was a compelling femme fatale of shady, but unspecified, European origins. No doubt similar such roles would have been planned for her had Selznick not run into financial difficulties and had to loan her out. It was her great fortune that among a series of undistinguished movies there was one that would come to be seen as the most compelling thriller of the early Cold War period. Her role as Harry Lime's Czech girlfriend Anna Schmidt in Carol Reed's *The Third Man* (1950) would cement her place in the imagination of international filmgoers.

Valli was compliant with many of the demands that were placed on her. For example, she joined other Hollywood stars in urging the Italians to vote against Communism in the divisive 1948 general election. But she refused to express gratitude to Selznick for the investment he had made in her and by the spring of 1949 had decided that she did not wish to continue her career with him. Her discontent at being traded 'like a package' manifested itself in various bouts of illness and demands for periods of leave.[31] Eventually, in 1952, she would free herself of her contractual obligations though she was required to register all her films for the next five years with the Selznick company. In fact, she would soon cease to do this. After appearing in some run-of-the-mill Italian melodramas with her old screen partner Amedeo Nazzari, she would win the career-changing role of Countess Livia Serpieri in Visconti's lavish Risorgimento drama *Senso* (1954). This would bring her critical success and enable her to embark on a new career path in European art films.

Though far from satisfactory for any of the parties involved, Valli's Hollywood experience was an improvement on the prewar disappointment of Isa Miranda and the contemporaneous ones of other Italians. Valentina Cortese, just two years younger than Valli, had made her screen debut in 1940 and, along with Carla Del Poggio, was one of few actresses in their early twenties to make a reasonably successful transition to postwar cinema. She was scouted by both Selznick and Twentieth Century Fox and would eventually accept the latter company's offer of a contract. She was initially more enamoured of the Hollywood lifestyle than Valli, who had a husband and a young baby, and was star-struck when she met Greta Garbo, Joan Crawford and many other luminaries.[32] But her experience was not gilded with the urgency and prestige of Valli's. Only after several months of idleness was she cast opposite Richard Conte in Jules Dassin's *Thieves' Highway* (1949). Rather than a scheming but glamorous dark lady, she was a prostitute picked up by a truck driver. Her surname was changed to Cortesa, mainly for pronunciation reasons, but otherwise she was not significantly repackaged. However, there were aspects of the studio system that she found unacceptable, such as when she was subjected to a sexual assault from the producer Daryl Zanuck.[33] Though she would make a number of successful films in the United States and in Europe for Fox, she too would break her contract and find greater satisfaction working in European cinema.

During her sojourn in Hollywood, Cortese encountered not only Valli but also Anna Magnani. The heroine of neorealism was not an obvious candidate for remoulding along Hollywood lines, and, in fact, there was no attempt to erase her particular identity. It was as a great actress that she was of interest. Tennessee Williams was an admirer, and he persuaded the producer Hal Wallis to cast her in the leading role in the screen adaptation of his play *The Rose Tattoo* (Daniel Mann, 1952). Though dubbed 'this dark Garbo' by Hedda Hopper, the gossip columnist recognized that 'her windblown, earthy looks are her trademark; she feels anything else false.'[34] For the Americans, she was a woman of the people, from the gutter, who had clawed her way up, like Sophia Loren later. This was completely different to the prewar image of European stars in the USA when their biographies were often upscaled to suggest aristocratic origins. The Best Actress Oscar that she won for her performance in *The Rose Tattoo* against competition from Bette Davis, Katherine Hepburn and Susan Hayward was a general tribute to her art and a mark of her difference.[35] Though she would make other American films,

Magnani, unlike her compatriots, was always an Italian, rather than a generically European, actress.

In the course of the 1950s, Hollywood continued to seek to recruit Italian talent. Several of the younger female stars who emerged in the postwar years accepted invitations to Hollywood, including Annamaria Pierangeli, twin sister of Marisa Pavan, who co-starred with Magnani in *The Rose Tattoo*. Recruited by Metro-Goldwyn-Mayer after her success in the teen drama *Domani è troppo tardi* (Tomorrow is Too Late, Leonide Moguy, 1950) and its sequel *Domani è un altro giorno* (Tomorrow is Another Day, 1951), Pierangeli also was subjected to an arbitrary name change, in this case to Pier Angeli. Others who were invited to Hollywood, but in the end returned without making a film there, were the young Gina Lollobrigida and Franca Faldini.[36] However, increasingly, to secure access to Italian talent, Hollywood had to negotiate with the powerful producers who were the arbiters of the Italian star system. The proliferation of runaway productions and the rise of the Italian film industry meant that not only were there many more opportunities for Italian actors to feature in Hollywood productions but also that the traffic was no longer only one way.

The Hollywood Star in Italy

No Hollywood star enjoyed greater popularity in postwar Italy than Tyrone Power. He was the leading heart-throb, a star of Latinate appearance notwithstanding his Irish origins, whose first films dated back to 1937–38. A box office champion, his films *Blood and Sand* and *The Mark of Zorro* were hugely successful among Italian audiences. When he arrived in the country to begin work on *Prince of Foxes* (Henry King, 1949), a drama set at the time of the Borgias, his appearances were greeted by ecstatic crowds of young people for whom 'he did not simply come from America: he was America.'[37] 'Even if he was a marine during the war, he is the classic Hollywood star, concerned only with the brilliantine in his hair and ensuring that the camera captures his best side', Rondi observed.[38] The publicity whirl around him, as Federico Vitella has shown, emanated from Twentieth Century Fox, but it was also an extraordinary product of the fan culture of the postwar years.[39] It reached fever pitch in the run up to his Rome wedding to the Italian-educated American starlet Linda Christian in January 1949. The press and newsreels talked of the 'wedding of the century', a phrase that also appeared on billboard posters promoting the event, and due coverage was given to the preparations and interminable stag nights that preceded the ceremony. The wedding was conceived and executed by Fox as an event to be consumed by a mass, worldwide audience. Permission was granted for newsreel cameras to be installed in the Santa Francesca Romana Church, which was chosen for its photogenic qualities by a Fox cinematographer,[40] and photographers took shots during the ceremony. Images were then rushed by motorcycle to the central telegraph office from where they were wired to newspapers around the globe. Photo-reporters hid in the bushes and hedges around the church and leapt out as soon as the couple emerged into the daylight and made towards the limousine that would take them to the Vatican for an audience with Pope Pius XII. 'An Italian style wedding...', observed Rondi, 'but the air of Hollywood is everywhere, tons of flowers, ladies in long pink dresses, almost all the men in morning dress. I was tempted a little to laugh, but the first effect was that of a film in technicolor.'[41]

Interest in the event was intense. 'For once the crowd did not gather to protest and the police did not have to protect ministries or politicians', wrote one journalist who described the crowds that filled the pavements along the Via dei Fori Imperiali, from Piazza Venezia to the Colosseum.[42] The gathering was so large, he said, reviving an adjective often used under Fascism, that 'it had what might be termed an "oceanic" character'. 'Summing up', he continued, 'one could say that Tyrone Power has beaten [Communist leader] Palmiro Togliatti.' It was composed of 'gossiping girls and mop-headed adolescents' *Il Tempo* observed,[43] while the *Corriere della sera* saw 'hundreds of youths who wear their hair like [Power] and who gesticulate and walk in a manner copied from his films ... hundreds of girls who had bunked school or slipped out of offices ... elderly ladies, lower class women, and old folk'.[44]

For many observers, the enthusiasm was new and undesirable. It had a brash, vulgar air that was reminiscent of the romantic plots that marked so many Hollywood films and that popular illustrated story magazines like *Grand Hotel* were churning out with great success. The left-wing press, which was wary of the creeping influence of American mass culture, picked up on the self-styling of members of the crowd. The Communist daily *L'Unità* deplored the sycophancy of 'modern girls, hysterical widows, and young dandies covered with brilliantine right down to their toe-nails',[45] while the Socialist *Avanti* gave a description of 'groups of young girls carrying books under their arms',[46] 'smart young guys wearing sky-blue ties, striped nylon socks, scruffy hair and suede moccasins' and 'distinguished ladies in furs', which made it clear the crowd was more middle- than working class. The wedding was an event for consumers rather than citizens. Not only were those present evident possessors of disposable income; attendees seem to have temporarily stopped shopping to watch. 'The halls of the big stores were rather empty yesterday morning, like during the flu epidemic', *Il Tempo* wrote. They, like schools and offices, were populated by those urban dwellers for whom film stardom was an aspect of wider practices of consumption.

The publicity machine set in motion by the Power Christian wedding was associated with the filming of *Prince of Foxes*, a historical drama set at the time of the Borgias that would open the following December. But it also served wider purposes. It offered an example of the way cinema helped to cement the alliance between the Christian Democrats, the Catholic Church and the American government, which had delivered a pro-western victory in the 1948 election. As Vitella argues, 'The new image of Power as a devout Christian implicitly affirmed the moral primacy of the Church of Rome over Hollywood Babylon.'[47] In the popular imagination, it would open the season of major runaway productions, which saw American companies take over the Cinecittà studios and bring leading stars to Rome. The imagery and lifestyle associated with them would become a significant factor in diffusing the imagery of mass consumption in the country. The first and in some ways most significant of these was MGM's *Quo Vadis*, which was shot in Rome between 1950 and 1951. The film's leading male star, Robert Taylor, a handsome, dark-haired romantic lead like Power, would quickly establish himself as the new heart-throb. A measure of his fame was offered in Vasco Pratolini's novel *Le ragazze di San Frediano*, in which the self-regarding protagonist, who simultaneously courts several girls of the district of Florence in which it is set, is nicknamed 'Bob'.[48]

Hollywood stars would make a significant contribution to the way stardom and celebrity evolved in postwar Italy. As 'human pseudo-events', to borrow Daniel Boorstin's term,[49] who inhabited the world of publicity, they brought a dimension of glamour to the film industry that was not fully developed in the peninsula. However, the fact that so many of them would visit Rome or work there was testimony not only to the extraordinary global influence of the American industry but also to the fact that it was no longer as powerful as it had once been. The decline of movie audiences in the USA from 1946 increased the importance of European and foreign markets, while the adoption of new forms of protectionism across Europe compelled the companies to decentralize production to the continent.

Though subject to restrictions of one sort or another, they found consolation in the fact that the Paramount ruling of 1949, which ended the majors' domination of the distribution and exhibition sectors, did not apply abroad.

However, by no means did all the stars who arrived in Italy do so under the auspices of a major company. Most of the Americans who appeared in Italian productions in the 1940s had gone to the country under their own steam. Faced with declining opportunities at home, they migrated to a country where film-making was recovering from the war and reconstruction. The most notable of these were the Dowling sisters, Doris and Constance. Doris had taken supporting roles in *The Lost Weekend* (Billy Wilder, 1945) and *The Blue Dahlia* (George Marshall, 1946). A sharp-featured brunette used to playing apparently tough but vulnerable characters, she was cast as the reluctant gangster's moll turned non-unionized rice weeder Francesca in *Riso amaro* (Bitter Rice, Giuseppe De Santis, 1949).

Italian producers like Ponti and De Laurentiis, who looked to the United States and took the Hollywood studio system as their model, soon moved from casually recruiting émigré actors to actively casting Americans in their films. The basic strategy consisted of casting a prominent American male star opposite a rising Italian female star, which was the same approach as that which would be adopted later by American studios with their European runaway productions. The casting of Kirk Douglas in *Ulisse* (Ulysses, Mario Camerini, 1954) was a turning point. It marked a shift in the ambitions and standing of the Italian industry, and in particular of the Lux company,[50] as it was the first time that a major American star had appeared in an Italian production. For Mangano, it represented a significant step towards her internationalization. The encounter of the two stars was crystallized in the screen kiss between Douglas's Ulysses and Mangano's sorceress Circe. The staging of this event and its precise dynamics were the subject of lengthy discussions. At the end of the scene, production secretary Anne Budyens asked Mangano how she felt about it. 'Her only reply', Budyens noted in her report of the conversation, 'was a slight lifting of the shoulders and a rolling of the slanted eyes of Circe. More eloquent, perhaps, is the fact that the following day she took off for a rest cure in the mountains and her husband, Dino De Laurentiis, took the opportunity to undergo a short liver treatment at Montecatini'.[51] Her unease was related to the difficulty of establishing a visual unity between Douglas, who was oriented towards action in the Hollywood manner, and her own customary statuesque iconography. For Steven Ricci, 'Camerini proved incapable of creating a world that was sufficiently abstract, sufficiently universal, to contain the heterogeneous cultural sources from which the film emerged.'⁵² Mangano nonetheless became the leading figure in the efforts of the joint Italian-American company Italian Film Export to promote Italian cinema in the United States.⁵³ Her films were repackaged to highlight her role (with *Il brigante Musolino* [The Brigand Musolino, Mario Camerini, 1950] becoming *Outlaw Girl*, for example), while publicity focused on her sex appeal.⁵⁴ Though the actress went along with the promotional campaign for *Ulisse* in Italy, according to her minder Irene Brin she was less co-operative in fulfilling her media obligations for IFE when on a trip to New York.⁵⁵

No migration from Hollywood testified to the new standing of Italian cinema than that of Ingrid Bergman. The Swedish star of *Casablanca* (Michael Curtiz, 1942), *For Whom the Bell Tolls* (Sam Wood, 1943) and *Notorious* (Alfred Hitchcock, 1946) was neither underemployed in Hollywood nor in decline, though, following the end of her contract with Selznick, the three films she made as an independent actress did not fare well. Tired of the artificiality of studio productions, she went to a screening of *Roma città aperta* one evening in spring 1948 and found the film's realism to be a revelation. The deep emotional impact that the film made on her was confirmed a few months later when, alone in New York, she saw *Paisà* on Broadway. Impressed with the immediacy of the films and their social importance, she wrote to Rossellini offering her services.⁵⁶ The director had to be told exactly who she was, but having been apprised of her standing, he set about meeting her and securing backing in Hollywood for a film with her.⁵⁷ With Bergman's good offices, RKO agreed to finance the film that would become *Stromboli* (1950).

Bergman's arrival in Rome in March 1949 was surrounded with publicity. Initially, it was the novelty of a major American star abandoning Hollywood for Italy that aroused press attention. Once it became clear that the relationship between the actress and the director was turning into a romance, the tone of the coverage changed.⁵⁸ The Italian press generally treated the affair as a love story, though there was considerable sympathy for the married Rossellini's acknowledged partner, Anna Magnani. In the United States and Bergman's native Sweden, however, rumours of an adulterous affair gave rise to a media scandal.⁵⁹ This would involve interventions from members of Congress, Churches, the Production Code Administration and others. It continued throughout the lengthy location filming on the island of Stromboli and reached a climax in February 1950, when the couple's son Robertino was born. RKO boss Howard Hughes hoped that the scandal would be good box office for the film and the advertising campaign overtly played on it by aligning the release with a piloted scoop announcing Bergman's pregnancy.⁶⁰

In fact, the content of the film was not controversial in any way and critics took a negative view of its artistic qualities. Re-edited against Rossellini's wishes for its American release, it was deemed by *The New York Times* 'a startling anti-climax'.[61]

For Italians, Bergman was not a star with the same profile that she had in the United States. The biopic of *Joan of Arc* (Victor Fleming, 1948), which would align her decisively with virtue and saintliness, had only just been completed when she arrived in Italy. Since little or nothing was known of her family and she was not a Catholic, the Church refrained from comment. Moreover, the press was not yet sufficiently powerful to perform any agenda-setting function or unscrupulous enough to regard scandal as a source of profit.[62] While the American press functioned according to modern criteria in so far as it participated in the creation and perpetuation of a moral panic in order to increase interest and sales, Italian news media still operated in a 'traditional' way.[63] That is to say, they pursued an approach to personal relationships that obscured or glossed over possible elements of transgression. With memories of the Power-Christian wedding still fresh, they saw an opportunity to recount a great love story. *Tempo* described Rossellini and Bergman as 'two characters in a romantic fable'.[64] Only later, and following the example of the Americans, did freelance journalists and photographers seek to draw advantage from the international scandal. Far more scandalous than adultery for a part of public opinion was Rossellini's abandonment of Magnani and move away from the social themes of his war trilogy.[65] Bergman's defection was not seen so much as a great coup for Italian cinema and a tribute to the global impact of neo-realism as a worrying confirmation of the director's desire to move beyond the methods and motivations of his great postwar films.

Magnani's decision to vent her anger by agreeing to star in William Dieterle's *Vulcano* (1950), which was shot on another Aeolian island at precisely the same time as *Stromboli*, in some respects appeared to confirm the subordination of Italian cinema to Hollywood. In fact, the film was produced by the Sicilian company Panaria Film, which was originally going to make Rossellini's film until he cast Bergman and reached an accord with RKO. But the recruitment of Dieterle gave the project an international image. That the country's top actress should have accepted to appear, for whatever personal reason, in a film that would be judged 'a mishmash, a melodrama in the worst Hollywood manner' was disappointing. 'She is good, of course', Rondi noted, 'but if she had avoided giving her support to a similar enterprise, it would have been for the best.'[66]

In fact, Rossellini's films with Bergman were anything but commercial (he strongly objected on the set of *Stromboli* when Bergman referred to herself as a star); the director would pay for his commitment to innovation with critical as well as commercial failure.[67] Magnani's role in *Vulcano*, however – though no more successful[68] – would pave the way to her brief but critically acclaimed Hollywood career. Her appeal to the Americans, Giuliana Muscio has noted, rested on her 'embodiment of diversity compared with the Hollywood star system; she was the incarnation of neorealism, of the "other" cinema'.[69] Though Bergman possessed too strong a screen image to be cast in Italian roles, her marriage to Rossellini and her long stay in Italy endowed her star persona with an Italian dimension that would be carried forward in later years by the couple's children.[70] More broadly, together with the Power-Christian wedding, her widely publicized relationship with Rossellini contributed to the development in Italy of a celebrity culture that, within a few years, would significantly change the coordinates of Italian stardom.

Notes

1. Betz, 'Co-productions', in Grant, *Schirmer Encyclopedia of Film*, 369.
2. J. Gili, 'European Co-productions and Artistic Collaborations: The Italian Response to the Hollywood Studio System', in Bondanella, *The Italian Cinema Book*, 213.
3. Ibid., 213–14.
4. Ibid., 214.
5. Burucoa, 'Gli accordi di coproduzione (1946–1995)', in Gili and Tassone, *Parigi-Roma: 50 anni di coproduzioni italo-francesi (1945–1995)*, 22.
6. M. Betz, 'Co-productions', in Grant, *Schirmer Encyclopedia of Film*, 370.
7. L. Bizzarri, 'L'economia cinematografica', in Di Monte et al., *La città del cinema produzione e lavoro nel cinema italiano (1930–1970)*, 43.
8. C. Burucoa, 'Gli accordi di coproduzione', in Gili and Tassone, *Parigi-Roma*, 19.
9. Rondi, *Le mie vite allo specchio: diari 1947–1997*, 28–29.
10. B. Corsi, 'La ripresa produttiva', in De Giusti, *Storia del cinema italiano*, Vol. VIII 1949–1953, 146–47.
11. Blasetti's judgement was confided to Rondi, *Le mie vite allo specchio*, 29. For Freda's view, see Freda, *Divoratori di celluloide: 50 anni di memorie cinematografiche e non*, 105–6.
12. There was no political problem, since she had suffered ostracism on her return from the USA. Moreover, her producer husband, Alfredo Guarini, had been active in the Resistance. Gundle, *Mussolini's Dream Factory: Film Stardom in Fascist Italy*, 274–75.
13. Rondi, in *Le mie vite allo specchio*, 34–35, describes meeting the director, who was waiting for the accords between the two governments to be settled before the film could start.
14. A. Aprà, 'Cross-Fertilization between France and Italy from Neorealism through the 1960s', in Burke, *A Companion to Italian Cinema*, 221.

15. Ibid., 218–19.
16. Quoted in Governi, *Nannarella*, 160.
17. Aprà, 'Cross-Fertilization between France and Italy', in Burke, *A Companion to Italian Cinema*, 221.
18. On Lux's French operations, see the contribution of Jean Gili to Farassino and Sanguineti, *Lux film: Esthétique et système d'un studio italien*.
19. Renzi, *Gina Lollobrigida*, 19, indicates that this film heralded a decisive turning point in her early career.
20. Phillips and Vincendeau, *Journeys of Desire: European Actors in Hollywood – A Critical Companion*.
21. On Valli's career up to 1943, see Gundle, *Mussolini's Dream Factory*, Chapter 10.
22. See Ellwood and Brunetta, *Hollywood in Europa: industria, politica, pubblico del cinema 1945-1960*.
23. Harry Ransom Humanities Research Center, The University of Texas at Austin (henceforth HRHRC), David O. Selznick Collection (henceforth DOS), Selznick Administration Talent Files 1939–51, b.3346, f.1, David O. Selznick to Neil Agnew, 6 July 1945.
24. For a detailed unofficial account of the American discovery of Valli, see H. Taubman, 'Fact vs Fiction in the Discovery of a Star', *New York Times*, 1 November 1948.
25. Gundle, 'Alida Valli in Hollywood: From Star of Fascist Cinema to "Selznick Siren"', 566.
26. HRHRC, DOS, Selznick Administration Correspondence 1940–50, Valli, b.589, f.5, Jenia Reissar to DOS, 8 May 1946; also see Reissar to DOS, 27 November 1946.
27. Phillips and Vincendeau, *Journeys of Desire*, 4–15.
28. Gundle, *Glamour: A History*, 179.
29. HRHRC, DOS, Selznick Talent Files, b.3346, f.6, Macnamara to Bolton, inter-office communication, 16 January 1947.
30. See, for example, HRHRC, DOS, Selznick Production Files, b.3374, f.6, DOS to Hitchcock, 23 January 1947; Gundle, 'Alida Valli in Hollywood', 572–73.
31. P. Cristalli, 'Alida dai cento volti', *Cineteca* 6: 2(3) (1990) 8–9; Gundle, 'Alida Valli in Hollywood', 578.
32. Cortese, *Quanti sono i domani passati: autobiografia*, 84–85.
33. Ibid., 98–99.
34. Academy of Motion Picture Arts and Sciences. Margaret Herrick Library. Hedda Hopper Collection. Anna Magnani notes (undated).
35. Governi, *Nannarella*, 165–67. See also Giachetti, 'Una rosa fiorì a Hollywood', *Epoca*, 23 September 1983, 15.
36. For Faldini's memories of the experience, see Faldini, *Roma Hollywood Roma: Totò, ma non soltanto*.
37. Vitella, 'Tirone, la volpe e il Papa: il matrimonio Power-Christian e la fan culture italiana del dopoguerra', in Dagrada, *Anna Cinquanta: il decennio più lungo del secolo breve*, 88. In English, see Gundle, 'Memory and Identity: Popular Culture in Postwar Italy', in McCarthy, *Italy Since 1945*, 190–92.
38. Rondi, *Le mie vite allo specchio*, 56.
39. Vitella, 'Tirone, la volpe e il Papa', in Dagrada, *Anna Cinquanta*, 85.
40. Ibid., 89.
41. Rondi, *Le mie vite allo specchio*, 76.
42. N. Salvalaggio, 'Linda e Tyrone acclamati dalla folla', *Il Tempo*, 28 January 1949, 3.
43. Ibid., 3.

44. F. Chiarelli, 'È costato un milione e mezzo l'abito di sposa di Linda Christian', *Corriere della sera*, 28 January 1949, 3.
45. M.F., 'Delusione per i mondani di Hollywood', *L'Unità*, 28 January 1949, 3.
46. F.G., 'Finalmente sposi Tyrone e Linda', *Avanti*, 28 January 1949, 3.
47. F. Vitella, 'Tirone, la volpe e il Papa', in Dagrada, *Anna Cinquanta*, 93–94.
48. 'Bob', whose real name in the novel is Aldo, is described as the nearest local equivalent to Robert Taylor, the postwar 'masculine ideal' of the girls of the San Frediano quarter of Florence, Pratolini, *Le ragazze di San Frediano*, 46.
49. Boorstin, *The Image: A Guide to Pseudo-Events in America*.
50. Farassino and Sanguineti, *Lux Film*, 144.
51. Wisconsin Center for Film and Theater Research, Kirk Douglas Papers, f. *Ulysses*, Anne Budyens' dailies, 26 August 1953.
52. S. Ricci, 'Camerini et Hollywood: questions d'identité (nationale)', in Farassino, *Mario Camerini*, 44.
53. On the role of IFE, see Nicoli, *The Rise and Fall of the Italian Film Industry*, 150–51.
54. The physical attributes of the stars were frequently mentioned in the promotional material for the American market prepared by IFE.
55. Brin, *L'Italia esplode: diario dell'anno 1952*, 138–40.
56. Bergman and Burgess, *Ingrid Bergman: My Story*, 17.
57. An eyewitness account of this moment is offered in Rondi, *Le mie vite allo specchio*, 74–75.
58. See Rondi, *Le mie vite allo specchio*, 80–84, 105–7.
59. On the dynamics of the scandal, see Gundle, 'Saint Ingrid at the Stake: Stardom and Scandal in the Bergman-Rossellini Collaboration', in Forgacs, Lutton and Nowell-Smith, *Roberto Rossellini: Magician of the Real*, 64–79. For a discussion of the Rossellini-Bergman collaboration, using mostly English-language sources, see Gelley, *Stardom and the Aesthetics of Neorealism: Ingrid Bergman in Rossellini's Italy*.
60. Gundle, 'Saint Ingrid at the Stake', in Forgacs et al., *Roberto Rossellini*, 70.
61. Quoted in Quirk, *The Films of Ingrid Bergman*, 133.
62. This situation would change in the late 1950s, when the rise of scandal-driven photographers would catch the eye of Fellini and his collaborators and form a key thread of the film *La Dolce Vita* (1960). From this film on, the photographers would be known as 'paparazzi'.
63. Gundle, 'Saint Ingrid at the Stake', in Forgacs et al., *Roberto Rossellini*, 72.
64. L. Sorrentino, 'La prova del volcano per Ingrid e Rossellini', *Tempo*, 16 April 1949, 4–7.
65. Gundle, 'Saint Ingrid at the Stake', in Forgacs et al., *Roberto Rossellini*, 73–74.
66. Rondi, *Le mie vite allo specchio*.
67. See A. Aprà, 'Cross-Fertilization between France and Italy', in Burke, *A Companion to Italian Cinema*, 219–20.
68. The Rome premiere of the film in February 1950 was overshadowed by the announcement of the birth of Bergman and Rossellini's son.
69. Muscio, *Napoli/New York/Hollywood: Film Between Italy and the United States*, 270.
70. Notably their daughter, Isabella Rossellini.

Conclusion

Several of the stars examined in this book remain household names today. Their films reappear on television, and scenes and moments from their films are regularly evoked in public discourse. They are so much a part of the collective consciousness that even people who have not seen their films recognize them. In *Roma città aperta* (Rome Open City, 1945), the last moments of Anna Magnani's character Pina, before she is gunned down in the street, is one of the best-known scenes of a film that occupies a central place in the shared Italian understanding of the experience of war and occupation. Aldo Fabrizi's well-timed (though unseen) blow with a frying pan to silence a garrulous old invalid during a police raid brings a touch of comedy to a film that is shot through with drama and suffering. Silvana Mangano's boogie woogie in *Riso amaro* (Bitter Rice, 1949) and Totò's innumerable physical and verbal gags also form part of a patrimony that postwar cinema transmitted to the Italians and that entered the national imagination. In each instance, these memorable scenes were instrumental in sustaining a star persona over time. Other figures who have been closely examined here did not generate such powerful images, and public perceptions of them were more diffuse. Amedeo Nazzari's movie stardom predated the war, and something of his ruggedly righteous masculinity survived into the 1950s. But it is mainly because of the forceful civilian roles that he took in Matarazzo's popular melodramas that he re-established himself as a fixed reference point in the mental universe of many Italians, and it is in the context of these films that he is best remembered. Silvana Pampanini's films are largely forgotten save for one or two for which there is a residual affection among *cognoscenti*.

Before the postwar years, few film stars occupied a significant place in the common culture of the nation. While the comics of the silent era, the great divas of the 1910s and, later, the numerous cinematic idols of Cinecittà in the 1930s and 1940s all had a following, their popularity remained circumscribed. They could not truly be regarded as national figures, because cinema itself was not a phenomenon to which all Italians had access. Many areas of the country remained outside the field of mass communications. It was only during and after the war that cinema became a genuine mass medium. Its expansion as a form of entertainment was the precondition for its impact on national identity. Moreover, the cinema that emerged from the ruins of Fascism and war aspired to speak to the whole nation. It placed itself at the centre of a real space that had been profoundly damaged by the dictatorship and foreign occupation. It charted changes in the Italian condition, entered everyday life and explored the world of personalities with commonplace names. It also sought to explore to some degree the experience of the whole country, including remote areas of the south and islands. This urgent embrace associated neorealism with the moral rebirth of the nation, with a washing away of the sins of the Mussolini era and the establishment of a new democratic sensibility. It turned cinema from a means of entertainment and escape, not to say propaganda, into a tool of enquiry, a form of citizenship and a part of the texture of shared experience. This is not to say that this inclusive approach was responsible for the expansion of the audience in areas of the country that had previously not been reached by the mass media. The steady increase in film-going was the result of four quite different phenomena: the impact of the Allied occupation forces, commercial development, political competition and material aspirations. It was American cinema and popular Italian cinema that provided the main fare of audiences in the south and the provinces. While neorealism sought to centre cinema's gaze on the common man, woman and child, both happily catered to the popular appetite for exceptional figures and stars.

This book has not separated neorealism from commercial cinema either by treating it as a distinct phenomenon or by ignoring the latter. Rather it has been treated as an influence, a factor of change and a site of innovation. Once the uncertainty of the immediate postwar period had passed, production companies once more entered the fray and became involved in making many neorealist films. The elements of hybridity that were present even in the earliest films consequently expanded. Commercial cinema borrowed from neorealism, too, especially its use of real environments and stories dealing with regular people. This led to situations of crossover and contamination in which neorealist films incorporated devices, situations and narratives that derived from genre cinema, while the latter centred dramas and comedies on social ills, everyday characters and ordinary dreams. There were nonetheless differences in orientation and in certain practices. Neorealism was always critical in its attitudes to stars and stardom. Visconti transfigured Massimo Girotti and Clara Calamai in *Ossessione*, while Rossellini bypassed established names in *Roma città aperta* and brought to the fore, in Magnani and Fabrizi, two actors known mainly for character parts. The persistent casting of non-professionals would confirm the detachment from existing screen talent. But stars soon came back. While Zavattini railed against actors and stars, seeing the latter as fundamentally undemocratic, De Santis believed that stars could be a positive force. He saw them as vehicles of popular taste aspirations, especially when they hailed not from professional environments but from real experience. He collaborated with De Laurentiis in selecting and launching Mangano and Lucia Bosè, and he used an entirely professional cast of popular names for his choral film *Roma ore 11* (Rome 11 O'Clock, 1952). In relation to Silvana Pampanini, he applied in *Un marito per Anna Zaccheo* (A Husband for Anna Zaccheo, 1953) the same sort of transformative techniques that Visconti had with Calamai, though with the intention of harnessing her star aura to a socially motivated film rather than destroying it.

The stars of the postwar years entered the world of cinema in a different way to those of earlier years. They came not from the theatre or the Centro sperimentale school but from popular theatre, beauty contests, sport and the street. Many of them initially had a low level of professional preparation and awareness. Since some did not speak on film with their own voices, they performed mainly with their bodies. It was their faces, their gestures, their physical beauty or ugliness that marked them out as screen presences. The stress on the physical went hand in hand with the huge growth of the audience for cinema. While middle-class tastes remained significant, increasingly it was lower-class preferences in humour, gender typologies, physical beauty and attitudes to life that counted. This did not mean that stars themselves were necessarily of humble extraction. Both Girotti and Vallone were educated and middle class despite their screen images. Moreover, the prevailing idea of the man or woman of the people was not confined to the working class or even to an urban underclass. It was broad enough to encompass the self-employed lower middle class as well as a variety of preindustrial categories. Thus, actors like Anna Magnani, Aldo Fabrizi, Totò and Pampanini could play workers, small business people, black marketeers, restauranteurs, entertainers and local government employees without their lower-class credentials ever being seriously doubted. They could also embrace ostentatious lifestyles – not quite yet on the scale of Hollywood – without losing popular affection. They all appeared genuine types who, with few adjustments, could seem to have stepped – to be sure, in some cases via the tropes of popular theatre – from street to screen.

Though some postwar stars were seasoned professionals, paths to celebrity multiplied after the war. The de-professionalization of screen acting was an aspect of democratization that saw the business of stardom expand to include new practices and media uses as well as aspects of celebrity. Nevertheless, the new stars were mostly groomed and launched in a rudimentary, even artisanal fashion. The way they responded to the public was largely in their own hands, unless, like Mangano, there was a producer carefully plotting out a career trajectory. Most were supported by one or more secretaries or family members. Only in the years following the period dealt with here did production companies evolve complex structures to exploit their assets and stars increasingly came to rely on agents, press agents, minders, fashion advisors and other mediators. In time, other producers would seek to gain exclusive control of an actress whose career they could plot to their advantage.

The period examined in this book was one of transition, first and foremost of the nation during the most calamitous and tragic years of its history. The disruption of film production, the drive to reform and innovation, the renewed distribution of American films and the efforts of production companies to compete with them meant that it was also an important phase of transition in the film industry. It was period in which old stars struggled to find a place and sometimes work, in which new names suddenly came to the fore and in which some star phenomena rose and fell. It was not a time of much stability, and the connections that even some of the most popular stars would forge with the public would not outlive the reconstruction by many years. Many of the figures explored here would sooner or later be substituted: Pampanini by Gina Lollobrigida; Magnani by Mangano and, a few years later, Sophia Loren; Totò by Alberto Sordi; Nazzari by a range of younger and more complex male actors. Massimo Girotti, Andrea Checchi and Raf Vallone would not be among them. Though they would all have long careers, their period as stars was soon over, if it ever really began (Checchi). Yet the very fact of their stardom having coincided with the emergence of Italy from the yoke of Fascism and war lent them an importance in defining a period in which divisions were sharp and displacement widespread. They did not shape the new republican constitution or the democratic party system, but they gave expression to a search for something new and better, something more dignified and democratic. If film spectatorship and political citizenship were aligned at this time, stars were the point at which this alignment occurred least problematically. They entertained the Italians at a time when entertainment was sorely needed. They provided vehicles for moral redemption, articulations of social, regional and gender tensions, and projections towards a future that, it was hoped, would be marked by peace and prosperity. Their beauty, their familiarity and their exuberance were part of the texture of the period, just as their faces were part of its iconography. Thus they made a contribution to the consolidation of a democratic culture. For this reason, some of them would never be forgotten. But even those who would soon fade played their part in the way Italy emerged from twenty years of belligerent Fascist rule and set itself on a new course.

Bibliography

Primary Sources

Archives

Academy of Motion Picture Arts and Sciences, Margaret Herrick Library,
    Hedda Hopper collection
        Motion Picture Association of America, Production Code Administration
Archivio Centrale dello Stato, Ministero del turismo e dello spettacolo
Centro sperimentale di cinematografia, Rome, Fondo Giuseppe De Santis
Cineteca di Bologna, Fondo Calendoli and Fondo Alessandro Blasetti
Harry Ransom Humanities Research Center, The University of Texas at Austin, David O.
    Selznick Collection
Istituto Luigi Sturzo – Rome, Archivio Andreotti
Wisconsin Center for Film and Theater Research, University of Madison at Wisconsin,
    Kirk Douglas papers

Newspapers and Magazines

Amica
Annabella
Araldo dello spettacolo, L'
Bollettino di informazioni dell'Associazione Generale Italiana dello Spettacolo
CIAK
Cine cocktail
Cinema
Cinema Nuovo
Cine moda
Cinémonde
Cine revue
Cinespettacolo
Corriere della sera
Domenica

Domenica degli italiani, La
Eco del Cinema, L'
Epoca
Europeo, L'
Festival
Film
Gente
Grazia
Hollywood
Illustrazione italiana, L'
Luna
Messaggero, Il
New York Times
Noi Donne
Novella
Oggi
Paese sera
Primi piani
Radiocorriere
Rassegna del film
Repubblica, La
Rinascita
Settimana Incom, La
Settimana Tv
Star
Stop
Tempo
Tempo, Il
Unità, L'
Verità, La
Vie Nuove

Autobiographies, Memoirs and Testimonies

Alberico, G. *Il corpo gentile: conversazione con Massimo Girotti*. Roma: Luca Sossella editore, 2003.
Brin, I. *L'Italia esplode: diario dell'anno 1952*. Rome: Viella, 2014.
Buffa, M.E. *Amedeo Buffa Nazzari*. Rome: Edizioni Sabinae, 2008.
Cortese, V. *Quanti sono i domani passati: autobiografia*. Milan: Mondadori, 2012.
Costa, A. 'Conversazione con Giuseppe De Santis'. *Cinema & Cinema* 9(30) (1982), 68–69.

De Matteis, S. et al. (eds). *Follie del varietà: vicende, memorie, personaggi, 1890–1970*. Milan: Feltrinelli, 1980.
Duranti, D. *Il romanzo della mia vita*. Milan: Mondadori, 1987.
Fabrizi, M. *Aldo Fabrizi, mio padre*. Rome: Gremese, 2006.
Faldini, F. and G. Fofi (eds). *L'avventurosa storia del cinema italiano: raccontata dai suoi protagonisti, 1935–1959*. Milan: Feltrinelli, 1979.
Freda, R. *Divoratori di celluloide: 50 anni di memorie cinematografiche e non*. Milan: Emme edizioni, 1981.
Freddi, L. *Il Cinema*. Rome: L'Arnia, 1949.
Gili, J.A. and M. Grossi (eds). *Alle origini del Neorealismo: Giuseppe De Santis a colloquio con Jean A. Gili*. Rome: Bulzoni, 2008.
Lajolo, D. *Il voltagabbana*. Milan: Il Saggiatore, 1982.
Lane, J.F. *To Each His Own Dolce Vita*. Cambridge: Bear Claw Books, 2013.
Lizzani, C. *Riso amaro*. Rome: Officina, 1978.
———. *Il mio lungo viaggio nel secolo breve*. Turin: Einaudi, 2007.
Macario, M. *Macario un comico caduto dalla luna*. Milan: Baldini & Castoldi, 1998.
Malaparte, C. *Diario di uno straniero a Parigi*. Florence: Vallecchi, 1966.
Olivieri, A. and A. Castellano. *Le stelle del varietà: rivista, avanspettacolo e cabaret Dal 1936 al 1966*. Rome: Gremese, 1989.
Padellaro, A. and G. Padellaro. *I non romani e Roma: testimonianze e confessioni*. Milan: Rizzoli, 1970.
Pampanini, S. *Scandalosamente perbene*. Rome: Gremese, 1996.
Pirro, U. *Celluloide*. Milan: Rizzoli, 1983.
Ramperti, M. *Quindici mesi al fresco*. Milan: Ceschina, 1960.
Rondi, G.L. *Un lungo viaggio: cinquant'anni di cinema italiano raccontati da un testimone*. Florence: le Monnier, 1998.
———. *Le mie vite allo specchio: diari 1947–1997*. Cantalupo in Sabina: edizioni Sabinae, 2016.
Savio, F. *Cinecittà anni trenta*. Rome: Bulzoni, 1979.
Steno. *Sotto le stelle del '44*. Palermo: Sellerio, 1993.
Totò. *Siamo uomini o caporali? Diario semiserio di Antonio De Curtis*, M. Amorosi and A. Ferraù (eds). Rome: Newton Compton, 1993.
Vallone, R. *Alfabeto della memoria*. Rome: Gremese, 2001.
Villani, D. *Come sono nate undici Miss Italia*. Milan: Editoriale Domus, 1957.
Zavattini, C. *Diario cinematografico*. Milan: Bompiani, 1979.

Collected Writing and Reviews

Aristarco, G. (ed.). *Il mito dell'attore: come l'industria della star produce il sex symbol*. Bari: Dedalo, 1982 (first published 1956).
Bianchi, P. *Maestri del cinema*. Milan: Garzanti, 1972.

———. *L'occhio di vetro: il cinema degli anni 1940–43*, O. Del Buono (ed.). Milan: Il Formichiere, 1978.
———. *L'occhio di vetro: il cinema degli anni 1945–1950*, O. Del Buono (ed.). Milan: Il Formichiere, 1979.
Blasetti, A. *Scritti sul cinema*, A. Aprà (ed.). Venice: Marsilio, 1982.
Calvino, I. *Saggi 1945–1985*, M. Barenghi (ed.). Milan: Mondadori, 1995.
Cardullo, B. (ed.). *André Bazin and Italian Neorealism*. New York: Continuum, 2011.
De Benedetti, G. *Al cinema*, L. Miccichè (ed.). Padua: Marsilio, 1983.
Marotta, G. *Al cinema non fa freddo*, G. Amelio (ed.). Cava de' Tirreni: Avagliano, 1997.
Overbey, D. (ed.). *Springtime in Italy: A Reader on Neo-Realism*. London: Talisman Books, 1978.
Prono, F. (ed.). *Le sirene immaginarie: dive raccontate da scrittori*. Florence: Vallecchi, 1995.
Soldati, M. *Cinematografo*. Palermo: Sellerio, 2006.
Viazzi, G. *Scritti di cinema 1940–1958*, C. Bragaglia (ed.). Milan: Longanesi, 1979.

Secondary Sources

Agnelli, M. and M. Caracciolo Chia. *Marella Agnelli: The Last Swan*. New York: Rizzoli, 2014.
Alberoni, F. *L'elite senza potere: ricerca sociologica sul divismo*. Milan: Vita e pensiero, 1963.
Anile, A. *I film di Totò (1946–1967): la maschera tradita*. Genoa: Le Mani, 1998.
———. *Totò proibito*. Turin: Lindau, 2005.
———. *Totalmente Totò: vita e opera di un comico assoluto*. Bologna: Cineteca di Bologna, 2017.
Anile, A. (ed.). 2018. *Guardie e ladri*. Rome: Edizioni di Bianco e Nero, 2018.
Anile, A. and M.G. Giannice. *La guerra dei vulcani: Rossellini, Magnani, Bergman – storia di cinema e d'amore*. Turin: le Mani, 2010.
Aronica, D. et al. *Totò: linguaggi e maschere del comico*. Rome: Carocci, 2003.
Arvidsson, A. *Marketing Modernity: Italian Advertising from Fascism to Postmodernity*. London: Routledge, 2003.
Aumont, J. *Du visage au cinéma*. Paris: Editions de l'Étoile, 1992.
Azzopardi, M. *Massimo Girotti: un acteur aux cent visages*. Paris L'Harmattan, 1998.
Bacon, H. *Visconti: Explorations of Beauty and Decay*. Cambridge: Cambridge University Press, 1998.
Baioni, M. *Risorgimento in camicia nera: studi, istituzioni, musei nell'Italia fascista*. Rome: Carocci, 2006.
Banti, A.M. *Sublime madre nostra: la nazione italiana dal Risorgimento al fascismo*. Rome: Laterza, 2011.
Baranski, Z. and R. Lumley (eds). *Culture and Conflict in Postwar Italy*. Basingstoke: Macmillan, 1990.

Baron, C. and S.M. Carnicke. *Reframing Screen Performance*. Ann Arbor: University of Michigan Press, 2008.

Barzoletti, G. et al. *Modi di produzione del cinema italiano: la Titanus*. Ancona: Di Giacomo, 1986.

Basinger, J. *A Woman's View: How Hollywood Spoke to Women 1930-1960*. London: Chatto & Windus, 1993.

Bayman, L. *The Operatic and the Everyday in Post-war Italian Film Melodrama*. Edinburgh: Edinburgh University Press, 2014.

Bazin, A. *What is Cinema?* Vol. 2, H. Gray (ed.). Berkeley: University of California Press, 1971.

Ben-Ghiat, R. 'Unmaking the Fascist Man: Masculinity, Film and the Transition from Dictatorship'. *Journal of Modern Italian Studies* 10(3) (2005), 336-65.

Bergman, I. and A. Burgess. *Ingrid Bergman: My Story*. New York: Dell, 1961.

Bertetto, P. (ed.). *Storia del cinema italiano: uno sguardo d'insieme*. Venice/Rome: Marsilio/Edizioni di Bianco & Nero, 2011.

Biess, F. and R. Moeller (eds). *Histories of the Aftermath: The Legacies of the Second World War in Europe*. Oxford: Berghahn, 2010.

Biondi, D. *Sottobosco del cinema*. Bologna: Edizioni Capitol, 1963.

Biribanti, P. *Boccasile*. Rome: Castelvecchi, 2009.

Bispuri, E. *Vita di Totò*. Rome: Gremese, 2000.

Bolton, L. and J.L. Wright (eds). *Lasting Screen Stars: Images that Fade and Personas that Endure*. London: Palgrave Macmillan, 2016.

Bondanella, P. (ed.). *The Italian Cinema Book*. London: BFI, 2014.

Boorstin, D. *The Image: A Guide to Pseudo-Events in America*. Harmondsworth: Penguin, 1962.

Bracalini, R. *Celebri e dannati: vita di Osvaldo Valenti e Luisa Ferida*. Milan: Longanesi, 1985.

Brice, C. *Histoire de Rome et des Romains de Napoleon 1er a nos jours*. Paris: Perrin, 2007.

Brunetta, G.P. *Storia del cinema italiano 1895-1945*. Rome: Editori Riuniti, 1979.

———. *Storia del cinema italiano: dal 1945 agli anni Ottanta*. Rome: Editori Riuniti, 1982.

———. *Cent'anni di cinema italiano*. Rome: Laterza, Chapters, 1991.

Brunetta, G.P. (ed.). *Identità italiana e identità europea nel cinema italiano dal 1945 al miracolo economico*. Turin: Edizioni della Fondazione Giovanni Agnelli, 1996.

Brunette, P. *Roberto Rossellini*. New York and Oxford: Oxford University Press, 1987.

Bruno, G. and M. Nadotti (eds). *Off Screen: Women & Film in Italy*. London: Routledge, 1988.

Buckley, R. 'National Body: Gina Lollobrigida and the Cult of the Star in the 1950s'. *Historical Journal of Film, Radio and Television* 20(4) (2000), 527-47.

———. 'The Female Film Star in Postwar Italy'. University of London PhD thesis, 2002.

———. 'Elsa Martinelli: Italy's Audrey Hepburn'. *Historical Journal of Film, Radio and Television* 26(3) (2006), 327-40.

———. 'Glamour and the Italian Female Film Stars of the 1950s'. *Historical Journal of Film, Radio and Television* 28(3) (2008), 267–89.
———. 'The Emergence of Film Fandom in Postwar Italy: Reading Claudia Cardinale's Fan Mail'. *Historical Journal of Film, Radio and Television* 29(4) (2009), 523–59.
Burchielli, R. and V. Bianchini. *Cinecittà: la fabbrica dei sogni*. Milan: Boroli, 2004.
Burke, F. (ed.). *A Companion to Italian Cinema*. Chichester: Wiley Blackwell, 2017.
Caldiron, O. (ed.). *Storia del cinema italiano*, Vol. V, 1930–1934. Venice: Marsilio/Edizioni di Bianco & Nero, 2006.
———. *C'era una volta il '48*. Rome: minimum fax, 2008.
Camerino, V. 'La vita del cinema in un piccolo-medio centro del salentino'. *Il Protogora*, third series, 1978.
Campari, R. 'America, cinema e mass media nel neorealismo italiano'. *Cinema & Cinema*, January–March (1977), 62–69.
Caponetti, G. *Il grande Gualino: vita e avventure di un uomo del Novecento*. Turin: UTET, 2018.
Cardullo, B. (ed.) *André Bazin and Italian Neorealism*. New York: Continuum, 2011.
Carluccio, G., E. Morreale and M. Pierini (eds). *Intorno al neorealismo: voci, contesti, linguaggi e culture dell'Italia del dopoguerra*. Milan, Scalpendi, 2017.
Carman, E.S. 'Mapping the Body: Female Film Stars and the Reconstruction of Postwar Italian National Identity'. *Quarterly Review of Film* 31(4) (2014), 322–35.
Carrano, P. *La Magnani*, Milan: Rizzoli, 1986.
Carrattieri, M. and M. Flores (eds). *La Resistenza in Italia: storia, memoria, storiografia*. Florence GoWare, 2017.#
Casavecchia, S. (ed.). *Amedeo Nazzari: il divo, l'uomo, l'attore*. Rome: Centro sperimentale di cinematografia, 2007.
Castello. G.C. *Il divismo: mitologia del cinema*. Rome: ERI, 1957.
Ceratto, M. *Caterina Boratto: la donna che visse tre volte*. Rimini: Edizioni Sabinae, 2015.
Champagne, J. *Aesthetic Modernism and Masculinity in Fascist Italy*. London: Routledge, 2013.
Chaplin, C. *My Autobiography*. New York: Simon & Schuster, 1964.
Chiappetta-Miller, T. 'Projecting the Diva's Voice: Anna Magnani in Visconti's *Bellissima*'. *Italian Studies* 70(3) (2015), 364–76.
Chiarini, L. *Cinema quinto potere*. Bari-Rome: Laterza, 1954.
Cigognetti, L. and E. Servetti. '"On Her Side": Female Images in Italian Cinema and the Popular Press, 1945–1955'. *Historical Journal of Film, Radio and Television* 16(4) (1996), 55–63.
Cimmino, G. and S. Masi. *Silvana Mangano: il teorema della bellezza*. Rome: Gremese, 1994.
Colonna, G. *Personaggi e interpreti*. Rome: Edizioni Filmcritica, 1955.
Comand, M. and S. Gundle (eds). 'Alida Valli'. Special issue, *Bianco & Nero* 586 (2016).
Conor, L. *The Spectacular Modern Woman: Feminine Visibility in the 1920s*. Bloomington: Indiana University Press, 2004.

Continanza, M. *Totò dopo Totò: il ricxordo dell'attore nella memoria collettiva dei napoletani*. Milan: Zambon, 1998.
Cooke, P.E. *The Legacy of the Italian Resistance*. New York: Palgrave Macmillan, 2011.
Corsi, B. *Con qualche dollaro in meno: storia economica del cinema italiano*. Rome: Editori Riuniti, 2001.
Cosulich, C. (ed.). *Storia del cinema italiano*, Vol. VII 1945–1948. Venice and Rome: Marsilio/Edizioni di Bianco & Nero, 2003.
Culhane, S. 'Street Cries and Street Fights: Anna Magnani, Sophia Loren and the *Popolana*'. *The Italianist* 37(2) (2017), 254–62.
Dagrada, E. (ed.). *Anna Cinquanta: il decennio più lungo del secolo breve*. Soveria Mannelli: Rubbettino, 2016.
Dalle Vacche, A. *Diva: Defiance and Passion in Early Italian Cinema*. Austin: University of Texas Press, 2008.
D'Attorre, P.P. (ed.). *Nemici per la pelle: sogno americano e mito sovietico nell'Italia contemporanea*. Milan: Franco Angeli, 1991.
Davis, R.L. *The Glamour Factory: Inside Hollywood's Big Studio System*. Dallas, TX: Southern Methodist University Press, 1993.
De Giusti, L. (ed.), *Storia del cinema italiano*, Vol. VIII 1949–1953. Venice and Rome: Marsilio/Edizioni Bianco & Nero, 2003.
De Grazia, V. *How Fascism Ruled Women: Italy 1922–1945*. Berkeley: University of California Press, 1992.
Della Casa, S. *Mario Mattoli*. Florence: la Nuova Italia, 1989.
——. *Romana Film: Fortunato Misiano e la sua avventura nel cinema*. Rome: Edizioni di Bianco & Nero, 2018.
Detassis, P. 'Corpi recuperati per il proprio sguardo'. *Memoria* 3(6) (1982), 24–31.
Di Chiara, F. *Generi e industria cinematografica in Italia: il caso Titanus (1949-1964)*. Turin: Lindau, 2013.
Di Monte, E. et al. *La città del cinema (produzione e lavoro nel cinema italiano (1930–1970)*. Rome: Napoleone, 1979.
Di Nolfo, E. *Le paure e le speranze degli italiani (1943–1953)*. Milan: Mondadori, 1986.
Duggan, C. *The Force of Destiny: A History of Italy Since 1796*. London: Allen Lane, 2007.
Dyer, R. *Stars*. London: BFI, 1979.
Ellwood, D.W. and G.P. Brunetta (eds), *Hollywood in Europa: industria, politica, pubblico del cinema 1945–1960*. Florence: Ponte alle Grazie, 1991.
Faldini, F. *Roma, Hollywood, Roma: Totò, ma non soltanto*. Milan: Baldini & Castoldi, 1997.
Faldini, F. and G. Fofi. *Totò: l'uomo e la maschera Totò*. Rome: minimum fax, 1977.
Farassino, A. (ed.). *Neorealismo: cinema italiano, 1945–1949*. Turin: EDT, 1989.
——. *Mario Camerini*. Locarno: Yellow Now, 1992.
Farassino, A. and T. Sanguineti. *Lux Film: Esthétique et système d'un studio italien*. Locarno: Editions du festival international du film de Locarno, 1984.
Finkelstein, N.H. *Jewish Comedy Stars: Classic to Cutting Edge*. Minneapolis: Kar-Ben, 2010.

Fofi. G. *Più stelle che in cielo*, Rome: e/o, 1995.
———. *Alberto Sordi: l'Italia in bianco e nero*. Milan: Mondadori, 2004.
Forbes, J. and S. Street (eds). *European Cinema: An Introduction*. Basingstoke: Palgrave, 2000.
Forgacs, D. '"Rome, Open City": Before and After Neorealism'. *Journal of Italian Cinema and Media Studies* 6(3) (2018), 301–13.
Forgacs, D. and S. Gundle. *Mass Culture and Italian Society from Fascism to the Cold War*. Bloomington: Indiana University Press, 2007.
Forgacs, D. and R. Lumley (eds). *Italian Cultural Studies: An Introduction*. Oxford: Oxford University Press, 1996.
Forgacs, D., S. Lutton and G. Nowell-Smith (eds). *Roberto Rossellini: Magician of the Real*. London: BFI, 2000.
Fusco, G.C. *Quando l'Italia tollerava*. Milan: Neri Pozza, 1995.
Gabrielli, P. *La pace e la mimosa: l'Unione delle donne italiane e la costruzione della politica della memoria (1944–1955)*. Rome: Donzelli, 2005.
———. *Il 1946: le donne, la repubblica*. Rome: Donzelli, 2010.
Gandin, M. *Il tetto di Vittorio De Sica*. Bologna: Cappelli, 1956.
Garcia Düttmann, A. *Visconti: Insights into Flesh and Blood*. Stanford: Stanford University Press, 2009.
Garofalo, A. *L'italiana in Italia*. Bari: Laterza, 1956.
Gauteur, C. and G. Vincendeau. *Jean Gabin: anatomie d'un mythe*. Paris: Nathan, 1993.
Gelley, O. *Stardom and the Aesthetics of Neorealism: Ingrid Bergman in Rossellini's Italy*. London: Routledge, 2012.
Gentile, E. *Fascismo: storia e interpretazione*. Rome: Laterza, 2005.
———. *25 luglio 1943*. Rome: Laterza, 2018.
Germani, S.G. *Mario Camerini*. Florence: La Nuova Italia, 1980.
Germani, S.M. et al. (eds). *Titanus: cronaca familiare del cinema italiano*. Rome: Edizioni Sabinae, 2014.
Giacci, V. *Carlo Lizzani*. Milan: Il Castoro Cinema, 2009.
Gili, J.A. and A. Tassone (eds). *Parigi-Roma: 50 anni di coproduzioni italo-francesi (1945–1995)*. Milan: Il Castoro, 1996.
Gledhill, C. (ed.). *Reinventing Film Studies*. London: Arnold, 2000.
Glenn, S.A. *Female Spectacle: The Theatrical Roots of Modern Feminism*. Cambridge, MA: Harvard University Press, 2000.
Gordon, R.S.C. *Rome Open City*. London: BFI, 2000.
Gottlieb, S. (ed.). *Robert Rossellini's Rome Open City*. Cambridge: Cambridge University Press, 2004.
Governi, G. *Vita di Totò: principe napoletano e grande attore*. Milan: Rusconi, 1980.
———. *Nannarella*. Milan: Bompiani, 1981.
Grant, B.K. (ed.). *Schirmer Encyclopedia of Film*. New York: Schirmer Books, 2006.
Grazzini, G. (ed.). *Cara Claudia...: lettere dei fans alla Cardinale*. Milan: Longanesi, 1966.

Grignaffini, G. 'Verità e poesia: ancora di Silvana e del cinema italiano'. *Cinema & Cinema* 9(30) (1982), 41–46.
Gubitosi. G. *Amedeo Nazzari*. Bologna: Il Mulino, 1998.
Gundle, S. *I comunisti italiani tra Hollywood e Mosca: la sfida della cultura di massa (1943–1991)*. Florence: Giunti, 1995.
———. 'Sophia Loren: Italian Icon'. *Historical Journal of Film, Radio and Television* 15(3) (1995), 367–85.
———. *Between Hollywood and Moscow: The Italian Communists and the Challenge of Mass Culture, 1943–1991*. Durham, NC: Duke University Press, 2000.
———. 'Hollywood Glamour and Mass Consumption in Postwar Italy'. *Journal of Cold War Studies* 4(3) (2002), 95–118.
———. *Bellissima: Feminine Beauty and the Idea of Italy*. New Haven and London. Yale University Press, 2007.
———. *Glamour: A History*. Oxford: Oxford University Press, 2008.
———. 'Alida Valli in Hollywood: From Star of Fascist Cinema to "Selznick Siren"'. *Historical Journal of Film, Radio and Television* 32(4) (2012), 559–87.
———. *Mussolini's Dream Factory: Film Stardom in Fascist Italy*. Oxford: Berghahn Books, 2013.
Gundle, S., C. Duggan and G. Pieri (eds). *The Cult of the Duce: Mussolini and the Italians*. Manchester: Manchester University Press, 2013.
Gundle, S. et al. *Dream makers: come i produttori hanno fatto grande il cinema italiano*. Bologna: Cineteca di Bologna, 2018.
Günsberg, M. *Italian Cinema: Gender and Genre*. Basingstoke: Palgrave Macmillan, 2004.
Haaland, T. *Italian Neorealist Cinema*. Edinburgh: Edinburgh University Press, 2012.
Harris, J.L. '"In America è vietato essere brutte": Advertising American Beauty in the Italian Women's Magazine *Annabella*, 1945–1965'. *Modern Italy* 22(1) (2017), 35–53.
Hess, T.B. and L. Nochlin (eds). *Woman as Sex Object: Studies in Erotic Art, 1730–1970*. London: Allen Lane, 1972.
Hewitt, N. (ed.). *The Culture of Reconstruction: European Thought, Literature and Film, 1945–1950*. New York: St. Martin's Press, 51–66.
Hill, J. and P. Church Gibson (eds). *The Oxford Guide to Film Studies*. Oxford: Oxford University Press, 1998.
Hipkins, D. *Italy's Other Women: Gender and Prostitution in Italian Cinema, 1940–1965*. Oxford: Peter Lang, 2016.
Hochkofler, M. *Anna Magnani*. Rome: Gremese, 2005.
Holdaway, D. and D. Missero. 'Re-reading Marina: Sexuality, Materialism and the Construction of Italy'. *Journal of Italian Cinema and Media Studies* 6(3) (2018), 348–58.
Hughes, S.C. 'Duelling After the Duce: Postwar Conflicts of Honour in Italy'. *Journal of Modern Italian Studies* 18(5) (2013), 615–26.
Innocenti, M. *Le signore del fascismo*. Milan: Mursia, 2001.
Isnenghi, M. *Storia d'Italia: i fatti e le percezioni dal Risorgimento alla societa' dello spettacolo*. Rome: Laterza, 2011.

Kezich, T. and A. Levantesi. *Dino: De Laurentiis, la vita e i film*. Milan: Feltrinelli, 2001.
King, G. *Film Comedy*. New York: Wallflower, 2002.
Koch, G. and M. Hansen. 'Bèla Bàlazs: The Physiognomy of Things'. *New German Critique* 40 (1987), 167–77.
Krämer, P. and A. Lovell (eds). *Screen Acting*. London: Routledge, 1999.
Lancia, E. and F. Melelli. *I film di Aldo Fabrizi*. Rome: Gremese, 2015.
Landes, J. *Visualizing the Nation: Gender, Representation and Revolution in Eighteenth Century France*. Ithaca: Cornell University Press, 2001.
Landy. M. *Stardom Italian Style: Screen Performance and Personality in Italian Cinema*. Bloomington: Indiana University Press, 2008.
Laura, E.G. (ed.). *Storia del cinema italiano*, Vol. VI 1940–1944. Venice and Rome: Marsilio/Edizioni di Bianco & Nero, 2010.
Livi. G. *Alberto Sordi*. Milan: Longanesi, 1967.
Lupano, M. and A. Vaccari (eds). *Fashion at the Time of Fascism: Italian Modernist Lifestyle, 1922–1943*. Bologna: Damiani, 2009.
Manzoli, G. *Da Ercole a fantozzi: cinema popolare e società italiana dal boom economic alla neotelevisione (1958–1976)*. Rome: Carocci, 2012.
Marcus, M. 'Visconti's *Bellissima*: The Diva, the Mirror and the Screen'. *Italian Culture* 17(1) (1999), 9–17.
Martellini, L. *Il "Cristo proibito" di Malaparte*. Viterbo: Universita della Tuscia, 2007.
Martini, A. (ed.). *L'antirossellinismo*. Turin: Kaplan, 2010.
Masi, S. and E. Lancia. *Stelle d'Italia: piccole e grandi dive del cinema italiano dal 1930 al 1945*. Rome: Gremese, 1994.
Masoni, T. and P. Vecchi. 'Totò al giro d'Italia di Mario Mattoli'. *Cineforum* 28(11) (1988), 53–55.
McCarthy, P. (ed.). *Italy Since 1945*. Oxford: Oxford University Press, 2000.
McLean, A. *Being Rita Hayworth: Labor, Identity and Hollywood Stardom*. New Brunswick: Rutgers University Press, 2004.
Meredith, G. *Vittoria*. London Constable, 1902.
Miccichè, L. (ed.). *Il neorealismo cinematografico italiano*, Venice: Marsilio, 1975.
———. *Signore e signori di Pietro Germi*. Turin: Lindau, 1997.
Minghelli, G. *Landscape and Memory in Post-Fascist Italian Film: Cinema Year Zero*. London: Routledge, 2014.
Mizejewski, L. *Ziegfeld Girl: Image and Icon in Culture and Cinema*. Durham, NC: Duke University Press, 1999.
Moneti, G. (ed.). *Lessico zavattiniano: parole e idee su cinema e dintorni*. Venezia: Marsilio, 1992.
Monza, M. and T. Scaroni (eds). *Cinquantanni di Miss Italia*. Rome: Ed. Organizzazione Miri, 1989.
Morandini, M. *Il Morandini: dizionario del film 2000*. Bologna: Zanichelli, 2000.
Morin, E. *Les stars*. Paris: Seuil, 1957.
———. *L'esprit du temps*. Paris: Grasset, 1962.

Morreale, E. *Mario Soldati: le carriere di un libertino*. Genoa: Le Mani, 2006.
———. *Cosi piangevamo il cinema melò nell'italia degli anni cinquanta*. Rome: Donzelli, 2011.
Morris, P. (ed.). *Women in Italy, 1945-1960: An Interdisciplinary Study*. New York: Palgrave Macmillan, 2006.
Moscati, C. *Aldo Fabrizi: l'ultimo Re di Roma*. Genova: Gruppo Editoriale Lo Vecchio, undated.
Moscati, I. (ed.). *Clara Calamai: l'ossessione di essere diva*. Venice: Marsilio, 1996.
Mosse, G. *The Image of Man: The Creation of Modern Masculinity*. Oxford: Oxford University Press, 1996.
Mulvey, L. 'Visual Pleasure and Narrative Cinema'. *Screen* 16(3) (1973), 6–18.
Muscio, G. *Napoli/New York/Hollywood: Film Between Italy and the United States*. New York: Fordham University Press, 2019.
Nicoli, M. *The Rise and Fall of the Italian Film Industry*. London: Routledge, 2017.
Noto, P. and F. Pitassio. *Il cinema neorealista*. Bologna: Archetipo libri, 2012.
Nowell Smith, G. *Luchino Visconti*. London: BFI, 2003.
O'Healy, A. 'Towards a Transnational Approach to the Study of Contemporary Cinema'. *The Italianist* 34(2) (2014), 268–71.
O'Leary, A. and C. O'Rawe. 'Against Realism: On a "Certain Tendency" in Italian Film Criticism'. *Journal of Modern Italian Studies* 16(1) (2011), 107–28.
Olivieri, A. *Totò, Scalfaro e la..."malafemmina"*. Rome: Daga, 1992.
O'Rawe, C. 'Italian Star Studies'. *Italian Studies* 65(2) (2010), 286–92.
———. '*Avanti a lui tremava tutta Roma*: Opera, Melodrama and the Resistance'. *Modern Italy* 17(2) (2012), 185–96.
———. *Stars and Masculinities in Contemporary Italian Cinema*. Basingstoke: Palgrave Macmillan, 2014.
Parigi, S. *Neorealismo: il nuovo cinema del dopoguerra*. Venice: Marsilio, 2014.
Paulicelli, E. *Fashion under Fascism: Beyond the Black Shirt*. Oxford: Berg, 2004.
Pellizzari, L. and C. Valentinetti. *Il romanzo di Alida Valli*. Milan: Garzanti, 1995.
Pezzotta. A. *Ridere civilmente: il cinema di Luigi Zampa*. Bologna: Cineteca di Bologna, 2012.
Phillips, A. and G. Vincendeau (eds). *Journeys of Desire: European Actors in Hollywood – A Critical Companion*. London: BFI, 2006.
Pierini, M. 'Recitazione e rotocalchi, movimento e fissità: Anna Magnani – 1945-1948', *Smarginature* 10 (2017): 407–12.
Pitassio, F. 'Popular Culture, Performance, Persona: Between *Rome, Open City* and *The Rose Tattoo*'. *Journal of Italian Cinema and Media Studies* 6(3) (2018), 373–88.
Pitassio, F. and P. Noto. *Il cinema neorealista*. Bologna: Archetipo libri, 2012.
Polhemus, T. (ed.). *Social Aspects of the Human Body*. Harmondsworth: Penguin, 1978.
Pratolini, V. *Le ragazze di San Frediano*. Milan: Mondadori, 1986 (first published 1951).
Pruzzo, P. and E. Lancia. *Amedeo Nazzari*, Rome: Gremese, 1983.
Quaglietti, L. *Storia economico-politica del cinema italiano 1945–1980*. Rome: Editori Riuniti, 1980.
———. *Ecco i nostri: l'invasione del cinema americano in Italia*. Turin: ERI, 1991.

Quarantotto, C. *Il cinema, la carne e il diavolo*. Milan: Edizioni del Borghese, 1962.
Quargnolo, M. *Quando i friulani andavano al cinema*. Udine: Edizioni Biblioteca dell'immagine, 1989.
Quinlan, D. *Quinlan's Illustrated Directory of Film Comedy Stars*. London: Batsford, 1992.
Quirk, L.J. *The Films of Ingrid Bergman*. New York: Citadel, 1970.
Reich, J. *Beyond the Latin Lover: Marcello Mastroianni, Masculinity and Italian Cinema*. Bloomington: Indiana University Press, 2004.
———. *The Maciste Films of Italian Silent Cinema*. Bloomington: Indiana University Press, 2015.
Reich, J. and P. Garofalo (eds). *Reviewing Fascism: Italian Cinema, 1922–1943*. Bloomington: Indiana University Press, 2002.
Reich, J and C. O'Rawe. *Divi: la mascolinità nel cinema italiano*. Rome: Donzelli, 2015.
Renzi, R. *Gina Lollobrigida*. Milan: Sedit, 1955.
Rigoletto, S. '(Un)dressing Authenticity: Neorealist Stardom and Anna Magnani in the Postwar Era (1945–48)'. *Journal of Italian Cinema and Media Studies* 6(3) (2018), 389–403.
Romano R. *Paese Italia: venti secoli di identità*. Rome: Donzelli, 1997.
Rondolino, G. *Rossellini*. Turin: UTET, 1989.
Rositi, F. 'Personalità e divismo in Italia durante il periodo fascista'. *IKON* 17(62) (1967), 9–48.
Sartre, J-P. *Being and Nothingness*. New York: Washington Square Press, 1968 (first published 1943).
Scaccabarozzi, L. 'Nuove ricerche e analisi intorno a Scalera Film'. Undergraduate dissertation, Università Ca' Foscari, Venice, 2017.
Scarlini, F. and L. Paloscia. *Il mondo dei fan club*. Milan: Adnkronos, 2000.
Schiavina, M.A. (ed.). *Alberto Sordi: storia di un commediante*. Milan: Baldini & Castoldi, 1999.
Schnapp, J. and M. Tiews (eds). *Crowds*. Stanford: Stanford University Press, 2006.
Schoonover, K. *Brutal Vision: The Neorealist Body in Postwar Italian Cinema*. Minneapolis: University of Minnesota Press, 2012.
Schwarz, G. *Tu mi devi seppellir: riti funebri e culto nazionale alle origini della Repubblica*. Turin: UTET, 2010.
Sciarra, S. *Quizario del cinema italiano*. Rome: Dino Audino, 2006.
Sedita, G. 'Vittorio Mussolini, Hollywood and Neorealism'. *Journal of Modern Italian Studies* 15(3) (2010), 431–57.
Sesti, M. *Pietro Germi: Life and Films of a Latin Loner*. Milan: Edizioni Olivares, 1999.
Setta, S. *L'uomo qualunque, 1944–1948*. Rome-Bari: Laterza, 1975.
Shingler, M. *Star Studies*. London: BFI/Palgrave Macmillan, 2012.
Sieglohr, U. (ed.). *Heroines Without Heroes: Reconstructing Female and national Identities in European Cinema, 1945–51*. London: Continuum, 2000.
Spinazzola, V. *Cinema e pubblico: lo spettacolo filmico in Italia 1945–65*. Milan: Bompiani, 1974.

Stael, Mme de. *Corinne, or Italy*. Oxford: Oxford University Press, 1988 (first published 1807).
Steimatsky, N. *The Face on Film*. New York: Oxford University Press, 2017.
Stewart, D.E. and A. Cornish (eds). *Sparks and Seeds: Medieval Literature and its Afterlife*. Yurnhout: Brepols, 2000.
Stewart-Steinberg, S. *The Pinocchio Effect: On Making Italians, 1860–1890*. Chicago: University of Chicago Press, 2007.
Synnott, A. 'Truth and Goodness, Mirrors and Masks – Part 1: A Sociology of Beauty and the Face'. *British Journal of Sociology* 40(4) (1989), 607–36.
Tapert, A. *The Power of Glamour*. New York: Crown, 1998.
Tapert, A. and D. Edkins. *The Power of Style*. New York: Crown, 1994.
Tassone, A. *I film di Michelangelo Antonioni*. Rome: Gremese, 2002.
Thomson, D. *Why Acting Matters*. New Haven and London: Yale University Press, 2015.
Tinazzi, G. (ed.). *Il cinema italiano degli anni '50*. Venice: Marsilio, 1979.
Treveri Gennari, D. *Postwar Italian Cinema: American Intervention, Vatican Interests*. London: Routledge, 2009.
———. '"If You Have Seen it, You Cannot Forget!": Film Consumption and Memories of Cinema-Going in 1950s Rome'. *Historical Journal of Film, Radio and Television* 35(1) (2015), 53–74.
Treveri Gennari, D. and J. Sedgewick. 'Memories in Context: The Social and Economic Function of Cinema in 1950s Rome'. *Film History* 27(2) (2015), 76–104.
Venè, G.F. *Mille lire al mese: la vita quotidiana della famiglia nell'Italia fascista*. Milan: Mondadori, 1998.
Ventrone, A. 'Tra propaganda e passione: "Grand Hotel" e l'Italia degli anni 50'. *Rivista di storia contemporanea* 17(4) (1988), 603–31.
Vitella, F. 'Forbice, album e carta da lettere: *Hollywood* come fan magazine'. *Fata Morgana* 27 (2015), 51–64.
———. 'Il diario intimo come fonte per la storia del fandom: ritratto di un Bobby-soxer di provincia'. *Bianco & Nero*, May–December (2015), 153–60.
Wagstaff, C. *Italian Neorealist Cinema: An Aesthetic Approach*. Toronto: Toronto University Press, 2007.
Zagarrio, V. (ed.). *Dietro lo schermo: ragionamenti sui modi di produzione cinematografici in Italia*. Venice: Marsilio, 1988.

Index

Abbasso la miseria!, 156, 164
Abbasso la ricchezza!, 156, 164
Achtung! Banditi!, 188, 189, 312
Addio amore!, 123
Addio giovinezza!, 121, 123, 269
Adultera, L', 126
AGIS, 75, 77
Agliani, Giorgio, 48n12
Agnelli, Marella, 236
Alfieri law (1938), 35, 36, 44
Alicata, Mario, 117
Alina, 257
Allies, the (in Italy), 22–25, 36, 57, 73, 345
Altri tempi, 68, 264
Amanti senza amore, 128, 129
Amato, Giuseppe, 39, 132, 155
Americano in vacanza, Un, 185
Amidei, Sergio, 118, 133, 136, 155
Amore, L', 146, 154, 167, 168
Amori di mezzo secolo, 274
Amorosa menzogna, L', 316
Andreotti, Giulio, 42, 294
Andreotti law (1949), 35, 44, 82
ANICA, 35, 36, 41, 46, 48, 75
Animali pazzi, 199
ANPI, 11, 37, 187
Anna, 295, 231
Anni difficili, 110
Antonio di Padova, 270
Antonioni, Michelangelo, 110
Apparizione, 105, 106
Aquila nera, 30, 38
Arrivederci papà, 268
Assedio dell'Alcazar, L', 55, 99, 176, 180
Au-delà des grilles (Le mura di Malapaga), 185, 328–29

Avanti a lui tremava tutta Roma, 157, 164, 165
Avanti c'è posto, 132–133, 143, 178, 189
Avventure di Mandrin, Le, 275, 287, 296–97
Avventuriera del piano di sopra, L', 123

Bacall, Lauren, 83
Bambini ci guardano, I, 101
Bandito, Il, 65, 158, 164, 165, 186, 246, 250
Barbaro, Umberto, 175, 199
Bartali, Gino, 203
Barzizza, Isa, 206, 207, 270
Barriera a settentrione, 257
Battisti, Carlo, 306, 308–9, 312, 325
Bazin, André, 64, 65, 154, 304
beauty contests, 65–66, 74, 79, 84–85, 218, 221, 223, 225, 226, 316, 346. See also Miss Italia
Bechi, Gino, 268
Bellezze in bicicletta, 202, 271–72
Bellissima, 1–4, 10, 147, 154, 168, 314–16
Benetti, Adriana, 268
Bengasi, 55
Bergman, Ingrid, 10, 61, 118, 168, 333–41
Berti, Marina, 57, 63, 189
Bisarca, La, 270
Blasetti, Alessandro, 1, 2, 25, 47, 65, 84, 95, 97, 107, 123, 140, 242, 243–44, 249, 317, 326, 328
Blood and Sand, 59, 85, 335
Blue Dahlia, The, 338
Boccasile, Gino, 80, 266–67, 272
Bode, Heinrich, 138
Bogart, Humphrey, 83
Bosè, Lucia, 66, 111, 217, 288, 295, 317, 346
Bovo, Brunella, 306
Bragaglia Carlo Ludovico, 204, 268

Brando, Marlon, 79
Brazzi, Rossano, 60, 125, 175
Brigante di Tacca di Lupo, Il, 257
Brigante Musolino, Il, 228–29, 257, 339
Brignone, Guido, 268
Bruno, Nando, 138, 139, 140, 166
Bufere, 275

Cabinet of Dr Caligari, The, 197
Caccia tragica, 107, 174, 187, 189, 217
Cagliostro, 39
Calamai, Clara, 13, 57, 59, 63, 93, 94, 97, 129, 183, 187, 223, 269
  as actor, 123–24
  beauty of, 117, 120, 123, 124, 125, 127, 128
  and fans, 120, 121, 124
  Fascist period roles, 121–23, 128
  and glamour, 114, 116, 118, 120, 121, 123, 124, 127
  in *Ossessione*, 114–21, 123, 126, 345, 346
  personal life, 121, 128–29, 129–30
  and *Roma città aperta*, 118–19, 120, 121
  screen persona, 118–20, 123, 126, 128, 131n31
Calvino, Italo, 219, 221
Calvino, Vittorio, 69
Camerini, Mario, 25, 37, 65, 119, 173, 242, 247, 287
Camicie rosse, 170, 294
Cammino della speranza, Il, 287, 289, 290
Campanini, Carlo, 200, 270
Campo dei fiori, 132, 134, 144, 153, 160
Canale, Gianna Maria, 66, 317
Canzoni, canzoni, canzoni, 276
Cardinale, Claudia, 85
Carmela, 54
Carnera, Primo, 96
Carosse d'or, La, 329
Casablanca, 339
Casilio, Maria Pia, 308, 314, 325
Castellani, Renato, 11, 137, 309
Catene, 78, 231, 253
Catholic Church, 2, 81, 82–85, 256, 268, 277, 291, 337, 340
Catholic Cinema Centre, 37, 82
Cavaliere del sogno, Il, 248

Cavalleria, 54
Cecchi, Emilio, 137
Cecchi d'Amico, Suso, 3, 137, 140, 165, 329
Cegani, Elisa, 96, 243–44, 257
Cena delle beffe, La, 97, 121, 123, 125, 128
Centa, Antonio, 59, 176
Centomila dollari, 243
Centro sperimentale di cinematografia, 12, 21, 24, 35, 52, 53, 63, 64, 175, 180–82, 199, 306, 316, 346
Cervi, Gino, 13, 42, 60, 63, 95, 157, 184, 291, 326
CGIL, 42
Chaplin, Charlie, 83, 195, 198, 199, 202, 211
Checchi, Andrea, 13, 60–1, 63, 65, 68, 78, 94, 120, 127, 173, 182, 188, 246, 347
  and Fascism, 180–82
  and Fosco Giachetti, 176–77, 180, 184, 190n27
  personal life, 180, 182
  physical appearance, 174, 182, 185, 186–87
  and the public, 176, 184
  as romantic lead, 177–79, 185
  screen persona, 174–75, 176, 178, 179, 183, 184, 185, 186–87, 189
  and Tuscany, 174, 176, 180
Chiari, Walter, 3, 4, 270
Chiarini, Luigi, 227
Christian Democrats, 2, 31, 42, 44, 75, 82, 145, 167, 206, 209, 228, 325, 337
Christian, Linda, 83, 85, 335–37, 340–41
Ciano, Galeazzo, 114, 181
Cinecittà, 1, 21, 22, 23, 34, 35, 39, 48, 54, 81, 97, 118, 120, 243, 311, 327, 328, 337, 344
Cinema (magazine), 21, 24, 25, 27, 60, 96, 115, 125, 174, 305
Cines, 35, 36, 53, 114
Cinque minuti a Cinecittà, 54
Clément René, 328
Coburn, Charles, 138
Come persi la guerra, 201
Come scopersi l'America, 201
Comencini, Luigi, 115, 123, 124, 205
Communist Party, Italian, 2, 42, 57, 81, 82, 83
  and stars, 83–85, 188, 217, 228, 285–87, 290, 295, 297, 312, 316, 336, 339

Conflicto inesperado, 251
Conte, Richard, 334
Contessa di Castiglione, La, 182
Coogan, Jackie, 304
Cooper, Gary, 54, 83
Coppi, Fausto, 203
Co-productions, 41, 323–36
Corona di ferro, La, 62, 95, 97, 101, 110
Cortese, Valentina, 60, 185, 189, 334
Crawford, Joan, 83, 334
Cristo proibito, 287, 291
Cronaca di un amore, 110
Cuny, Alain, 291
Cuori senza frontiera, 287

D'Angelo, Salvo, 3, 4, 37, 39, 47, 146, 326, 328
Davis, Bette, 58, 83, 334
De Benedetti, Aldo, 137, 255
De Curtis, Antonio. See Totò
De Filippo, Eduardo, 30, 198
De Filippo, Peppino, 194, 209, 270, 274
De Gasperi, Alcide, 42, 83
De Giorgi, Elsa, 59
De Laurentiis, Dino, 38, 48, 65, 67, 186, 191, 212, 216, 217, 218, 224, 228, 230–31, 233, 236, 246, 247, 251, 253, 329, 338, 346
De Marco, Gustavo, 196, 198
Del Poggio, Carla, 187, 189, 334
De Robertis, Federico, 61, 305
De Santis, Giuseppe, 11, 13, 24, 25, 27, 51, 60, 61, 84, 103, 105, 107, 115, 117, 174, 175, 187, 189, 191, 225–26, 268
  and *Riso amaro*, 216–28, 283, 285, 346
De Sica, Vittorio, 7, 10, 25, 28, 38, 42, 43, 52, 60, 61, 64, 101, 154, 156, 174, 233, 234, 242, 262, 304, 306–10, 312, 318
Delitto di San Giovanni Episcopo, Il, 138
Denis, Maria, 57, 59, 62, 200
Desiderio, 105, 121
Di Vittorio, Giuseppe, 42
Dieci commandamenti, I, 22, 182, 244
Dietrich, Marlene, 124, 266, 328, 332
Dilian, Irasema, 54, 60, 249, 257, 268, 330
Domani è troppo tardi, 335
Domani è un altro giorno, 335

Domenica d'agosto, 303, 309, 312, 315
Donne e briganti, 257
Dopo divorzieremo, 243
Dora Nelson, 95
Douglas, Kirk, 101, 233, 338
Dov'è la libertà, 205
Dowling, Doris, 217, 219, 222, 328
Due lettere anonime, 37, 119, 120, 157, 183
Due orfanelle, Le, 200
Due orfanelli, I, 200, 209
Due soldi di speranza, 303, 310, 314
Dunne, Irene, 83
Duranti, Doris, 54, 70n18, 182

elections of 1948, 2, 42, 82, 83, 228, 329, 337
Emmer, Luciano, 309, 315
Emigrantes, 145, 146
Eroe della strada, L', 201
Eroi della domenica, Gli, 287, 295–96
Ettore Fieramosca, 121, 122, 176
Excelsa-Minerva, 12, 34, 37, 38

Fabiola, 10, 47, 101, 109, 110, 315, 326–28
Fabrizi, Aldo, 12, 13, 51, 60, 61, 66, 93, 118, 153, 178, 194, 195, 211, 264, 270, 329
  and Anna Magnani, 134, 140, 144, 147
  and Ave Ninchi, 139, 145, 147
  and comedy, 133, 134–35, 142–43, 144, 147
  and food, 135, 148
  and love, 137, 143
  and neorealism, 136, 140
  in *Roma città aperta*, 132, 133, 134, 135, 136, 137, 147, 344, 346
  and Rome, 132, 133, 138, 141, 144–45, 148
  Passaguai film series, 146–47
  performance style, 134, 136, 137, 138, 142, 143–44, 146
  personal life, 143, 147–48
  physical appearance, 140–41, 143, 144, 148
  and theatre, 141–42
Fairbanks, Douglas, 98, 146
Faldini, Franca, 211, 335
Famiglia Brambilla va in vacanza, La, 101, 110, 147
Famiglia Passaguai film series, 146–47

Fanfan la tulipe, 330
Fascism and cinema, 20–24, 26, 52–57
Fascism and the star system, 52–56
Fatalità, 101, 248–49
Fellini, Federico, 133, 136
Ferida, Luisa, 54, 95, 241
Fermo con le mani, 199
Fernandel, 330
Fiammata, La, 257
Fifa e arena, 201, 202
Figli di nessuno, I, 254, 256
Figlia del capitano, La, 247, 249
Figlia del corsaro verde, La, 54
Film Europe, 324
Fiore, Maria, 314
Flaiano, Ennio, 138
Flynn, Errol, 54, 62, 297
Fonda, Henry, 109
For Whom the Bell Tolls, 339
Francesco giullare di Dio, 12, 136
Franco, Fulvia, 203
Freda, Riccardo, 30–31, 38, 101, 107, 317, 328
Freddi, Luigi, 22, 36, 44, 45, 53, 56, 62, 182, 240–41

Gabin, Jean, 253, 328–29
Gable, Clark, 257
Gallone, Carmine, 30, 157, 200, 268
Garbo, Greta, 84, 232, 236, 266, 328, 332, 333, 334
Garson, Greer, 84
Gassman, Vittorio, 84, 185, 231, 234, 250, 253, 256, 295
Geiger, Rod, 38
Gelli, Chiaretta, 59
Genina, Augusto, 55
Germi, Pietro, 11, 105, 107, 274, 287, 292
Ghenzi, Sandro, 317
Ghergo, Arturo, 264
Giachetti, Fosco, 30, 54–56, 57, 59, 62, 65, 68, 85, 98, 184, 190n27
    and Andrea Checchi, 176–77
Giannini, Guglielmo, 206
Giarabub, 54, 137
Gigli, Beniamino, 268

Gilda, 58, 59, 219
Gioi, Vivi, 54, 57, 187
Giorno di nozze, 147
Giorno in pretura, Un, 274
Giorno nella vita, Un, 105, 106, 243–44, 249
Gioventù perduta, 107, 253
Girotti, Massimo, 13, 51, 61, 62, 84, 85, 93, 99, 100, 109, 115, 159, 187, 297, 326
    and Amedeo Nazzari, 105–6, 111, 243, 249, 347
    and the Communist Party, 198
    and fans, 96, 184
    and Fascist aesthetics, 101–2, 104
    and homosexuality, 103, 104, 110, 113n55
    in *Ossessione*, 97–8, 101, 103, 104, 107, 111, 115–16, 174, 345
    passivity of, 104, 105, 111
    personal life, 108, 109, 113n55
    physical appearance, 95–6, 98, 101, 102, 105, 108, 109, 110, 111, 180, 183
    and social class, 106–7, 109, 346
Gisa, Erno, 290
glamour, 53, 59, 62, 67, 78, 80, 81, 98, 114, 154–55, 163, 169, 219, 227, 230, 246, 333
Gloria, Leda, 54
Gone With The Wind, 76
Grable, Betty, 76, 84
Grandi magazzini, I, 173, 179, 180, 181, 186
Grido della terra, Il, 187, 189
Gualino, Riccardo, 36, 44, 212, 217, 330
Guardie e ladri, 205, 213
Guarini, Alfredo, 57, 314, 329

Harlem, 105
Harlow, Jean, 53
Hayward, Susan, 334
Hayworth, Rita, 58, 59, 68, 79, 84, 218–19, 229
Hepburn, Katharine, 83, 84, 334
Herrand, Marcel, 328
Hollywood, 40, 44–46, 52, 56, 58, 59, 73, 76–79, 81, 83, 85, 88, 89, 255, 233–26, 330–1, 346
    Italian stars in, 330–35
Hollywood (magazine), 58, 85, 86–88, 212, 256

Imperatore di Capri, L', 205, 212

In nome della legge, 107
Inafferabile 12, L', 270, 273
Incantevole nemica, L', 275
Innocente Casimiro, L', 201
Interlenghi, Franco, 314–15
Io sono il capitaz, 270
Io suo padre, 123, 126, 137
Joan of Arc, 340
Jourdan, Louis, 332

Kitzmiller, John, 138
Koch, Carlo, 95
Koenigsmark, 330
Kubrick, Stanley, 101

Ladri di biciclette, 10, 64, 137, 188, 303, 304, 306, 310, 313
Lake, Veronica, 58, 59
Lamour, Dorothy, 58
Lattuada, Alberto, 140, 146, 158, 186, 231, 246, 254, 287
Laughton, Charles, 138, 332
Lebbre bianca, 257
Lizzani, Carlo, 11, 13, 27, 29, 121, 174, 175, 188, 220, 221, 285–86, 287
Lollobrigida, Gina, 66, 67, 68, 78, 79, 85, 86, 189, 257, 264, 290, 330, 335, 347
Lombardo, Goffredo, 39, 251, 256
Loren, Sophia, 66, 67, 86, 233, 334
Lost Weekend, 338
Lotti, Mariella, 59, 62, 243–44, 248, 249, 257, 269, 330
Luce Institute, 21
Luce nelle tenebre, 123
Luci della ribalta, 146
Luciano Serra pilota, 54, 137, 240, 251, 255
Lulli, Folco, 185, 288
Lupi, Roldano, 68, 184
Lupo della Sila, Il, 86, 225, 229, 232, 251, 256–57
Lux film, 34, 36, 37, 38, 40, 44, 48, 69, 156, 187, 212, 216, 217, 218, 228, 246, 287, 329, 338
Luxardo, Elio, 264

Macario, Erminio, 66, 194, 201–2, 262

Maggiorani, Lamberto, 65, 188, 306, 308–9, 312–4, 317, 320n37
Magnani, Anna, 3, 4, 12, 13, 42, 43, 51, 61, 67, 78, 80, 110, 118–19, 264, 314, 329, 339, 340, 341, 347
  and Aldo Fabrizi, 153, 166
  in *Bellissima*, 1–4, 168
  decline of, 164, 347
  and Hollywood, 334–35
  and jewellery, 155, 170
  and motherhood, 150–1, 158, 164, 170
  performance style, 154, 157, 158–59, 161, 165, 167, 168–70
  personal life, 161–62, 163, 168–69, 170, 171n14
  physical appearance, 154–55, 162, 164, 169
  as *popolana*, 155, 156, 159–61, 163, 164, 166, 169
  and popular cinema, 156–59, 164–65, 166–67, 168
  and Roberto Rossellini, 166–68
  in *Roma città aperta*, 118, 119, 150–53, 155, 156, 158, 160, 163, 344, 346
  and Rome, 150, 151, 154, 156, 159, 161–63, 165–66, 169, 170
  and theatre, 153–54, 158, 169
Malacarne, 248
Malaparte, Curzio, 208, 287, 292, 293–94
Maliconico autunno, 255
Mambo, 233
Mangano, Silvana, 13, 52, 66 67, 68, 78, 80, 86, 89, 93–4, 191, 192, 212, 213, 317, 334, 346, 347
  and Amedeo Nazzari, 225, 228–29, 231, 234, 253, 257
  in *Anna*, 231–33, 295
  and the public, 229
  beauty and sex appeal, 216, 219–23, 228, 230, 231, 232, 234, 236, 238n62
  compared to Garbo, 232, 236
  and Dino De Laurentiis, 218, 218, 224, 228, 230–33, 236
  family background, 224–25, 232, 236
  international roles, 338–39, 344
  personal life, 229, 250

in *Riso amaro*, 216, 220, 228, 231, 234, 284, 317
Marchal, Georges, 328
Marcuzzo, Elio, 174, 189n2
Marito per Anna Zaccheo, Un, 106, 258, 268, 275–76, 271, 346
Mark of Zorro, The, 335
Martin, Dean, 78
Martini, Rossana, 86, 262–63
Matarazzo, Raffaello, 231, 253
Michi, Maria, 105, 249
Minerva. *See* Excelsa-Minerva
Mio figlio professore, 137, 144
Miracolo a Milano, 200, 306, 310, 312
Miranda, Isa, 13, 25, 57, 59–60, 63, 185, 262, 334
Misiano, Fortunato, 39
Miss Italia, 66, 80, 86, 111, 191, 203, 217, 261–64, 317. *See also* beauty contests
Molti sogni per le strade, 110, 159
Monaco, Eitel, 35, 46
Monicelli, Mario, 146, 205, 225
Montand, Yves, 85, 298
Moore, Gar, 138
Morante, Elsa, 84
Moravia, Alberto, 84
Morgan, Michèle, 47, 326–28
Morlay, Gaby, 329
MPEA, 40, 46, 324–25
Mulino del Po, Il, 253
Musco, Angelo, 200
Mussolini, Benito, 11, 20–22, 26, 28, 36, 37, 44, 52, 56, 60, 69, 103, 114, 160, 161, 180, 182, 197, 205, 240, 250, 325, 332, 345
Mussolini, Vittorio, 21

Natale a campo 119, 10, 138
Nazzari, Amedeo, 8, 12, 13, 54, 55, 56, 57, 60, 62, 65, 78, 80, 86, 98, 105, 106, 111, 158, 177, 182, 184, 186, 191, 212, 229, 231, 275, 288, 297, 331, 333, 347
and Anna Magnani, 246, 250
and Fascism, 240–41, 243
and masculinity, 246–47, 253
and Massimo Girotti, 248–49

performance style, 243–44, 250
personal life, 257–58
and the public, 242, 255, 256–57
and Raffaello Matarazzo, 254–58, 344
screen persona, 240–41, 242, 246–48, 253, 255–56, 259n33
and Silvana Mangano, 251–53, 257
in Spain and Argentina, 242, 250–52
war activity, 241–42, 244
and Yvonne Sanson, 254–56
neorealism, 2, 9, 10, 20, 27, 28, 30, 278, 303–5, 345
demise of, 45, 65, 175
and film industry, 10, 28–29, 31, 40, 47
and stars, 4, 5, 10, 28, 29, 51, 60–65, 78, 184, 310–11, 316–19, 345–47
Neufeld, Max, 127, 157
Ninchi, Ave, 139, 145
Ninchi, Carlo, 13, 63, 127, 184
Non c'è pace tra gli ulivi, 287, 289
Non-professional actors, 13, 61, 64, 66, 303–22, 347
Noris, Assia, 54, 59, 63, 174, 261
Notorious, 335
Nuvolari, Tazio, 203

Onorevole Angelina, L', 165, 166, 170
Onorevoli, Gli, 205
Orbis, 37, 243
Ore 9 lezione di chimica, 177
Oro di Napoli, L', 211, 233
Osiris, Wanda, 164, 270
Ossessione, 3, 10, 24, 26, 27, 60, 93, 95, 97–98, 101, 103, 104, 107, 110, 111, 117, 119, 123, 152, 154, 168, 174, 223, 345
Otello, 39

Padovani, Lea, 68
Pagliero, Marcello, 105
Paisà, 10, 26, 61, 138, 249, 303, 305, 307, 339
Pampanini, Silvana, 13, 80, 86, 89, 110, 111, 191, 192, 202, 206, 258, 344, 346, 347
costumes, 269, 273
as cover girl, 265, 272
family and lifestyle, 273, 277–79, 281n50

and France, 275, 330
and Giuseppe De Santis, 275–76, 281n48
glamour and sex appeal, 266–68, 272–73, 274
and Miss Italia, 261–64
Parisian associations, 265, 273–75
personality, 270–71
physical appearance, 263, 270, 271
and the public, 277–79
and Rome, 264, 278
screen persona, 269, 272–73, 275–76
and Totò, 269, 271, 277
Pane, amore e fantasia, 78
Paradine Case, The, 332–33
Parigi è sempre Parigi, 315
Parvo, Elli, 105, 121, 263
Passaporto rosso, 145
Patellani, Federico, 155, 264–66
Pavan, Marisa, 335
Pavolini, Alessandro, 182
Peck, Gregory, 332
Perilli, Ivo, 157
Petacci, Claretta, 60, 114
Petacci, Miriam (Maria di San Servolo), 60, 114, 330
Petrolini, Ettore, 133, 180, 198
Phillipe, Gerard, 330
Pierangeli, Annamaria, 335
Pietrangeli, Antonio, 49n38, 62, 63, 183
Pilota ritorna, Un, 95, 99, 127
Pinelli, Tullio, 126, 247
Pirati della Malesia, I, 123
Pittaluga, Stefano, 36
Pius XII, 81, 83, 336
Pizzi, Nilla, 276
Pompieri di Viggiù, I, 193, 195, 201, 203, 212, 269, 270
Ponti, Carlo, 25, 37, 38, 48, 67, 191, 212, 228, 329, 338
Porta del cielo, La, 22
Power, Tyrone, 58, 73, 83, 85–6, 89, 335–57, 340–41
Presidentessa, La, 274–75
Presle, Micheline, 328
Prima comunione, 146, 317, 329

Primula bianca, La, 187
Prince of Foxes, 73, 335, 337
Processo alla città, 258, 275, 276
Puccini, Gianni, 114, 115, 175, 285

Quai des brumes, 328
Quando gli angeli dormono, 251
Questa è la vita, 136
Quo Vadis, 337

Raft, George, 109
Ragazze di San Frediano, Le, 337
Ramperti, Marco, 57, 59, 197
Rascel, Renato, 194, 270
Ratto delle sabine, Il, 200
Re d'Inghilterra non paga, Il, 181
Reggiani, Serge, 187, 291
Regina di Navarra, La, 121
Renzetti, Gastone, 3, 314
Resistance, the, 2, 24–25, 31, 57, 62, 93, 150–53, 165, 183, 189–90, 206, 221, 243–44, 256, 285
women and, 151–52, 165
Ribelle di Castiglia, Il, 251
Riento, Virgilio, 189
Righelli, Gennaro, 156
Rigoletto, 30
Risate di gioia, 213
Risi, Dino, 120, 121, 307
Riso amaro, 5, 68, 84, 185, 191, 192, 216–25, 231, 234, 253, 261, 283–86, 288, 289, 290, 338, 344
Roma città aperta, 4, 9, 12, 26, 31, 37, 38, 51, 61, 93, 118, 120, 121, 135, 138, 139, 147, 150–53, 155, 156, 160, 163–67, 183, 194, 223, 244, 249, 329, 339, 344, 346
Roma città libera, 185, 189
Roma ore 11, 287, 295, 346
Romana film, 39
Romanticismo, 257
Rose Tattoo, The, 4, 334–35
Rossellini, Roberto, 10, 12, 25, 26, 37, 61, 93, 95, 98, 104, 105, 118, 119, 127, 132, 140, 205, 242, 249, 305, 306, 307, 345–46
and Anna Magnani, 166–68

and Ingrid Bergman, 339–41
and *Roma città aperta*, 133–36, 167
Rovere, Luigi, 39
Ruggeri, Ruggero, 196

San Giovanni decollato, 200
Sanson, Yvonne, 86, 88, 254–55
Scala, Delia, 202, 270, 271
Scalera film, 34, 36, 38, 126
Scalfaro, Oscar Luigi, 209, 211
Scelba, Mario, 145
Schubert, Emilio, 81
Sciecco bianco, Lo, 316
Sciuscià, 38, 308, 314
Schiava del peccato, La, 276
Secchia, Pietro, 83
Segreto di San Giovanni, Il, 268
Selnick, David O., 12, 331–34
Semeraro, Gabriele, 167
Sensani, Gino, 125, 127
Senso, 111, 333
Sensualità, 257
Sernas, Jacques, 253
Siamo donne, 4, 154, 168–69, 311
Siamo uomini o caporali, 206, 211
Signora senza camelie, La, 316
Signoret, Simone, 85, 208
Silvi, Lilia, 59
Simon, Michel, 326
Simoneschi, Lydia, 276
Sinatra, Frank, 78
Socialist Party, Italian, 2, 42, 336–37
Solari, Laura, 59
Solaroli, Libero, 115
Soldati, Mario, 25, 95, 126, 138, 144, 182, 186, 199, 206
Sole sorge ancora, Il, 25, 121
Sorelle Materassi, Le, 118
Sordi, Alberto, 347
Sorprese del vagone letto, Le, 123
Sotto il sole di Roma, 308, 303, 312
Spartaco, 101, 110
Squadrone bianco, Lo, 55, 176
Starace, Achille, 180
Steno (Stefano Vanzina), 101, 146, 205, 225

Stoppa, Paolo, 206
Stromboli, 118, 168, 339, 340, 341

Tamburella, Paolo William, 38
Taranto, Nino, 194, 269
Tellini, Piero, 165–66, 247
Tempo massimo, 153, 157, 203
Teresa Venerdì, 153, 154, 157
Terra madre, 54
Terra trema, La, 3, 10, 61, 303, 310
Tetto, Il, 307, 318
Thieves' Highway, 334
Third man, The, 339
Tiranno di Padova, Il, 127
Titanus, 34, 36, 39, 47, 69, 78, 231, 251, 254
Togliatti, Palmiro, 226, 336
Tombolo, paradiso nero, 138, 139
Tormento, 254, 256
Tosca, 95, 102
Toso, Otello, 249, 328, 331–32
Totò (Antonio De Curtis), 7, 8, 13, 36, 60, 66, 191, 193, 195, 269, 344, 346, 347
  and Anna Magnani, 213
  and Charlie Chaplin, 195, 198, 199, 208, 211
  costume, 198
  language of, 208–9
  and Mario Mattoli, 201, 204
  and Naples, 194, 197, 198, 208, 211
  and neorealism, 205
  personal life, 208, 209–11
  physical appearance, 194, 199
  and the public, 193, 194, 201, 205, 209, 211–12
  screen persona, 195–96, 199, 200, 204
  and Silvana Pampanini, 202, 206
  and theatre, 193, 195, 196, 197, 197–98, 199, 203, 204, 205, 211
Totò a colori, 193
Totò al giro d'Italia, 201, 203
Totò cerca casa, 195, 205, 212
Totò le Mokò, 195–96
Totò, Peppino e le fanatiche, 209
Totò terzo uomo, 196
Tototarzan, 195, 206
Tracy, Spencer, 83, 109

Tragica notte, 186

Ulisse, 233, 338–39
Ultima carrozzella, L', 132, 134, 135, 153
Ultimi giorni di Pompei, Gli, 328
Ultimo amore, 127, 128, 187
Umberto D, 303, 306, 309, 314, 325
Universalia, 37, 47, 146, 326–29
Uomo qualunque (political movement), 206
Uomo ritorna, Un, 157

Valenti, Osvaldo, 96, 241
Valentino, Rudolph, 85, 109, 143
Valli, Alida, 7, 8, 12, 13, 30, 54, 57, 60, 83, 177, 200, 257, 331–34
Vallone, Raf, 13, 62, 84, 192, 219, 222, 319, 334
    and the Communist Party, 285–86, 287, 290, 295, 297, 299n19
    compared to Amedeo Nazzari, 297, 289, 347
    in *Cristo proibito,* 291–94
    and Elena Varzi, 291–93, 297–98
    family and other background, 285, 294–95, 298, 346
    and Giuseppe De Santis, 285–86, 287, 288, 295, 297
    physical appearance, 282, 283, 286, 288–89, 292, 294–95, 297
    in *Riso amaro,* 219, 222, 231, 283–85, 286, 287, 288, 289, 295
    screen persona, 282, 283, 287, 295

Vanni, Vanna, 62
Varzi, Elena, 291, 292, 293, 297–98, 317
Venice film festival, 21, 35, 228, 327
Vergano, Aldo, 25, 241
Viale della speranza, 316
Vidal, Henri, 326–27
Vie dell'amore, Le, 114
Villa, Roberto, 59, 95, 96, 175
Villani, Dino, 80, 261–62
Visconti, Luchino, 2–4, 24, 26, 60, 61, 82, 84, 93, 95, 126, 68, 183, 242, 249, 262, 304, 315, 317, 333, 345, 346
    and *Ossessione,* 97, 103, 104, 111–18, 174, 346
Vita ricomincia, La, 30, 37
Vivere in pace, 138
Volver la vida, 251
Vortice, 110
Vulcano, 340–41, 168

Wayne, John, 78
Weissmuller, Johnny, 98
Welles, Orson, 39

Yvonne la nuit, 193

Zacconi, Ermete, 196
Zampa, Luigi, 140, 146, 165, 287, 312
Zavattini, Cesare, 3, 4, 28, 146, 199, 262, 305–8, 311, 314, 321n51, 328–29, 340
Zeffirelli, Franco, 166

www.ingramcontent.com/pod-product-compliance
Lightning Source LLC
Chambersburg PA
CBHW071330080526
44587CB00017B/2786